THE FASHION INDUSTRY
AND ITS CAREERS

THE FASHION INDUSTRY
AND ITS CAREERS

FOURTH EDITION

MICHELE M. GRANGER, EdD, ITAA
Missouri State University

SHERYL A. FARNAN, MBA, PhD
Metropolitan Community College, Kansas City, Missouri

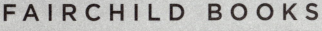

FAIRCHILD BOOKS
NEW YORK · LONDON · OXFORD · NEW DELHI · SYDNEY

FAIRCHILD BOOKS
Bloomsbury Publishing Inc
1385 Broadway, New York, NY 10018, USA
50 Bedford Square, London, WC1B 3DP, UK

BLOOMSBURY, FAIRCHILD BOOKS and the Fairchild Books
logo are trademarks of Bloomsbury Publishing Plc

Second edition published 2012
Third edition published 2015
This edition first published in the United States of America 2020

Cover design by Eleanor Rose | Cover image: Models pose for a photographer during a fashion
shoot in a tunnel left empty due to the road being occupied by by pro-democracy protesters,
in the Admiralty district of Hong Kong on October 8, 2014. © ED JONES / AFP / Getty Images

Library of Congress Cataloging-in-Publication Data
Names: Granger, Michele (Michele M.), author. | Farnan, Sheryl A., author.
Title: The fashion industry and its careers / Michele M. Granger, Sheryl A. Farnan.
Description: Fourth edition. | New York, NY : Fairchild Books, an imprint
of Bloomsbury Publishing Inc., 2020. | Includes index.
Identifiers: LCCN 2019026136 | ISBN 9781501339004 (paperback) | ISBN 9781501338601 (pdf)
Subjects: LCSH: Fashion—Vocational guidance. | Fashion—Study and teaching. |
Clothing trade—Vocational guidance. | Clothing trade—Study and teaching.
Classification: LCC TT507 .G68 2020 | DDC 746.9/2023—dc23
LC record available at https://lccn.loc.gov/2019026136

ISBN: 978-1-5013-3900-4

Typeset by Lachina Creative, Inc.
Printed and bound in the United States

To find out more about our authors and books visit
www.fairchildbooks.com and sign up for our newsletter.

To my mom and dad, Tom and Darlene Farnan, my first teachers, most truthful critics, and biggest cheerleaders. Thank you!

CONTENTS

EXTENDED CONTENTS

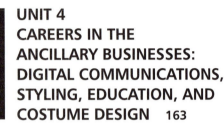

PREFACE

The Fashion Industry and Its Careers: An Introduction, fourth edition, provides an overview, or survey, of the global fashion industry with a focus on the career paths available within each level of the industry. It is written for the reader who is exploring career options, whether as a career change or as an entry-level position. It is designed to support introductory college or university courses in fashion design, fashion merchandising, product development, textiles, apparel, interior design, and career exploration. The fourth edition is fully updated with recent developments in technology, world economics and globalization, and effects on industry sectors and career opportunities. Through current, applied industry information and personal assessments throughout, students gain a critical understanding of what careers match their aptitudes, skill sets, and interests—and how to begin heading down a path toward a successful career in the fashion industry.

The book is based on the following four broad assumptions of postsecondary education and the fashion industry:

1. *People immerse themselves in studies they find personally and professionally relevant.* By examining the different levels or sectors of the fashion industry and exploring the career options that exist at each level, students have the opportunity to see themselves on career paths and, subsequently, define career goals to enhance and individualize their educational experiences.
2. *Fashion is a lifestyle that permeates many industry segments, from apparel and accessories to home fashions to beauty and wellness.* It includes all products and services that are influenced by changing trends in form, materials, theme, and color.

3. *The careers within the sectors of the fashion industry provide an ideal way to define and explain the industry and illustrate its various levels, from raw materials to ancillary services.* Exploring the industry by highlighting the careers in each industry segment provides a framework that allows students to see how the various levels work together.
4. *Effective career preparation requires across-the-board understanding of the following concepts:*
   - The apparel and textile industry operates in a global and high-tech market, making an understanding of cultural diversity, the world economy, and technological advances essential.
   - Activities of product development, manufacturing, and retailing are interrelated, from fiber and textiles to design and production to sourcing and merchandising.
   - Successful companies recognize that product decisions are consumer-driven.

ORGANIZATION OF THE TEXT

The Fashion Industry and Its Careers: An Introduction, fourth edition, is organized into four units, or parts, beginning with the creators and providers of raw materials and the manufacturers of products, followed by the manufacturers' designers who develop the concepts that will be produced, to the retailers who create and/or sell the products to the consumer, and ending with the auxiliary industries that support the work done by the product creators and product retailers. The text is organized in the following sequence: Unit 1, Careers in Forecasting, Textiles, and Manufacturing; Unit 2, Careers in Fashion

Design, Product Development, and Fashion Promotion; Unit 3, Careers in Fashion Retailing; and Unit 4, Careers in the Ancillary Businesses: Digital Communications, Styling, Education, and Costume Design.

Unit 1:
Careers in Forecasting, Textiles, and Manufacturing

The primary level of the fashion industry begins with the people responsible for the inspiration and conception of the fashion product's parts and raw materials (e.g., the forecasters, designers, and sourcing personnel). Unit 1 starts at the beginning of fashion product development and production. It provides an overview of the firms that supply the information, components, production, and design of fashion products that manufacturers produce. In addition, the back office departments of manufacturing firms are examined, to include sales, accounting, finance, and human resources. Chapter 1, Trend Forecasting, presents the trend forecasters who research, interpret, inspire, and predict shifts in fashion preferences and influence both the raw materials and the actual outcomes of fashion production. Chapter 2, Textile Design and Development, examines the textile product developers and designers who use colors, textures, patterns, and finishes to create the foundation on which fashion products are built. In Chapter 3, Sourcing, the personnel who locate the components and manufacturers of products are explored in greater depth. Chapter 4, Production and Sales, presents production processes in which employees work together to manufacture and sell the final product, such as showroom and manufacturer's representatives. The section of this chapter that discusses trends affecting careers in production has been updated with information on career areas such as merchandise coordinator, sustainability officer, and transparency officer.

Unit 2:
Careers in Fashion Design, Product Development, and Fashion Promotion

Unit 2 is composed of three chapters, Chapters 5 through 7, which explore the design sector of the fashion industry in greater depth. In Chapter 5, Designing Apparel and Accessories for the Manufacturer, careers related to designing apparel and accessories for the manufacturer are discussed, to include the fashion designer, assistant fashion designer, technical designer, specification technician, and pattern maker. Some retailers purchase finished fashion merchandise from manufacturers or wholesalers; others develop and manufacture products specifically for their clientele; many large retailers do both. Several large retail operations own a product development division that functions as a design and production source exclusively for them. In Chapter 6, Product Development by the Manufacturer and Retailer, the career tracks for director of product development, merchandiser, sourcing staff, product development designer, product manager, colorist, textile technical designer, product development patternmaker, and quality control manager are presented. Whether the fashion product is created and manufactured by the retailer or purchased from a manufacturer or wholesaler, it must be marketed to appeal to the consumer. In Chapter 7, Promotion for the Designer and Manufacturer, these marketing activities are explored through the career tracks of fashion stylist, public relations and social media directors, advertising research and promotion positions, and fashion event producer.

Unit 3:
Careers in Fashion Retailing

The third level of the fashion industry represents the retailers of fashion products, from apparel to home furnishings, and those involved with creating a desire in the consumer for the retailer's fashion goods. Unit 3 focuses on marketing, merchandising, and management for the brick-and-mortar and/or e-commerce fashion retailer. As shown in Chapter 8, Marketing for the Retailer, the marketing, or promotion, division of a retail operation does just that through such professionals as the marketing director; product, brand, digital, and Web site marketing managers; art director; and copywriter. Chapter 9, Merchandising for the Retailer, explores the merchandising division of the retail operation— the buying and marketing of products. General merchandising managers, divisional merchandising managers, buyers/fashion merchandisers, assistant buyers, planners, distribution managers/allocators, and merchandising trainees work on the selection, pricing, and placement of merchandise on retail sales floors.

In Chapter 10, Management for the Retailer, essential management careers in the retail sector are examined, to include those in stores—regional, store unit, associate, assistant, and department managers—as well as customer service managers. This chapter culminates in presenting the retail operation owners—all-in-one entrepreneurs who own and operate their retail businesses. Whether product or service—or brick-and-mortar, brick-and-click, or solely e-retailing—these entrepreneurs are rapidly contributing innovation and jobs to the fashion industry.

Unit 4:
Careers in the Ancillary Businesses: Digital Communications, Styling, Education, and Costume Design

Unit 4 presents a range of ancillary businesses that promote, educate, and provide support to the producers, retailers, and consumers of fashion goods. Whether working as freelancers or within a company, these ancillary business professionals frequently offer services, rather than tangible products. In a new Chapter 11, Digital Communication, the ever-growing careers in digital media are explored from the digital media director to the fashion journalist and blogger. In Chapter 12, Fashion Styling, Photography, and Costume Design, career options are discussed from the perspectives of company-employed and freelance positions. Fashion scholarship is discussed in its own chapter, Chapter 13, Fashion Curatorship and Scholarship, and includes coverage of museum and historical costume study, as well as teaching opportunities in high school and postsecondary education. Opportunities in the fashion or costume division of a museum discussed in this chapter include museum director, museum curator, assistant curator, collections manager, museum archivist, and museum conservator. The star of the fashion scholarship segment of the industry is the fashion educator, who instructs and/or conducts research in historical costume or many other facets of the fashion industry, from production to design and product development, to merchandising and entrepreneurship.

Chapter 14, Visual Merchandising and Retail Design, encompasses careers in visual merchandising, store planning, and mall management. Visual merchandising has become an important component of not only manufacturers' showrooms and retailers' sales floors, but it is also integral to online sales, social media, branding, and promotion. Fashion producers, designers, Web site and store retailers, and stylists all hire visual merchandisers to create a setting or an environment that will attract consumers and visually sell the merchandise. The primary career tracks discussed in Chapter 14 include visual merchandising professional, store planning director, mall manager, and assistant mall manager.

Appendix A provides a list of key career areas and Web sites to research salaries by region. New online resources presented at the end of each chapter also provide current information on careers and industry trends. Appendix B features an assortment of résumé examples from several careers as well as suggestions for writing a résumé, researching employers, and interviewing. A glossary of key terms is also included at the end of the text.

Each chapter of *The Fashion Industry and Its Careers: An Introduction*, fourth edition, provides current visuals, online resources, discussion questions, and key terms—the terminology used in the industry. These text features are developed to help clarify concepts, stimulate class discussion, and encourage critical thinking with applications and illustrations. Relevant education, work experience, personal characteristics, and career challenges are examined for each career track.

New to This Edition

- *Case Studies in Career Exploration* showcase profiles of companies, interviews with individuals, industry scenarios, and insider tips.
- *The Job Search* boxes feature sample advertisements for actual positions in fields discussed within each chapter.
- *Social Media Strikes* boxes in each chapter explore how social media trends are integrated into the various levels of the industry and describe the impact of Facebook, Twitter, Pinterest, Instagram, LinkedIn, and more. As new social media forces will continue to impact our lives and the fashion industry world, understanding the why and the how of social media today will help us anticipate the future.
- *In-depth job titles and descriptions* for a wide range of careers now include *Sustainability Officer* (Chapter 4) and *Transparency Officer* (Chapter 4), which help demonstrate industry shifts toward greater attention

to preservation of natural resources and consumer demand for more open communication regarding manufacturing practices of fashion goods.

- *Organizational changes* to the unit structure of this fourth edition align the content with current industry practice, emphasize career areas with the greatest growth potential, and provide specific focus to careers that benefit most directly from fashion education.
- A *fully updated photo program* contains more than seventy new photographs.

Instructor's Resources

This edition includes an Instructor's Guide, Test Bank, and chapter PowerPoint presentations. The Instructor's Guide includes syllabi, class discussion topics, exercises/assignments, and guest speaker suggestions. The Test Bank includes a separate answer key and a mixture of true/false, multiple-choice, and open-ended questions.

Resources can be accessed via www.fairchildbooks.com.

ACKNOWLEDGMENTS

In preparing this fourth edition of *The Fashion Industry and Its Careers: An Introduction*, my sincere thanks and appreciation is extended posthumously to Dr. Michele M. Granger for her dedication and work in the field of fashion education. Thank you to my colleagues and mentors who have provided encouragement and guidance throughout this process and throughout my academic career. And appreciation to my students, who, year after year, work very hard to overcome significant personal trials to learn, study, and follow their dreams. You are a continual inspiration to me.

I am indebted to industry professionals who have provided guidance and direction throughout this process. Comments from readers and educators selected by the publisher have also been very helpful. Thanks to reviewers Gargi Bhaduri, Kent State University; Cheryline Calcagni, Marist College; Lori Faulkner, Ferris State University.

My gratitude and sincere appreciation go to the staff at Fairchild Books. I would like to thank Emily Samulski, Acquisitions Editor; Joseph Miranda, Editorial Development Manager; Edie Weinberg, Art Development Editor; and Jenna Lefkowitz, Editorial Assistant. You are all professional, kind, and encouraging—it is an absolute joy to work with each of you!

On a personal note, I wish to thank the many teachers throughout my life who approached their work with passion, sincerity, and the desire to help students succeed. You not only taught subjects and information, but you taught me how to teach. I think of many of you often.

I would not, and could not, do this work without the support and encouragement of my dear husband, Jay Leipzig. He always sees possibilities where others usually see obstacles. He has taught me to lead with "yes!"

I welcome comments from students and instructors who use this book. You should feel free to send those through Fairchild Books.

CAREERS IN FORECASTING, TEXTILES, AND MANUFACTURING

Unit 1 starts at the beginning of fashion product conception and production. It explores the firms and people supplying the information, components, production, and support needed to manufacture fashion products to bring them to the retailers. In addition, the departments of manufacturing firms that support the people and profitability of fashion lines are examined, to include sales, human resources, finance, and accounting. Chapter 1, "Trend Forecasting," presents the trend forecasters who research, interpret, inspire, and predict shifts in fashion preferences. Trend forecasters have tremendous influence on both the raw materials and the actual fashions. Chapter 2, "Textile Design and Development," looks at the textile designers and developers who use color, texture, pattern, and finishes to create the foundation on which fashion products are built. In Chapter 3, "Sourcing," the careers of sourcing professionals, who locate the components of products, are explored. Sourcing involves locating the materials that become part of the fashion merchandise

and also finding factories, particularly overseas, to produce the merchandise. Chapter 4, "Production and Sales," examines the careers of employees who work together to manufacture the final product.

When people who are interested in building a career in the fashion industry initially consider career tracks in the field, they often do not think about the primary level of the industry where fashion products begin. It is another world with a full range of job opportunities. The prospective fashion executive with a penchant for design can explore the world of textiles. Those with an interest in putting products together have vast opportunities in manufacturing. Others who have the skills and drive to sell fashion products are not limited to doing so in retailing; selling fashion lines to retail buyers provides both a new perspective and an array of new potential employers. It's a world the fashion consumer often does not think about, but it's one that you will next explore to broaden your career options and build your understanding of the fashion industry.

CHAPTER 1
TREND FORECASTING

Whenever you open a *Vogue* magazine, click on to Haute-Look.com, or tune into *Project Runway*, you are introduced to the latest trends in fashion. From where do these concepts come? Who decided what the latest themes, colors, silhouettes, styling details, or fabrics would be? How far in advance of seeing these fashions on the runway (Figure 1.1), online, or in the fashion publication pages were these trends determined? What will next season's, or next year's, fashion trends be? No person or company uses a crystal ball to foresee the future of fashion. The people responsible for making these predictions are referred to as **trend forecasters**, *fashion forecasters*, or *creative directors*.

Customers are often unaware of the amount of lead time that fashion products require. **Lead time** refers to the number of days, weeks, months, or years needed for the intricate planning, purchasing, and production steps to be implemented before fashion products actually land on the sales floors or Web sites of the retail operations. Lead time includes the time fashion forecasters need to analyze and project colors, design themes, silhouettes, fabrics, patterns or prints, and styling details—often years in advance of the actual manufacturing of the products. Without that proverbial crystal ball, fashion forecasters must combine their knowledge of fashion design, marketing, current world trends, and history with consumer research and business information. When trend forecasters identify and market their visions of the fashion future effectively, designers, retailers, and manufacturers in the textiles, apparel, accessories, and home environment sectors who subscribe to the forecasters' ideas have an edge, and their lines will be on point for their specific target markets. They will have lower purchasing risks and greater opportunities to increase their customer following and, ultimately, their sales volume.

Figure 1.1
The introduction of a designer's seasonal collection, as shown here at Valentino's Spring 2019 Haute Couture runway show in Paris, is an important time for fashion forecasters, because these industry leaders have a great influence on future fashion trends.

The position of trend forecaster is one of the most influential career options in the fashion industry. Most fashion consumers and many prospective fashion industry executives wonder where the latest and greatest fashion trends originate. Trend forecasters continually monitor consumers and the industry through traveling, reading, networking, listening, and, most important, observing. Trend forecasters attend trade shows, where they analyze the wholesale end of the business by looking at new products and fresh designs from established and new designers. They gather information from the media on population, design, manufacturing, and retail trends to determine what the new looks, silhouettes, colors, and fabrics will be for upcoming seasons. This career is illustrated in Box 1.1, an interview with fashion forecaster David Wolfe.

Many large corporations in all sectors—from agriculture to medicine—have research and development (R&D) departments. In the fashion sector, trend forecasters form the "R" component of the R&D departments in fashion businesses. They lead the research activities of the fashion industry and may also be involved in developmental functions. As researchers, trend forecasters (a) provide new knowledge to designers, buyers, and product developers; (b) assist in the development of new products; and (c) look for ways to update old products or to extend the life of popular products through modifications that rejuvenate them.

Forecasters search for consumer and business facts, as well as creative occurrences, and then analyze the findings to identify common threads that will become trends. Their goal is to isolate the major trends that will positively affect the amount and types of fashion products consumers will buy. Once the trends are classified, trend forecasters use words and images to communicate these to designers, buyers, product developers, and manufacturers in fashion. Images of the trend's mood and key terms, fabrications and colors, and styling details are composed on a "board," referred to as a **trend board**. In the past, these boards were created by hand; today, they are more likely created and disseminated to design and merchandising personnel digitally.

Technology is also impacting the way trend forecasters conduct research and development, market product concepts, and listen to the consumer. Box 1.2 provides more detail about the ever-changing world of trend forecasters by exploring how social media options reach out to creative people around the world.

Few career opportunities in fashion relate to all levels of the industry. Trend forecasting is one of the few. Population trends and interests, availability of raw materials, manufacturing capabilities, retail changes, merchandising and management developments, and entrepreneurial endeavors influence trend forecasting. This chapter introduces the world of trend forecasters, from those in color and textile forecasting to those in theme, style, and detail forecasting.

THE JOB OF A TREND FORECASTER

Types of Forecasters

In general, there are four primary types of trend forecasting firms: fiber and textiles, color, consumer population, and broad spectrum. First, there is the forecaster who works for a **fiber house**, or *fabric or textile house*, a company that represents a fiber source or a fabric. Examples include Cotton Incorporated or the Mohair Council of America. Second, there is the forecaster who specializes in color trends and is employed by a firm such as Color Association U.S. This forecaster provides information on color preferences and palettes for a wide variety of clients, from automobile manufacturers to flooring producers to apparel designers. Next, there is the forecaster who projects population trends and explores the social, economic, geographic, and technological changes in the world, as well as shifts in the population. The population trend forecaster tracks a population's age shifts; residential and geographic preferences; changes in family sizes and structures; entertainment preferences; spending patterns; influences by celebrities, films, and art; as well as other people-related topics, such as values and beliefs. Finally, there is the forecaster who is employed by a **broad-spectrum firm**, a company that provides forecasting services for a wide range of target markets and product categories or industries.

The clients of broad-spectrum firms represent a variety of product categories, as illustrated by the following list of Li Edelkoort's clientele: the paper industry, automobile manufacturers, the food and drink industry, beauty products, and high-tech firms from telecommunications to electronic devices.

CASE STUDIES IN CAREER EXPLORATION

BOX 1.1   Interview with David Wolfe, Creative Director of The Doneger Group

Interviewed by Jared Bajkowski

Could you give us a little introduction?

I'm a Creative Director at The Doneger Group. There are four of us with very different functions, but my position probably overlaps the most with all the others. My focus is the youth market, which includes kids up to tweens and juniors. I also cover accessories, intimate apparel, and beauty (which is my other specialty).

What does an average day look like? What is the time frame for your work?

There's really no typical day, especially when we have markets. Then, I could be doing ten to twenty presentations with clients. Other days, I could be analyzing runway shows, doing consultancy project meetings, or meeting with clients on more forecasting-driven stuff. Our publications are released eighteen to twenty-four months in advance. With the Internet, we can constantly post updates. We can say, "This trend has reached saturation, you should pull back on it," or "This is a color we saw turn up that we weren't anticipating, and you should get into it." We can definitely update and react more often.

At what point did you realize that this was something you wanted to do?

Similar to many students, I didn't even know this career existed. I knew I had an interest in fashion, but prior to that, I had interests in art, history, and writing, so those were probably my strengths. When I first got into FIT [Fashion Institute of Technology], I thought I wanted to be a buyer or a stylist. After taking some buying courses, I realized that math was probably not my strength. By exploring and getting out into the industry, I was lucky enough to do two internships at the same time. One of them was with Vogue-Butterick and the other was with JC Penney. The Vogue-Butterick was really *The Devil Wears Prada* type of fashion office with the fashion director coming in with the little dog in her bag every day. JC Penney was very down-to-earth and let me actually work with the fashion director on children's, men's, and women's wear.

Figure Box 1.1 David Wolfe, Creative Director at The Doneger Group.

JC Penney hired me, and I moved to Plano, Texas, into a position they created in which I covered all the areas. When it moved its fashion office back and forth from New York to Plano a couple of times, I moved and, in between, worked at J. Crew in the fashion office. At the JC Penney fashion office in New York, I had an opportunity to see David Wolfe speak and Doneger was at the top of my list. Abbey [Doneger] came over to look at some video equipment, and that's when he asked me if I wanted to come over and talk. I was very fortunate that I was in the right place at the right time, and there was an opening for a Creative Director. I've been here for fourteen years.

(continued on next page)

BOX 1.1 *(continued)*

What kind of skills does somebody in your position need?

It's important to be very analytical and have strong editing and writing skills. You need to have a good eye, which you really can't teach somebody. Either you have it or you don't. We're all required to speak a lot. We give all sizes of presentations. Initially, that was something I had a problem with, and I probably still do. Normally, I'm a very shy person. I had a professor at FIT who said, "From your test scores you're probably the brightest person in the class, but if you don't learn how to speak up, you're never going to make it in this industry." From that point on, I just pushed myself.

At what point in your career did you really get to hone those skills?

I would say here [at Doneger]. At JC Penney, I was making presentations to the buyers and product development people, but it was not until here that I could be thrown into an audience of 200 people—or working with two people. In China last summer, I had an audience of 800. You have to have a certain comfort level with working all of those types of audiences.

What traits are really important for trend forecasters?

Flexibility. The people we've hired who go the furthest and stay the longest can be thrown into any kind of situation and rise to the occasion—you know, real team players. I think those are the people who get the most out of the experience. It just really helps to have a down-to-earth personality and always be willing to pitch in on anything. We could get a phone call from a client and have to turn around a project in a couple of days. We're a small team, so everyone has to be super flexible—and *nimble*.

How do you get inspired?

Literally, being like a sponge. I'm that weirdo on the subway looking at everybody, from the person who's not interested in fashion to the fashionista. I'm really interested in everybody. When I have time to travel and to open myself up to everything around me, that's when I get most inspired.

What motivates you?

I never have a typical day. Every day is so different and so creative. I really have a great outlet for all of the things I love to do. To be able to write and do it creatively and feel like I'm helping my company, and to go out on the streets and photograph—I have no complaints.

How do you think trend forecasting has changed over the years?

When I first started, we used to cut and paste trend images down on sheets. It was crazy. We had a slide library of the collections and put them in carousels and did literal slide shows of the collections. If David [Wolfe] said, "Everybody in San Tropez is wearing lilac this summer. Everybody has to go buy lilac for next summer," it would happen. It doesn't work that way anymore. Once the Internet came along, our jobs changed tremendously, not just because of online free resources and competition, but also because clients can't wait a year to react to something. Our processes are *completely* different.

When did you realize that things were changing?

Once we subscribed to First View and then Style.com popped up, we were getting all these images. This drastically changed the way we did things as a department. I remember going to every fashion show and every party afterward—we would just be doing all-day-long shows. Then, suddenly, we were sitting at our desks, analyzing. Now, I really pick and choose which one of the shows I'm going to, because I see less when I'm at the shows and I see more when I'm sitting at my desk. It's definitely changed the way that we look and analyze, and for everybody else, too. Most of our clients can instantaneously access the materials. The way that we provide value is that the clients don't have time to look through that many images and come up with an informed opinion.

BOX 1.1 *(continued)*

Do you think there's any kind of drawback to predicting what is going to happen?

We always tell clients that we're making our best educated guess based on what we know now, and where we see things going. We're fortunate because of the way the office functions. Part of our office is merchandising, so they often hear back from stores firsthand what's happening in terms of sales results and what the customer is reacting to in terms of colors and hot items. They keep us grounded because, being creative people, we can make things very esoteric or kind of out-there. They bring us down to earth because they can say from experience that the customer is never going for that, or it's unrealistic. They keep us grounded and we push them.

Have you had any experiences where you were totally wrong or you left out something big from a report?

There are times when a client will say we missed something. Early in my career, when I first went to Barcelona, I thought there was a red pant trend. It wasn't until I went to Barcelona a couple of times that I realized that they just like red pants (laughs). We make our best educated guess, and sometimes we say things that don't make our clients happy. Take flared jeans, for example. When I first talked about flared jeans (at least three years ago), a lot of the clients said, "That's never gonna happen; we just got them into skinny jeans. It took them a long time to accept the skinny jean. They just found the right fit." Then they started seeing the sales and went—(throws hands up). I ultimately have to be the person to push it.

What kinds of applications are there for forecasting beyond fashion?

When I first started, I never anticipated we'd work with a lot of financial companies who have clients with investments in some of the designers and retailers that we're looking at. They ask, "Do you think it's a strong season for them?" They want to be able to tell their clients who have stock in the brand whether or not it's a strong season for that company.

Could you walk us through a case study of a past trend on which you worked?

There are several trends that we keep renaming and recycling. We're going to make a bigger deal out of the whole aspect of comfort going forward. I think it is related to the whole athletic sport idea. I can't tell you how many clients were asking, "Can we have a resource like Birkenstock?" When we first started talking about that, everybody said, "Nobody's going to want to wear Birkenstocks." It's so funny that the impact of the ugly shoe went upward. It was one of the few trends that I've seen that started with the feet and then worked its way up. Now, apparel is sort of matching, as is the whole attitude and the lifestyle. It's a big umbrella trend in every area—the idea of comfort.

Any advice for anybody who is aspiring to become a forecaster?

There are so few trend companies left, but I don't like to discourage anybody. I think that the best step is to pursue something in product development. I'm working with a retailer now that has as much access to the fashion services and the shows and all of the research tools that I do but has an even bigger budget. It would be useful to do something for a retailer in its product development department. It's also important to have retail background to understand the psychology and lingo.

Courtesy of Henry Doneger Associates, Inc.

BOX 1.2   Consumer Behavior and Trend Forecasting

Consumers of every age, race, geographic, social and economic background provide limitless data about themselves every single day, and on a plethora of topics through text, photos, and videos. If only there were a way for researchers to break all of this information down and use it to learn more about how customers live with the products that brands manufacture and market . . .

Ah, but there is! Technology companies continue to develop a wide range of tools to collect, examine, and define social media to help brands better understand and relate to their consumers. Social Native uses artificial intelligence (AI) and robotic process automation to survey social media content and organize information for client brands. Heuritech, partnering with Louis Vuitton and Christian Dior, also use AI to mine information about their brands on social media to learn more about how people use products to develop personal identity and to find potential emerging trends. IBM has developed software to search on specific styles, cuts, and fabrics and can use the information to identify trends and even design uniquely proprietary patterns. Epytom created a Facebook Messenger bot that takes stock of one's personal wardrobe, proposes outfit choices based on highly localized factors like weather or planned calendar events, and, with enough information, can even make suggestions of items for the potential shopper to add to their wardrobe. GAN is an AI company that provides wardrobe suggestions based on body measurements submitted by the customer.

And all of this data is considered in some respects way better than a focus group or a survey in learning authentic information about consumers, their lives, and how they interact with brands. Analyzing social data is considered by some researchers to be more organic and authentic, eliminating the "Hawthorn Effect," also known as the observer effect, which is a reactivity of individuals to modify their behavior in response to their awareness of being watched or observed.

These data miners can help brands ask and answer questions: Who is using my brand? What do these users say about my brand or products? What advice do consumers give to others who are considering buying our product? And, very importantly, what are the demographics of those who use the product, or who are engaged with that platform?

Sources:

Shadpour, D. "How social media can serve as the new focus group for your brand," Forbes, March 21, 2018, https://www.forbes.com/sites/forbesagency-council/2018/03/21/how-social-media-can-serve-as-the-new-focus-group-for-your-brand/#71d210743d7b

The Next Brick, "The crystal ball of fashion is in your hands," January 3, 2019, https://www.thenextbrick.com/retail-trends/predict-fashion-trends

Companies like Trend Union, The Doneger Group, and Promostyl provide information on all of the trend areas for many target markets and product categories, including color, fabrications, silhouettes, fashion influences, design themes, and population trends. In essence, they offer a one-stop trend forecasting and strategy planning service, as illustrated in Box 1.3, an interview with Trend Forecaster, Li Edelkoort.

Sources of Information

Where do forecasters go for information? It depends on the market sector in which they specialize (e.g., color, demographics, apparel, or home) or consumer segment they are investigating (e.g., contemporary women, preteens, or men). There is, however, a range of information sources that most trend forecasters find to be valuable. Following is a list of popular trend forecasting resources:

- *Market research firms.* These companies provide specific information on consumer market segments for a fee. Population changes that can be quantified are referred to as **demographic data**, such as age, education, residence, family size, occupation, income, and expenditures. Additionally, more general government data on demographics is available on similar subjects at no cost through resources such as the U.S. Census Bureau (www.census.gov).
- *The couture collections.* Dior, Chanel, Celine, Gucci, Armani, Prada, Issey Miyake—the list of prominent and influential designers is a long one. The introductions of their seasonal collections are important times for trend forecasters, because these industry leaders have a great influence on future ready-to-wear and home trends.
- *New designers.* Trend forecasters often view the collections of up-and-coming designers with as much enthusiasm and interest as those of the established

Figure 1.2

Trend forecasters often view the collections of innovative designers, such as Moon Choi, with as much enthusiasm and interest as those of time-honored couturiers.

couturiers (Figure 1.2). Trend forecasters are often seeking new places for design talent, such as prestigious fashion schools around the world, or in countries providing government support and new opportunities for fashion entrepreneurial businesses, such as India, Canada, and Hong Kong.

- *Other fashion services.* Apparel and accessories forecasters may subscribe to other services, such as color forecasting services. Some subscribe to competitors' services to stay on top of what the competition is doing. The primary tangible product of a trend forecasting firm is referred to as a **trend book**, or *look book*, which features the recommendations and predictions of the company for the upcoming seasons.

- *Trade shows.* International fiber and fabric markets, such as International Textile Fair in Dubai and Premiere Vision in Paris (Figure 1.3), are primary information sources for forecasters who are researching color and textile trends. There are apparel and accessories trade shows at the markets in New York City, Dallas, Los Angeles, Las Vegas, and Chicago, to name a few. High Point, North Carolina, offers markets in home textiles and furnishings.

- *Communication with peers.* Networking is a key activity for trend forecasters. Updates from designers, buyers, and manufacturers can provide significant information on what is selling and what is not. Communication

Figure 1.3

Premiere Vision in Paris is among the world's premiere international fabric trade shows.

CASE STUDIES IN CAREER EXPLORATION

BOX 1.3   Trend Forecaster Li Edelkoort

Interviewed by Jared Bajkowski

Could you give us a brief introduction?

As Strategic Director of New Business, I help The Doneger Group as a company to realize new projects and new assignments that will take us into branding and marketing worlds. The second role I have is Men's Fashion Director. As a retail and merchandising organization, we have found that menswear is a growing and opportunistic category, so it makes some natural sense to use my skills and background in menswear to leverage it and market it to the menswear community.

Does strategy apply to everything you approach?

I think strategy is at the root of so many organizations and marketplace opportunities—and especially in our world of fashion today. Being strategic allows a business to bloom and grow. I think any successful organization today is more balanced between strategy and creativity, which means left-brain to right-brain, and I really try to balance that out. I think that's important.

What kind of recurring actions fill your time here?

Well, I think there's always recurring seasons, retail concepts, and marketplace shifts. At one time, you only worried about seasons four times a year and how they affected the consumer or the store. I think today we operate on 365 days a year. It is: You're living for today, you're worried about tomorrow, you're looking to next year, but you understand what last year was about as well. Right now, we are still talking about this season and researching the same season a year from now, but as a company we are past that and beyond. And we have to deal with every day.

What kind of skills does an aspiring trend, branding, or strategic executive need to develop?

I think you have to be a generalist, not a specialist. You have to be left-brain and right-brain. You have to be very cognizant that, even if you are in the merchandising

Figure Box 1.3 Li Edelkoort of Trend Union.

world, you have to interface with the marketing and retail worlds. It all connects, and, therefore, you have to find out what the connectors are and what your role is in each and every part of it. I have always found that the most successful efforts and programs are those where corporate and marketing come to the table, interface with product, and then deliver the right thing in the right way. I will say the most important skillset for every executive at every level is a digital knowledge bank and project experience, and a consumer connection to it.

BOX 1.3 *(continued)*

What inspires you?

I'm still inspired by the worlds that are in front of me every day, no matter what city I'm in. Culture, consumer, and experience. I've always prided myself on saying, "Give me 24 hours in a city and I will know the downtown area, the suburban area, the hot alternative destination area, the collegiate area, and the typical shopping area. Once I see that I will have a very good perspective on what is going on. Even if I go on a vacation, I can see it from that level. It's just how I'm wired.

What's so important about what you're doing?

Every time I get involved with something, I say the bottom line of the business is so important. No matter how great a program, if it doesn't move the needle, it's not considered successful in corporate measurement style. One of my biggest challenges day in and day out in advertising and marketing was making sure that I was relevant and that the projects delivered. You have to show the results. You have to merchandise it; you have to sell it. I always say, "Show me. Don't tell me." Show the results in order to get the embrace.

Do you think the public is becoming more aware of marketing?

The consumer is very aware of everything today, and the consumer has a role and a voice. You can't ignore it. Ten years ago, the consumer would take anything that came out of fashion. Now, the consumer wants to see something that they've contributed to. It's true participation, and that is an ingredient that changes everything.

What have been the toughest challenges you've had to face in your career?

I've learned that you may not get the reward that is due you. You may have to look for other ways to get achievements. The entrepreneurial, start-up thing was not available to my generation because we were so traditionally schooled. Being a Pittsburgher brought up in a hard-working middle class, I wanted to work and work with passion.

I wanted to believe in what I worked in and for. The hardest thing for me was to leave my emotion at the door. At the end of the day, it's either about the client or the product. Yes, you can be excited, but that can't be the only driver. As a young person, you have to realize that sometimes your passion has to stop for the reality of what the business is or what the opportunity can be. That's hard when you're truly impassioned by it.

Is there any last advice to anybody with an aspiring fashion mind?

I keep hearing from industry executives that, in this virtual world, everything is transparent. Marketing executives will say about job candidates, "I want to see what they're doing and how they're doing it." If I see they are a part of a student group that's impacting the world, I know that is real and relevant. If they are online and they're making a difference with their message on Facebook, Instagram, or Tumblr, that's a very credible way for me to gauge them. If I see that they're self-promoters, and all they're doing is their pics of them and their friends in the coolest way, I'm not getting that they're hard-working individuals. Consider that whatever you put out there has to represent you and your brand, and it has to reinforce what you are going to contribute to the organization, because it is very accessible to anyone. I had a communications company say, "We will only hire a young person who has 5,000 Facebook followers, runs his or her own blog, and is tweeting 20 times per day. Why? Because they're approaching social media as part of their own, and that can help my business as well." What I see in young people today that is so dynamic is that they've got a great base of education; they're more worldly or have some type of international experience; and they've all had great internship experiences. That's pretty great. If you don't have that equation today, you need to figure out how you're going to get it, because you're kind of behind the eight ball without it.

Courtesy of Henry Doneger Associates, Inc.

with representatives of key suppliers can assist the forecaster in identifying trends. Membership in professional organizations, such as the Fashion Group International, Inc. and the American Society of Interior Designers (ASID), also provides trend forecasters with the opportunity to network with others in the know in the fashion industry.

- *E-sources.* Web sites, blogs, online music programs, chat rooms, news sites, e-catalogs, and social networks are valuable resources that are easily accessible to trend forecasters. Also, forecasters may subscribe to specific online trend forecasting resources. Some of these sites are provided at the end of this chapter.
- *Design sources.* Reference books, historical costume collections and texts, vintage clothing shops, antique dealers, museums, bookstores, and libraries are excellent resources for forecasters who are exploring the influence of past eras on fashion, as in Figure 1.4. Videos and photographs of recent designer collections, fashion shows, trade show exhibitions, and fashion or art books are some examples of design resources that trend forecasters use for information on current designer and trend information.
- *Publications.* Trade journals and international consumer magazines are common, obvious sources for trend information. It is less apparent, however, that many apparel and accessories forecasters subscribe to home furnishings and home accessories magazines to identify color, fabric, and theme trends in the home. New colors in automobiles are often gleaned from successful hues in home furnishings and apparel. Auto, health, and celebrity magazines are also part of the trend forecaster's reading materials. Trend forecasters often read it all.
- *The arts.* Music concerts, visual art presentations, museum exhibits, dance performances, and theater plays can influence or interrelate with fashion trends. For example, a photography or apparel exhibit that travels internationally can influence fashion trends, as in Figures 1.5 and 1.6.
- *Entertainment headliners.* Celebrities greatly influence fashion trends. People in music and the news, on talk shows, on the red carpet, in videos, and on the big screen have the ability to set trends. For example, celebrity gowns are copied and made available to consumers in weeks (Figure 1.7). Forecasters often watch

Figure 1.4
Vintage clothing and antiques are excellent resources for forecasters who are exploring the influence of past eras on today's fashion.

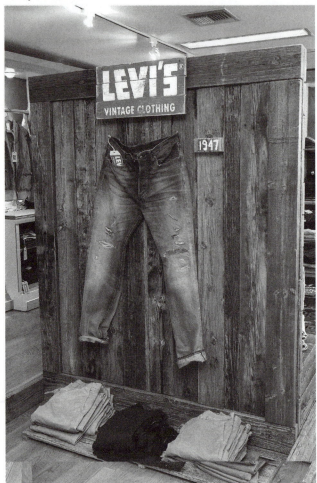

up-and-coming celebrities and project which newcomers have the star quality and visibility that will make them future stars. Forecasters observe what they wear, who their favorite designers are, how they style their hair, and where they hang out with friends. Because forecasters have to anticipate the actual trends before they happen, identifying the people who will influence future trends is a critical part of the forecaster's job.
- *Fabrics.* Cotton Incorporated is a company that represents the cotton industry and provides trend information to designers and retailers. Fabric companies, such as Burlington Industries Group, also develop trend information, which is often available on their Web sites.

Figure 1.5
"Fashion is not something that exists in dresses only. Fashion is in the sky, in the street, fashion has to do with ideas, the way we live, what is happening."
—Coco Chanel

Figure 1.6
The 2013 Esprit Dior exhibition at the Museum of Contemporary Art in Shanghai presented nine themes, grouping collections together from 1947 to the present day, and displayed eight of China's emerging artists as an homage to the designer of Avenue Montaigne.

Figure 1.7
Jennifer Lopez attends the 91st Annual Academy Awards wearing a shimmering gown by designer Tom Ford.

Figure 1.8

Designer Dries Van Noten and his dog, Harry, on the rooftop of his Antwerp, Belgium headquarters. With its vacation appeal and fashion focus, Antwerp is an example of a travel destination where fashion trends develop.

- *Travel.* Vacation hot spots are often filled with people who influence fashion trends. Additionally, certain fashion trends develop in specific geographic locations. China and its fun fur fashions, Belgium with its deconstruction techniques in apparel, and Japan and its young and creative street fashions are all examples of the travel destinations where fashion trends have developed (Figure 1.8).

- *Consumer tracking.* **Consumer tracking information** refers to data that relates to customer spending, such as how much money is spent on clothing, entertainment, or food. It can also relate to how a customer makes a purchase—cash, Bitcoin, credit card, debit card, or (rarely) check. Purchases can be correlated with credit card data to examine who is actually buying what.

- *Lifestyle trends.* **Lifestyle trends** refer to a population segment's values, interests, attitudes, dreams, and goals. Think about the following lifestyle trends: an increasing interest in health and fitness, the baby boomers' desire to entertain at home, and couples deciding to have fewer children and to start their families at a later age than previous generations. Next, ask yourself how these lifestyle trends influence fashion. Workout wear sales have increased. Patio furniture, cookware, and table-top accessories have received a renewed interest in the home furnishings and accessories industries. The number of pieces sold in children's wear has decreased, but sales in this merchandise classification have increased as a result of higher unit prices. Two working parents who have launched their careers and waited to have

Figure 1.9
Working parents, who have
launched their careers and
waited to have children, often
have the finances and desire to
provide their children with more.
Celebrities have a tremendous
impact on consumer preferences.
Jennifer Lopez, working mother
and celebrity, exemplifies both of
these lifestyle trends.

children often have the finances and desire to provide
their children with more. Lifestyle shifts influence what
the customer wants to buy (Figure 1.9). **Psychographics** take this idea a step further: these include people's
lifestyles and behaviors—where they like to vacation,
the kinds of interests they have, the values they hold,
and how they behave. Forecasters endeavor to become
aware of these changes before they occur and identify
the products that will meet consumer needs before
customers know what they need.

- *Places where people gather.* Airports, concert stadiums,
  shopping malls, dance clubs, and Times Square on
  New Year's Eve are some of the locations where groups
  of people can be observed. Trend forecasters examine
  where these people are going, what they are wearing,
  and from whom and what they are buying.

- *Street scenes.* "I watch people anywhere and everywhere," one successful trend forecaster explains. "You
  never know where a trend will start." Worth Global
  Style Network (WGSN), a key forecasting resource
  discussed later in this chapter, recruits people from
  colleges and other locations worldwide to submit
  trend information from their various communities.
  Every street in every city of the world, from WGSN's
  perspective, has the potential for fashion leadership
  (Figure 1.10).

Figure 1.10
A young woman on the street during London Fashion Week
February 2019.

Figure 1.11

When a particular sport or activity, such as cycling, gains consumer interest, its active sportswear is often imitated or modified for streetwear.

- *Sports.* When a particular sport or activity gains consumer interest, its active sportswear is often imitated or modified for street wear. High-top boxing boots, surfer shorts, and yoga pants illustrate the influence of sports trends on ready-to-wear. As Figure 1.11 depicts, cycling is one of the sports currently impacting active and streetwear fashions.

THE CAREER PATH

Securing a position in trend forecasting does not happen quickly. Typically, many years of industry experience are required. Some successful forecasters have previously worked as designers or buyers before moving into the trend forecasting career field. A few of the fortunate begin with internships or assistantship positions in forecasting firms to gain direct experience, exposure, and contacts in the forecasting world.

Qualifications

Successful trend forecasters often meet or exceed the following qualifications:

- *Education.* At the very least, a bachelor's degree in one of a wide range of disciplines is required. These disciplines most frequently include business administration (e.g., marketing or consumer behavior), visual arts, fashion design, or fashion merchandising.
- *Experience.* Forecasters often begin in entry-level positions in the areas of retail, product development, design, merchandising, or fashion coordination. Some successful forecasters have held positions in several sectors of the industry, such as design, product development, and retailing.
- *Personal characteristics.* There are a few specific and unique qualities that trend forecasters display. Among them is an excellent understanding of people and human behavior, global population and industry shifts, and fashion trends. Successful trend forecasters have effective visual, written, and oral communication and presentation skills. They are often curious and creative people with superior networking abilities. Most important, they have an exceptional capability to analyze, synthesize, and organize observations into categories that are clearly communicated to clients. Think about viewing fifteen couture collection presentations in a five-day period and then identifying the consistent trends among them. Trend forecasters have the ability to find the common threads and, later, classify and describe these trends for designers, manufacturers, and retailers who use the trend services.

The Trend Forecaster's Typical Career Path

Although the majority of college graduates prefer to start at the top, it is an essential advantage for a trend forecaster to understand all levels of the industry from a holistic perspective. Even the most entry-level retail sales positions provide valuable experience for future forecasters. As a sales associate, one is directly exposed to the customers' preferences and dislikes. Effective sales associates endeavor to understand who the customers are and identify their buying habits. As future trend forecasters progress to higher positions within the industry (e.g., product development or merchandising), it is important that they always keep in mind who the customers are and how they are changing. The work experience trend forecasters have acquired through the years is used on a daily basis when assisting designers, manufacturers, or merchandisers with future designs and purchases for upcoming seasons.

The Job Market for Trend Forecasters

The fashion industry has a limited number of trend forecasting positions in the areas of color, textile design, apparel and accessories design, and home furnishings. Because trend forecasting positions are limited, successful trend forecasters are well compensated for their knowledge and skills. Sometimes, a commission will be paid to trend forecasters based on how well their companies perform with their assistance.

Career Challenges

The pros of a trend forecasting career have been discussed, but what about the challenges? Because there are a limited number of successful forecasting firms, there are only a few jobs for a few good men and women. The job of a trend forecaster requires a tremendous amount of intelligence, skill, and exposure and, perhaps, a sixth sense. Forecasters must be aware of all of the external influences that may affect consumer behavior. The ability to observe, organize, and prioritize these outside influences is a rare skill. Trend forecasters who consistently identify the right trends develop strong reputations. Many wannabes who provide the wrong information for a season or two are no longer hired by clients, who depend on accurate fashion direction to make a profit. It can be stressful for trend forecasters to identify significant fashion influences seasonally or annually. Additionally, trend forecasters must be able to market their companies, their ideas, and themselves. The forecaster's knowledge, intuition, and experience truly form the ultimate product.

Examples of Trend Forecasting Companies

There are several successful trend forecasting companies around the world, with new firms constantly entering the mix. Some focus on a certain target market, such as teens or contemporary men, whereas others emphasize a specific fashion variable, such as color or fabric. Some offer a wide breadth of personal service, whereas others provide online reports. Whatever your fashion interest, there is a trend forecasting company to fill the bill.

Doneger Creative Services

Doneger Creative Services (doneger.com), based in New York City, is the trend and color forecasting and analysis division of The Doneger Group. Doneger Creative Services offers a broad range of products and services, such as printed publications, online subscriptions, and live presentations. This division addresses the forecasting needs of retailers, manufacturers, and other style-related businesses. Doneger's creative directors and trend analysts cover the apparel, accessories, and lifestyle markets in the women's, men's, and youth merchandise classifications.

Promostyl

Promostyl's (promostyl.com) mission is to pinpoint fashion, design, and lifestyle trends and help companies adapt to changing trends. The company bases its work on the currents of society, cultures, and lifestyles, believing that society makes fashion. The company creates trend books, develops visual presentations, consults with companies, and maintains an international network of subsidiaries and agents. Three main offices are located in Paris, New York City, and Tokyo.

Worth Global Style Network (WGSN)

Founders Julian and Marc Worth launched WGSN (wgsn.com), based in London, in 1998. It is one of the most successful online forecasting services to emerge. WGSN offers research, trend analysis, and news to the fashion, design, and style industries. Members of the 100-person staff travel extensively around the world. The WGSN team includes experienced writers, photographers, researchers, analysts, and **trendspotters**. Trendspotters are people located at universities and other locations worldwide who provide information to WGSN on the latest trends in each locale. The company tracks not only the latest fashion trends but also hot retail stores, new designers, emerging brands, and business innovations. WGSN maintains offices in London, New York City, Hong Kong, Seoul, Los Angeles, Melbourne, and Tokyo. Its client list is long and impressive and includes such designers and retailers as Giorgio Armani, Target, Mango, and Abercrombie & Fitch.

SnapFashun

To meet the needs of designers and manufacturers, members of SnapFashun (snapfashun.com) have access to its entire online archive of vector sketches and flats, based on thirty years of retail, street, and runway reporting from the fashion capitals of the world. The fashion library is updated with new details and silhouettes up to fourteen times per year. SnapFashun is a source for Los Angeles and European retail reporting, merchandising trends, and original design ideas. The firm monitors up-to-the-minute looks at top-selling items in trendsetting cities.

Paris Trend Forecasters

Several trend forecasting services and trade shows are based in Paris, France. Carlin Creative Trend Bureau is a forecasting and marketing firm dedicated to fashion trend information. The company's Web site (carlin -creative.com) is available in English and French. Peclers Paris (peclersparis.com) is a fashion trend forecasting service that specializes in textile design, fashion, beauty, consumer goods, and retailing. Première Vision (premier-evision.com) is the world's leading trade show in fabric forecasting, promoting fabric trends for designers and manufacturers in the fashion industry.

Color Forecasters

The Color Association of the United States is a color forecasting service. According to its Web site, colorasso-ciation.com, it is the oldest such company in the United States. Since 1915, the Color Association has been issuing color reports in fabric-swatched booklets. A committee panel of eight to twelve industry professionals selects seasonal color palettes. Another player in the color forecasting business is Doneger Creative Services. The company's trend and color forecasting division is devoted to the apparel, accessories, beauty, and lifestyle markets.

Cool Hunting

Cool Hunting seeks out trends in the form of "all things cool." Founder Josh Rubin believes that there are no new ideas, just great executions. A self-proclaimed "interaction designer," he is always looking for both creative inspiration and an understanding of the way people do things. In 2003, he decided to start a catalog of what he found and haphazardly named it Cool Hunting. Today, Cool Hunting has a global team of editors and contributors sifting through innovations in design, technology, art, and culture, and then reporting on the coolest of these at coolhunting.com. Cool Hunting is synonymous with seeking inspiration—its stories and videos highlight creativity and innovation in design, technology, style, culture, food, and travel. With a global team of editors and contributors, the company creates an award-winning publication, consisting of daily updates and weekly mini-documentaries (videos). Started as a designer's personal reference, Cool Hunting now has an international audience of like-minded creative people, who find its content on its Web site, its iPad app, and on Vimeo, Instagram, Twitter, and Facebook.

Trend Union

Trend Union (trendtablet.com), created by Lidewij Edelkoort, specializes in forecasting trends, consulting, and developing trend books for the fashion and textile industries, among others. With offices in Paris and New York, Edelkoort is assisted by a highly qualified team of creative professionals: graphic artists, designers, artists, and consultants. Every six months, Edelkoort personally designs the majority of the notebooks that become a collection of biannual trend forecasting books, setting forth the colors, materials, shapes, and lifestyles for seasons to come. These books are available to Trend Union's clients two years in advance of the major trends in the fields of fashion, textile, and consumption. Twice a year, Edelkoort creates a twenty-minute audiovisual presentation of images and music that portray the significant future trends featured in the books. This presentation is shown in Paris to the clients of Trend Union, with sessions in other major cities around the world.

Summary

Trend forecasters are central to the fashion industry. Accurate forecasting can make or break a company. Every designer and merchandiser must be aware of trend predictions to ensure their lines will appeal to their specific target market. Trend forecasters may be employed by broad-spectrum firms, fiber or fabric houses, companies specializing in color trends, or businesses that project population trends. They gather information by examining market research firms, couture collections, new designers, trade shows, art, design, e-sources, travel trends, lifestyle trends, entertainment, and street styles. Fashion forecasting is one of the few careers that encompasses all of the aspects of the industry; therefore, it is essential for trend forecasters to possess a strong understanding of the fashion industry, from creative product development to retail selling. Seldom does one gain a position in this field without a number of years of prior experience and education. As a trend forecaster, you may anticipate a challenging career that encourages you to create, read, listen, travel (online and off), observe, absorb, organize, and research always!

Key Terms

broad-spectrum firm
consumer tracking
   information
demographic data
fiber house
lead time

lifestyle trends
psychographics
trend board
trend book
trend forecaster
trendspotters

Online Resources

bigthink.com
businessoffashion.com
coolhunting.com
fashionising.com
featureshoot.com
inhabitat.com
nowness.com

pantone.com
reddit.com
ssense.com
trendhunter.com
trendwatching.com
wgsn.com

Discussion Questions

1. How conscious are you of current trends? Identify current color, design, art, textile, entertainment, and sociocultural trends for this season and the next.

2. Spot trends within the current season and trace their sources. Did these trends originate from the streets, art exhibitions, new technology, couture collections, or some other source?

3. Analyze current fashion publications and Web sites and compare the trends with fashion six months ago. Describe three themes cited as next year's top fashion trends.

4. What are some examples of companies outside of the fashion industry that rely on trend forecasting? Why are trends important to these businesses?

CHAPTER 2
TEXTILE DESIGN AND DEVELOPMENT

Take a look at one of your favorite prints. It can be a blouse, a shirt, or that great pair of patterned shorts. Think about the colors, the texture, the weave or knit, and the art of the print. There are designers and design houses who have made their places in fashion history with their textile designs. Can you name a few? Louis Vuitton, Missoni, Gucci, and Emilio Pucci may come to mind. Somebody has to be the creative force behind textile designs, and that somebody is a textile designer.

A **textile designer** creates original designs for the fabrics used in all sorts of industries. This person understands how to combine visual arts with technical and usage concerns. **Textile design** is the process of creating patterns, motifs, or surface interest for knitted, woven, or printed fabrics. Pattern and print designs are evaluated in terms of how they can be combined with printing, knitting, weaving, embossing, and embroidery processes.

Textile designers often specialize in one type of textile or another (e.g., knits or wovens), and they collaborate with textile colorists. A **textile colorist** works with a design to determine **colorways**, the specific color selections for a particular pattern or print; these are sometimes referred to as a *color palette*. Figure 2.1 provides an example of a colorway for a woven print.

These two creative positions are examples of the numerous career paths in the textile industry, which is a high-touch, high-tech industry. In the high-tech sector of the textile industry, there are several other career options, including textile engineering and textile production. A **textile engineer** works with designers to determine how designs can be applied to a fabric. A **textile technician** works with the issues that are directly related to the production of **piece goods**, such as finishing. Newly constructed knit or woven fabric must pass through various finishing

Figure 2.1

An example of a colorway for a woven print presented on Kaledo by Lectra.

processes to make it suitable for its intended purpose. **Finishing** enhances the appearance of fabric and also adds to its suitability for everyday wear or rugged use. Finishes can be solely mechanical, solely chemical, or a combination of the two. Finishes that simply prepare the fabric for further use, such as scouring and bleaching in blue jeans, are known as **general finishes**. **Functional finishes**, such as durable press treatments, impart special characteristics to the cloth, such as waterproofing or flocking.

Job opportunities in actual textile production have dramatically declined in recent years because of inexpensive labor costs overseas. About 650 textile plants closed between 1997 and 2009, draining thousands of jobs and depressing communities.[1] Textile manufacturing in the United States declined significantly in the 1990s and 2000s as cheaper labor pulled jobs overseas. In addition, automation and increased productivity of textile mills also cost jobs. More than 200,000 textile manufacturing jobs have been lost to automation in the last decade. However, things are changing overseas as well. Increasing wages in China and other countries, combined with higher transportation costs and tariffs, have prompted foreign and domestic companies to consider American manufacturing sites. The tide may eventually turn.

For now, a great number of U.S. fashion companies outsource much of their production work to companies in foreign countries. **Outsourcing** refers to having an aspect of a company's work performed by nonemployees in another company and, perhaps, in another country. Most outsourced jobs in the textile industry are low-paying production positions in countries with lower labor costs than those in the United States, such as those in the Pacific Rim, as well as South and Central America. The majority of American textile companies design domestically, but they outsource goods for production to take advantage of the free-trade agreements with low-wage countries. Despite the dramatic decline in U.S. jobs in the textile manufacturing industry, there is some light in that some job losses have been offset by creative and scientific tracks in design and product development.

In this chapter, the creative and scientific career opportunities in textile design and textile technology are examined. Whether one has a creative personality and an eye for pattern and color or a scientific mind that is interested in engineering and production, a job path in the textiles field can provide a fulfilling career.

FASHION DIRECTOR

A **fashion director** for a textile company is responsible for determining the trends, colors, themes, and textures for piece goods or fabrics that the firm will feature for a specific season. Fashion directors are primarily interested in identifying the most important fashion trends for their companies and communicating these trends to textile designers, production managers, and customers. Fashion directors often work with trend forecasting firms to determine trend possibilities in color, form, theme, and fabric needs for each season.

Qualifications

The following is a list of qualifications for a career as a fashion director for a major textile firm:

- *Education.* A bachelor's degree in textiles, fashion design, fashion merchandising, visual arts, or a related field is a minimum requirement for employment as a fashion director.
- *Experience.* The majority of fashion directors moved up the ladder from within the ranks. Many of them were textile designers, product developers, buyers, or assistant fashion directors before obtaining key positions as fashion directors.
- *Personal characteristics.* The fashion director often has similar characteristics to the trend forecaster: curiosity, strong communication skills, a strong visual sensibility, leadership abilities, a good understanding of who the customers actually are, and the ability to work with a variety of constituencies—from designers to production managers to technical assistants.

Career Challenges

The challenges of the fashion director's career relate to two primary areas: securing the job and keeping it. Fashion directors are expected to have a strong foundation of work experience in the industry. It takes time, skill, and effort to be promoted through a variety of positions, for example, from technical textile designer to product developer to buyer. The best and the brightest climb quickly up the career ladder. Once in the position of fashion director, there is a great deal of pressure to be right—to be accurate about the color, pattern, style, and theme trends.

If, for example, a fashion director determines that olive green is the color for a season, and it bombs at the retail level, then the company may lose a great deal of money from a high investment in olive green fabrics. As a result of this error, this fashion director may be searching for a new job. Additionally, the fashion director must collaborate successfully with a wide variety of people—designers, production personnel, and clients. It takes a person with a solid educational foundation in textiles, a well-balanced personality, and excellent communication skills to work effectively with so many different people.

TEXTILE DESIGNER

Textile designers create the images, patterns, colors, textures, weaves, and knits of the fabrics we wear and use, from our clothing and interiors to our automobiles and awnings (Figure 2.2). They can be classified as **surface designers**—knitters, weavers, or embroiderers for industries ranging from apparel to upholstery. To assist in textile design, there are **print services**, companies that sell art that becomes print designs to mills, wholesalers, product developers, and retailers. Many textile designers utilize **computer-aided design (CAD)**, which is the process of developing garments, prints, and patterns on a computer screen. This process has greatly influenced the field of textile design, as it provides faster, more varied, and more personalized design options in textiles than were possible in past years. Box 2.1 provides information on Lectra, one company that offers optimized processes to the fashion industry through integrated computer technologies.

Technological advances in CAD software and digital printing, several of which will be presented later in this chapter, offer unlimited creative opportunities to designers. For instance, a customer can now have a photograph of her pet pug transferred to canvas, which will then be used to create a handbag. An image of a Parisian street scene can be scanned and printed on fabric that will later become bedroom curtains. Once the print or pattern is developed, a strike-off is produced by the textile manufacturer. A **strike-off** is a test sample of printed fabric made to show and verify color and pattern before entering into production on larger quantities. Figure 2.3 shows a digitally printed textile design, and Box 2.2 provides information on the development of digital textile design and some of its designers.

Figure 2.2
Italian textile designer Donatella Ratti with fabric swatches of her work.

Figure 2.3
A model on the runway wearing a digitally printed textile design by Basso and Brooke.

PROFILE: Lectra and Its Impact on Textile Design and Development

With more than forty years' experience in fashion and apparel, Lectra's mission is to provide a complete spectrum of design, development, and production solutions to confront twenty-first-century challenges. From first creative spark to final product, Lectra addresses an end-to-end process, supporting the day-to-day operations of companies in more than 100 countries. From fast fashion to luxury to ready-to-wear, Lectra's 23,000 customers in markets as diverse as casual, sports, outdoor, denim, and lingerie represent every development and sourcing model imaginable.

Lectra Fashion PLM

Lectra Fashion PLM connects planning, design, development, and sourcing teams to help companies master the entire collection lifecycle from design to development to production. Specifically designed for the fashion and apparel industry, this collaborative environment combines collection creation and management, textile and fashion design, product specifications, and design-to-cost for real-time decision making.

Lectra's Fashion and Textile Design Solution

Lectra's collaborative design solution keeps fashion and textile design teams focused on creative activities, allowing them to do digitally what they could never do by hand. With sketching and boarding tools, knit, print and woven textile design, and color development, Lectra's design solution provides tools for fashion companies to create new designs and trends.

Designers can easily share their creative work with other teams right from the beginning of the collection process, ensuring design quality and production feasibility. Better collaboration between designers and product development teams reduces the number of errors and supports early decision making to significantly accelerate the design process.

Sketching tools help designers stay on top of trends and reduce the time it takes to get products from the drawing board to development and sampling. Fashion-specific tools cut down the time needed to create new styles and carry over bestsellers. Range plans and quick sketches jump-start fast visual concept development by turning creative trends into product ideas quickly. Detailed specification and production instructions reduce the need for clarifications when communicating product ideas to teams and suppliers.

Collaborative Textile Design Modules

Lectra's textile designer modules help textile designers create original concepts or adapt existing ideas from a textile archive by supplying industry-specific tools for woven, knitted, and print design production. Creating these visuals helps deliver clear specifications and design proposals with essential color, pattern, repeat, and scale information.

- Lectra's collaborative print solution turns creative ideas into production-ready, cost-effective prints. Print-specific tools help designers change repeat ideas, overlap, and dimensions; respect color limitations; group colors for tonal prints; and

Figure Box 2.1a Sketching tools that give the designer flexibility, creativity, and options while saving time and money.

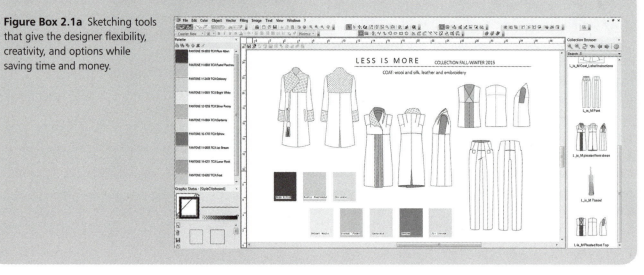

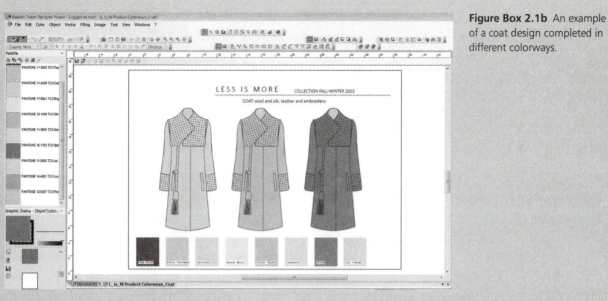

Figure Box 2.1b An example of a coat design completed in different colorways.

Figure Box 2.1c Coat details are illustrated on the Lectra screen.

recolor from a seasonal palette to create unlimited colorways.

- Lectra's collaborative weave solution contains visual libraries of industry-standard weaves for an easy start, as well as the tools to customize and build on existing patterns. A yarn creation tool encourages designers to explore the effects of fibers, twist, and diameter on weave and knit patterns.
- Lectra's collaborative knit solution is driven by a unique three-dimensional stitch simulator that generates realistic knit fabric simulations. Designers can preview and check complex combinations of multi-color yarns and structured knits to get designs right the first time. An extensive library of knit structures

coupled with this unique three-dimensional stitch simulator reduces the designer's time and the need for costly samples.

From palette creation to the preparation of print specifications, Lectra supports designers in the key steps of the print design process: (1) combine artistic tools and scanned images to create new print designs; (2) reduce and recolor flat and tonal prints; (3) create and vary print repeats; and (4) prepare print specifications with callouts, color information, text, and images for accurate communication with design, product development, and production teams.

Figure 2.4

A knit design and its colorways are presented on Kaledo by Lectra.

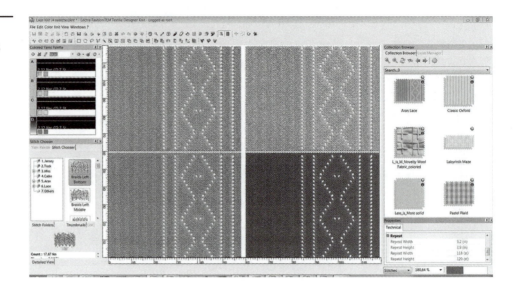

Figure 2.5

Croquis of a sweater design developed using CAD software.

A textile designer using CAD likely knows how to paint and draw well, but works specifically on the computer to create designs. A textile designer can take several different specialized career paths, including working with wovens, knits, or prints. For example, a textile designer may choose to focus on fibers and processes that are commonly used for knit goods such as sweaters, as illustrated in Figure 2.4. Another textile designer may decide to specialize in creating textile prints for woven fabrics by painting or by using CAD to create a **croquis** (Figure 2.5), a rendering or miniature visual of a textile pattern or print for a garment or an accessory, such as a scarf or handbag. The **assistant textile designer** supports the textile designer in accomplishing all of these tasks. What is the most important personal trait needed to be a successful textile designer? The key characteristic is to possess a mind that is simultaneously creative, business-oriented, and technically savvy.

TEXTILE STYLIST

A **textile stylist** is the creative person who modifies existing textile goods, altering patterns or prints that have been successful on the retail floor to turn them into fresh, new products. The textile stylist may resize the image or develop new colorways for the modified textile print or pattern, sometimes collaborating with a textile colorist to accomplish this task.

TEXTILE COLORIST

A textile colorist chooses the color combinations that will be used in creating each textile design. Colorists frequently travel to fashion markets and belong to color forecasting organizations to stay on top of current and future color trends. There is a wide range of industries in which textile designers, stylists, and colorists are employed. They include the following:

- Knitted and woven textiles, used to make clothes and soft-good products, as well as upholstered products, such as home furnishings and automotive seats
- Rugs and carpets
- Prints for wallpapers, paper goods, flooring, or tiles

The responsibilities of textile designers, stylists, and colorists are as follows:

- Interacting with customers (e.g., apparel manufacturers or designers) to understand their needs and interpret their ideas accurately

- Collaborating with marketing, buying, and technical staff members, as well as design colleagues
- Understanding how textiles will be used, what properties textiles will need to function optimally, and how the addition of color dyes or surface treatments will affect these properties
- Conducting research for ideas and inspiration, from antique embroidery to modern architecture to children's storybooks
- Experimenting with texture and pattern as it relates to color
- Producing design or color ideas, sketches, and samples and presenting them to customers
- Producing designs or color options for designs using CAD software
- Checking and approving samples of completed items
- Working to meet deadlines
- Working within budgets
- Keeping up to date with new fashions and population trends—current and projected
- Staying on top of new design and production processes
- Attending trade and fashion shows

Textile designers, stylists, and colorists need to consider such factors as how the designs will be produced, how the finished articles will be used, the quality of the materials used, and the budgets. They work standard hours, but they need to be flexible to meet deadlines. They are based in studios or offices. Prospective employers require a strong and relevant portfolio of work for review. Employers include large manufacturing companies and small, exclusive design houses. Some textile designers, stylists, and colorists are self-employed.

Qualifications

Requirements for employment in textile design, stylist, or colorist positions include the following:

- *Education.* A bachelor's degree in textiles, visual arts, computer-aided design, graphic design, fashion design, or a related discipline is a minimum requirement.
- *Experience.* Entry-level design positions provide the ideal starting place for college graduates. Additional experience in technical design (i.e., CAD) and color will assist the candidate in moving up the career ladder. Lectra's Kaledo Suite for textile design is becoming

increasingly important in textile design, and experience in this program will give the job candidate an edge.
- *Personal characteristics.* Flexible computer skills; a strong visual sense for color, texture, and pattern; a creative personality; knowledge of how textiles are produced; effective business skills; an awareness of fashion trends; a practical understanding of skills such as sewing, knitting, weaving, and embroidery; and knowledge of the target consumer help make the textile designer, stylist, and colorist successful.

Career Challenges

The challenges for textile designers, stylists, and colorists are similar. They must interpret the trends designated by the fashion director. Sometimes, converting the words of the fashion director into the fabrics the director has envisioned can be difficult. Textile designers, stylists, and colorists also must be aware of the technical requirements of fabric development, such as the printing requirements, durability, and application of finishes. Most important, they are often under pressure to meet quick deadlines and work within budget constraints.

TEXTILE TECHNICIAN

A textile technician either supervises the production facilities of a company or oversees the production as it is done by a **contractor**, a firm that is hired to manufacture the product line, either domestically or abroad. If a textile company owns its manufacturing facility, then the textile technician is responsible for the smooth running of the equipment used in textile production to maximize production. If a textile company contracts its production out to another company, then the textile technician works with the contractor to accomplish these goals. The primary responsibilities of the textile technician are as follows:

- Overseeing the regular routine maintenance of equipment or the efficient production of the contractor
- Checking performance levels of equipment and/or contractors for optimal production
- Carrying out regular checks on production, spotting any difficulties, and dealing with them before they become problematic

CASE STUDIES IN CAREER EXPLORATION

BOX 2.2 The Fabric as the Designer's Canvas

Digital printing technologies continue to offer faster production and may grow to become the technology that provides the majority of the world's printed textiles.

Lights, cameras, fabrics . . . Digitally manipulated prints have become big news on the runways. Martin Margiela, Peter Pilotto, and Mary Katrantzou belong to a new generation of designers who are literally creating not only the designs but also the printed fabrics they envision. "My training is as a textile designer and in traditional screen printing, but because of the nature of what I was doing with trompe l'oeil, digital collages give greater plasticity," explains Mary Katrantzou, a Central Saint Martins graduate, speaking of digital design's benefits. "With a screen print, 10 or 15 color separations need great expertise. With digital, there is no limitation. You can print a photographical version of anything," she adds.

Previously an instructor at the Royal College of Art and now a fabric consultant for Louis Vuitton in Paris, Susannah Handley compares the difference between traditional and digitally printed textiles as being similar to that of painting and photography. She tells the *International Herald Tribune*: "Directly from computer to cloth is how many patterns are realized these days—it is a more clinical, faster method with the advantage that an instant result can be achieved."

The inkjet printing technology used in digital printing was first patented in 1968. In the 1990s, inkjet printers became widely available for paper-printing applications. You likely have one on your desk right now. The technology has continued to develop, and there are now specialized wide-format printers that can process a variety of substrates, everything from paper to canvas to vinyl and fabric. Although digital textile printing has been around for decades, it has only recently taken its place in the fashion industry. Digital textile printing provides the ability to print designs on fabric, directly from a PC or Mac. Inkjet printing is done on fabric in the same manner as it is completed on paper, and just as easily. This versatile technology is being used in many apparel and nonapparel markets. Digitally printed textiles can be used for a vast range of applications, including apparel, handbags, footwear, umbrellas, flags and banners, exhibition signage, furniture, curtains, drapes, bedding, towels, wall coverings, and carpets or other floor coverings.

Although digital textile printing has been around for decades, it has only recently taken its place in the fashion industry. Digital textile printing provides the ability to print designs on fabric directly from a PC or Mac. Inkjet printing is done on fabric in the same manner as it is completed on paper—and just as easily. This versatile technology is being

Figure Box 2.2 Digital printing technologies continue to offer faster production and may grow to become the technology that provides the majority of the world's printed textiles.

used in many apparel and nonapparel markets. Digitally printed textiles can be used for a vast range of applications, including clothing, handbags, footwear, umbrellas, flags and banners, exhibition signage, furniture, curtains, drapes, bedding, towels, wall coverings, and carpets or other floor coverings.

For some companies and some products, digital textile printing can significantly reduce the costs associated with screen printing on textiles. Presently, the textile industry produces the majority of its printed textile fabric by screen printing, also referred to as analog textile printing. However, as we move through the digital age, developments in the digital printing of paper are increasingly being adapted for the textile market. Inkjet textile printing is growing, while growth in analog textile printing remains stagnant.

As digital print technologies continue to offer faster production and larger cost-effective print runs, digital printing may grow to become the technology that provides the majority of the world's printed textiles. Currently, digital printing on textiles has several advantages over traditional textile printing methods, as follows:

- Lower production costs for short runs
- High productivity because of shorter lead times
- Fast turnaround

The only special requirement is that the fabrics used must be pretreated to hold the ink better and reproduce a wider range of high-quality hues. There are various types of treatments applied, according to the fabrics and the inks being used.

Unlimited creative opportunities are often at the top of the designer's list when it comes to digital textile printing. Think about printing photographs on fabrics, using art as inspiration, creating a color palette that is unique to your design collection, and customizing products to meet an individual customer's desires. Digital printing on fabrics has also opened new opportunities for designers, manufacturers, merchandisers, and salespersons. For example, it is now possible to print a small piece of fabric, or just enough for a garment, to create a sample of a new design.

Sources:

Bumpus, J., "Special effects," *Vogue* UK, April 13, 2003, https://www.vogue.co.uk/article/the-digital-print-revolution

Desmond, J., "Introduction to digital fabric printing," Fashion-Incubator, June 24, 2010, www.fashion-incubator.com/archive/introduction-to-digital-fabric-printing/

Ujiie, H., *Digital Printing of Textiles*, Centre of Excellence in Digital Ink Jet Printing, Philadelphia University, Woodhead Publishing Series in Textiles No. 53.

In a large textile factory, a technician may specialize in one type of production technique, such as knitting or weaving; however, in a smaller company, the responsibilities of the technician may be more wide ranging. Technicians work approximately forty hours per week, sometimes on shifts.

Qualifications

Requirements for employment as a textile technician include the following:

- *Education.* A bachelor's degree in textile technology, textile production, computer science, textile engineering, industrial technology, or a related field is required.
- *Experience.* Some textile technicians begin in entry-level technical design positions. They may move up into management of a team of technical designers that covers specific merchandise classifications, such as menswear or children's wear. Some technicians move into management or into specialized areas, such as quality control and research.
- *Personal characteristics.* High levels of technical knowledge and computer skills are extremely important personal qualifications in this career path. Strong practical and problem-solving skills are also essential. A thorough understanding of textile applications and usage assists the textile technician in making decisions about product development.

The career challenges for a textile engineer and textile technician are similar and are presented after the following discussion of the textile engineer's position.

TEXTILE ENGINEER

Manufacturers are merging textiles with technology to create new products for the market. For instance, instead of being just wrinkle-resistant, fabrics have become truly

Figure 2.6

An enlarged image of a crochet-look bioimplantable surgical patch.

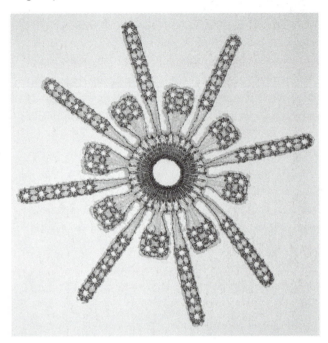

wrinkle-free through a process patented by TAL Corporation of Hong Kong. The process involves baking a special coating onto the fabric, as well as innovative use of adhesives along the seams to prevent puckering. Other fabrics are coated with Teflon to resist stains. Materials have been developed to change color with body temperature changes, which is particularly appealing for hospital use. Figure 2.6 shows an additional example of innovative fiber technology. The career path that directly relates to these new products is that of textile engineer.

A textile engineer works with designers to determine how designs can be applied to a fabric while considering practical variables, such as durability, washability, and colorfastness. A person in this position will have a background in textile science that often includes chemistry and manufacturing, in addition to textile analysis.

Qualifications

Requirements for employment as a textile engineer include the following:

- *Education.* A bachelor's degree in textiles, textile technology, textile production, computer science, textile engineering, industrial technology, or a related discipline is a minimum requirement.

- *Experience.* Many textile engineers working for companies that own and operate their own manufacturing facilities move up from the production line to this position. Textile engineers working with firms that contract out production may have a greater job emphasis on information technology in their positions. Some textile engineers begin in apprentice positions as assistant textile engineers.

- *Personal characteristics.* A textile engineer has a broad knowledge of how textiles are produced. In addition, this position requires an understanding of technical considerations as they relate to textile applications, an awareness of consumer wants and needs, and a comprehension of textile science.

Career Challenges

Textile technicians and engineers face the challenge of understanding and anticipating the continually changing technologies in textile design and production. Deadlines are a constant potential source of stress. Communicating and problem solving with a variety of co-workers in different divisions, such as design and production, require a proactive approach, patience, and flexibility by textile technicians and engineers. The ability to identify a problem and solve it quickly is an ongoing task in these positions.

In addition to design, color, and technical positions in the textile industry, there are ancillary career paths. The resource room director or reference librarian and the account executive are two career paths that relate to the textile industry, yet require different sets of skills and backgrounds from those of the creative and scientific positions.

RESOURCE ROOM DIRECTOR/ REFERENCE LIBRARIAN

Many large companies maintain a **resource room**, or *reference library*, of textile samples, source books and magazines, Internet resources, print and pattern images, and, possibly, actual garments constructed from the company's fabrics or those of competitors. As portrayed in Figure 2.7, these items are used by fashion directors, designers, technicians, and sales representatives for design inspiration and reference. The **resource room director** oversees the procurement, organization, and removal or replacement of these materials.

Figure 2.7
Bunny Williams' design resource room. Resource rooms, also called reference libraries, hold items that are used by fashion directors and designers for inspiration and reference.

Companies such as large apparel manufacturers, fashion publishers, and fiber/fabric houses maintain reference libraries. The **reference librarian** is responsible for managing the inventory of books and resources and procuring new ones.

Qualifications

Requirements for employment as a resource room director or reference librarian include the following:

- *Education.* A bachelor's degree in textiles, fashion merchandising, fashion design, or a related discipline is a minimum requirement.
- *Experience.* For recent graduates with work experience in fashion retailing and textiles, strong academic performances, and impressive references, these can be entry-level positions. Some resource room directors or reference librarians later move into the design divisions of firms. Exposure to the references of a particular firm helps build the potential designer's background.
- *Personal characteristics.* Strong organizational skills, effective time management, first-rate communication skills, and attention to detail are personal qualities that fit the position of resource room director or reference librarian.

Career Challenges

Managing a resource room or reference library can be a daunting task. There is a constant flow of new acquisitions that need to be inventoried, labeled, and stored, often in minimal space. There must be a high level of organization for the resource room director or reference librarian to be able to pull samples quickly for the fashion director or designer who needs them immediately.

ACCOUNT EXECUTIVE

An **account executive**, also referred to as *sales* or *manufacturer's representative*, sells to and manages the accounts, or clients, of textile manufacturers. The account executive is responsible for the sales of textiles and usually is assigned to a specific territory, such as the southern or midwestern United States. As illustrated in the classified advertisement of Figure 2.8, account executives can be paid in several ways: a salary, commission, quota, or a combination of these. This is a great career for someone who prefers working independently and enjoys business, budgets, and sales, as well as the textile, fashion, and home furnishing markets. Box 2.3 provides a look at how manufacturer's representatives are using social media to generate sales and build relationships with clients.

SOCIAL MEDIA STRIKES
BOX 2.3 How Manufacturer's Reps Can Use Social Media to Generate Sales

Social media is the perfect tool for manufacturer's reps of fashion brands to engage their customers online. A recent study found that salespeople using social media on the job outperformed their peers who were not using it by an incredible 73 percent. They also exceeded their quotas 23 percent more often than their counterparts who were not using social media. Both social media and fashion are all about self-expression. Customers recognize that the way they dress reflects their emotions, personality, and how they want to be viewed by others—just like their tweets or Instagram posts. Fashion and social media—it's a perfect fit. Here's a look at social media strategies that can be applied to any fashion rep's business:

- *Super-size your audience.* Connect with your retail buyers *and* their customers, your ultimate end users who buy your line from the retailers' store and wear the fashion items all over town. Be available and credible, because clients-to-be do research before they walk into a showroom or talk to a sales rep. Make initial connections on LinkedIn and create a link to the manufacturer's Web site to give them more content to peruse.

- *Keep the goods coming.* Social media users don't take nights and weekends off. Neither should a media director. Facebook pages that are frequently updated with captivating posts are much more likely to generate likes and attract new fans. To keep fresh content that is needed for regular posts and interactions, think about asking Facebook users to contribute new material with a special theme, such as stories of where they wore—and what they did while wearing—your fashion line. For example, Tiffany & Co.'s Facebook page asks fans to post their love stories with photos of their engagement and/or wedding rings. There's also a place for the story-telling strategy on Twitter.

- *Provide customer service extraordinaire.* Facebook and Twitter give your customers constant accessibility and *personalized service*. Delivering personalized service is nothing new to a seasoned salesperson, but scaling this with social media is key to building sales productivity and effectiveness. Today's customers expect reps to do their homework and to reach out at the right time with the right message. Successful salespeople do not annoy prospects before they are ready to hear from them. There simply are not enough hours in the day to be in touch with everyone all the time, so the smart salesperson strives to provide immediate customer service when it is needed. The days of waiting "forever" for a representative to be available to take the buyer's calls are over. A tweet is much simpler and quicker. Do you offer your buyers Twitter or Facebook customer service?

- *Instagram and Pinterest are your two new best friends.* Both sites provide a visual experience for your clients. Every user can instantly post photos of his or her looks from your lines; you can post looks from your new line with the speed of light—well, the speed of fashion anyway. Bring your fashions to the masses.

- *Reach out to bloggers.* Contact bloggers who relate to your line and suggest a giveaway (that sample line can come in handy here) to boost blog visits and your line's visibility. The resulting positive press can mean a whole new crowd of customers—buyers and wearers.

- *You're too square to be hip?* Think about your target market and find someone who is like them to help you with your social media. Check out examples of a youthful approach at OscarPRGirl, a site that uses the persona of a PR girl who reports from inside the Oscar de la Renta fashion house as its moderator.

- *Social media is a way to start a conversation with your buyers and customers and to make new friends.* It is also key to getting ahead of your competition. Post on Facebook, tweet on Twitter, create a board on Pinterest, take an Instagram, and then tally up your sales. It is the power of social media.

Sources:

Fidelman, M., "Study: 78% of salespeople using social media outsell their peers," *Forbes*, May 19, 2013, www.forbes.com/sites/markfidelman/2013/05/19/study-78-of-salespeople-using-social-media-outsell-their-peers/

Marsh, B., "6 tips for using social media to boost sales," *Inc.*, March 5, 2014, www.inc.com/bob-marsh/6-tips-for-using-social-media-to-boost-sales.html

Newberry, C., "Social selling: What it is, why you should care, and how to do it right," *Hootsuite*, April 23, 2019, blog.hootsuite.com/social-media-for-sales

Odden, L., "How should salespeople use social media?" *ClickZ*, February 27, 2012, www.clickz.com/clickz/column/2155088/salespeople-social-media

Shih, C., "How sales reps can succeed in the social era," *Harvard Business Review*, April 10, 2013, blogs.hbr.org/2013/04/how-sales-reps-can-succeed-in/

Figure 2.8

Classified advertisement for a textile company representative. As illustrated in this classified advertisement, sales executives are responsible for the sales of a company's textiles and the solicitation and maintenance of accounts.

Fashion Sample Design Manager Coordinator ✕

Saachistyle Fashion - White Plains, NY

Saachistyle is a fast-growing fashion accessories wholesale company in White Plains, NY near the Kensico Dam Plaza

See us at **www.saachistyle.com**

See us at **www.instagram.com/saachistyle/**

Description

We are looking for a Sample Coordinator/Manager to **keep track of every sample and product that moves across our company.** The Sample Manager is responsible for the flow of samples in and out for each internal group (sales, manufacturing, marketing, photography). You will support and be a key part of the merchandising process.

This is a tough fast-paced job that requires being hands-on with merchandise and having excellent organizational skills and a great memory of where everything is. Be prepared to work with multiple teams having fast turn-around asks all day and not get frustrated. Be prepared to be on your feet all the time.

If you are looking for a fun exciting fashion job and love to learn how it all works and are willing to put in the time - this is a great opportunity.

Responsibilities

This role will receive, organize, and maintain a physical and digital record for all samples and requests for those samples among the teams. Some idea of the parts of the job.

- Manage internal tracking system for real-time status of samples, from order to delivery across any group and through final archiving. Keep track at all times
- Apply organizational tools for tracking receipt - Create your own if you need to
- Check-in/out all physical samples out of the showroom. Create a system of checking in and chacking out.
- Ship your sample packets for customers.
- Provide status on all samples
- Create SKU/take pictures for each new sample
- Archive and classify all samples.
- Maintain archive, storage rooms.
- Owner of all samples and merchandise lines.
- Process daily package deliveries/sample returns and put them back
- Communicate with the overseas office regarding estimated timelines of delivery.
- Track all master samples and predict the need for additional; samples for key items.

Qualifications

Qualifications include the following:

- *Education.* A bachelor's degree in fashion merchandising, general business administration, or marketing is preferred.
- *Experience.* Retail or wholesale sales experience is most often required; however, an internship or employment as an assistant to an account executive is an excellent way to open the door to this career path.
- *Personal characteristics.* A strong understanding of accounting, effective sales skills, good communication abilities, and excellent follow-up skills are important attributes of successful account executives.

Career Challenges

Account executives are challenged to continually beat last season's or last year's figures. For some people, it is difficult to work independently and motivate oneself, despite rejections during sales calls and a fluctuating economy. Monitoring income and expenses, including many costs related to generating sales, is a juggling act for many account representatives, who must ask themselves, "Will I make enough commission to earn a living and offset the costs of this travel to trade markets or to clients' offices?" Maintaining a positive outlook and a high energy level are requirements for the successful account executive.

EXAMPLES OF COMPANIES EMPLOYING TEXTILE DESIGNERS AND PRODUCT DEVELOPERS

Several large companies employ textile personnel, from designers to resource room managers. Many of these firms are located in New York City and Los Angeles; some have satellite offices in Dallas, San Diego, and Atlanta, as well as cities abroad. In this section, eight of the top textile firms are examined, encompassing fur as a type of textile.

Cotton Incorporated

Cotton Incorporated is a not-for-profit corporation established pursuant to the Cotton Research and Promotion Act of 1966. It provides fabric, color, and trend

Figure 2.9
Cotton Incorporated conducts research and promotion for cotton and cotton products, with the primary goals of increased demand and profitability.

Figure 2.10
If you check the label of any quality wool or blended wool item you own, you are likely to find the famous Woolmark symbol, as shown here.

information for textile manufacturers, soft goods, and soft-good products for manufacturers, designers, and retailers. Funded by U.S. growers of upland cotton and importers of cotton and cotton textile products, Cotton Incorporated conducts research and promotion for cotton and cotton products with the primary goal of increasing the demand for and profitability of U.S. cotton and cotton products; its logo is illustrated in Figure 2.9.

The company offers technical services, such as fiber processing, fabric development, dyeing and finishing, and cotton quality management assistance. Information services provide data on cotton supply and demand, fiber quality, and consumer research trends. To keep cotton on the runway, Cotton Incorporated's fashion trend analysis team provides color and trend forecasts for cotton apparel and home products, highlighting the company's trend research and supplier information. Cotton Incorporated World Headquarters is located in North Carolina. Offices are located worldwide, including New York, Mexico City, Osaka, and Shanghai. The company's Web site, cottoninc. com, provides corporate information, research reports, and employment opportunity postings.

Australian Wool Services Limited (The Woolmark Company)

With more than sixty years of expertise in the wool industry and textile innovation, Australian Wool Services Limited is the world's leading wool fiber textile organization. The company provides unique global endorsement through ownership and licensing of the Woolmark, Woolmark Blend, and Wool Blend brands. The Woolmark

Company, a subsidiary of Australian Wool Services, specializes in the commercialization of wool technologies and innovations, technical consulting, business information, and commercial testing of wool fabrics. If you check the label of any quality wool or blended wool item you own, you are likely to find one of the famous Woolmark symbols, as illustrated in Figure 2.10.

These brands and their corresponding brandmarks are protected by strict and extensive control checks to ensure product quality. Australian Wool Services Limited operates globally, working with textile processors, designers, and retailers in both the apparel and interior textile markets.

Fur Council of Canada

The Fur Council of Canada is a national, nonprofit organization incorporated in 1964, representing people working in every sector of the Canadian fur trade. This includes fur producers, auction houses, processors, designers, craftspeople, and retail furriers. The goals of the Fur Council programs include the following:

- Encouraging linkages between designers and other sectors of the fashion industry
- Sponsorship of competitions for both professional designers and students in Canadian fashion colleges
- Promotion of the work of innovative Canadian fur designers through advertising in top national and international fashion publications
- Providing accurate information about the Canadian fur trade to consumers, educators, and the public to counter criticisms that the industry's practices are cruel to

Figure 2.11

The Fur Council of Canada can be further studied on its Web site at www.furcouncil.com.

animals. For example, in Canada, trappers must pass a mandatory course in which they learn how to use new humane trapping methods and how to apply the principles of sustainable use established by wildlife officials and biologists.

The Fur Council of Canada can be further investigated on its Web site at furcouncil.com; its logo is featured in Figure 2.11.

International Luxury Outerwear Expo

Chicago is the site of a major luxury outerwear international expo. Launched in 2014, The International Luxury Outerwear Expo (ILOE) is a fur and outerwear fashion fair of attracting thousands of professional buyers from the world's finest specialty boutiques and department stores with its wide array of luxury furs, boutique furs, shearlings, leathers, cashmere, and accessories. In 2018, the show hosted eighty exhibitors representing designer labels and upscale women's and men's outerwear in fur and precious fabrics. The lines range from formal looks to casual wear, sportswear, and streetwear. Buyers come from the United States and abroad. Another area of the trade show features unique international accessory collections, including handbags, gloves, scarves, hats, wraps, and jewelry. The ILOE show can be investigated more by visiting the organization's Web site at iloeshow.com.

Mohair Council

The Mohair Council is an organization exclusively dedicated to mohair, the fleece of the Angora goat. Established in 1966, the Mohair Council concentrates on marketing, education, and research as it relates to the mohair industry. The Mohair Council was created for mohair producers and is still financially sustained primarily by producers. It is a nonprofit organization funded by interest and dividend dollars from the now-defunct Wool Act, a current voluntary producer mohair assessment program, and funds from the U.S. Department of Agriculture.

The council headquarters is located in San Angelo, Texas, on the edge of Edwards Plateau in the southwest part of the state. This rugged ranching region is prime goat country and has long been home to many of the finest Angora goat breeding flocks in the world. Ninety percent of the U.S. Angora goat population grazes within a 150-mile radius of the Mohair Council's national headquarters, making Texas the primary mohair region of the United States. The United States has developed into one of the three largest mohair-producing nations in the world, with an annual production in excess of 2.4 million pounds. The other principal mohair sources are South Africa and Turkey.

The main function of the Mohair Council is to promote American mohair and to find viable worldwide markets for this unique commodity. To market its product, the Mohair Council has a team of eleven professionals who travel the world in search of profitable foreign markets for American mohair. These individuals meet one on one with prospective buyers, discover their needs, and then work to put the mohair buyer and supplier together.

Another objective of the Mohair Council is to educate designers, manufacturers, retailers, and consumers about mohair and mohair products (logo illustrated in Figure 2.12). For example, did you know that, as a decorating fabric, mohair is valued for its flame resistance and high sound absorbency? It is ideal for public places such

Figure 2.12
A primary objective of the Mohair Council is to educate designers, manufacturers, retailers, and consumers about mohair and mohair products.

as theaters, hotel lobbies, and offices, as well as homes. In addition, mohair draperies are effective insulators, keeping heat in during cold weather and serving as a barrier against hot outdoor temperatures in the summer. The Mohair Council's Web site is mohairusa.com.

Cone Mills

Cone Mills, LLC, is one of America's leading textile manufacturers. Cone Mills is a privately held company owned by W. L. Ross and Company as part of the International Textile Group. It is headquartered in Greensboro, North Carolina, with three manufacturing facilities located in China and Mexico. The company operates regional sales offices in Greensboro, New York, Dallas, Los Angeles, Kansas City, and San Francisco. Established in 1891, Cone Mills aims to be the largest producer of denim fabrics in the world. It has been selling denim and casual sportswear fabrics internationally for more than 45 years, serves markets in more than 35 countries, and is the largest U.S. exporter of denim and apparel fabrics. Cone Industries has a strong interest in and commitment to safeguarding the environment. The company provides internship opportunities in textile production and environmental protection. Further information about the company and its job opportunities can be found at its Web site, conedenim.com.

Springs Global

Founded in 1887, Springs Global supplies leading retailers with coordinated home furnishings. The company's U.S. headquarters is located in Fort Mill, South Carolina. Springs Global also produces and markets bed and bath products for institutional and hospitality customers, home sewing fabrics, and baby bedding and apparel products. This range of products is truly mind-boggling. Springs' bedding products include sheets and pillowcases, comforters and comforter accessories, bedspreads, blankets, bed skirts, quilts, duvet covers, pillow shams, decorative and bed pillows, and mattress pads. Its bath products include towels, bath and accent rugs, shower curtains, and ceramic and other bath accessories. Its window products include window hardware and decorative rods, blinds, shades, and soft window treatments, such as drapes, valances, and balloon shades.

Through licensing agreements, Springs Global has extended its product lines to include kitchen and table accessories, flannel and knit sheets, blankets and throws, and lampshades. In 2001, the company merged with Brazilian firm Coteminas, forming the North American division of Springs Global. In 2019, the Springs Global North American division merged with private label producer Keeco. Keeco operates design offices in New York and San Francisco. Springs Global US Inc. is headquartered in Lancaster, South Carolina, with manufacturing sites throughout South Carolina in Rock Hill, Fort Mill, Fort Lawn, and Lyman. Springs Global's Web site is ir.springs.com and Keeco's Web site is keecohome.com.

DuPont

When it was founded in 1802, E. I. du Ponte de Nemours was primarily an explosives company. Today, it is a company that has shown explosive growth. DuPont offers a wide range of innovative products and services for numerous markets, including agriculture, food and beverage, electronics, chemicals, packaging and printing, safety and protection, home and construction, transportation, and apparel. DuPont operates in more than 90 countries and is a Fortune 500 company.

DuPont's mission includes research and development as high priorities. The company has more than forty research, development, and customer service labs in the United States and more than thirty-five labs in eleven other countries. The productive results of DuPont's research are illustrated by its products. DuPont's brands include Teflon coatings, Corian solid surfaces, Kevlar high-strength material, and Tyvek housing protective material. DuPont's innovative fabrics run the gamut of uses from hospital and medical care applications to firefighters' gear and sportswear. The company can be located online at DuPont.com.

Summary

As fashion companies in the United States now, more than ever, outsource much of their production work to companies in foreign countries, domestic job opportunities in textile production have dramatically declined. The majority of American companies design domestically but outsource goods internationally to take advantage of the free-trade agreements with low-wage countries. Although there is a loss in U.S. production jobs in the textile industry, there is an increase in the creative and scientific track, such as design, product development, and textile technology. Some of the key career tracks in the creative sector of textiles include fashion director, textile designer, textile stylist, and textile colorist. In the scientific and manufacturing areas of textiles, career options include textile engineer and textile technician. Additionally, there are ancillary career paths in textiles in a variety of areas, such as reference libraries and sales. The director of a resource room or reference library for a fiber association, such as Cotton Incorporated, maintains the fabric samples, garments, books, and trade journals that company employees use for inspiration and reference. The account executive is the sales representative for a fabric producer, selling piece goods to clients, such as the designers and manufacturers of apparel, accessories, or home furnishings. Whether you are interested in sales, technology, or design, there are career opportunities in the primary level of the fashion industry, the sector that includes fiber, fabrics, and manufacturing.

Endnote

1. Mercer, M., "Textile industry comes back to life, especially in South," *USA Today*, February 5, 2014.

Key Terms

account executive
assistant textile designer
colorways
computer-aided design (CAD)
contractor
croquis
fashion director
finishing
functional finish
general finish
outsourcing
piece goods

print service
reference librarian
resource room
resource room director
strike-off
surface designer
textile colorist
textile design
textile designer
textile engineer
textile stylist
textile technician

Online Resources

artdesignfashion.com/textile
cowtan.com
designworksintl.com
fashiondex.com
marimekko.com
pierrefrey.com

printsourcenewyork.com
surfacedesign.org
texprint.org.uk
textilesocietyofamerica.org
textilesource.com

Discussion Questions

1. In light of the trend toward outsourcing in textile production, what new career options do you believe will develop in the fiber and fabric sector of the fashion industry? What types of knowledge, training, and skills will best equip a job candidate to succeed in this industry over the next decade?

2. What are the differences between the textile designer, stylist, and colorist? The similarities?

3. Using the Internet, locate and describe two new technology programs, one that assists with textile design tasks and another that facilitates textile production.

CHAPTER 3
SOURCING

If you have ever taken a clothing construction class, you have a head start into the world of sourcing. You likely worked with interfacing, elastic, zippers, and buttons. As a result, you probably have an idea of how many components go into a garment, including some we do not even see. There is a person in the fashion industry whose job is to buy the materials that make up your favorite winter coat, your great leather belt, or your comfortable reading chair. Yet another person locates the manufacturing facility that produces the coat, belt, or chair. Both of these people are involved in the work of sourcing. **Sourcing** primarily refers to one of two activities: (1) the task of locating the suppliers of components needed to make a product, or (2) the job of securing manufacturers to produce end products and then collaborating with the manufacturer, contractor, or vendor while the products are being created. A **vendor**, or *supplier*, is any firm, such as a manufacturer or a distributor, from whom a company purchases products or production processes. Sourcing includes the following activities:

- Determining the amount of product needed
- Negotiating the best possible price and discounts
- Problem solving throughout the procurement and production activities
- Following up on actual shipments to make certain that due dates are met
- Assuring quality control is maintained
- Scheduling deliveries

Whether locating the components of a product or securing a manufacturer to produce it, sourcing takes a product from its conception stage to the sales floor or Web site.

Let's say a designer of an apparel line comes up with several amazing **collections**, or groupings of related styles. According to the designer's sketches, to actually turn the illustrations into apparel, the company will need several tapestry fabrics for jackets, silk chiffons for blouses, and colored denim for bottoms. Additionally, there will be the need for faux fur for the detachable collars, buttons for the jackets and tops, lining fabrics, interfacing, belting, and zippers—the list goes on and on. In some companies, the designer and an assistant locate the places from which to purchase these items. In larger companies, buyers source fabrics and related products for the items in the designer's line. In many midsized to large companies, the sourcing manager takes the designer's vision and helps turn it into reality.

SOURCING THE PRODUCT

How do design companies locate the fabrics and other product parts necessary for producing their lines? Some career options focus on sourcing fabrics and other product components. Fashion production planners, piece goods buyers, and findings buyers are three examples of these career paths. Sourcing can encompass buying goods domestically and abroad. If products are purchased from an overseas vendor and shipped to the United States, then they are referred to as **imports**. In contrast, products that are bought by an overseas company from a vendor in the United States and sent out of the country are referred to as **exports**. Imports and exports are examined in further detail throughout this chapter.

FASHION PRODUCTION PLANNER

Fashion production planners have the significant responsibility of material planning, anticipating all of the parts needed to make the final product. The primary tasks of fashion production planners are as follows:

- Reviewing forecasts of sales generated by the manufacturers' representatives and/or by analyzing past sales performance of line items
- Planning fabric production based on current orders and projected reorders
- Scheduling and monitoring works in progress
- Working with material manufacturers to determine the availability of goods
- Collaborating with key departments, such as design and product development, to anticipate future needs
- Meeting strict deadlines to keep shipments on time

Qualifications

A career as a fashion production planner requires the following qualifications:

- *Education.* A bachelor's degree in fashion merchandising, fashion design, business administration, marketing, international marketing, project management, or a related field is a requirement.
- *Experience.* Skills in a similar role within the fashion manufacturing sector of the industry are a hiring plus. Knowledge of offshore raw materials planning and purchasing as it relates to sales forecasts is essential. Experience in a large and varied manufacturing fashion company would be highly regarded. An internship

with a manufacturer during college is an added bonus to postgraduate employment.
- *Personal characteristics.* The ability to communicate clearly is essential. Fabrics and findings are often sourced overseas; therefore, a multilingual background may be extremely valuable. A few of the languages that are currently important in the sourcing field are Mandarin, Taiwanese, and Spanish.

PIECE GOODS BUYER

The **piece goods buyer** works for a company that uses textiles in the production of its final products. This can be an apparel company, a home furnishings firm, an automotive manufacturer, or an accessories producer. The responsibilities of a piece goods buyer include the following:

- Shopping for textile supplies at trade markets and through textile manufacturers' representatives (Figure 3.1)
- Planning the amount of fabric, referred to as **yardage**, to purchase from various sources or determining from which vendors the piece goods will be purchased and communicating with these vendors
- Coordinating with production managers who advise on the delivery status of purchase orders; a **purchase**

Figure 3.1

A piece goods buyer for an apparel manufacturer shops for textiles at trade markets and textile manufacturers' showrooms.

order (PO) is a contract for merchandise between buyers, as representatives of their firms, and vendors

- Communicating with accounts payable on payments and financing, to include proof of payments, wire transfers, and letters of credit; a **letter of credit** is a document issued by a bank authorizing the bearer to draw a specific amount of money from the issuing bank, its branches, or associated banks and agencies. It allows importers to offer secure terms to exporters
- Working with warehouse managers on inventory management, such as availability and accessibility of fabrics
- Monitoring quality control by inspecting shipments and dealing with **chargebacks**, credits for damaged merchandise and returns on defective goods

An **assistant piece goods buyer** often works with the piece goods buyer to accomplish this long list of responsibilities and as training for the position of piece goods buyer in the future.

Qualifications

A career as a piece goods buyer requires the following qualifications:

- *Education.* A bachelor's degree in fashion merchandising, fashion design, textiles, or a related field is a minimum requirement.
- *Experience.* Many piece goods buyers are promoted from the position of assistant piece goods buyer; others move into piece goods buying from the textile design track or the merchandising career path.
- *Personal characteristics.* A piece goods buyer has excellent quantitative skills, which are needed for calculating cost of goods, delivery expenses, and yardage amounts. This person must be able to work effectively under pressure, have excellent follow-up and communication skills, and be a successful negotiator.

FINDINGS AND/OR TRIMMINGS BUYER

The **findings buyer** is responsible for ordering findings and trimmings. **Findings** include such product components as zippers, thread, linings, and interfacings. Findings are functional and may not be visible when viewing the final product. **Trimmings**, however, are decorative components designed to be seen as part of the final product.

Trimmings include buttons, appliqués, and beltings. The **trimmings buyer** is responsible for ordering these product components.

Locating findings and trimmings is an important job in which timing is critical. Think about the production line, quality control, and the end product. If the findings buyer orders skirt zippers that are too short, either the zippers will be installed and the customers will not be able to get into the skirts or production on the skirts will be halted until the correct zippers are received. If a button shipment is late, the trimmings buyer is held accountable, as the entire production has to be held until it arrives. Figure 3.2 shows a photo of Tender Buttons, a well-known boutique in New York City.

Figure 3.2

On a tree-lined street in Manhattan is a tiny brick townhouse, Tender Buttons, one of a few shops in America devoted entirely to the sale of buttons.

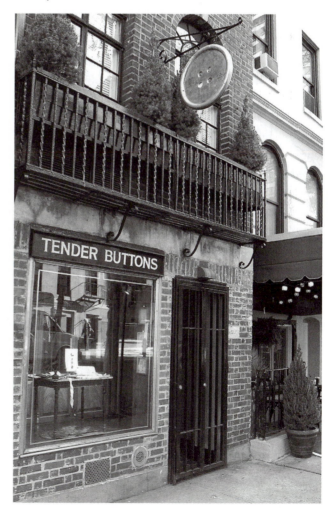

Qualifications

The education, experience, and personal characteristics required for findings and/or trimmings buyers are as follows.

- *Education.* A bachelor's degree in fashion design, fashion merchandising, product development, or a related discipline is a minimum requirement.
- *Experience.* Most findings and trimmings buyers work as assistants to the buyers before moving into this position, or they have worked in retail fashion merchandising. Internship experience and/or employment in either the manufacturing or design sector of the fashion industry are beneficial to securing these positions.
- *Personal characteristics.* High attention to detail is a critical asset to findings and trimmings buyers. Understanding product construction, sewing techniques, and product quality are essential skills. The abilities to locate vendors and negotiate with them are critical, as is following up on deliveries.

Career Challenges

Planners and buyers of raw materials, piece goods, and findings and trimmings share similar job struggles. It can continually be a source of stress to follow up on shipments needed to meet deadlines. Negotiating with vendors for priority shipping and competitive pricing can be a challenge. Written and oral communication skills may be tested when the buyer is putting together a deal with an overseas supplier. Currency exchanges, shipping costs, language barriers, and cultural differences can contribute to communication breakdowns. Attention to detail and written agreements are critical to minimizing these challenges. Finally, the buyer in sourcing is faced with constantly recalculating costs of goods. Shipping prices can change overnight. Handling fees may be added. Taxes may change. The dollar may fluctuate in currency exchange. Reviewing costs is a task that must be reexamined from the time an order is placed until the products reach the receiving dock. Fortunately, most buyers in sourcing enjoy quantitative work that demands a high level of attention to detail.

SOURCING MANAGER

In addition to the positions responsible for sourcing materials needed to create the end product, some midsized to large companies have a position entitled sourcing manager, in which an individual is responsible for sourcing production. The **sourcing manager** communicates with the company manufacturing the product, referred to as the **contractor**. Sourcing managers work with overseas or domestic producers, discuss product specifications with them, and negotiate contracts. Next, the sourcing manager monitors the controls put into place to make certain that production is executed correctly by the outside vendor. After production begins, the sourcing manager oversees quality control and delivery schedules. Throughout the process, there are, more often than not, problems to be resolved.

Qualifications

Sourcing managers should possess the following qualifications:

- *Education.* A bachelor's degree in fashion merchandising, fashion design, product development, business administration, or a related field is a requirement.
- *Experience.* Strong knowledge of product construction is necessary for sourcing production, fabric, and findings. Also, a general technical knowledge of fabric applications, construction, and care is required. This position requires prior work experience. Two to three years as a retail buyer, a wholesale merchandiser, or a production manager provide a good background.
- *Personal characteristics.* Flexibility is often cited as the number-one quality for the successful sourcing manager. Keen observation skills and strong communication abilities are also important attributes. A large network of contacts in product components and manufacturing can make the sourcing manager's job easier. This network often results from professional relationships built during prior work experiences.

Career Challenges

The sourcing manager has to see far enough down the road to anticipate changes and potential problems and then be flexible enough to keep the work on track. Top sourcing managers are proactive, rather than reactive. Stamina is also a critical characteristic, as the job demands long hours that require tremendous focus and effort. Frequent travel may be required. Particularly for overseas travel, sensitivity to cultural differences is an asset. The abilities

BOX 3.1 SOURCING AND LOGISTICS MANAGER

Maker of custom clothing seeks a Materials Sourcing Coordinator to improve the fabrics and trims in existing garments as well as source new materials to support new product launches. Men's shirts, suits, jeans, chinos, and tees as well as women's jeans made to measure with smartphone camera technology.

Location: San Francisco

Work closely with our team in Bangladesh to find local suppliers and develop new products.

- Maintain fabric library for approved, ongoing qualities
- Evaluate existing fabric choices. Develop superior replacements in terms of cost and quality
- Establish direct relationships with current and future vendors
- Identify opportunities for material quality consolidation
- Source new materials for future product launches, including sweatshirts, polos, and overcoats

Requirements

- Bachelor's Degree
- 3+ years experience in apparel product development, sourcing or retail buying
- Professional experience and expertise in the manufacturing of yarn and textiles
- Experience with at least some relevant garment types: dress shirts, denim, chinos, tees, and suits
- Experience with fabric testing for shrinkage, stretch, and other quality measures
- Strong written and verbal communication skills

Benefits

- Generous monthly credit and internal discount
- Generous stock compensation
- Huge capacity for impact at a small and growing company

to learn from experience, negotiate effectively, and maintain a cool head reduce the stress level a sourcing manager can face. Box 3.1 is a sample of an online classified advertisement for a sourcing manager.

MERCHANDISER FOR A MANUFACTURER

The position of **merchandiser**, or *merchandise planner*, on the wholesaler's or manufacturer's side of the industry is very important to all departments, as this person works as the liaison among the design, production, and sales teams—from the showroom to the factory (Figure 3.3). Box 3.2 features a position description of a merchandise planner for a major lifestyle brand. One of the primary responsibilities of the merchandiser is to develop a merchandise line plan by month and by piece count or by **stock-keeping unit (SKU)**, a type of identification data for a single product. Some of the other duties of the merchandiser for a manufacturer include the following:

- Determining top sellers, referred to as **volume drivers**, and essential programs, retail pricing, and fabric recommendations for the collections based on past retail selling history
- Shopping the market and competition and, later, presenting a merchandising strategy to the design team
- Communicating changes in strategy, assortment planning, and allocation to technical, visual, and licensing teams
- Updating and maintaining the purchasing sheets on a weekly basis
- Providing input on budgets, sales, gross margin, and receipt flow
- Recommending line changes at department weekly meetings, based on actual sales trends as opposed to the sales plan for each style
- Identifying product opportunities for future seasons by translating trends
- Analyzing the current season's opportunities from retail sales
- Working with the sales teams to make sure their specific product needs are being addressed

Figure 3.3
One of the key duties performed by the merchandiser is shopping the market, reviewing the lines of current suppliers, and looking for new vendors.

Box 3.3 discusses social media trends and changes in marketing and sales.

Qualifications

Merchandise planners should possess the following qualifications:

- *Education.* A bachelor's degree in fashion merchandising, fashion design, product development, business administration, or a related field is a requirement.
- *Experience.* Strong knowledge of product components and product construction is necessary, as is general knowledge of production capabilities and technology. This position often requires prior work experience as a buyer or assistant merchandise planner. Applicants with work experience in both manufacturing and retailing have an edge over other candidates, as they have the ability to view the product from the manufacturer's and retail buyer's perspectives.
- *Personal characteristics.* Attention to detail, the ability to work accurately with numbers, and a futuring perspective are personal qualities that successful merchandise planners often have.

Career Challenges

Merchandisers (merchandise planners) must continually look ahead, preparing today for tomorrow's sales. They are constantly juggling several seasons at one time. It is a daunting task to be able to predict sales trends and to adjust production for the current season from slow-selling products into top-selling ones. Strong work relationships and effective communication skills help offset these challenges.

IMPORT PRODUCTION COORDINATOR

An **import production coordinator** is the apparel or home furnishings company's liaison with the manufacturer or contractor. The import production coordinator is involved in all aspects of the production process, works closely with the design team, and is the link between overseas factories (e.g., in China, Japan, Taiwan, India, and South America, to name a few locations) and the company's design and buying teams. The import production coordinator works on establishing the best possible **first cost**, or wholesale price, in the country of origin. The **country of origin** refers to the nation in which the goods were located and purchased.

The main goal of import production coordinators is to ensure on-time delivery and quality of production. In addition, production coordinators negotiate price and track the supply chain from sample production to bulk delivery. A more detailed listing of the main responsibilities of an import production coordinator is as follows:

BOX 3.2 MERCHANDISER (MERCHANDISE PLANNER)

An international brand and a leader in the design, marketing, and distribution of premium lifestyle products for more than forty years in four categories: apparel, home, accessories, and fragrances. Seeking a merchandise planner at corporate headquarters.

Purpose and Scope:

The merchandise planner is responsible for partnering with the merchandising team to create annual and seasonal merchandise plans, forecasting the business based on changes in strategy and business climate, and managing inventory to support forecasts for our newest online business. In addition, this individual will have the opportunity to work on special projects to support the strategic and operating initiatives critical to success of the Web site and our continued growth and profitability.

Responsibilities:

- Forecast sales, margin, and inventory turn by month, at a department/class level, and communicate business performance during the monthly forecast
- Partner with merchant team to analyze current sales trends and on order at a brand level and adjust the forecast accordingly
- Create department and category level quarterly hindsight reports to drive strategic assortment decisions for future quarters and in-season management
- Plan and project receipt flow for basic items to support sales forecasts
- Prepare weekly sales recaps to aid in business analysis
- Track current selling to the plan and provide analysis around promotional events, as needed

Job Requirements:

- Expertise in retail math; strong analytical skills
- Ability to make confident and independent recommendations and accountability for managing and achieving business goals
- Decision-making capability clearly driven by conceptualizing future opportunities and developing strategic business initiatives
- Creative, assertive, and solution-oriented approach when faced with difficult business performance and/or challenging directives from senior management
- Ability to influence, present, and defend a business argument both one-on-one and in a group setting
- Superb presentation and communication skills, both spoken and written
- Ability to prioritize and direct multiple activities
- High level of organizational skills and attention to detail

An equal opportunity employer, offering dynamic career opportunities with growth potential and a generous company discount.

- Scheduling sample and line production in collaboration with design team
- Coordinating sample production and communicating any changes to the factory
- Establishing and maintaining strong relationships with offshore suppliers
- Anticipating the length of time it will take goods to be shipped and received from factories abroad
- Knowing import and export laws and how to complete the necessary documents to ship and receive goods and understanding how to work with customs
- Completing final sign-off on samples to begin production
- Managing critical time to ensure on-time deliveries
- Updating in-house computer systems on styling information
- Monitoring the production process and updating management on any changes or needs to create quality products
- Having an eye for detail and quality
- Identifying and resolving issues quickly and with cost efficiency
- Having the accounting knowledge needed to determine **landed costs**, the actual price of goods after taxes, tariffs, handling, and shipping fees are added to the cost of goods

SOCIAL MEDIA STRIKES
BOX 3.3   The Rise of the Micro-Influencer

Certain early adopters of social media found stardom and prosperity through gaining high numbers of "followers." Part model, part photographer, part scribe, these fashion enthusiasts used their own personal sense of style to gather interested followers. And these followers translated into dollars. A popular influencer with 100,000 followers could earn upwards of $5,000 for a single brand endorsement.

With a playbook firmly in place for fame and success as a social media brand influencer, soon came a wave—a tidal wave—of young wannabes. And with such high stakes for a huge number of followers, these influencer-hopefuls have found themselves spending a fortune to promote their accounts and gain followers. The *New York Times* dubbed the phenomenon "The Follower Factory." Schemes arose to sell huge numbers of followers through bot networks, outsourcing, and pyramid schemes.

Once uncovered, brands became wary. Fake followers do not translate into real sales and real dollars. As a result, the reputation of the social media influencer failed.

Micro-influencers, on the other hand, still provide a valuable marketing resource for brands, and this is an important distinction for brand managers and merchandisers. Micro-influencers have far fewer followers—10,000 to 100,000—but these followers are carefully cultivated. In a survey by Markerly, a social media and influencer marketing firm, they concluded that micro-influencers have an optimal combination of reach and engagement with their followers. In other words, the relationship between influencer and follower is more authentic. And if the right influencer has been chosen by the brand, the followers are a good match for the brand's target market.

Brand marketers are learning that one of the best marketing strategies is to let micro-influencers tell their stories. Through their blogs and social media accounts, they tell their stories on a regular basis. They are part of a niche, and they help their fans and followers sort through their problems. Because of this relationship, the influencer's first loyalty is to his or her followers. They know a great deal about their passion, and love to share what they know with other enthusiasts, and, through this, they build respect from their fans and followers. They happily recommend brands and products if they believe it will help their followers.

Sources:

Bergstrom, B., "The best social media template to show your results," CoSchedule Blog, https://coschedule.com/blog/social-media-report-template/

Confessore, N., Dance, G.J.X., Harris, R., and Hansen, M., "The follower factory," The New York Times, January 27, 2018, https://www.nytimes.com/interactive/2018/01/27/technology/social-media-bots.html

Hausman, A., "The rise and fall of the social media influencer," Marketing Insider Group, January 17, 2019, https://marketinginsidergroup.com/influencer-marketing/the-rise-and-fall-of-the-social-media-influencer/

Influencer Marketing Hub, "Digital Marketing and the Rise of the Micro Influencer," October 24, 2018, https://influencermarketinghub.com/digital-marketing-and-the-rise-of-the-micro-influencer/

Markerly.com, "Instagram Marketing: Does Influencer Size Matter?" http://markerly.com/blog/instagram-marketing-does-influencer-size-matter/

Assistant importers work for the import production coordinator and follow up on orders with overseas suppliers. They also communicate with freight companies and customs agents, process documents, and check pricing agreements. They may also be responsible for arranging payments to overseas suppliers and serving as a liaison with internal customers to ensure goods arrive as expected.

Qualifications

The required qualifications for the import production coordinator are as follows:

- *Education*. A bachelor's degree in fashion design, fashion merchandising, product development, business administration, or a related field is essential.

- *Experience*. To secure this position, a prospective employee will need several years in previous import production experience within the apparel or home furnishings industry. The position of import production coordinator often requires fluency in a foreign language (e.g., Japanese, Spanish, or Mandarin, to name a few). Intermediate to advanced Microsoft Office skills (e.g., Microsoft Word and Excel) are expected. Work experience may be obtained in the position of intern and/or assistant importer. This position often requires extensive travel. A proven background in importing, shipping, and client relationships is helpful.

- *Personal characteristics*. To be successful, import production coordinators need keen attention to detail, self-motivation, and the ability to work on a team. Excellent written, visual, and oral communication skills are required. They must be highly organized and able to work in a fast-paced environment. This person must have strong analytical skills and materials-planning knowledge to review product forecasts and plan raw materials to manufacture domestically and internationally. Effective negotiating and time-management abilities are key attributes, as problems often need to be resolved quickly and with consensus.

Career Challenges

The sourcing manager, import production coordinator, and assistant importer are faced with the primary challenge of effective communication to ensure on-time deliveries, the best prices, and top-quality products. They are often juggling many balls, working with the numerous vendors, production managers, and designers simultaneously. Although global travel may be an exciting adventure in the beginning of these careers, it can become a burden to pack a suitcase, jump on a plane to put out a production "fire," and return to the office, ready to work the next day. It takes a great deal of flexibility, stamina, and organizational skills to rise above the potential stress of a worldwide business operation.

LICENSING AND SOURCING

Globalization is the process of interlinking nations of the world with one another; this is a growing trend in the fashion industry. **Global sourcing** refers to the process of locating, purchasing, and importing or exporting goods and services from around the world, and has created a new fashion career path in licensing. Think of European designer names such as Dior, Chanel, Versace, and Gucci; American designers such as Donna Karan, Calvin Klein, and Ralph Lauren; American characters such as Mickey Mouse, Spider-Man, and Barbie; or manufacturers such as Harley-Davidson, Nike, and Hershey's. All of these companies offer product lines that are not central to their primary product lines. For example, in addition to a Fat Boy motorcycle, you can purchase Harley-Davidson belts, apparel, and sunglasses. Another example of international appeal for character product lines can be found at EuroDisney SCA in Paris, which features a range of Disney character products. The Disney boutique on the Champs Elysées is a prime retail location for the French and tourists alike.

Many well-known celebrities, fashion designers, and companies offer alternative product lines by working with manufacturers to produce goods under their names.

For example, Fossil Inc. produces a line of watches for Donna Karan International Inc. The timepiece line fits the Donna Karan image, coordinates with her DKNY clothing and accessories, and features her name; however, Donna Karan International Inc. does not own the watch company. Fossil Inc., owner of the line, is the timepiece company that manufactures this product classification for and pays a fee and/or royalties to Donna Karan International Inc. The company also licenses its name to the likes of Estée Lauder (beauty products), Liz Claiborne (activewear), PVH (men's shirts), Oxford Industries (children's clothes), and Luxottica (eyewear).

This arrangement is referred to as a **license**, an agreement in which a manufacturer, the **licensee**, is given exclusive rights to produce and market goods that carry the registered name and brandmark of a designer (e.g., Ralph Lauren), celebrity (e.g., Jessica Simpson), character (e.g., Lego), or product line (e.g., Porsche). The owner of the name or brandmark is called the **licensor**. The licensor receives a percentage of wholesale sales or some other compensation for the arrangement.

Figure 3.4 provides an example of footwear licensed under Tory Burch. Camuto Group, Inc., based in Greenwich, Connecticut, coordinates the design, development, and distribution of women's fashion footwear as women's lifestyle brands on a global scale. The company sources

Figure 3.4
Footwear under the Tory Burch label is licensed through Camuto Group, Inc.

the Tory Burch footwear collection. Camuto Group, Inc. also develops and manages several exclusive brands for Max Studio, Sole Society, Lucky Brand, and Madewell.

Today, many companies combine sourcing merchandise from overseas with importing and licensing. Additionally, many of these firms have finished products delivered from overseas manufacturers to retail operations abroad rather than solely importing the merchandise to the United States. It is truly a global market for many licensed products, one that can establish and strengthen brand identity. As international distribution continues to develop, particularly in Asia, manufacturers in the United States need specialists with knowledge of sourcing, importing, exporting, and licensing regulations. These specialists are referred to as licensing directors.

LICENSING DIRECTOR

Licensing directors are responsible for overseeing the look, quality, labeling, delivery, and distribution of their companies' product lines. Sourcing is an integral part of this job. They work with the foreign and domestic manufacturers of various product lines, the licensees, to make certain that the products are branded correctly. The style, placement, size, and color of the brandmark and labels must be consistent across all product lines. Additionally, licensing directors make sure product lines meet quality expectations and fit within the design concepts of their company's primary line, whether it be apparel, accessories, or footwear. For example, sourcing for Tory Burch

footwear must coordinate with the designer's aesthetic and resonate with other products in the line, such as jewelry, handbags, and apparel. The results that the manufacturers and designer desire are multiple sales to the consumers and a greater visual presence on retail floors (Figure 3.5).

Qualifications

The job requirements for licensing directors are as follows.

- *Education.* A bachelor's degree in fashion design or merchandising, business administration, marketing, international marketing, business law, or a similar field is a minimum requirement.
- *Experience.* Many licensing directors begin on the showroom floor of a manufacturer or as account representatives. Prior to this, retail sales experience during college provides a solid foundation in working with various product lines and customers. The position of licensing director is one that a candidate is promoted into after showing knowledge and skills in the business.
- *Personal characteristics.* The licensing director must manage many tasks at one time. The abilities to manage time, stay calm under pressure, and prioritize tasks are significant. Strong negotiation skills are a plus. Comprehension of product construction, quality, and design is a necessity. An understanding of import and export laws, branding regulations, and different cultures is critical to this career path.

Career Challenges

One of the greatest challenges in a licensing career is the need to clearly understand and stay up to date in a wide range of areas. The licensing professional must have a thorough knowledge of design and product development, branding specifications, import and export legislation and regulations, and manufacturing processes—all for a variety of products, such as sunglasses, gloves, sportswear, and footwear. If a product of poor quality that does not reflect the licensor's vision slips out from under the licensing director's radar, then the image and sales of the licensor can be negatively affected. Therefore, coordinating the work of many manufacturers located around the world that produce a range of product types is a tremendous task and responsibility.

Figure 3.5
Licensing directors are responsible for making sure that product lines meet quality expectations and fit within the design concepts of their company's primary line, as with the Tory Burch footwear license with Camuto Group, Inc. Designer Tory Burch favors an aesthetic of bold, stylized, classic designs.

Summary

From locating vendors to collaborating with manufacturers, sourcing is the process of taking a product from its conception stage to the sales floor. In some companies, designers and their assistants locate the places from which to purchase piece goods. Larger companies may employ buyers to source fabrics and related products for the items in the designer's line. The career options that focus on sourcing fabrics and findings necessary for producing collections include fashion production planner, or raw goods buyer, and piece goods buyer. Production managers, who act as contacts between buyers and vendors, advise on the delivery status of purchase orders. Sourcing managers work with overseas or domestic producers to figure out product specifications and negotiate contracts. An import production coordinator is involved in all aspects of the production process and is often the link between the overseas factories and the design and buying teams.

Today's global market has inspired many companies to combine sourcing merchandise from overseas with importing and licensing. As international distribution continues to develop, manufacturers employ sourcing, importing, exporting, and licensing directors—all who understand licensing regulations.

Although education and field experience are important qualifications for a career path in sourcing, the qualifications that are key to success are flexibility, organization, and communication. Knowledge of import and export laws, branding regulations, foreign languages, and different cultures is important to those working within all aspects of the global industry. If you are interested in sourcing as a future career, you must have the ability to work effectively when under pressure and possess excellent negotiation skills. Sourcing is an ideal profession for the curious, creative, and detail-oriented person. It is an exciting and satisfying journey to take a design from dream to reality.

Key Terms

assistant importer	letter of credit
assistant piece goods buyer	license
chargebacks	licensee
collection	licensing director
contractor	licensor
country of origin	merchandiser
exports	piece goods buyer
fashion production planner	purchase order (PO)
findings	sourcing
findings buyer	sourcing manager
first cost	stock-keeping unit (SKU)
globalization	trimmings
global sourcing	trimmings buyer
import production	vendor
coordinator	volume driver
imports	yardage
landed costs	

Online Resources

apparelresources.com
gasl.biz
pinterest.com/internationalap
sourcingjournal.com
ubmfashion.com/shows/sourcing-magic
www.forbes.com/sites/walterloeb/2014/04/25/j-c-penney-
   must-fix-its-sourcing-to-fix-its-business/

Discussion Questions

1. How many different components, or parts, make up the clothes and accessories you are wearing today? Determine the fabrics, trimmings, and findings that were sourced to assemble each garment. How likely is it that all of these parts have come from the same producer or even the same country?

2. Research to discover how many licensing agreements your favorite designer shares with manufacturers. Generate a list of three key designers and the licensing arrangements they have by product and manufacturer. Do the manufacturers produce similar lines for other fashion companies?

3. Why do piece goods buyers rarely source fabrics and findings from the United States? Construct a list of six reasons for the movement in outsourcing.

4. Which countries host the largest number of manufacturing companies for fashion products? In what specific merchandise classifications, fabrics, or production processes does each country specialize? What are some reasons for specialization? Develop a spreadsheet to answer these queries.

CHAPTER 4
PRODUCTION AND SALES

Some prospective employees find the construction and manufacture of fashion products to be the most interesting part of the industry. Others are drawn to the more quantitative tasks, such as buying, costing, and production planning. Many are fascinated with the technical and computer-oriented aspects of the fashion business. Still others enjoy the creative and artistic parts of the fashion industry. Whether construction, manufacturing, numbers, computers, or creativity appeals to you, there is a career path in production that relates directly to each area.

The basic stages of the production process can be mapped as follows:

- Sourcing parts and producers for the product
- Securing bids for piece goods, findings, and trimmings
- Costing out the product
- Ordering product components
- Scheduling production
- Creating the production pattern
- Grading
- Marker making
- Spreading and cutting
- Assembling/constructing the product
- Controlling the quality of the product
- Packing and shipping
- Producing and shipping reorders

Production, or manufacturing, of **end products**, the products that will actually be purchased by the customer, is an area that offers diverse career opportunities. Many technological and management concepts relevant to the fashion industry have created or affected career tracks in this area. These include computer-integrated manufacturing, electronic data interchange, mass customization, supply-chain management, and radio-frequency identification technology. These manufacturing trends are examined later in this chapter. First, an exploration of career options relating to these concepts, in both domestic and overseas production, includes employment opportunities in the following positions: product manager, production planner, production manager, traffic manager, production efficiency manager, quality control manager, pattern production (pattern grader and marker maker), and spreader and cutter.

PRODUCT MANAGER

Depending on the size of the company, a **product manager**, or *product design manager*, may be responsible for all of the products within a company's product line in a small firm, or for a specific product category in a line for a large company. Product managers often work with one foot in the creative part of the business and the other foot in the production part of the business. On the creative, design-focused side, product managers monitor market and fashion trends related to their assigned product lines. If a team of product managers is responsible for a variety of the company's product categories, it works to integrate the products for a consistent and cohesive fashion look. Product managers are also responsible for comparison shopping the lines of competitors. They compare assortment, quality, price, and trend representation. They will also shop merchandise lines outside of their product categories, making certain that their product lines will blend in terms of the color, style, and fabric trends being shown for the season in all departments.

For example, the product manager of Fenty X Puma by Rihanna may review the new line for trend representation, fabric selections, and key colors for the season. She may then meet with the product managers of the Savage X Fenty line of lingerie and with the product manager of the footwear category to ensure that color, pattern, fabric, and fashion trends are in common. The goal is to create a clear and forward fashion image for the company as a whole, as illustrated in Figures 4.1a–d. The product manager will also examine the product lines of other manufacturers that appeal to the Fenty brand target market, such as footwear, lingerie, and apparel lines that compete for the line's target customers. The product manager reviews competitive lines by looking at product line similarities and differences, pricing, and product voids. **Product voids** refer to merchandise categories in which there are few, if any, items to fill consumer needs and desires. The product manager's objective is to guide the product line to higher sales by creating a timely fashion presence that fits with trends, meshes with the company's total image, and fills product voids.

On the production side, the product manager works with sourcing personnel, production managers, and quality control directors, among other departments involved with the manufacturing of the product lines for which they are responsible. The product manager monitors the manufacturing of his or her product line(s) from start to finish by checking deliveries of product components, overseeing timelines as the products move through the manufacturing process, assessing quality, and assuring on-time delivery to the retailers. The effective product manager has a dual perspective on the product line—the creative viewpoint of fashion trends and a cohesive fashion image, and the business viewpoint of quality and timely production—both combining to place the right products in the consumers' hands at the right time.

Qualifications

The qualifications for this career are as follows:

- *Education.* A bachelor's degree in fashion merchandising, fashion design, product development, production, apparel manufacturing, or a related field is commonly a requirement.
- *Experience.* A sales representative for a manufacturing company may climb the career ladder into the position of product manager. An assistant in a trend forecasting firm may leave that sector of the industry to move up to a product manager position. Large firms have assistant product manager positions, for which product manager positions are the next step up the career ladder.

- *Personal characteristics.* Successful product managers have the ability to analyze their firm's market for opportunities and threats. Assessing competition, communicating fashion trends, and investigating retail trends require the personal attributes of curiosity, observation, and creativity, as well as strong skills in communication, organization, and presentation. They also have an in-depth knowledge of the manufacturing processes for their particular product categories.

Career Challenges

Many small companies do not employ product managers; instead, designers are responsible for evaluating competitors and determining fashion trends for the line. As a result, the number of positions in this area is limited to mid- and large-sized firms. Product managers are "under the gun" when it comes to being correct on the fashion colors, styling, and themes that will be featured in product lines. If, for example, rhinestones are the key fashion trend the product design manager chooses for the season, and it turns out to be trend a company's target market does not buy, then the product manager may be job hunting. Additionally, product managers face great challenges with manufacturing products abroad in terms of quality, fit, and deadlines. Because there is much at stake when a company produces the wrong product or ships the right product too late, product managers must conduct detailed research to make accurate decisions, which makes this position exciting and never dull.

PRODUCTION PLANNER

The majority of large manufacturing firms have production planners on staff. **Production planners** estimate the amounts and types of products a company will manufacture, based either on previous seasonal sales or on orders received by sales representatives on the road and in the showroom. There are two primary methods of production planning: cut-to-order and cut-to-stock. **Cut-to-order** is considered the safest method of projecting manufacturing needs. It entails waiting until orders are received from buyers and then working within tight timelines to purchase product parts, construct product lines as ordered, and ship them to the retail accounts on

Figure 4.1a
Grammy-winning recording artist Rihanna built on her style, beauty, and fame by launching Fenty Beauty in 2017, celebrating diversity and inclusivity with a 40+ shade palette of foundation colors.

Figure 4.1b
With 67 million Instagram followers, and 31 million subscribers to her YouTube channel, the pop queen used this hefty reach to launch Fenty X Puma, a line of urban sportswear and footwear.

Figure 4.1c
Fenty X Puma footwear styles are sleek and urban, with a nod to their parent sneakers.

Figure 4.1d
Rihanna's recent launch is Savage X Fenty, a line of lingerie with inclusive design and sizing from Small to 3X.

time. Which types of fashion companies prefer the cut-to-order option? This technique is most often used by designer firms that feature higher-priced, high-fashion merchandise. For these companies, forecasting the sales of products that reflect new fashion trends is more difficult. Also, the costs of being wrong may be much higher than for less expensive, less fashion-forward merchandise because of the more expensive fabrics and, often, more detailed workmanship these high-fashion companies include in their products.

Cut-to-stock involves purchasing fabrics and other product components before orders are acquired. Production planners using the cut-to-stock method examine several variables before projecting manufacturing needs. They look at the economy and how, when, and on what consumers are spending their money. They investigate what the competition is doing, including new companies entering the market and targeting their customers. They study sales histories of products in the line, focusing on sales by style, color, size, and price for each season. They analyze the strength of new lines by discussing sales potential with the design staff and sales representatives.

What are the advantages of the cut-to-stock option? It enables production to be spread out over a longer period. This permits the manufacturer to keep factories in production mode throughout the year (Figure 4.2), rather than working around "peaks and valleys." Cut-to-stock also allows for a longer **lead time**, the amount of time needed between placing a production order and receiving a shipment of the products. With international production gaining importance, lead times have become longer for manufacturers using overseas factories. Which types of firms find the cut-to-stock alternative to be most efficient and cost effective? A manufacturing company that produces a significant number of basic products, such as a T-shirt company, has the ability to project sales more closely than does the producer of more expensive, fashion-sensitive goods (refer to Box 4.1).

Figure 4.2
Garment workers sew at the American Apparel factory in downtown Los Angeles.

CASE STUDIES IN CAREER EXPLORATION

BOX 4.1   Production Planning and Control in Apparel Manufacturing

Production planning and control (PPC) is one of the most important departments in the garment manufacturing process. Production planning refers to the prearranged process of turning raw materials into finished goods, while control refers to the procedures put in place to assure timely results, quality products, and anticipated costs. There are six primary functions of PPC:

- Scheduling jobs or tasks for the line styles
- Planning material needs (e.g., fabric thread, zipper)
- Determining which styles and quantities will be loaded into production and when
- Selecting facilities and planning manufacturing processes
- Estimating costs of production
- Delivering goods, following up, and executing improvements to the process

Precision in PPC results in on-time shipments and the most economical use of resources, often because labor and appropriate supplies and equipment are available for each order. Garment manufacturers cannot afford to lose time or materials in the production process.

Late fees or product returns can result when products are not delivered as promised. In the highly competitive apparel industry, that's too risky. Buyers will quickly find other companies to replace manufacturers who cannot deliver, or who do not deliver on time. In addition, raw material prices rise consistently, and poor planning can lead to missed opportunities and higher costs. Approximately 60 to 70 percent of the cost of a garment is in the fabric, according to smallbusiness.chron.com. Styles are changing rapidly as customers want new looks regularly,

not just at the start of each season. To keep up with changing trends, buyers are making smaller orders more frequently with shorter lead times between ordering and delivery. Manufacturers who purchase materials at the right price and the right time and can meet short lead times have a distinct competitive advantage. As a result, the planning phase of each production piece must be as accurate as possible.

What types of problems does effective PPC avoid? If the cutting room falls behind in its production schedule, for example, the sewing and finishing lines must wait. This can lead to backlogs on the production line and, as a result, missed deadlines for shipment. To avoid lost time in the production process, the production planner must oversee each step of the production process daily. Anticipating problems and keeping the entire production line updated on any delays allows time for plans to be made and implemented to pick up any slack. In addition, PPC adds to the bottom lines of the manufacturer and the retailer in that the necessary materials are purchased in the right amount at the best possible prices. PPC—profitable, prompt, and consumer-driven—brings the manufacturer and buyer together and remains one of the most important departments in the garment manufacturing process.

Sources:

Ray, L., "Production planning for garment manufacturing," Chron, smallbusiness.chron.com/production-planning-garment-manufacturing-80975.html

Sarkar, P., "Functions of production planning and control (PPC) department in apparel manufacturing," Online Clothing Study, December 4, 2011, www.onlineclothingstudy.com/2011/12/functions-of-production-planning-and.html

Qualifications

Whether the production planner uses the cut-to-order or cut-to-stock option, the education, work experience, and personal characteristics needed for successful employment in this career track are similar, including the following:

- *Education.* A bachelor's degree in fashion merchandising, fashion design, product development, apparel manufacturing, or a related field is commonly required.

- *Experience.* Work experience with a manufacturer is needed, possibly beginning in the showroom and later moving into product development or purchasing. An understanding of how products are constructed, the materials they are made from, and the manufacturing processes required to bring them to fruition is critical.

- *Personal characteristics.* The successful product planner has strong quantitative abilities, effective communication skills, excellent time management, and top organizational skills.

PRODUCTION MANAGER

Production managers, also referred to as *plant managers*, are responsible for all of the operations at production facilities, whether domestic or overseas locations, contracted or company owned. The job responsibilities of production managers include:

- Supervising or completing the estimation of production and employee costs scheduling work flow in factories
- Ensuring product quality control
- Hiring, training, and motivating production employees

Think about the number of employees, tasks, and potential problems associated with cutting, constructing, pressing, and shipping a product line. This is a challenging career track, but one that pays well and is critical to the success of a company. Box 4.2 is an example of a classified ad for a plant manager position.

Production assistants often support production managers with detail work, scheduling, and record keeping. Assistants may track fabric, trim, and findings deliveries; help with developing production schedules; and communicate the workflow of the factory to production managers. They also follow up on outgoing shipments, often keeping customers informed on the progress of their orders and expediting deliveries when needed. Additionally, production managers may have the assistance of traffic managers. **Traffic managers** supervise workflow on factory floors, monitoring products from start to finish. They anticipate problems that may stall production, whether in materials, personnel, or equipment. The goal of the traffic manager is to make certain that the factory employees have all they need to manufacture products with efficiency and in good quality.

THE JOB SEARCH

BOX 4.2 PLANT MANAGER

Plant Manager—Textile Manufacturing and Production Company

Location: Dallas, Texas
Base Pay: $50,000–$80,000 annually
Industry: Fashion, Apparel, Textile, Manufacturing, Industrial
Required Education: Two-year degree
Required Experience: More than five years
Relocation Covered: Yes

Job Responsibilities

- Manage production facility of approximately 15 employees, consisting of supervisors, drivers, and production crew
- Manage day-to-day operations of the production process, including quality control and productions checks
- Hire, train, review, promote, and discharge employees as required
- Manage service technicians and maintenance crews as necessary
- Meet operational efficiencies by implementing process improvement and monitoring work flow and production

- Create and continuously promote a safe work environment by ensuring that all staff understands and adheres to safety-related policies and procedures
- Maintain appropriate safety and waste disposal records/logs
- Resolve day-to-day issues for production facility
- Monitor and order supplies
- Develop and maintain operational budget

Job Requirements

- Management experience within a production/manufacturing facility environment
- Excellent management skills with the ability to delegate responsibilities and tasks
- Solid understanding of budgeting and plant operations
- Associate's degree or higher

We offer a competitive salary, a comprehensive benefits package, incredible growth potential, and learning opportunities. If you have more than five years of management experience within a production/manufacturing facility environment, please apply for immediate consideration.

Qualifications

The qualifications for a production manager, production assistant, and traffic manager are similar. The production assistant and traffic manager positions usually precede that of production manager.

- *Education*. A bachelor's degree in fashion merchandising, fashion design, product development, apparel manufacturing, or a related field is commonly required.
- *Experience*. Hands-on experience in the industry, which may include work experience in computer-aided pattern design, grading and marker making, product costing, and quality control, is required for this position. The ability to produce flat sketches and specification drawings using a computer is helpful. A production assistant position is often posted as an entry-level position with the potential of moving into a production manager opening. Larger manufacturers offer assistant traffic manager positions as a starting place.
- *Personal characteristics*. Knowledge of raw materials and manufactured processes, design and product development, and production technology is required. An understanding of textiles, product construction, the capabilities and limitations of production equipment, and the principles of pattern assembly is essential. The ability to work as part of a team, as well as independently with little supervision, is critical to success. Good communication skills, both oral and written, are also required. Because apparel production workers represent many nationalities, the ability to speak Mandarin or Spanish, for example, is an asset. An appreciation of cultural diversity is essential.

Career Challenges

What are the challenges for production managers, assistant production managers, and traffic managers? All of them face the obstacles of tight deadlines, sometimes worsened by external factors that are difficult to foresee or control. Manufacturing equipment breakdowns, delayed textile shipments, defective zippers, or thread in the wrong color are types of problems that can halt the workflow of the manufacturing facility and cause the manufacturer to miss shipping commitments. This can be a high-stress area in which to work. Effective communication and excellent follow-up skills are essential to making it in this career path.

PRODUCTION EFFICIENCY MANAGER

Some large manufacturing firms offer the position of production efficiency manager. These companies are usually quite large and conduct global manufacturing activities. **Production efficiency managers** are responsible for monitoring the speed and output of the manufacturing facilities and for managing waste (Figure 4.3). Production efficiency managers often work closely with quality control managers to ensure that products meet quality standards while costs are under control. For example, the production efficiency manager of a handbag company may find an accessory firm to purchase leather scraps left over from the cutting tables to use them for belts.

QUALITY CONTROL MANAGER

Quality control managers, or *quality control engineers*, develop specifications for the products that will be manufactured. They are responsible to see that those standards are met during all phases of production, identifying quality problems and working with manufacturing personnel to correct them. The quality control manager works with such issues as fit, fabric performance, construction difficulties, packaging and shipping needs, and production pace.

In large companies, a manufacturer's factories may be located worldwide. The quality control manager frequently travels to several manufacturing sites,

Figure 4.3
Production efficiency managers are responsible for monitoring the speed and output of the manufacturing facilities.

coordinating production and deliveries, while checking to be certain that quality standards are being met at all locations. Because quality problems can run the gamut from the original product specifications to a defective button-holer machine, the quality control manager collaborates with personnel in various company divisions—from the design staff to plant employees.

Qualifications

The qualifications for production efficiency managers and quality control managers are related, with similar requirements in education, work experience, and personal characteristics:

- *Education.* A bachelor's degree in fashion design, fashion merchandising, textiles, production, or a related discipline is needed.
- *Experience.* Knowledge of product construction, textile technology, and manufacturing capabilities is required. Some quality control managers enter the field from design, merchandising, and/or production backgrounds.
- *Personal characteristics.* Personal characteristics that enhance the work of quality control managers include organizational abilities, effective time-management skills, and communication skills. Effective quality control managers are strong problem solvers with good follow-up skills and are detail oriented. This position requires people skills to gain the commitment of factory workers to produce high-quality products.

Career Challenges

Production efficiency managers and quality control managers face the challenge of working with a wide range of constituencies, from designers and patternmakers to plant managers and workers located in the United States and abroad. It is a significant challenge to communicate with so many people on such diverse levels in, possibly, global locations in different time zones. Strong communication skills and superior organizational abilities are keys to being successful in these two career tracks.

PATTERN PRODUCTION

Career paths in the area of pattern production include patternmaker, pattern grader, and marker maker. The career track of patternmaker is explored in Chapter 5.

Figure 4.4
If a single pattern piece is one-quarter of an inch too large, the garment will not likely flow through the production process. If by chance it does, the consumer will not purchase a product that does not fit correctly or look attractive.

Marker makers and pattern graders share common characteristics: a superior level of accuracy, an understanding of how textiles perform, and an ability to adjust to increasing technological advances in pattern production. Pattern development, fit, and production require sharp focus and strong attention to detail (Figure 4.4). If a single pattern piece is one-quarter of an inch too large, then the apparel or home furnishing product will likely not flow through the production process. If by chance it does, the consumer will likely purchase a product that does not fit correctly or look attractive. If details and accuracy are in your realm of expertise, pattern production offers career options for you.

Pattern Grader

Working from the **master pattern**, the pattern that evolves after adjusting and perfecting the sample pattern, **pattern graders** develop the full pattern range of sizes offered by the manufacturer. For example, the master pattern may be graded in misses' dress sizes 12 to 20 or sizes 6 to 14, depending on the garment style, the company, and its target market. By enlarging or reducing the pattern within a figure-type category, all of the pattern pieces of a particular design are developed for each size. Pattern grading is technical and precise work. It is often work that must be done at a fast pace under the pressure of production deadlines. Although most large manufacturing companies use computers to do grading work quickly, many smaller

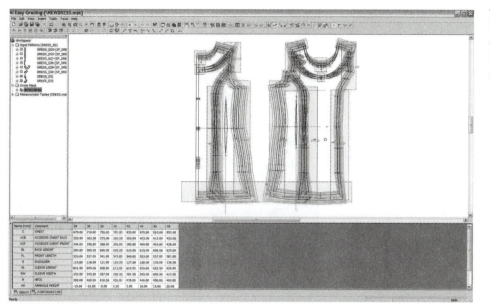

Figure 4.5
A pattern that has been graded into a size range using CAD software.

companies cannot initially afford this technology and/or prefer the hands-on skills of a grader. Figure 4.5 depicts a pattern that has been graded using CAD software.

Qualifications

Pattern graders should have the following background in terms of education, experience, and personal characteristics:

- *Education.* A bachelor's degree in fashion design, apparel production, or a related field is a minimum requirement.
- *Experience.* Effective skills in patternmaking, drafting, and product construction are necessary. Experience in pattern draping is a plus. An understanding of pattern grading technology and related work experience are needed.
- *Personal characteristics.* Strong attention to detail, the ability to work independently and under tight deadlines, and quantitative skills are job requirements for successful pattern graders.

Marker Maker

After the pattern is graded, it is time to develop a marker. A **marker** is the layout of pattern pieces on the fabrication from which the pieces will be cut, as illustrated in Figure 4.6. There are two main purposes of a marker: (1) a good marker minimizes fabric waste; and (2) it generates an accurate end design. Fabric prints and patterns,

textures and naps, and sheens and matte finishes must be taken into consideration when creating a marker. Think, for example, about a corduroy jacket. If the fabric in the back of the jacket is cut in a different direction from the front, the front and the back will appear to be two different colors. **Marker makers** manipulate and trace the pattern pieces, by hand or by computer, into the tightest possible layout, while keeping the integrity of the design in mind. In some cases, a marker is generated in hard copy, or print; in other cases, it is computer-generated and stored in the computer.

Figure 4.6
A marker is the layout of pattern pieces on the fabrication from which the pieces will be cut.

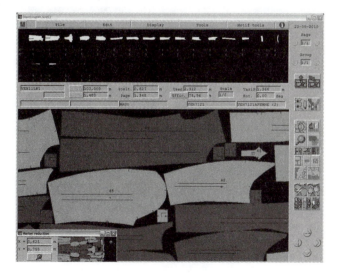

Qualifications

The qualifications required for a marker maker are as follows:

- *Education.* A bachelor's degree in fashion design, apparel production, or a related field is a minimum requirement.
- *Experience.* Effective skills in patternmaking, drafting, and product construction are necessary. Experience with marker making technology is often required.
- *Personal characteristics.* Like pattern graders, marker makers must have strong attention to detail, the ability to work independently and under tight deadlines, and strong quantitative skills. Additionally, marker makers must have the ability to "see" the product in its final form when determining pattern piece layout.

SPREADER AND CUTTER

After the marker is developed, it is ready to be placed on the fabric as preparation for cutting the pattern pieces. A **spreader** lays out the selected fabric for cutting. The spreader guides bolts of material on a machine that lays the fabric smooth and straight, layer over layer. In mid- to large-sized companies, a machine (as shown in Figure 4.7) does this function. In smaller companies or computerized factories that require fewer employees, this job may be done by cutters. A **cutter** uses cutting machines to cut precisely around the pattern pieces through layers of fabric,

Figure 4.7
The spreading machine lays the fabric smooth and straight, layer over layer, in anticipation of the next step—cutting.

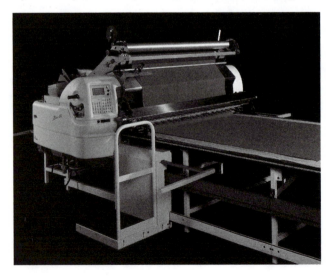

Figure 4.8
A cutter uses an electronic cutting machine to cut precisely around pattern pieces through layers of fabric.

often several inches in thickness, as shown in Figure 4.8. Although firms with advanced technology may use water jets or lasers to cut out garments quickly and accurately, some companies specialize in merchandise classifications that require hand cutting. A firm that produces beaded eveningwear or a couture design house that creates bridal wear may choose to have fabrications manually spread and cut in consideration of the delicate nature and high cost of the fabrics.

For the spreader and the cutter, vocational training or training with the manufacturer are usually considered adequate. In addition to these positions, there are a number of skilled or semiskilled workers on the production assembly line. These employees run the sewing machines, press or steam the final products, and package them for shipping, among other tasks. The production picture is a broad one with a variety of personnel opportunities.

SALES

You likely know people who are natural-born salespersons. You may even be one of these people with the enthusiasm, drive, and persuasive skills to consistently sell products, services, or ideas. These people enjoy the thrill of the chase and the excitement of the closing. The best salespersons are skilled at, almost instantly, building a rapport with customers. Through observation and active listening, sales gurus can determine the customers' needs and desires and then, by emphasizing the benefits of particular products, effectively explain how the products will fit those needs. The finish line is in sight when the customer's concerns are alleviated and the sale is closed. As a grand finale, additional products or services are offered to build the sale. If you have ever purchased an automobile, a cellular phone, a sofa, or a suit from a sales pro, then you know the feeling of a smooth sale.

In this section, sales careers in the wholesale sector of the fashion industry are explored. These include employment opportunities in the following positions: manufacturer's representative or company salesperson and merchandise coordinator.

MANUFACTURER'S REPRESENTATIVE

A **manufacturer's representative** is also referred to as a *manufacturer's rep*, an *independent rep* or *sales rep*. For the purposes of this chapter, we use the general term of *manufacturer's rep* and, later, discuss the differences between a company salesperson and a manufacturer's rep. No matter what this person is titled, his or her job is to sell a wholesale line(s). If he or she is self-employed, then the manufacturer's rep is, in essence, often a business owner. Manufacturer's reps sell the product line, or lines, of one or several manufacturers to retail store buyers. Reps who choose to sell several lines usually work with noncompetitive product lines and manufacturers. This type of manufacturer's rep is classified as a **multiline rep**, or *multiple-line rep*. For example, the manufacturer's rep may represent a handbag line from one manufacturer, a jewelry line from another vendor, and a glove line from yet another manufacturer. Such a rep can call, for instance, on the accessories buyers of retail stores and offer a selection of products. Occasionally, manufacturer's representatives decide to sell lines that are seasonally opposite, such as swimwear and outerwear. This way, the reps have better opportunities to generate sales income year-round. The manufacturer's rep who prefers to sell solely one manufacturer's line as an independent salesperson rather than as a company employee is a **single-line rep**.

The main task of a manufacturer's representative is to sell the products manufactured by the company to the buyers of retail operations. The manufacturer's rep holds meetings with prospective clients (i.e., retail buyers of brick-and-mortar stores or Web sites) in order to engage the buyers into purchasing the products and to support them in selling the products to the ultimate consumer. The manufacturer's rep's job responsibilities include:

- Solicit orders from new and current clients in a specific geographic area
- Provide samples, catalogs, and illustrations of the company's product line
- Handle product inquiries of clients and address product-related issues
- Arrange special events, such as employee training or a trunk show, or product launches for new merchandise
- Collaborate on marketing and advertising strategies to increase sales
- Nurture partnerships and build new key accounts to maintain excellent customer relations and repeat business
- Survey clients, analyze data, and prepare proposals for new and current clients

Typically, employers look for fashion sales representatives who have strong sales and marketing skills. Sales representatives are increasingly using social media to communicate effectively with retail buyers and the ultimate consumer.

The manufacturer's representative usually works within a given territory, as negotiated with the manufacturer, such as the East Coast, Florida and Georgia, or Canada. In their territories, manufacturer's reps travel to the buying offices of retail companies, the locations of small store operations, and trade marts to sell their lines to retail buyers. **Trade marts**, also called *apparel marts*, house temporary sales booths and permanent showrooms leased by either the sales representatives or the manufacturers. **Market weeks**, also called *trade shows*, are scheduled at apparel and trade marts throughout the year in conjunction with the introduction of the new, seasonal lines presented by manufacturers. Although apparel marts are located across the United States, some of the larger ones are situated in New York City, Dallas, Los Angeles, Chicago, and Atlanta.

In Figure 4.9, manufacturers' product lines are featured on the runway at MAGIC in Las Vegas, one of the premier trade shows. Manufacturer's representatives arrive at the apparel marts a day or two ahead of the market opening to set up booths or showrooms, as in Figures 4.10a and b. When the market opens, it is show time. The manufacturer's reps show the line to buyers with whom prearranged appointments have been set or to buyers who stop by, hoping to find new lines that their customers will purchase. Market weeks are key times for representatives to gain new retail clients, meet with current accounts, and secure a part of the retailers' buying dollars.

Figure 4.9
Manufacturers' product lines are featured on the runway at MAGIC in Las Vegas, one of the premier trade shows.

Figures 4.10a and b
For market week, the sales reps set up booths or showrooms with the new lines and other materials, such as company brochures, USBs containing line sheets, and displays that will help sell the new merchandise.

Company Salesperson

What is the difference between the general title of manufacturer's representative and the specific title of company salesperson? Many large manufacturing firms hire company salespeople. The **company salesperson** is a sales representative who is employed and paid directly by a particular firm and who carries just one line, that of the employer. Like manufacturers' representatives, company salespeople travel to retail buying offices, retail stores, or trade markets to show and sell their company's line. They often receive employee benefits, such as health insurance and vacation pay. Employers of company salespeople may also cover some of the expenses that manufacturers' representatives must incur, such as trade show fees, the cost of sample lines, and retail advertising contributions.

Showroom Salesperson

The majority of large manufacturers in the apparel and accessories industry have showrooms in New York City, Dallas, Chicago, Atlanta, Los Angeles, and other major metropolitan areas where large fashion trade markets take place. **Showrooms**, unlike typical apparel and accessories retail stores, rarely sell merchandise from the floor. Items are generally for display only, to allow the buyers to see pieces that would otherwise be visible only in a catalog or online.

Showroom salespeople, also called *showroom representatives*, are a type of company salesperson. They work at a manufacturer's or designer's showroom, where they meet with visiting retail buyers, present the latest product line to them, and assist with placing their purchase orders.

Qualifications

The education, work experience, and personal characteristics needed for successful employment as a manufacturer's representative, company salesperson, and showroom salesperson are similar and are listed next:

- *Education.* A bachelor's degree in fashion merchandising, fashion design, product development, business administration, marketing, or a related field is most often a minimum requirement.
- *Experience.* Sales, sales, and more sales are the key experiences needed for a career as a manufacturer's representative. Working as an assistant to a manufacturer's representative is an excellent route to understanding the responsibilities of this career and to building a network of industry contacts. Working in a showroom as a receptionist and then moving into sales is yet another option. Working on a retail sales floor or selling advertisements for the campus newspaper provides important knowledge and skills in sales. In essence, all types of sales experience provide a foundation for future employment as a company salesperson. In addition, an understanding of accounting and computers is also necessary, as is a willingness to travel.
- *Personal characteristics.* Self-discipline, self-motivation, good follow-through skills, perseverance, organizational abilities, a contagious enthusiasm, and the ability to handle rejection are key attributes of top manufacturer's reps. Successful reps are highly competitive and believe in the products they sell. They have excellent communication skills, both written and oral. Knowledge of fashion industry trends and manufacturers' competitors is critical. Understanding how products are constructed, the materials from which they are made, and the manufacturing processes helps reps educate their clients—retail buyers, in this case—about the product.

Career Challenges

Many manufacturers' reps are faced with the uncertainty of not knowing how much their next paychecks will be. In this career, income is primarily based on sales performance. Sometimes, external factors beyond a rep's control may decrease the amount of money the rep receives. Unshipped orders, late deliveries, and incorrect shipments can reduce the remuneration reps expect based on merchandise they sold.

Company salespeople must work under the guidelines of their employers. In some cases, new accounts, trade market participation, and travel plans must be approved by the administration. This position is not as autonomous as that of the manufacturer's representative. When working with a single company, if the product line for a certain season is not strong, the company salesperson does not have another line to rely on for income. If competitive lines become stronger in terms of securing the retail buyers' orders, the company salesperson faces the challenge of staying afloat during a tough sell period or securing a position with a new employer.

Manufacturer's reps can incur some expenses in the process of doing business. Some manufacturer's representatives are required to purchase their sample lines, often at a discounted price, from manufacturers. A **sample line** includes a prototype of every style within the line. Each prototype is tagged with fabric swatches, color options, sizes available, and its wholesale price, also referred to as **cost price**, or *cost*. Depending on the size of the product line, a sample line can cost a manufacturer's representative thousands of dollars. Some manufacturers buy back the sample lines, possibly to sell at factory outlets. In other cases, reps may sell sample lines independently. Additionally, there are costs associated with showing lines during market weeks. There are travel expenses; rental fees for booths, showrooms, and fixtures; as well as trade organization dues. Manufacturer's representatives who have large businesses may employ administrative and sales assistants. As independent contractors, manufacturer's representatives are business owners who share the risk, potential, and challenges associated with being their own bosses.

TRENDS AFFECTING CAREERS IN PRODUCTION

At the start of this chapter, five trends in the production of apparel and home soft goods products were mentioned: computer-integrated manufacturing, electronic data interchange, mass customization, supply-chain management, and radio-frequency identification technology. Because these trends will undeniably shape the requirements for production careers in the fashion industry of the future, a brief discussion follows.

As technology develops at a rapid pace globally, the ability to link computers together has introduced amazing advances in production. Computers tied together, referred to as **computer-integrated manufacturing (CIM)**, can be used to communicate throughout the entire product development and manufacturing processes, from design to distribution. Computer-aided design and computer-aided manufacturing are linked to form a system in which design and product development activities move smoothly into patternmaking, grading, marker making, cutting, and product construction activities. Examples of manufacturers and retailers using CIM include Talbots, Zara, and H&M (Figure 4.11). A related trend is **electronic data interchange (EDI)**, which refers to the electronic exchange of computer-generated information between one company's computer system and another's. Through EDI, manufacturers and retailers share data about the styles, colors, sizes, and price points that consumers are buying or those that are not selling and require markdowns.

Figure 4.11

Talbots uses computerized information systems to develop costing reports and specification sheets; later, shipping and sales data are analyzed.

Yet another strategy to gain market share is **mass customization**, a process that allows manufacturers or retailers to provide individualized products to consumers. Consumers desire products that can be personalized through fit preferences, color selection, fabric choices, or design characteristics. A solution to the fit preference is a scanner that takes a customer's measurements digitally, creating what is referred to as a **digital twin**. **Body-scanning** software defines and captures all of the measurements necessary for actually producing the garment or shoe. This data is forwarded online to the manufacturer, whose production technologies ensure an exact fit. Nike provides a Web site (https://store.nike.com/us/en_us/pw/nikeid-shoes/1k9Zoi3?ipp=120) to give customers the opportunity to design their own shoes. They can select from a variety of athletic shoe styles, choose colors, and add design details from an assortment of options. Figures 4.12a–c depict the body-scanning process utilized by Brooks Brothers.

In the fashion industry, manufacturers and retailers continue to work to decrease the amount of time required from design and the purchase of raw materials to production and distribution of the final product into the consumer's hands. This goal requires a partnership among the supplier, manufacturer, and retailer in which open and honest communication is the key to success. Top-selling products can be reordered and received faster. Modifications of these products give the consumer more options through preferred merchandise assortments. This activity of sharing and coordinating information across all segments of the soft goods industry is referred to as **supply-chain management (SCM)**. SCM comprises all of the activities required to coordinate and manage every step needed to bring a product to the consumer, including procuring raw materials, producing goods, transporting and distributing those goods, and managing the selling process. The goals of SCM are to reduce inventory, shorten the time for raw materials to become a finished product in the hands of a consumer, and provide better service to the consumer.

Referred to as Quick Response in the past, "SCM goes beyond Quick Response in that SCM companies share forecasting, point-of-sale data, inventory information, and information about unforeseen changes in supply or demand for materials or products."[1] As SCM strategies grew, new technologies also increased to provide companies with tools for communication and integration. One such tool is radio-frequency identification technology.

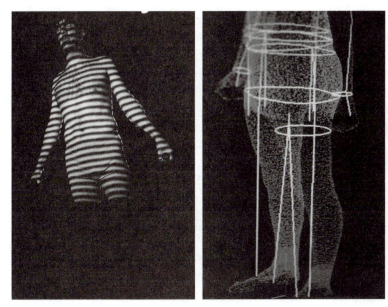

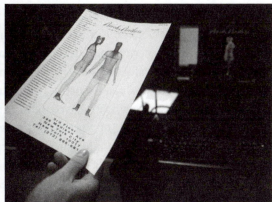

Figures 4.12a–c
The body-scanning process utilized by Brooks Brothers for digital tailoring.

Figure 4.13
RFID technology refers to tags that are called the next-generation barcode. A sales clerk holds up an RFID tag.

Radio-frequency identification technology (RFID) is referred to as the next-generation barcode, because its primary functions are to increase SCM through the tagging of containers, pallets, and individual items so that they can be accurately tracked as they move through the supply chain. "However, unlike barcodes, RFID tags do not rely on line-of-sight readability. In fact, multiple RFID tags can be read simultaneously; they have memory and, therefore, can store and update data, and they provide fully automated data collection."[2] This technology has proven to be so effective that major global retailers, such as Walmart and Target, are requiring all suppliers to apply RFID tags to pallet and case shipments. With these major retailers requiring RFID technologies of their suppliers, RFID equipment, tags, and accessories are becoming more affordable and available to a broader range of companies (Figure 4.13).

MERCHANDISE COORDINATOR

In the early 1990s, the number of specialty stores began declining, and large department stores began increasing in size and number of units. Many of these massive department stores did not offer the customer service that most specialty stores provided. In the department stores, there were fewer sales associates. The few sales staff members in the department stores were often part time, seasonal, or floaters, a term for sales associates who moved from department to department as needed, leaving little time for the retail sales staff to get to know the products and customers in order to provide excellent customer service. As a result, some of the large manufacturers were compelled to find a way to assist the department stores and, ultimately, help their firms to achieve higher sales volume. These manufacturers, among them Liz Claiborne, Ralph

Lauren Polo, and Fossil, developed a new career path in the fashion industry, that of merchandise coordinator.

Merchandise coordinators assist with a manufacturer's line in retail stores and are employed by the manufacturer, rather than the retailer. Merchandise coordinators are hired to service the manufacturer's key retail accounts in a specific geographic area. **Key accounts** are the large retailers, in terms of sales volume, carrying the manufacturer's line. Today, specialty stores have made a comeback as customers seek personalized service. Key accounts can include boutiques, specialty stores, Web sites, and large department stores, depending on the amount of inventory of a particular manufacturer's product line they carry. Merchandise coordinators travel to the retail sites to work with the owners, buyers, management personnel, sales staff, and customers. Most of these retail sites can be visited by car, as they are frequently in large metropolitan areas.

In most cases, it is not the merchandise coordinator's primary responsibility to sell the line to the buyer or customer; coordinators may write reorders, fill-ins on merchandise that is selling well. Another service that merchandise coordinators may perform is moving merchandise that has been shipped and is waiting in the stockroom to the sales floor. Reorders and stock placement on the floor are commonly referred to as **inventory replenishment**. **Visual merchandising** is another job responsibility of merchandise coordinators and may include changing displays, straightening racks, and arranging shelved goods to present the best possible visual image to the customer. In essence, merchandise coordinators are somewhat like dedicated store owners, except the "stores" are the manufacturers' departments in the retailers' stores. Some retailers collaborate with merchandise coordinators on promotional events. For example, the merchandise coordinator may be featured in an advertisement as the line's representative, and customers are invited to meet the merchandise coordinator for personal assistance with line purchases.

Career Outlook

The future for merchandise coordinators is bright. This career track has been so successful for manufacturers that many large companies have added merchandise coordinator positions. Ralph Lauren Polo employs merchandise coordinators for children's wear, misses' sportswear, and menswear, among other divisions, in New York City, St. Louis, Chicago, Atlanta, and other large cities. Another example, Jones Apparel Group, Inc., employs about 100 merchandise coordinators who are trained by its apparel designers to make product recommendations to customers. Box 4.3 is a sample classified advertisement for a merchandise coordinator of footwear with a major online retailer.

Qualifications

Successful merchandise coordinators may meet or exceed the following job criteria:

- *Education.* A bachelor's degree in fashion merchandising, fashion design, product development, business administration, marketing, sales, or a related field is commonly required.
- *Experience.* Hands-on experience in the industry, which may include work experience in retail or wholesale selling, is required for this position. Many companies will hire new college graduates with strong selling skills and an enthusiasm for the manufacturer's line.
- *Personal characteristics.* Knowledge of the product line and marketing is required. An understanding of sales, visual merchandising, textiles, and product construction is helpful. The ability to work independently with little supervision and guidance is critical to success. Strong communication skills, both oral and written, are also required.

Career Challenges

Merchandise coordinators walk a fine line between several parties—the manufacturer, the manufacturer's sales rep, the retail buyer, the retailer's sales staff, and the customers. This career requires strong attention to the goals of all parties. Merchandise coordinators are constantly challenged to find ways to help retailers generate sales, while keeping their focus on their manufacturer's profits. There may be many client stores in a merchandise coordinator's territory, requiring carefully scheduled travel plans and exceptional time management. Additionally, they have to complete many tasks in each retail location. It is a fast-paced job, but it is an excellent position for someone who enjoys sharing the retailers' and manufacturers' worlds.

BOX 4.3 WEB SITE MERCHANDISE COORDINATOR OF SHOES

Detailed Description:

Do you love shoes? Have a passion for fashion retail? The Shoes team is looking for a meticulous and tenacious self-starter to coordinate our merchandising process. The Merchandise Coordinator we are looking for is someone who is highly organized and obsessed with providing excellent customer experiences while continually improving existing processes. This position is a great opportunity for someone with talent, energy, and a love for fashion to join a fast-paced, growing e-business.

Responsibilities:

- Drive smooth execution of Shoes merchandising process from beginning to end
- Collaborate with merchandisers, vendor representatives, designers, and photo studio managers
- Streamline current processes and create efficiencies where needed
- Work cross-functionally to ensure accurate, on-time inputs for promotions
- Coordinate photo shoot samples and create shot lists
- Monitor featured items for receiving and stocking
- Assist with creation and accuracy of keywords, trends, and special features, and content and accuracy of features and site flips
- Produce and distribute weekly merchandising update reports
- Prioritize appropriately when process inputs may be at risk
- Provide support for special projects as assigned

SUSTAINABILITY OFFICER

Sustainability is the practice of maintaining profitability while avoiding depletion or exploitation of natural, human, and economical resources. The three pillars of corporate sustainability have been informally dubbed "Planet, People, Profits." As more and more companies engage in efforts around sustainability, a professional role has emerged among the corporate ranks to champion and monitor these efforts.

The primary level of sustainability practices in a firm usually include activities like recycling projects and "green teams." These efforts are not necessarily centralized through a formal position or office.

Once an organization becomes more strategic about using sustainability practices to achieve efficiencies that will save money, such as reducing water use or carbon emissions in the manufacturing process, or examining packaging or printing design and practices, a company is more likely to hire an official **Sustainability Officer**. This professional is charged with building a business case in the organization to make improvements that enhance profitability as well as improve the company's public image. The sustainability officer's responsibilities include:

- Lead and influence the organizations global commitments to enable the organization to make a significant impact on the planet.
- Set environmental targets and implement strategies focused on sustainability commitments.
- Manage strategic partnerships with sustainability consultants and organizations to identify and prioritize sustainability initiatives aligned with the organization.
- Prepare and lead responses to sustainability audits and/or assessments to organizations such as the Carbon Disclosure Project (CDP), and the Global Reporting Initiative (GRI). Determine appropriate measurement and tracking model and reporting requirements.
- Identify areas of concern, such as in packaging, fiber or yarn process, milling, or other aspects of the supply chain that will make the biggest impact on the environment. Manage environmental corporate footprint data collection.
- Lead measurement and evaluation process to assess impact of efforts focused on the environment.
- Partner with Communications to identify and coordinate internal and external communications opportunities.

Qualifications

A career in sustainability requires the following qualifications:

- *Education.* A bachelor's degree in apparel and textiles, business administration, environmental science, or a related field is a minimum requirement. Most firms specify a preferred qualification of a master's degree in business, environmental science, public policy, strategic communications, environmental law, or related field.
- *Experience.* This level of experience and exposure to the apparel production process requires a candidate with upwards of five to seven years working in the industry. A sustainability officer for an apparel brand should have knowledge of the apparel production supply chain, environmental issues, human rights issues related to labor, governmental and legal issues related to doing business in vendor countries, and environmental issues related to fiber, fabric, and garment production and finishing. Because of the reporting arm of this position, transparency officials often have specific experience in public policy and communication.
- *Personal characteristics.* Strong communication skills, collaboration skills, and decision-making skills, with the ability to identify areas for change and improvement, build programs, and serve as a change agent for the organization.
- *Challenges.* This role in an organization continues to evolve. Sustainability requires cultural shift in an organization and often rethinking and reworking complex production systems and supply chains.

TRANSPARENCY OFFICER

One of the principal issues related to product sourcing and manufacturing is **transparency**, which is the full disclosure of information from the company regarding all aspects of the product, including materials used in the product, human rights and wage issues related to production processes, and impact to the environment along the supply chain. To monitor, ensure compliance, identify gaps and develop and provide open communication of these practices, a new position has emerged among corporate leadership in larger companies: the **Transparency Officer**.

Emerging in importance only since the early 2000s, the role of this position continues to evolve. However, as more and more consumers demand clear and transparent information about the products they buy, and how those products are produced, this role has increased, and experts predict it will continue to do so.

Qualifications

- *Education.* A bachelor's degree in apparel and textiles, business administration, or a related field is a minimum requirement. Most firms specify a preferred qualification of a master's degree in business, public policy, strategic communications, law, accounting, or related field.
- *Experience.* This level of experience and exposure to the apparel production process requires a candidate with upwards of five to seven years working in the industry. This is not an entry-level position. A transparency officer for an apparel brand should have knowledge of the apparel production supply chain; vendor selection and relations; environmental issues; human rights issues related to labor; governmental and legal issues related to doing business in vendor countries; and environmental issues related to fiber, fabric, and garment production and finishing. Because of the reporting arm of this position, transparency officials often have specific experience in public policy and communication.
- *Personal characteristics.* Strong communication skills, collaboration skills, and decision-making skills, with the ability to identify areas for change and improvement, build programs, and serve as a change agent for the organization.
- *Challenges.* This is a newer position and continues to evolve. Because of the historically fragmented and complex nature of the apparel production process, even the best efforts to document, comply, and report often fall short. To learn more about the growing demand for transparency among consumers, see Box 4.4.

Summary

Within fashion firms, large and small, there is a vast range of employment opportunities in the production sector, whether the firms manufacture their lines domestically, overseas, or both. Career tracks exist in production for those interested in fabrics, numbers, or technology. Careers that relate directly to manufacturing include product manager, traffic manager, production planner,

BOX 4.4   #whomademyclothes

Fashion Revolution is a global initiative based in the UK and comprised of fashion industry professionals as well as other fashion enthusiasts from around the world. Their goal is to achieve greater transparency in the fashion product supply chain. Based on a belief that the fashion industry values people, the environment, creativity, and profit equally, this group endeavors to radically change the way clothes are sourced, produced, and consumed to achieve a safe, clean, and fair industry.

Born from the April 24, 2013, Rana Plaza factory collapse, killing 1,138 people with many more injured, this anniversary marks the group's annual observance with Fashion Revolution Week and the social media campaign #whomademyclothes. Since the launch of #whomademyclothes in 2015, the social media impact expands each year, with greater numbers of consumers wanting to know how their fashion products are produced. In 2018, there were 720 million impressions from the social media campaign, up 30 percent from the previous year.

Brands and retailers are responding. According to Fashion Revolution, 3,838 have responded to consumers with real information about suppliers, workers, and more. In reply, the #imadeyourclothes response campaign emerged, where brands posted images of actual apparel workers from around the world.

The Fashion Transparency Index reviews and ranks 150 of the largest global fashion and apparel brands and retailers, measuring how much information these firms disclose about their supply chain policies, practices, and social and environmental impact. Here is a list of the ways Fashion Revolution encourages companies to build a greater commitment to transparency:

1. Answer customers' #whomademyclothes questions with specific information, not just your policies.
2. Share photos and personal stories of workers in the supply chain using the hashtag #imadeyourclothes
3. Publish direct contact details for your Corporate Social Responsibility or Sustainability department on the company website.
4. Publish suppliers publicly – in a searchable and downloadable format.
5. Publish details about suppliers, including the results of supplier assessments. Make this information easy to understand.
6. Publish information about the way the progress on social and environmental issues is tracked.
7. Publish information about the real-world effects of supply chain practices and sustainability efforts.
8. Make one product completely transparent. Companies could do this through tools like Provenance (provenance.org) or traceable QR codes.
9. Make at least one whole supply chain transparent. Companies could do this through tools such as Sourcemap (Sourcemap.com) or Cotton Connect (Cottonconnect.org).
10. Offer customers both product and price transparency, like the pioneering brand Honest, founded by Jessica Alba, The Honest Company (honest.com).

Sources:

Fashion Revolution, "Why Transparency Matters," https://www.fashion revolution.org/about/transparency/

Ley, R., "Not so fast: Millennials press fashion brands for greater transparency," Ethical Corporation, October 20, 2017, http://www.ethicalcorp.com/not-so -fast-millennials-press-fashion-brands-greater-transparency

Figure Box 4.3 The "Fashion Revolution" movement calls for a fairer, safer, cleaner, and more transparent fashion industry.

production manager, production efficiency manager, and quality control manager. After the designer has created the line, development of the actual product before it goes into production is facilitated by the patternmaker and marker maker. Grading, spreading, and cutting are three phases of production in which computers are quickly impacting job opportunities. Additionally, several technological trends will undeniably impact the requirements for production careers in the fashion industry of the future. These include computer-integrated manufacturing, electronic data interchange, mass customization, supply-chain management, and radio-frequency identification technology. Growing in importance for consumers of fashion products is sustainability and transparency. As a result, more firms include professionals to coordinate and communicate these activities to their customers.

Endnotes

1. Burns, L.D., Mullet, K.K., and Bryant, N. O., *The Business of Fashion: Designing, Manufacturing, and Marketing*, 5th Edition. New York, Fairchild Books, 2016.
2. Ibid.

Key Terms

body scanning
company salesperson
computer-integrated
    manufacturing (CIM)
cost price
cutter
cut-to-order
cut-to-stock
digital twin
electronic data interchange
    (EDI)
end product
inventory replenishment
key accounts
lead time
manufacturer's representative
market week
marker
marker maker
mass customization
master pattern
merchandise coordinator
multiline representative
pattern grader

product manager
product void
production assistant
production efficiency
    manager
production manager
production planner
quality control manager
radio-frequency identification
    technology (RFID)
sample line
showrooms
showroom salesperson
single-line representative
spreader
supply-chain management
    (SCM)
sustainability
sustainability officer
trade marts
traffic manager
transparency
transparency officer
visual merchandiser

Online Resources

www.latimes.com/business/la-fi-american-apparel-made-in-
    usa-20140810-story.html#page=1
www.interviewmagazine.com/fashion/the-row/
www.apparelnews.net/news/2019/feb/21/sustainable-fashion-
    forum-will-examine-how-help-en/
www.fashionindustrynetwork.com/group/garmentproduction

www.lectra.com
www.just-style.com/sectors/apparel_id128
www.apparelnews.net/news/manufacturing/
www.cdp.net/en
www.wwd.com/markets-news/textiles/the-american-way-
    7309282?navSection=package&navId=7313534
www.globalreporting.org/Pages/default.aspx
www.fashionrevolution.org
www.americanapparel.com/en/aboutus/social-compliance.jsp
apparel-sourcing-usa.us.messefrankfurt.com/new-york/
    en.html

Discussion Questions

1. Consider apparel and home soft-goods production a decade from now. What education, experience, and personal qualities will the production manager of a large domestic manufacturer in home furnishings need? Develop a classified advertisement to recruit a qualified candidate for this position.

2. Select three of the following production trends discussed in this chapter: computer-integrated manufacturing, electronic data interchange, mass customization, supply-chain management, and radio-frequency identification technology. Locate and copy articles that provide illustrations of each of these technologies being implemented in fashion companies for discussion in class.

3. Practice "futuring" by researching manufacturing trends and innovations in technology not presented in this chapter that will impact apparel manufacturing over the next decade. Construct a chart of the top-five innovations (e.g., software programs or hardware inventions, processes of production, new locations for manufacturing) and their creators, and briefly describe the impact these advances will have on soft-goods manufacturing.

CAREERS IN FASHION DESIGN, PRODUCT DEVELOPMENT, AND FASHION PROMOTION

Unit 2 looks at the field of fashion design and product development from two perspectives, those of the manufacturer (Chapter 5) and the retailer (Chapter 6). The move into outsourced production, the customer's need for speed in purchasing new looks, and the proliferation of technology in design and manufacturing have come together to generate new career opportunities in fashion design and product development. In Chapter 5, "Designing Apparel and Accessories for the Manufacturer," careers related to designing apparel and accessories for the manufacturer are discussed. There are several relatively new positions, in addition to those of the fashion designer, assistant fashion designer, and patternmaker; among them are the career paths of the technical designer and specification technician.

Some retailers purchase fashion merchandise from manufacturers or wholesalers at markets where all of the retail buyers are selecting from the same product lines. Other retailers create exclusivity in their inventory offerings by developing and manufacturing their own products, or by collaborating with a manufacturer who will supply exclusive products that fit their customers' needs. Many large retail operations own a product development division functioning as a design and production source exclusively for them. In addition, many manufacturers are either specializing in creating and/or manufacturing product-developed goods specifically for their client retailers. As a result, Unit 2 examines design and product development for and by the fashion retailer. The career paths in this field, as discussed in Chapter 6, "Product Development by the Manufacturer and Retailer," include the following: director of product development, merchandiser, sourcing staff, product development designer, project manager, colorist, textile technical designer, product development patternmaker, and quality control manager.

Whether the fashion product is created and manufactured by the retailer or purchased from a manufacturer, it must be marketed to appeal to the consumer. In Chapter 7, "Promotion for the Designer and Manufacturer," we examine the promotion division of a manufacturer that does just that—markets the designer and/or the line of the manufacturer to the retail buyer and ultimate consumer. Promotion career opportunities in the primary level of the fashion industry, as examined in Chapter 7, include fashion stylist, public relations director, advertising research and promotion positions, social media director, and fashion event producer.

In the next unit (Unit 3), Chapter 8 explores promotion for the retail operation. As a result of the growth of social media and Internet marketing, career opportunities are exploding in promotion and public relations. Although there is some overlap in promotion tasks for the manufacturer and retailer, this growth and their differing goals and responsibilities warrant examining each separately and from their individual perspectives.

Unit 2 explores the growth of design and product development divisions in the retail sector of the fashion industry, which has added another area of job opportunities for the fashion design and product development professional. He or she is no longer limited to the manufacturing or wholesale levels of the industry. As fashion lines have become more prolific, more competitive, and more available via e-commerce, differentiating a line and highlighting it in the consumer's eyes have become essential and challenging tasks. As a result, promotion and public relations have become critical keys to the success of designers', manufacturers', and retailers' lines. The central line from the movie *Field of Dreams*, "If you build it, they will come," doesn't reflect the work of fashion designers and product developers today. For them, it is: "Build it well, promote it well, and they will come."

CHAPTER 5

DESIGNING APPAREL AND ACCESSORIES FOR THE MANUFACTURER

Either a creative individual or a team of creatives came up with the design concept for your favorite shirt, jeans, or iPad case. The season after you purchased this product, a new and exciting version of this apparel or accessory item was introduced. How do these designers do this season after season, year after year? From all around the world, fashion designers share their trend and consumer knowledge, as well as their imaginations, personalities, and aesthetic preferences, as they develop their creations. They put themselves out there each fashion season. Think about Betsey Johnson, who has a love for detail and design that is evident in everything she has done in life and in business for nearly fifty years. She says, "Making clothes involves what I like, and color, pattern, shape, and movement, and I like the everyday process and the people, the pressure, the surprise of seeing the work come alive walking and dancing around on strangers."[1] Fashion design is about knowing your customer, as described by footwear designer Manolo Blahnik (Figure 5.1): "About half my designs are controlled fantasy, 15 percent are total madness, and the rest are bread-and-butter designs."[2] Fashion design is about creativity, self-expression, and change—always change. Karl Lagerfeld (Figure 5.2) explains this: "Fashion keeps me designing: the love of change, the idea that the next one will be the right one, the nonstop dialogue."[3]

Fashion design is the development and execution of wearable forms, structures, and patterns. Just as fashions have changed over the years, the field of fashion design has changed dramatically. Designers rely heavily on social media to market brands and build relationships

SOCIAL MEDIA STRIKES
BOX 5.1   Designers and Brands—Finding the Best Fit on Social Media!

By most accounts, social media first emerged around 1997, and since that time designers and brands have continuously strived to harness its power. In the constantly evolving array of social media platforms, designers can now engage their customers and tell their story in a variety of ways.

Twitter can spread news like wildfire! This is a great format for a designer or brand to gain a huge number of followers, quickly let their customers know about new products and projects, and read what is being said about them. The trending topics and hashtag features allow Twitter users to easily see what others are talking about. The "retweet" feature for the most bold and newsworthy posts increases brand awareness and consumer engagement.

For browsers, Pinterest is the platform of choice. Brands and designers can create a variety of boards focusing on different categories of the product offerings – like "denim," "weekend," and "accessories." According to one study, fashion accounts for 45 percent of Pinterest searches and pins, and consumers are 10 percent more likely to make a purchase when directed by Pinterest than from any other social media platform.

For the authentic, personal, "behind-the-scenes" of it all, Snapchat is the go-to! The platform boasts over 150 million global active users a day, with 60 percent in the 18 to 34 age category. This platform is favored for its captivating video format, far less static than the text and images used in most other platforms. Subscribers can choose from hundreds of designers to follow and get regularly updated content on fashion shows, ongoing teases about new product lines, and a general feel of the day-to-day things that go on behind the scenes in a big fashion brand.

YouTube is the second largest search engine and the third most visited site after Google and Facebook. On mobile devices alone, YouTube reaches more 18- to 49-year-olds than any single broadcast or cable TV network. The platform has launched in over ninety countries and available in eighty different languages. Vloggers and how-to fashionistas have found a home on YouTube for some time. But as the YouTube reach continues to expand, fashion designers and brands can now effectively advertise on any video that reaches their target audience with pre-roll, mid-roll, and post-roll ads.

The imaging power of Instagram is a natural fit for fashion designers and brands. With 1 billion active users, the potential consumer reach is enormous. The "see more" feature adds to this power. Through swipe technology, viewers can be taken directly to a Web site where they can buy the item viewed moments earlier in the Instagram post. This literally drops the item right into the palm of their hand—and all the consumer has to do is buy it.

Fashion marketing is ever evolving and changing, and social media is proving to be an essential part of the communication mix for any successful designer or brand.

Sources:

Arthur, R., "10 fashion brands nailing their Snapchat strategy," Forbes, November 30, 2016, https://www.forbes.com/sites/rachelarthur/2016/11/30/10-fashion-brands-nailing-their-snapchat-content-strategy/#35413d0b4e9e

Brandwatch, "52 fascinating and incredible YouTube statistics," July 15, 2019, https://www.brandwatch.com/blog/youtube-stats/

GreenBuzz, "Social media's effect on the fashion industry," June 21, 2018, greenbuzzagency.com/social-media-effect-fashion-industry

with consumers (Box 5.1). The move into outsourcing (or overseas production), the customer's need for speed in purchasing new looks, and the rapid evolution of technology in design and manufacturing have generated new career opportunities in fashion design. There are several new positions in addition to that of the fashion designer, assistant fashion designer, and patternmaker. Among them are the career paths of the technical designer and specification technician. In this chapter, all five career paths are explored, beginning with the fashion designer.

FASHION DESIGNER

Working as a **fashion designer**, an artist dedicated to the creation of apparel and accessories, can mean supervising a team of design assistants, working under the label of a big-name designer or manufacturer, freelancing for a line or group of lines, or designing and producing a line under your own name. Although the first two options may not appear to be as alluring as the others, they may be less stressful and, quite possibly, more lucrative. Designing

Figure 5.3
Ralph Lauren.

Figure 5.4
Michael Kors.

Figure 5.5
Nicolas Ghesquière.

and manufacturing your own label takes a great deal of money, time, dedication, and hard work.

There are as many different ways designers embark upon a fashion career as there are styles of design. Ralph Lauren started with a small tie collection that he sold to Bloomingdale's (Figure 5.3). Helmut Lang opened his own clothing store because he couldn't find "the right" T-shirt. Michael Kors (Figure 5.4) built a following of customers by selling his designs in an NYC boutique. Nicolas Ghesquière (Figure 5.5) is a globally recognized fashion designer who is currently creative director for LVMH's Louis Vuitton, replacing Marc Jacobs. He learned the job hands-on as an assistant at Jean-Paul Gaultier and later as creative director for Balenciaga. The paths in fashion design are diverse, but most people find that the best foundation for a design career is a college degree and the work experience needed to truly know what it takes to be a fashion designer.

Fashion designers often choose to work in a specific area of fashion, such as the merchandise categories of men's, women's, and children's apparel, or accessories. Accessory designers create such items as handbags, belts, scarves, hats, hosiery, and eyewear. Jewelry designers work in the areas of costume jewelry or fine jewelry using precious stones and metals (Figure 5.6). Footwear designers create different styles of shoes and boots. Although most fashion designers specialize in a specific area of fashion (e.g., knitwear, wovens, fur, children's wear, handbags), a few work in all areas. Regardless of the merchandise category in which a designer works, the steps in the design process are very similar.

Figure 5.6
Alexis Bittar.

From conceiving the initial design to producing the final product, the design process can take between eighteen and twenty-four months. Listed next are the general steps the fashion designer takes to place a new collection or a full line in the retailers' hands:

1. Researching current fashion and making predictions of future trends. Some designers conduct their own research, whereas others turn to fashion industry trade groups or trend forecasters, who publish trend reports that project the particular styles, colors, and fabrics for a season (as examined in Chapter 1)

2. Sketching preliminary designs. Many designers sketch initial designs by hand; more designers use computer-aided design (CAD) software to transfer these hand sketches to the computer, or to draw first sketches

3. Attending trade shows or visiting manufacturers to peruse fabrics and procure samples in order to decide which fabrics to use

4. Determining a color palette

5. Designing the styles to be part of the new collection or line, knowing that some of these will later be eliminated due to cost or merchandising decisions

6. Costing out styles to make certain they fit within the price range of the line

7. Creating a prototype or sample of the garment and then trying the sample on the fit model for design adjustments

8. Creating the full collection or line of samples and reviewing the full line to determine which styles to keep or delete

9. Having sample lines constructed to market to retail buyers in the showroom or at trade markets

10. After buyers have placed their orders, distributing the garments to retail operations and identifying top-selling items for the next collection

Qualifications

The qualifications for a fashion designer are presented in the following list:

- *Education.* A bachelor's degree in fashion design or product development is commonly required. Supplementing a fashion design degree with a business, marketing, or fashion merchandising degree or minor gives a job candidate an edge.

- *Experience.* A fashion designer needs basic skills in drawing, patternmaking, clothing construction, and CAD. Fashion designers are expected to present a portfolio of work at interviews. Industry experience is necessary. Many fashion designers started out as interns, patternmakers, or design assistants for more experienced designers. Salaried designers as a rule earn higher and more stable incomes than do self-employed designers. However, a few self-employed fashion designers who have become very successful earn many times the salary of even the highly paid salaried designers. The largest concentrations of fashion designers are employed in New York and California. Designers with many years of experience can earn much greater than the average national salary, in addition to bonuses or commissions for exceptional seasonal sales.

- *Personal characteristics.* A strong eye for color and detail, a sense of balance and proportion, aesthetic appreciation, and knowledge of historical fashion are important competencies for a designer. Fashion designers also need effective communication and problem-solving skills. Strong sales and presentation skills and knowledge of the business end of the fashion industry are vital to a successful fashion design career.

Depending on the size of the design firm and the designer's level of experience, fashion designers have varying levels of involvement in different aspects of design and production, as shown in Box 5.2, a profile of fashion designer, Vera Wang. In large design firms, fashion designers often are the lead designers who are responsible for creating the designs, choosing the colors and fabrics, and overseeing technical designers who turn the designs into a final product. (Technical designers are discussed later in this chapter.) Large design houses also employ their own patternmakers, who create the master patterns for the design and sew the prototypes and samples. Designers working in small firms, or those new to the job, usually perform most of the technical, patternmaking, and sewing tasks, in addition to designing the clothing. A few high-fashion designers are self-employed and create custom designs for individual clients. Other high-fashion designers sell their designs in their own retail stores, specialty stores, or department stores.

Yet other fashion designers specialize in costume design for performing arts, film, and television productions. Although the work of costume designers is similar

PROFILE: Fashion Designer Vera Wang

From the moment she unlaced her competitive figure skates for the last time, Vera Wang set her sights on a life in fashion. In the forty-plus years since, hers has been a singular ride, one that took her first on a sixteen-year editorial stint at *Vogue* magazine, where she learned that no one disturbed the calm of Mr. Penn's set with chatter, to Ralph Lauren, where she experienced the creative joys of limitless resources, and finally, almost thirty years ago, to her own company.

Vera Wang, a design leader in bridal gowns, continues to be a leader in fashion and social media. She tweeted that, for her spring bridal collection, she was inspired

Figure Box 5.2
Fashion Designer,
Vera Wang.

by the "lightness of being." Vera Wang then went on to unveil her Spring 2015 bridal collection in a film available online and via mobile devices. "The opportunity to create a visual and expressive experience of the clothes, as interpreted by my fashion vision, is a whole new way for me to communicate with not only brides, but women everywhere," explained Wang.

As one of fashion's most daring designers, Wang also stands out in ready-to-wear. Fall 2019 channels the garb of Celtic warriors with a fabric-first approach. A departure from the very classic and broad appeal of her wedding collections, she used a *tonnag*, a traditional plaid shawl, as a point of departure for inspiration. From this point, Wang reworked classic plaids and even included surface design prints inspired by artwork from the ancient "Book of Kells." On inspiration for her modern, forward collections, Wang explains "things that came before, people and things and experiences—that does mean something to me. It doesn't mean I don't embrace the new, but I don't forget the past, either."

Sources:

BrainyQuotes, "Vera Wang quotes," https://www.brainyquote.com/authors/vera-wang-quotes

Daily News, "Vera Wang unveils Spring 2015 bridal film to show off newest collection," Casa de Novia, April 14, 2014, www.nydailynews.com/life-style/fashion/vera-wang-unveils-spring-2015-bridal-film-article-1.1755906

Elevology, "Vera Wang debuts spring 2015 bridal film," April 14, 2014, http://www.casadenoviabridal.com/blog/entry/vera-wang-debuts-spring-2015-bridal-film

Foley, B., "Vera Wang: A life in fashion," WWD, May 12, 2010, www.wwd.com/fashion-news/designer-luxury/vera-wang-a-life-in-fashion-3068440

Foley, B., "Vera Wang RTW fall 2019," WWD, February 12, 2019, https://wwd.com/runway/fall-ready-to-wear-2019/new-york/vera-wang/review/

to that of other fashion designers, it is different in that costume designers often perform extensive research on the styles worn during the period in which the performance takes place or collaborate with directors to select and create appropriate attire. They sketch the designs, select fabric and other materials, and oversee the production of the costumes for television and film. Costume designers are discussed in Chapter 12.

Career Challenges

A fashion design career is not for the meek. Fashion designers must be able to work in a high-pressure environment with an assortment of personalities—with the common goal of meeting tight deadlines. Those entering this occupation must be willing to work as part of a team. Designers are expected to handle criticism, and critics in this field can be brutal. Successful fashion designers know how to learn from a critique while maintaining their individual styles. Many designers tend to have sporadic working hours, often needing to make adjustments to their work days (or work nights) to accommodate company deadlines (e.g., market week timing, fashion show plans, production due dates). Constant interfacing with suppliers, manufacturers, and co-workers throughout the world requires excellent communication skills and patience. Most fashion designers can expect frequent travel. Finally, they must stay on top of consumer and fashion trends, competition, and how their lines are performing at retail. As trend reporter and marketer Jason Campbell states, "Spotting trends is an ongoing exercise."[4]

ASSISTANT FASHION DESIGNER

In the fashion design field, as well as any other career field, you have to start somewhere. This is where assistant designers, or design assistants, come in. **Assistant fashion designers** support designers by helping them create new materials, styles, colors, and patterns for fashion brands and labels. Like fashion designers, design assistants usually specialize in a particular line, such as woven garments, knitwear, footwear, or accessories. The design assistant uses product knowledge and, in some firms, strong apparel and accessories construction, patternmaking, and computer-aided design skills to create prototypes or to modify existing garments. The assistant designer may also be responsible for managing parts of the design process, for example, making certain products arrive on time by working closely with factories and suppliers.

The duties of an assistant designer typically include the following:

- Assisting with the design and development teams to execute the seasonal concept direction, line plan style needs, margin requirements, and completion of product
- Communicating with vendors and other departments under the direction of the designer, such as sourcing fabrics and trimmings
- Participating in meetings with vendors, sales representatives, representatives of other company departments, and retail clients, as determined by the designer
- Communicating technical and creative ideas to the designer, using sketches, fabrics, and trims
- Assisting the designer in creating the product collections at the beginning of each season

- Preparing development creative packages and specification packets under the direction of the designer, such as clear and detailed technical sketches
- Assisting in the preparation of seasonal product review meetings
- Creating new artwork for trims, appliqués, and such for items in the collection
- Supporting the design and development team by preparing necessary visual tools (e.g., sketches, presentation boards, fabric swatches, and color standards)
- Checking for quality by inspecting products during the design process and, when a product is completed, ensuring that samples are constructed accurately and on time

With experience, the assistant designer may take part in seasonal market research to help the design team develop a new product range and forecast trends for the following season. Some companies hire interns, and it is often the assistant designer's responsibility to supervise and guide them. Although the assistant designer usually works in a studio, he or she may have the opportunity to travel and visit manufacturers or go on research trips to art galleries, trade shows, or particular places or countries that inspire a design theme (Figure 5.7).

Qualifications

The qualifications required for an assistant designer position vary with employers, but there are two common prerequisites: training in patternmaking and experience in **computer-aided design (CAD)**. CAD is increasingly being used in the fashion design industry. Although most designers initially sketch designs by hand, a growing number translate these hand sketches to the computer or draw completely on the computer. CAD allows designers to view apparel styles on virtual models and in various colors and shapes, saving time by requiring fewer adjustments of prototypes and samples later. A listing of qualifications commonly required for an assistant designer follows:

- *Education.* A bachelor's degree in fashion design and/ or product development is commonly required, to include coursework in patternmaking, illustration, and CAD. Training in draping, tailoring, and specialized merchandise categories (e.g., swimwear, menswear, or children's wear) is a plus when it matches the employer's product line.

Figure 5.7
Although the assistant designer usually works in a studio, he or she may have the opportunity to travel and visit manufacturers or go to trade shows.

- *Experience.* The assistant designer should have computer skills in design-related software, such as Adobe Illustrator, Excel, Kaledo, and Photoshop. Working on CAD updates and color, color cards, fabric swatches, and tech pack updates requires strong computer skills. Experience in design or product development with some background in fit, fabric development, finishes, and construction details is often required. Experience often separates the candidate who receives the job offer from other applicants. This can begin in the form of volunteer work, such as costuming for a community theater, as well as an internship with a design or manufacturing firm during college years.

- *Personal characteristics.* Excellent organizational and verbal communication skills are needed. A high level of attention to detail and accuracy is important. The abilities to follow instructions, anticipate what will need to be done, and work as part of a team are mandatory. A strong aesthetic sense and abilities in color, proportion, and fit are critical skills for the assistant designer.

TECHNICAL DESIGNER

Technical design is a career path that evolved from the manufacturer's move into outsourcing. As the majority of apparel and accessories production relocated from domestic production factories to overseas manufacturing facilities, these offshore manufacturers began producing a wide range of products across several categories. Many of the products were new to the manufacturers. Someone was needed to oversee what the factories were doing—the measurements they were using, the construction techniques that were being applied, the dates products were going through the different stages of production, and more. A specialist was needed to provide product specifications and to communicate with the various contractors. Technical design was born.

Technical design (also called *tech design*) refers to using drawings, measurements, patterns, and models to develop the "blueprints," or technical plans, needed for the manufacturing of products. Technical design includes determining specifications of trim colors, construction, and components of products as needed by the manufacturer. Fashion is a perfect fit for technical design because the manufacturer's work with overseas contractors mandates strict oversight of specifications to ensure consistent quality, good fit, and standardized sizing. In addition, technical design impacts manufacturing efficiency and cost effectiveness through reduced errors and quicker turnaround.

Today's technical designer essentially does parts of the job that designers used to do when companies were smaller and production was completed domestically. In years past, the technical design position did not exist because companies had their own production facilities.

Their products were similar and used the same types of construction, and these processes were often standardized in-house. As production crossed borders and oceans, the designer needed help—badly. The technical design position provided the designer with time to focus on design again.

A **technical designer** is the liaison between the designer and the factory and is responsible for working closely with the designers to communicate their specific product requests to the factory overseas. An apparel technical designer's focus is on the fit, construction, and quality of the garment, more than the actual design of it. Technical designers are, in essence, the architects of fashion products. They work with flat measurements, construction, and pattern corrections from the first sample to production. They are responsible for creating the prototypes, or samples, and patterns, and they work with the manufacturers and suppliers during the production stages. Technical designers may also work with the sales team to figure out how they want the fit executed, depending on the trend for that season. In Box 5.3, a day in the life of a technical designer is explored.

Responsibilities of the technical designer vary with each company, as with any industry. Some companies require the technical designer to be more involved with design and computer work in such programs as Adobe Illustrator and Kaledo, whereas others require the technical designer to work heavily with patterns. The general responsibilities of the technical designer are as follows:

- Managing the fit process of production garments from first sample fitting through stock delivery
- Ensuring that garments adhere to the company's quality and fit standards
- Conducting fittings and issuing all fit corrections
- Resolving construction and fit issues to ensure consistent fit and quality
- Generating complete and accurate production specifications and corrections
- Organizing and tracking production samples
- Interfacing with manufacturing to identify any issues that may prevent timely fit approval
- Monitoring/resolving any problems with samples
- Providing care-labeling instructions
- Conducting stock review
- Communicating daily and troubleshooting with overseas offices

- Overseeing adherence to design and production calendar, responding to change as appropriate, and, if applicable, partnering with design and manufacturing team to ensure timely delivery of line

Qualifications

The qualifications for the position of technical designer are as follows:

- *Education.* Technical designers are typically required to have at least an associate's degree, likely a bachelor's degree in fashion design or product development. Basic training includes computer skills in common programs (e.g., Microsoft Excel) and program-specific skills (e.g., Adobe Photoshop, Illustrator, and Kaledo).
- *Experience.* Patternmaking and CAD experience are expected. Many technical designers are hired from the position of specification technician. An internship with a fashion design firm and work in the technical design department can help open the door to a position in this area. A strong portfolio of a job candidate's best work is the ideal way to showcase his or her creativity and can go a long way toward convincing potential employers that the candidate would be an asset to their business.
- *Personal characteristics.* An understanding of numbers, business, and technology can be very helpful to a technical designer, as are an eye for detail and strong interpersonal skills, because this position often requires working with a cross-disciplinary team. Technical designers often work within specialized niches, gaining field-specific knowledge as they continue to climb the professional ladder. As companies continue to outsource their work, often expanding overseas in the process, there will also continue to be a growing demand for technical designers.

Career Challenges

The technical designer serves as the liaison between the manufacturer and the designer. Tasked with the responsibility of upholding the creative integrity of the fashion, while ensuring excellent fit and production efficiencies, this role requires exceptional communication skills, as well as diplomacy, organization, and time management. The fashion industry, and its related technology,

CASE STUDIES IN CAREER EXPLORATION

BOX 5.3   A Day in the Life of a Corporate Fashion Designer and a Technical Designer

Do you aspire to work in the fashion industry? Do you have dreams of spending your days out shopping for inspiration? While there may be a glamorous side to being a fashion designer, there is also the not-so-glamorous (but equally rewarding, nonetheless) side of the job that you may not be aware of. Here is a day in the life of a corporate fashion designer:

9–10:30 a.m. Answer e-mails from factories overseas and explain or rework any outstanding issues they have on tech-packs in order to get either knit downs, hand looms, or samples in (depending on time of season).

10:30–11 a.m. Meet with sourcing team to discuss timeline and any issues relating to fabric development.

11–11:30 a.m. FedEx delivers proto samples (prototypes/samples) from the factory. They all have to be checked for mistakes before handing them off to technical design team for fittings. (We have specific days for fittings with models.)

11:30 a.m.–12 p.m. New e-mails are sent to factories giving my design comments of proto samples.

12–1 p.m. Lunch break. This might be at the desk, while continuing to work.

1–3 p.m. Design meeting with sales team to review current line that is under development. We show CADs (computer-aided designs), hand looms and knit downs, etc. Sales team members give their comments. We get new directions for styles that are needed.

3–6 p.m. Back to the boards. Either "CAD" anything needed to complete line, do sketches, or work on tech packs. Review afternoon mail; approve lab-dips, trim cards, fabrics, wash panels or other items.

6–7:30 p.m. Time to go home!

Squeezing in time for trend research, sketch inspiration, and shopping can prove to be quite a challenge, and has to be worked in when time is available.

For a technical designer, the day-to-day tasks may vary from company to company, but they all have the same goal at the end of the day: to produce a well-fitting garment at a marketable price. This is a day in the life of one technical designer:

The day starts by reading e-mails from the factories to see what issues or questions they might have or what they need. From there, I begin my day and focus on my priorities. I may send comments or production tech packs out to the factory, do a fitting with the design team, and/or correct a pattern. We also have meetings with the sales staff to go over new styles or a meeting on production issues that need to be solved with the production team.

Most technical designers work very closely with the factories, and sometimes we get the opportunity to fly over to meet the people we speak to overseas on a daily basis. Unfortunately, these days it's very rare to see that happen, due to the economy, but I think once the industry picks up, we will be able to experience that once again.

The working hours can be very exhausting, but each position is quite different. My hours do not allow for any personal time. I am always one of the first to arrive, and the last one to leave, with about a ten-minute lunch that requires me to swallow food whole while still reading e-mails. It's tiring, to say the least. That is why it is very important to like the people with whom you work; in this respect, I have been very fortunate.

When looking at the workday of each of these two types of designers, what is the same? What differences are there between these two positions?

Sources:

http://www.design-training.com/fashion-design/a/a-day-in-the-life-of-a-fashion-designer.html

https://www.technical-designer.com/a-day-in-the-life-of-a-technical-designer/

is constantly evolving, so the technical designer must be highly adaptable to these changes. As deadlines near, overtime is often necessary to meet these demands, often with little time left for personal activities. Extensive travel, both domestic and international is sometimes required to meet with manufacturers, designers, and other vendors. More likely, however, most communication happens remotely through email or phone between the technical designer and the factory, which is most likely in another country and another time zone.

SPECIFICATION TECHNICIAN

The typical duties of a **specification technician**, or a *spec tech*, are to attend the fittings of the sample garments, take measurements, and compile these measurements into packets to hand off to production. These packets are referred to as **spec packs**, or *tech packs*. They contain detailed information taken from the designer's sketch, translated into measurements in order to ensure desired fit and styling details, such as the placement of pockets, the length of zippers, the size of buttons, etc., as illustrated in Figure 5.8. Spec tech is usually an entry-level position, because the primary responsibility of the spec tech is to measure the product. Spec techs are usually promoted to technical designers after they gain a few years of experience, depending on their abilities and progress. The qualifications for a spec tech are equivalent to those of a beginning technical designer.

PATTERNMAKER

Patternmakers play a key role in the design and production processes. They are responsible for translating the design concept into a pattern for the actual garment. Patternmakers develop a **first pattern**, which is used to cut and sew the **prototype**, or first sample garment. The first pattern is made in a **sample size**, the size used for testing fit and appearance in addition to selling purposes. Although sample sizes vary by company, they are generally as follows:

- For juniors, sample sizes are 5, 7, or 9
- For misses, they are 6, 8, or 10
- For women's wear, sample sizes are 18 or 20, depending on the line and its target market
- For menswear, sample sizes are 34 for trousers and 38 for tailored suits

- For infants' apparel, size 3–6 months is the sample size
- For toddlers' apparel, size 2 is often the sample size
- In children's wear, it is usually a size 7

Patternmakers may use three different techniques to develop the first pattern: draping, flat pattern, or computer-aided patternmaking. With the **draping method**, patternmakers shape and cut muslin or the garment fabric on a dress form, or model, to create a pattern, as shown in Figure 5.9. Draping is the preferred strategy for soft, flowing designs. It allows the patternmaker to adjust the design as it evolves three-dimensionally, as with a piece of sculpture. When the designer approves the look, the patternmaker removes the muslin from the form and then draws the pattern on heavy paper.

Alternately, the **flat pattern method** uses angles, rulers, and curves to alter existing basic patterns, referred to as **blocks** or *slopers*. The term "block" is used to describe a pre-pattern template for which additional manipulation is required at the end to generate a pattern (e.g. changing the bust dart, adding seam allowances) for a variety of other garments. Finally, computer-aided patternmaking is utilized by many large firms that can afford the expense of the equipment and software programs. With **computer-aided patternmaking**, patternmakers can manipulate graphics of pattern pieces on a computer screen or make patterns manually using a **stylus**, a computerized pen, or a **puck**, a mouselike device.

Another tool in computer-aided patternmaking is the **digitizer**, a program integration feature used to make or alter patterns. Patternmakers and technical designers can copy and paste measurements to a design, as well as grade patterns. With a digitizer, they can also import appliqués, screen graphics, and embroideries from other programs for pattern placement. The digitizer can also be used to create or alter markers. Whether draped, created by flat pattern, or developed on a computer, the first pattern must accurately reflect the style, proportion, and fit the designer had in mind when conceiving the product.

Qualifications

Following are the qualifications for a patternmaker:

- *Education.* A bachelor's degree in fashion design, product development, apparel manufacturing, or a related field is commonly required.
- *Experience.* Preparation for the career of patternmaker includes knowledge of flat patternmaking,

Figure 5.8

Spec packs contain detailed information taken from the designer's sketch, translated into measurements in order to ensure desired fit and styling details, such as the placement of pockets, the length of zippers, the size of buttons, etc.

		Graded Measurement (1-12) - 1: MY Missy - Short Womens							
Style #	COPY 62263	Product Group		Season	SP		Status	
Division	Womens	Office/Agency		Year	2004		Create Date	Aug-01-2003
Department	Woven Btms	Prod Desc	UTILITY POCKET SHORT LEVEL - FAVORITE				Revise Date	Aug-01-2003
Fabrication	uniform ctn						Development #	

Product Type	Short Womens	Size Category	MY Missy	Tolerance Level	Standard
Style Number		Size Scale	0 - 16	Status	Other
Sample Size	8	S/Q/V		Prod Type	Short Womens
Comments					

*	Code	Points of Measure	Tol -	Tol +	0	2	4	6	8	10	12	14	16		
*	555	Waist Circ-Along Top Opening Edge	1/2	1/2	29	30	31	32	33	34	35 1/2	37	38 1/2		
*		Waist Circ. Along Bottom Edge	1/2	1/2	30 1/2	31 1/2	32 1/2	33 1/2	34 1/2	35 1/2	37	38 1/2	40		
*	201	Low Hip Placement Below Waistband	0	0	4 1/2	4 1/2	4 1/2	5	5	5	5 1/2	5 1/2	5 1/2		
*	1566	Low Hip Circ X" Below WB	1/2	1/2	37	38	39	40	41	42	43 1/2	45	46 1/2		
*	240	Front Rise Blw WB - Along Curve	1/4	1/4	7 1/2	7 3/4	8	8 1/4	8 1/2	8 3/4	9 1/8	9 1/2	9 7/8		
*	241	Back Rise Blw WB - Along Curve	1/4	1/4	13	13 1/4	13 1/2	13 3/4	14	14 1/4	14 5/8	15	15 3/8		
*	205	Thigh Circ 1" Below Crotch	3/8	3/8	23	23 3/4	24 1/2	25 1/4	26	26 3/4	27 7/8	29	30 1/8		
*	255	Leg Opening Circumference - Short	3/8	3/8	22	22 3/4	23 1/2	24 1/4	25	25 3/4	26 7/8	28	29 1/8		
*	208	Inseam	3/8	3/8	5	5	5	5	5	5	5	5	5		
*	1567	Photo Inseam	3/8	3/8	6	6	6	6	6	6	6	6	6		
	209	Outseam Below Waistband	3/8	3/8											
*	210	Waistband Height at CB	0	0	1 3/4	1 3/4	1 3/4	1 3/4	1 3/4	1 3/4	1 3/4	1 3/4	1 3/4		
*	215	Front Fly Length	1/4	1/4	4 1/2	4 1/2	4 1/2	5	5	5	5 1/2	5 1/2	5 1/2		
*	194	Zipper Opening	1/4	1/4	4	4	4	4 1/2	4 1/2	4 1/2	5	5	5		
*	216	Front Fly Width	0	0	1 3/8	1 3/8	1 3/8	1 3/8	1 3/8	1 3/8	1 3/8	1 3/8	1 3/8		
*	211	Belt Loop Height	0	0	2 1/4	2 1/4	2 1/4	2 1/4	2 1/4	2 1/4	2 1/4	2 1/4	2 1/4		
*	212	Belt Loop Width	0	0	1/2	1/2	1/2	1/2	1/2	1/2	1/2	1/2	1/2		
*	1697	Belt Loop Placement frm CF	0	0	4 1/8	4 1/4	4 3/8	4 1/2	4 5/8	4 3/4	4 7/8	5 1/8	5 3/8		
*	1698	Belt Loop Placement from SS	0	0	2 5/8	2 5/8	2 5/8	2 5/8	2 5/8	2 5/8	2 5/8	2 5/8	2 5/8		
*	223	Patch Pocket Width at top edge	0	0	6 7/8	6 7/8	6 7/8	6 7/8	6 7/8	6 7/8	6 7/8	6 7/8	6 7/8		
*	1568	Patch Pkt Placement -blw SS at Front of pkt	0	0	2 1/8	2 1/8	2 1/8	2 1/8	2 1/8	2 1/8	2 1/8	2 1/8	2 1/8		
*		Patch Pkt Placement blw SS at Center of pkt	0	0	2 1/4	2 1/4	2 1/4	2 1/4	2 1/4	2 1/4	2 1/4	2 1/4	2 1/4		
*	1569	Patch Pkt Placement - blw SS at Bk Side of Pkt	0	0	2 1/2	2 1/2	2 1/2	2 1/2	2 1/2	2 1/2	2 1/2	2 1/2	2 1/2		
*	227	Patch Pocket Height at Center	0	0	7 3/4	7 3/4	7 3/4	7 3/4	7 3/4	7 3/4	7 3/4	7 3/4	7 3/4		
*	232	Visible Welt Pocket Width	0	0	5	5	5	5	5	5	5	5	5		
*		Visible Welt Pocket Height	0	0	1/2	1/2	1/2	1/2	1/2	1/2	1/2	1/2	1/2		
*	235	Side Pocket Flap Width at Top Edge	0	0	5	5	5	5	5	5	5	5	5		
*	233	Side Pocket Flap Height at Center	0	0	2	2	2	2	2	2	2	2	2		

		(Construction) - Sketch (L) - 1							
Style #	COPY 62263	Product Group		Season	SP		Status	
Division	Womens	Office/Agency		Year	2004		Create Date	Aug-01-2003
Department	Woven Btms	Prod Desc	UTILITY POCKET SHORT LEVEL - FAVORITE				Revise Date	Aug-01-2003
Fabrication	uniform ctn						Development #	

Sketch Organizer:\ SP04\SHORT IMAGES\MISSY\WMS WOVEN BOTTOMS\D22754.dwg\SIDE

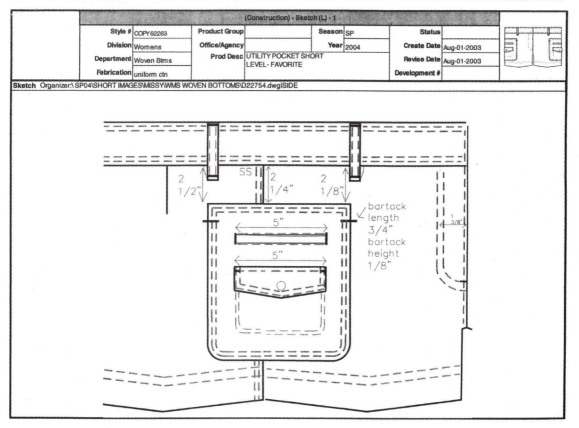

Figure 5.9

With the draping method, patternmakers shape and cut muslin or the garment fabric on a dress form or model to create a pattern.

computer-aided design, and, depending on the manufacturer, draping. Many patternmakers begin their careers as an assistant patternmaker or a pattern grader.

- *Personal characteristics.* Patternmakers must have an understanding of mathematical calculations as they pertain to sizing and fit. They must have keen eyes for proportion and line, as well as the ability to achieve perfect fits. The successful patternmaker is a design technician with a critical eye for detail and accuracy.

Career Challenges

As the initial translator of the designer's concept into a saleable product, the patternmaker is part technician, part scientist, and part artist. You must be able to exercise exceptional organization and communication skills. In addition to well-developed technical skills, the ability to work collaboratively is essential. The designer may desire a skirt to hang and sweep in just a certain way, creating a specific type of stylish silhouette. It is up to the patternmaker to know exactly how this is achieved through artistic nuances of pattern shape and cut. Textile behavior is also key—a clear knowledge of textile science is essential. The patternmaker must be able to factor in elements such as the fiber, stretch, weight, bulkiness, pile, or surface design and how these various elements affect the pattern design. Figure type and age of the target consumer are rapidly becoming important aspects of fit. As the population ages and becomes more pluralistic, standard size, fit, and desired comfort continues to shift.

Summary

What are the differences in the careers of a technical designer, patternmaker, and specification technician? A technical designer's responsibilities encompass most of the duties that a patternmaker and specification technician would have. If a company offers all three positions (technical designer, patternmaker, and specification technician), then the team works together, each member with a different focus. The patternmaker focuses on adjusting patterns, correcting and balancing them so the garment fits properly. The technical designer works with measurements. The specification technician prepares the spec pack.

Endnotes

1. Biography.com editors, "Betsey Johnson biography," July 23, 2019, https://www.biography.com/people/betsey-johnson-23182

2. Brainyquote, "Manolo Blahnik quotes," www.brainyquote.com/quotes/quotes/m/manoloblah110627.html

3. NewsCore, "Karl Lagerfeld to launch affordable collection for Internet customers," FoxNews.com, October 25, 2011, https://www.foxnews.com/entertainment/karl-lagerfeld-to-launch-affordable-collection-for-internet-customers

4. Herman, D., "Stylish Sarah's Q & A with Jason Campbell: Judge of cool," A Shaded View on Fashion, May 30, 2010, https://ashadedviewonfashion.com/2010/05/30/do-you-ever-screen-phone-calls-look-at-the-number-and-decide-to-take-the-call-or-not-why-and-do-you-ever-feel-guilty-1/

Key Terms

assistant fashion designer
block
computer-aided design (CAD)
computer-aided patternmaking
digitizer
draping method
fashion design
fashion designer
first pattern
flat pattern method
patternmaker
prototype
puck
sample size
spec pack
specification technician
stylus
technical design
technical designer

Online Resources

businessoffashion.com
fashionista.com
hugoboss.com
jimmychoo.com
karl.com
louisvuitton.com
viviennewestwood.com/
www.wwd.com/fashion-news/designer-luxury/all-eyes-on-nicolas-ghesquires-debut-at-louis-vuitton-7511207
www.nytimes.com/2014/03/06/fashion/Nicolas-Ghesquire-Debuts-Louis-Vuitton-Collection-paris-fashion-week.html
www.dailymail.co.uk/femail/article-2487213/Balenciaga-designer-Nicolas-Ghesqui-replaces-Marc-Jacobs-Louis-Vuittons-artistic-director.html
cdn.businessoffashion.com/reports/The_State_of_Fashion_2018_v2.pdf
wwd.com/fashion-news/designer-luxury/chanel-names-virginie-viard-as-successor-to-karl-lagerfeld-1203035015/
fortune.com/2019/02/19/fendi-karl-lagerfeld-death/
www.nbcnews.com/business/business-news/michael-kors-just-bought-versace-2-1b-n912811
www.forbes.com/sites/laurengensler/2017/07/25/michael-kors-buys-jimmy-choo-for-1-2-billion/#17b8301f2664

Discussion Questions

1. Select one of each: a new and relatively unknown designer, a current contemporary designer, and a legendary designer of the past. Construct a report examining the following aspects of these designers' careers: background (e.g., birthplace, education, experience), career startup and path (e.g., internships, jobs, and current position), signature looks, licenses in other product areas, and future plans.

2. Select three well-known apparel manufacturers that would likely require a patternmaker to have exceptional abilities in one of each of the following skill areas: draping, making flat patterns, and computer-aided patternmaking. Why did you choose these manufacturers?

3. Compare and contrast two classified advertisements for technical designers. How are the position descriptions similar and different? Among many other Web sites, you can locate classified ads for the fashion industry at www.wwd.com/wwdcareers, www.style-careers.com, and www.fashion.net/jobs.

JENNIFER LOPEZ
ONLY AT **KOHL'S**

CHAPTER 6
PRODUCT DEVELOPMENT BY THE MANUFACTURER AND RETAILER

To compare product development with fashion design in apparel, you may want to envision (1) an illustration and a completed sample of a garment (i.e., fashion design) and (2) an illustration, the sample, the garment hanging in a store, and the customer walking away from the store with the garment in a shopping bag (i.e., product development). So what exactly does product development consist of? Product development is the creation, production, and marketing of a product from start to finish. This is not a new process.

Manufacturers in many industries, from automobiles to household appliances, have engaged in product development for many decades. However, in the 1980s, it became widespread for large fashion retailers to develop products of their own instead of solely selling the lines of manufacturers. The Gap, for example, used to carry a variety of national brands, such as Levi's. Now it carries only Gap-branded merchandise that is designed and developed in-house. Forever 21, H&M, and Banana Republic are other examples of retailers carrying fully product-developed goods. In contrast, Macy's, Neiman Marcus, and Saks Fifth Avenue are examples of retailers that carry both manufacturers'/designers' lines and their own product-developed lines.

Product development may be the function of one department in a retail operation or a division within an organization. For example, Macy's, Inc., with corporate offices in Cincinnati and New York, is one of the nation's premier retailers, with fiscal 2018 sales of $24.9 billion. The company operates Macy's and Bloomingdale's brands, with about 870 stores in forty-three states, the District of Columbia, Guam, and Puerto Rico, as well as macys.com, bloomingdales.com, and bluemercury.com. The diverse workforce of Macy's, Inc., includes approximately 130,000 employees.[1]

Within Macy's there is a division called Macy's Merchandising Group (MMG). MMG is responsible for conceptualizing, designing, sourcing, and marketing privately developed and privately branded goods sold at Macy's and Bloomingdale's. These private brands, available "Only at Macy's," are developed to appeal to a certain customer lifestyle and are supported with marketing programs Macy's builds to create a precisely defined image. Some of MMG's fifteen highly successful private brands include I.N.C., Charter Club, Maison Jules, Alfani, Bar III, Belique, Thalia & Sodi, Style & Co., and Hotel Collection.

Regardless of the company and whether it is a manufacturer or a retailer, many steps need to be taken when developing a line, although the details may change depending on the type of product, on whether the line is to be produced overseas or domestically, or if the company has an in-house sample department. The general steps that are taken for each season, as described as follows:

1. Inspiration sources (e.g., fabrics, art and museum exhibitions, travel destinations, films, color palettes, and so on) are reviewed. Market research is conducted. The previous year's sales and markdowns are analyzed. Product categories are decided.
2. Trend forecasts are discussed. The preliminary line is planned. The company decides "what it believes in." Color stories are selected.

3. Fabrics and trims are researched, then selections are made. Prints are designed.

4. Concepts are developed, storyboards are created, and designs are sketched. Sample fabrics and trims are ordered. Labdips, colored samples of selected fabrics, are requested.

5. Merchandising meetings are held. The line may be edited from sketches.

6. Specifications are written, and technical packages are compiled.

7. Sourcing is completed. Samples, or prototypes, are constructed, and preliminary costing is requested.

8. Patterns and first samples are produced by a sample room or contractors. Often 20 to 50 percent more designs are made than those that actually will be manufactured. Factories advise on costs.

9. Samples are fitted, edited, and adopted into the line during a line review. The fitting process continues until the sample is approved or dropped. Costs are negotiated. Quantity may be an integral part of cost negotiations, or it may be determined when orders are generated. Quantities may be finalized and orders may be placed at this time, depending on factory lead time.

10. Samples, or prototypes, are produced. Private label goods may require only a meeting sample. Costs are finalized. Photo and production samples are requested.

11. For a private brand in a retail operation with decentralized buying, the styles will be "sold" internally to buyers who quantify the purchase. **Decentralized buying** refers to the process used by individual stores or groups of stores within a retail chain that have a buyer who selects from the company's primary buyer's purchases.

12. Production fabric and trim are ordered as soon as the factories receive orders.

13. Production goods are manufactured, and quality control is completed.

14. Goods are packed and shipped to the retailer.

15. Merchandise is received by the retailer and delivered to the warehouse or selling floors.[2]

In the fashion industry, there are three key types of businesses that produce merchandise: manufacturers, contractors, and retailers. As discussed in Unit 1, manufacturers are companies that create, produce, market, and distribute product lines on a continual basis. This may be a designer who owns a company or a company that employs designers. Manufacturers may own their own factories or use contractors to construct their products. A growing area of product development is the manufacturer that establishes a product development division to service its clientele of retailers, as illustrated in Box 6.1.

SOCIAL MEDIA STRIKES
BOX 6.1 The Product Development Manufacturer Reaches Out

Manufacturers who offer product development to retailers provide innovation, flexibility, and cost control for retailers. Many are responsible for a traditional manufacturer's tasks, such as bringing innovative fabrics to the retailer or producing garments from a product sample; however, others may be expected to work closely with the retailer's strategic plans to build products that are best suited for creating customer/brand familiarity—from start to finish. Some product development teams employed by manufacturers identify important trends and develop innovative products reflecting those trends. Whether providing a selection of textiles or working on the creation of new designs, the retailer's target market and budget, or price points, are at the heart of decisions made by the manufacturer's product development team.

Product development divisions of manufacturers use social media to listen to the retailer's target market. This 360-degree mode of communication provides interactive outlets that offer direct engagement with their clients' target customers. Collaborating with the retailer, the product development manufacturer announces new products on YouTube, Pinterest, and Instagram. They can have a dialogue on Twitter with the retailer's customers about which styles to produce. With more than one billion people on Facebook worldwide (Smart Insights), it has become essential for fashion manufacturers to spend time and money on social media advertising and campaigns. Nike has the most followers of any fashion brand on Instagram, by far! With 47.7 million followers in 2018 (Jumper Media), the next fashion brand in line isn't even close. Their communication is a mixture of ad campaign images and inspirational athlete stories—all of which clearly resonates with the Instagram community.

Sources:

Chaffey, D., "Global social media research summary 2019," Smart Insights, February 12, 2019, https://www.smartinsights.com/social-media-marketing/social-media-strategy/new-global-social-media-research/

Kart, K., "33 of the best brands on Instagram right now," Jumper Media, February 24, 2019, https://jumpermedia.co/33-of-the-best-brands-on-instagram/

Contractors, factories that make and finish goods, may be domestic, meaning in the United States, or off-shore, such as those in China, India, or Taiwan (refer to Figure 6.1). **Retailers** are businesses that sell products to the ultimate consumer and may include the vast range of brick-and-mortar stores (e.g., department stores, mass merchants, specialty stores, boutiques, discount stores, and outlet stores), as well as catalogues, brick-and-click stores, and online stores. **Brick-and-mortar store** refers to retail operations in a facility, such as a building or a store in a mall. **Brick-and-click store** refers to a retail operation that offers products both through actual stores and online. Some retailers sell through all or several of these channels. JCPenney, Saks Fifth Avenue, and Nordstrom's, for example, sell their product lines through brick-and-click stores and catalogues. Nearly all of the large retailers are currently engaging in some form of product development. Next, the focus is on the product development and design activities of retail operations.

WHY RETAILERS BECAME DESIGNERS

There are four main reasons why retailers moved into the business of developing their own products or lines of products. First, retailers wanted to be able to satisfy specific customer demands. Sometimes, the retail buyers were unable to locate the products, looks, prices, or fit for their customers' needs. The second reason retailers went into the business of creating products is fashion exclusivity. **Fashion exclusivity** refers to a company having merchandise that is unique to that particular company (Figure 6.2). You may have remarked or may have overheard a customer saying, "Everything in the mall looks the same. I don't want to see myself coming and going."

Figure 6.2
Fashion exclusivity refers to having merchandise that is unique to a particular company, sometimes in a specific geographic territory.

Retailers wanting to project fashion images that are unique to their particular companies established product development departments or divisions. Most important, product development provided higher profit margins. Retailers reasoned that by producing directly through contracted or company-owned factories instead of buying from manufacturers, they could make more money on each item, even while charging the customers less than they charged for nationally branded merchandise. Finally, retailers needed to reduce lead time between ordering new merchandise and receiving it on the sales floor. This trend is referred to as fast fashion.

Fast fashion is a phrase used to describe apparel and accessories trends that are designed and manufactured quickly and affordably to allow the mainstream consumer to take advantage of current fashions at a lower price. This philosophy of quick manufacturing at affordable prices is the business model of many large retailers, such as H&M, Forever 21, and Zara. Fast fashion is achieved through the retailers' understanding of the target market's wants, in that the latest runway trends, and new variations of products the customer is buying are delivered to the sales floor as fast as possible.

In most cases, the product developer's first objective is a high-fashion-looking garment at a mass-market price. His or her second objective is often to create modifications of the items that sell and have these manufactured quickly. The product developer, buyer, and manufacturer collaborate to maximize sales and profits by satisfying customer needs. Fast fashion brings more product options to the consumer more frequently.

Initially, retailers who developed their own product lines ran into some roadblocks. There is a long tradition in the fashion business of knocking off the hot or successful designs offered by top designers, rather than creating new looks. A **knockoff** is a copy of another style, often of lesser quality and with minor modifications. Knockoffs of Hermès' Birkin and Kelly bags, carried by celebrities like Victoria Beckham and Sarah Jessica Parker, can be found at midpriced retail stores (Figure 6.3). Although the practice is less common today, retailers were historically known for creating private-label lines that were collections of knockoffs. **Private label** refers to a line name or brand that the retailer develops and assigns to a collection of product development goods. Because many of the retailers were knocking off products that were already on the market, the majority of the private-label products

Figure 6.3

Knockoffs of Hermès' Birkin and Kelly bags can be found modified at mid- to low-priced retail stores, or copied by counterfeiters.

lacked fashion newness. Retailers also had to take responsibility for securing fabrics, avoiding fit problems, and shipping goods. Another obstacle was that many overseas factories required retailers to open letters of credit to pay for goods. As a result, retailers were faced with tying up large amounts of their operations' dollars in advance of shipping, rather than paying for merchandise thirty days after they received shipment.

As retail-driven product development matured, retailers began to build highly skilled design and merchandising teams to remove some of the roadblocks. Some major retailers do not attempt to develop products in certain specialized apparel categories because these areas are too precarious or too dependent on major brand names. A few of the product categories that retailers place in product development are basic apparel, because of ease of fit; jeans, because of the low risk and ease of entry into the market as a price-point alternative (lower and higher) to major brands; and product categories that have a lower level of competition from major brands. Some retail operations prefer to leave development of highly specialized apparel, such as swimwear and hosiery, or categories that require major advertising investments, such as cosmetics and fragrances, to the major brand manufacturers. As styling in basic products makes it difficult to distinguish a major brand from a private label, some retailers have found that they are safer developing this type of merchandise. Other retailers choose private-label lines to create unique and exclusive products that are not available in the market. Retailers often evaluate the risk of trying to develop trendy, high-priced merchandise, knowing that customers often prefer a designer name attached to their investment purchases.

TYPES OF PRODUCT DEVELOPMENT BUSINESSES

Several product development classifications have evolved as retailers increasingly engage in the customizing of product lines. These classifications include retail label, private label, private brand, direct market brand, and licenses. A **retail label** is a brand with the retailer's name on it, such as Neiman Marcus, Custom Interiors, or Barney's. A retailer may negotiate with a manufacturer to put its label on a group of items instead of or in addition to the manufacturer's label. Some of the items carrying a retail label may be **exclusives**, or items that only one retailer carries.

In some cases, a retailer may negotiate to be the only one in a geographic region to carry a particular item or the only one in the country to carry a particular color or style. For example, the label may read, "Burberry Exclusively for Neiman Marcus."

Similar to a private label, yet with a greater level of market penetration primarily through advertising, a **private brand** is a name owned exclusively by a particular store that is extensively marketed with a definite image, such as Target's Mossimo brand, Macy's I.N.C. brand (Figure 6.4), and JCPenney's Stafford brand. A **direct market brand** describes a brand that is the name of the retailer. This is often a specialty store chain, such as Ann Taylor, IKEA, or Gap (Figure 6.5).

Today, large retail companies and manufacturers/designers are major employers of product development staffs, as illustrated by Macy's Product Development Executive Development Program in Box 6.2. The career paths in this field include the following: director of product

Figure 6.4
Macy's partners with designer Anna Sui on the I.N.C., International Concepts Collection, a private brand or label.

CASE STUDIES IN CAREER EXPLORATION

BOX 6.2 Macy's Product Development Executive Development Program

The Product Development Executive Development Program is a part of Macy's Merchandising Group (MMG); this group is responsible for conceptualizing, designing, and sourcing Macy's private brands. Some of the exclusive brands you may be working with include: Charter Club, Club Room, Thalia, Material Girl, Children's Epic Threads, Alfani, Style & Co., Tools of the Trade, American Rag, Bar III, Jenni, Ideology, Home Hotel Collection, and The Cellar.

In this role, you'll learn to identify emerging trends, conceptualize branded styles, partner with our overseas offices, and negotiate pricing strategies with global and domestic vendors to create the next wave of private label goods. You'll also react to sales performance, analyze consumer trends, and anticipate market needs to promote the visibility of private label goods—and this is only the beginning of what it means to pursue a career in Product Development. This Executive Development Program takes place exclusively in New York, NY.

Job Description

- Collaborate with key partners from merchandising, marketing, stores, fashion research and development, and color analysis
- Analyze and competitive shop to gain market awareness
- Partner with MMG overseas offices on sourcing, development, garment fit, quality, sampling, sales, and price negotiation
- Contribute business and trend strategy ideas in Line Development meetings with the Design Team
- Participate in tactical meetings with vendors and manufacturers to develop business driving strategies
- Gain exposure to supply chain management including purchase order creation and agreements, order tracking, and collaboration with customs and Macy's Logistics team
- Manage the Product Development Time and Action Calendar for Design, Technical, Quality Control, Manufacturing, and Customs to ensure accurate and timely delivery of shipments

- Create and analyze selling reports to develop strategic recommendations based on merchandise sales performance, present top seller product summary in monthly meetings
- Partner with the Private Brands Marketing team to identify new packaging and branding needs
- Track advertising and marketing samples, and monitor marketing related sales trends
- Assist in preparation for Market/Buy Meetings by creating style placement packages and line presentation materials

Requirements

- Bachelor's degree, all majors welcome
- Solid academic performance—minimum 3.0 GPA preferred
- Proficiency on PCs and MS Office; excellent Excel skills critical
- Strong analytical skills and attention to detail
- Strong communication and presentation skills
- Ability to prioritize multiple projects to achieve productivity and business goals
- Ability to promote teamwork, solve problems, and manage complex relationships
- Experience in retail; sales, management, or buying exposure a plus

The Product Development career path includes tracks in Product Management, Brand Management, and Retail Divisions. Each path is outlined below.

Training Program

In the Product Development Executive Development Program, you'll gain the fundamental tools and strategies needed in your first position as a Product Assistant. This layered program includes formal training classes that supplement hands-on experiences; working directly with Product Managers, Designers, Buyers, Planners, and Vendors, you'll learn the key strategies and techniques needed to successfully manage a specific brand classification within the Private Brands Business. Training Program highlights include:

- Product Development Lifecycle: This dynamic class teaches the fundamentals of the product development lifecycle through the eyes of a specific business. You'll walk through the struggles, revisions, and successes of a Private Brands style. Conducted in a learning environment, experience on-the-job examples regarding business, strategy, partnerships, systems, and retail terminology.
- Design and Technical Design Overview: Experience the function of Design and Technical Design through guiding a style from the conceptual sketch stage to a tangible product sample. Learn to successfully navigate the dynamic and important collaboration between the product development and design teams.
- Retail Math: Taught by a Professor from the Fashion Institute of Technology with a seasoned career in retail, you will learn the fundamentals of retail math and how to analyze your business and utilize sourcing negotiations to maximize your bottom line. This course is taught in stages as you progress in your business and financial acumen.

- Sales Reporting: Learn how to build a report used to analyze your business and in turn maximize profitability. Focus on the use of sales tracking to address fast and slow turning merchandise to react to and anticipate the needs of the business.
- Trend and Color Research and Development: Gain exposure to our in-house trend research and developers, while gaining insight on how forecasts of style and color trend are translated and represented within our Private Brands.

You will complete a collaborative group project and present your recommendation to key leaders. At the end of the eight weeks, you will receive performance feedback from your assigned team and leave the internship program with a greater understanding of how to analyze and drive sales.

Macy's, Inc. is an Equal Opportunity Employer, committed to a diverse and inclusive work environment.

Source:

Macy's Careers After College, www.macyscollege.com/Careers/ProductDevelopment/; Courtesy of Macy's, Inc.

Figure 6.5
The Gap features a full merchandise assortment of its own direct market brand at its stores in the United States, Canada, Mexico, the United Kingdom, France, Italy, Ireland, Japan, China, and, most recently, Taiwan.

development, merchandiser, sourcing staff, designer, colorist, textile technical designer, patternmaker, and quality control manager.

DIRECTOR OF PRODUCT DEVELOPMENT

A **director of product development** is ultimately responsible for the strategic planning of the division, specifying exactly what the company will make and market, as well as when it will do this. After selecting a general product category, such as junior T-shirts, the director of product development must narrow the focus. The fashion market is extremely segmented, with each brand filling its particular niche. It is not enough simply to decide to create a line of junior T-shirts, because that is far too broad a category to allow for effective line development. Instead, the director of product development will decide, for example, to create vintage-inspired T-shirts for fashion-forward, young female customers in junior sizes extra-small to large. A key product segmentation decision is specifying the target market niche, which can be accomplished only by knowing the customer well—who she is, what she likes, and where she lives, works, and plays.

Other product segmentation decisions that product development directors must make relate to the product, price, size, and taste level. Next, the director of product development will work with the staff to build a brand by creating an image or personality for the line. An image is the way the product developer wants the brand to be perceived, the way that will best attract the target customer. With the abundance of fashion products on the market, image may be the only means of product differentiation. Carefully defining target customers will allow brands to develop images and product lines that will appeal to them.

There are two main approaches the director of product development may take toward the branding of a line: a design-driven brand or a merchandising-driven brand. A **design-driven brand** is led by a designer who is expressing a personal artistic vision and sense of taste, such as Target's collaboration with Missoni. This type of brand appeals to customers who relate to the designer's particular style

and flair and includes most brands with designer names. These apparel brands tend to be more original and creative. Design-driven brands also have the peculiar distinction of representing both a particular designer's viewpoint and a line of products. In the case of a manufacturer's line, such as Ralph Lauren's apparel and accessories, the brand has several faces, including English gentleman, East Coast aristocrat, African safari adventurer, and Western individualist, as shown in Figures 6.6a–c.

Merchandising-driven brands, or *void-filling brands*, do just that. These market-based brands search for a void in the market or an underserved customer and create a product to fill that void and appeal to that distinct customer. Styling decisions are based on careful monitoring of past sales successes and failures in conjunction with customer desires. Customer comfort and competitive pricing are of utmost importance to merchandising-driven brands. Many private labels are merchandising-driven brands.

The director of product development has an important overall task. Retailers' brands must have a fashion image consistent with that of the customer the operation attracts. It is the director of product development's responsibility to make certain that the designed products add up to a marketable line that matches the retail operation's image. If, for example, a retailer of women's conservative career

Figures 6.6a–c
A few of the many faces of designer Ralph Lauren's lines: (a) English gentleman, (b) world adventurer, and (c) Western Americana.

wear brings in a private-label line of Indian cotton bohemian blouses and skirts, the customer may be turned off by the confusing look of the inventory.

Market knowledge is as critical to the success of a fashion brand as is customer knowledge. The director of product development must examine the competition. **Direct competition** is any other brand producing a similar product at roughly the same price point, targeted toward the same customer or market niche. It is important for product developers to be attentive to what direct competitors are doing, if only to refrain from duplicating their products or brand image. These direct competitors are fighting to be the consumer's choice. Ideally, a company wishing to grow a brand will have such a great product and know its customers so well that customers feel they must buy it. In a broader sense, competition is any other brand vying for consumers' retail dollars.

Types of competition change as retailing venues change. Think about the Internet as a shopping mall of new competitors. As the face of retail changes, a brand's product line may be competing with brands online, at different price ranges and from global companies. Consumers are less loyal to retailers today, because there is no stigma attached to cross-shopping. **Cross-shopping** refers to the customer's inclination to purchase a wide variety of products in an array of brands from various providers—directly from the manufacturer, in a resale store, at a flea market, or a retailer of high-end designers (Figure 6.7). For today's consumer, it is cool to buy smart. Think about wearing a $60 BCBG top with $232 Baldwin jeans and $4.99 Target flip-flops; now, that's cross-shopping. The new consumer mentality puts added pressure on the director of product development, who must now be aware of price, quality, and look of products in all categories, not just one narrow market niche.

Qualifications

The qualifications for the position of director of product development include the following:

- *Education.* A bachelor's degree in fashion merchandising, fashion design, product development, or a related field is required.
- *Experience.* The director of product development holds an executive position that often requires five to seven years of successful work experience as a merchandiser or designer.

Figure 6.7
Cross-shopping is when a customer purchases a wide variety of products in an array of brands at various retail outlets.

- *Personal characteristics.* Creativity, a strong marketing sense, and an understanding of consumers, quantitative skills, and networking abilities are key attributes for directors of product development. They are excellent communicators—orally, in writing, and visually. Also, the director of product development has other diverse characteristics: curiosity, leadership abilities, and the ability to work with a variety of constituencies, from designers to merchandisers to colorists.

A classified advertisement for a senior product development director is featured in Box 6.3.

CAREER CHALLENGES

The director of product development is the leader of the pack. It is a high-pressure job in which one must be a motivator, guide, and, sometimes, the "take-charge" person. It takes a strong person with vision to manage a team of executives. In the position of product developer for a manufacturer, this person is likely guiding product design for several retail clients. He or she will have to learn exactly who each retailer's customers are and what they

BOX 6.3 SENIOR PRODUCT DEVELOPMENT DIRECTOR

Employer: Growing Contemporary Sportswear Manufacturer
Location: Los Angeles, California
Type: Supervisor in Product Development
Job Status: Full-time

Duties and Responsibilities:

- Research and coordinate all phases of the development process—beginning with fabric and trim selection/development, following through to the sealed tech pack for bulk production
- Responsible to coordinate approval for all fabric/wash/trim/print/color details between design and vendors in a timely manner following the company product calendar
- Responsible for setting up costing sheets, coordinating, and following up costing communications with vendors
- Effectively update beginning of the month reports (BOM) and communicate any changes, corrections, or suggestions to the sourcing partner (technical designer) and design
- Research the market for innovations in materials and fabric wash/finish technologies

Knowledge, Skills, and Abilities Required:

- Five to ten years' experience in an apparel development–based position working with domestic and international vendors
- BA, BS, or BFA in a related apparel or business major
- Very knowledgeable of apparel construction, fabrics, fabric washes, trims, costing, color approval process, and overall manufacturing processes for both women's wear and men's wear markets
- Highly organized with the ability to manage multiple projects/seasons at various stages of the development process at the same time
- Ability to work effectively in a team environment
- Very proficient in Microsoft Office, Kaledo, Illustrator, and Adobe programs, especially Excel
- Proven analytical and problem-solving abilities, with a keen attention to detail
- Ability to effectively prioritize and execute tasks in a high-pressure environment
- Good written, oral, and interpersonal communication skills
- Team-oriented and skilled in working within a collaborative environment

want, likely without ever setting foot in their stores. This takes a great deal of research and superior communication skills. If this person is the director of product development for a retailer, he or she may have the opportunity for excellent customer knowledge, but less daily experience in the production end of the business. Maintaining strengths while building expertise in weak areas in the fast-paced world of fashion are challenges for the product development director.

MERCHANDISER

A merchandiser's responsibilities vary widely depending on company requirements. A product development **merchandiser** collaborates with the director of product development in deciding what to produce and then organizes and manages the entire product development process.

Merchandisers are responsible for the development of a balanced, marketable, profitable, and timely line. In some manufacturing companies, merchandisers oversee the design function and may serve as liaisons between design and sales. They will create the initial line plan and project target wholesale costs by analyzing sales from previous seasons, fashion trends, and customer wants. As Figure 6.8 illustrates, merchandisers work closely with designers on seasonal themes and guide designers on the development of cost-effective and marketable styles. In some manufacturing companies, merchandisers may also have responsibilities in sourcing and marketing functions. In other companies, there is a sourcing staff to locate the suppliers and manufacturers for the product.

The merchandiser is responsible for constructing the **merchandising calendar**, the product development team's schedule. The goal of the calendar is to deliver the right product (i.e., correct style, quality, and price) at the

Figure 6.8

A merchandiser discusses design and color concepts with a product developer.

Typical responsibilities of the merchandiser include the following:

- Researching the market, including tracking market trends and attending trade shows
- Fashion forecasting
- Attending consumer focus groups
- Shopping the competition
- Scouting fabric and trim markets
- Analyzing past sales, markdowns, and market trends within the retail operation
- Developing the merchandising calendar and line plan
- Creating design concepts with the product developers
- Calculating cost estimates for new products
- Directing and participating in line presentations
- Choosing and quantifying which styles will actually be produced, sometimes prior to sales (referred to as **production authorization**)
- Sourcing, in some cases
- Fostering a creative environment so technical design and sourcing staffs can do their best work

Qualifications

To achieve a career as a retail merchandiser, consider obtaining the following qualifications:

- *Education.* A bachelor's degree in fashion merchandising, fashion design, product development, retailing, or a related field is required.
- *Experience.* The merchandiser is sometimes promoted from within the product development department or division, having worked on the sourcing or technical design staff, for example. Three to five years of on-the-job experience in product development is preferred. In some cases, highly skilled merchandisers from the retail side of the business may be hired for this position in a manufacturing firm, and vice versa.
- *Personal characteristics.* The merchandiser is an excellent communicator—orally, visually, and in writing. Thorough market knowledge, a keen fashion sense, strong analytical skills, creativity, and an astute marketing instinct are essential characteristics. Successful merchandisers are continually cognizant of the market environment and the target customer and make well-informed decisions quickly and confidently. In companies that manufacture the majority of their product lines overseas, fluency in the languages of the countries where production takes place can be very helpful.

right time. When creating a new line, developers carefully plan how often they want goods to flow into the stores. Once they complete the delivery schedule, merchandisers create a calendar by working backward from in-store delivery dates, listing all of the tasks in the product development cycle, with deadlines for each. Next, merchandisers develop detailed line plans. The **line plan** shows the number of styles in the line, the number and general types of fabrics and yarns to be used, the colors per style, the anticipated stock-keeping units (SKUs), and the approximate preferred costs. The line plan not only gives product developers guidelines from which to work and focuses their efforts in a distinct direction but also takes into account fabric and yarn minimums and lead times. Merchandisers often work on different phases of several seasons at once.

Career Challenges

The merchandiser is a planner. You know—or perhaps you are—this type of person, with your schedule drafted months in advance, telephone numbers and addresses at your fingertips, and a to-do list in a constant state of addition and completion. The merchandiser thinks creatively and quantitatively. The product lines are viewed from many perspectives—what will be in fashion, how much will it cost to manufacture a product, which items will the customer purchase, and what is the competition doing. The successful merchandiser must be a sponge, soaking up all of the variables that affect whether a product will sell. When a line doesn't sell, the merchandiser may be held responsible for figuring out why it didn't sell and for making certain it doesn't happen again. Stressful? It can be.

SOURCING STAFF

Sourcing—locating components and producers of the final product—was discussed in Chapter 3 as it relates to the primary level of the industry, manufacturers of fashion merchandise. Sourcing in product development for the retailer is much the same as it is for the manufacturer. The primary difference, in most cases, is that the retailer often finds and hires contractors to produce private-label lines, rather than building or purchasing factories to manufacture the lines. The sourcing staff of a product development team is responsible for finding the best possible fabrics, findings, trims, and manufacturers to make the designers' lines reality. Members of the sourcing staff may specialize in specific categories, such as belting or trims. They may also travel extensively to locate parts of the product or a manufacturer for the product.

The sourcing staff often works with a sales forecast to determine the amount of product components needed. A **sales forecast** is created by the product development director and merchandiser, in conjunction with the sourcing staff. It includes projections of sales by category, style, color, and size based on historical data and statistical analysis. This information may be used to place preliminary fabric and trim orders and block out production time in factories. As the sourcing staff must often place orders early, an accurate sales forecast is critical to deliveries made at the right time and in the right amount.

Qualifications

To become a member of a company's sourcing staff, one should have the following qualifications:

- *Education.* Usually employers require a bachelor's degree in fashion design, fashion merchandising, product development, project management, or a related field.
- *Experience.* In many corporations, sourcing personnel are promoted from the technical design staff or are hired with assistant designer experience from outside of the company.
- *Personal characteristics.* Sourcing personnel pay attention to detail and have efficient organizational skills and strong written and oral communication abilities. They are "born to shop," comparing quality, price, and availability in product parts and production requirements.

Career Challenges

Sourcing staff personnel face the task of finding the best product or product parts at the best price, in the right quantity, and in a timely fashion. Many are required to travel globally and frequently. Negotiations can be tough when working with people from different cultures, with or without an interpreter. The abilities to shop until you drop and then communicate effectively and negotiate successfully take a great deal of flexibility and stamina.

PRODUCT DEVELOPMENT DESIGNER

Product development designers (sometimes called *private-label designers*) are the creators of the product line for a manufacturer or a retailer. For example, in addition to its own brand, Fossil manufactures a collection of watches under a number of brands such as Michele, Relic, Skagen, Zodiac, Adidas, Burberry, Diesel, DKNY, Emporio Armani, Armani Exchange, Karl Lagerfeld, Kate Spade New York, Marc Jacobs, Tory Burch, and Michael Kors. Fossil has product development designers working on these collections each season. From a retail perspective, MMG at Macy's has design teams working on each of its company-branded lines, from I.N.C. to Hotel Collection. They are trend forecasters in their own right by determining what their customers will be ready for next. They go through the design process with each new season. Table 6.1 shows monthly activities for product development by season.

The **design process** refers to the conception of a style, to include its inspiration or theme, color palette, fabric selection, form, and fit. Product development designers must be adept at synthesizing a variety of fashion influences while acknowledging marketability and fulfilling customer wants and needs. An important designer trait is the art of compromise. These designers must balance the desired fashion look of a product and the highest possible quality standards with a price tag that is acceptable to the target customer.

After determining the style, color, fabric, and trend concepts, designers begin sketching individual styles, usually with a particular form, or silhouette, in mind that epitomizes the fashion trends for the upcoming season. They may repeat versions of this silhouette throughout the line. Some styles may be completely original, but sometimes designers will adapt a style from an actual garment found on a shopping expedition or in a magazine. Most lines include at least a few **carryovers**, updated bestsellers from a previous season. The designers will be careful to include important basics and to balance each group with the help of the merchandiser. Many companies ask for estimated costs from factories before samples are made, so that styles can either be dropped or adjusted when the line is still in sketch form. Oversampling is quite expensive, so the merchandiser will generally try to keep it under control. When a complete group of styles is finalized, all of the sketches are placed on a line sheet so the group may be seen at a glance.

Typical tasks of the designer may include the following:

- Shopping the retail market, sometimes with merchandisers or a member of the sourcing staff, for design ideas and knowledge of the competition; buying samples
- Shopping the fabric, yarn, and trim markets
- Attending trend forecasting meetings
- Developing **color palettes**, groups of colors, and **colorways**, combinations or pairings of colors
- Determining the styling direction of the line and creating concept boards or storyboards
- Shopping the print market and buying print paintings for textile development
- Developing styles through sketching garments by hand or on a computer
- Recoloring garments or prints
- Designing embroideries, screen prints, and appliqués
- Writing specification sheets
- Corresponding with factories or in-house sample departments regarding drapes, patterns, and garment construction
- Attending fit meetings

These tasks vary, often depending on the size of the company for which the designer works. Some of the larger companies may assign some of these tasks, such as writing specifications or developing color palettes, to more specialized personnel, such as technical designers or colorists.

TABLE 6.1

PRODUCT DEVELOPMENT ACTIVITY CALENDAR

Activity	Fall	Holiday/Resort	Spring	Summer
Design/Development	January/February	April/May	July/August	November/December
Selling and Show Dates	February/March	June/August	September/October	January
Producing Orders Begins	May	August	November	February
Shipping Starts	July	October	January	April
Shipping Completed	September	Early December	Early March	Early May

Qualifications

Designers on product development teams are likely to have the following qualifications:

- *Education.* A bachelor's degree in fashion design, product development, fashion merchandising, or a related field is a minimum requirement.
- *Experience.* Employment as an assistant designer or technical designer is an excellent stepping-stone to the position of designer. These entry-level positions provide knowledge of fabrics, construction, and fit. Additionally, the designer needs prior experience in PC software, such as spreadsheets, imagery, and word processing. Many employers require designers to have CAD experience.
- *Personal characteristics.* Successful designers have excellent organizational skills and pay attention to detail. They can create an image of the final product, either on a drawing pad or on the computer. Because much business is conducted in Asian countries, foreign language skills in languages such as Mandarin and Japanese are a plus.

Career Challenges

The successful designer must know the retailer's customer well, because knowing the customer's likes and dislikes minimizes the designer's fashion risks. Designers must be able to multitask with the best, often working on two or more collections at one time. Working with color, silhouettes or forms, fabric, and trend themes, they are challenged to create collections. It may be difficult to find new sources of inspiration and to find a common theme to weave among the items in a collection. In addition, product development designers must balance aesthetics with price, a decision that sometimes compromises their vision of the initial design concept. They must constantly remember the customer for whom they are designing, rather than incorporating their personal tastes.

COLORIST

A **colorist** in product development chooses the color combinations that will be used in creating the product lines. Colorists need a strong knowledge of textiles. They need to be able to ascertain, for example, how a print design will be produced, how the finished article will be used, how the fabric will react to dyes and finishes, and how big or limited the budget is.

Colorists frequently travel to trade and fashion markets and subscribe to color-forecasting publications to stay on top of current and future color trends. They observe what the customers purchase, or do not buy, to understand their needs and interpret their color preferences accurately. Colorists collaborate with marketing, buying, and technical staff members, as well as design colleagues, on color trends and preferences. They often conduct research for ideas and inspiration, in such diverse areas as historical costume, architecture, art, and global destinations. Color inspiration can come from anywhere. After determining a color palette for the season, the colorist produces boards, swatches, or other visuals to present the color ideas to the product development team.

Colors and patterns are constantly changing in the fashion industry. Specific terminology is used to describe outcomes in this area of product development: labdips, colorways, and strike-offs. As soon as colors and fabrics have been determined, the design and color staff must decide whether any of the colors will be custom dyed in any of the fabrics. If so, original color standards must be sent to the dyeing mills or fabric companies so that dye formulations may be created. The mills will send **labdips**, small swatches of the dyed fabric, to the product development team for color approval before dyeing large yardages of fabric. Organizing and approving labdips may consume a significant amount of a colorist's time.

Printed fabric may be purchased from different companies, but sometimes a designer will want to include a print on the line that is exclusive to the company. This requires that the designer develop a print on the computer or by hand, or that the company buy a **croquis**, a painting of the print. It will be examined in terms of its repeat and colorways, or the color composition, will be decided. When these projects are finalized, the print image is sent to a printing mill. The mill will print a few yards of fabric, called a **strike-off**, and send it to the product developer (i.e., colorist or designer) for approval before it is made into a sample (Figure 6.9).

Qualifications

Following are the qualifications for a successful colorist:

- *Education.* A bachelor's degree in visual arts, fine arts, computer-aided design, graphic design, fashion

Figure 6.9

An example of a dress design and the fabrics selected to construct it from Todd & Duncan and Pitti Textiles.

Prospective employers often require the candidate to have a strong and relevant portfolio of work for review.

- *Personal characteristics.* The colorist must keep up to date with fashion and population trends—current and projected—while staying on top of new design and production processes. Flexibility, computer skills, the ability to meet deadlines, and effective business skills make colorists successful. They have an exceptional eye for discerning and recalling colors. A strong network of color expertise, from trade organizations to publications to peers, supports the colorist's own expertise. The successful colorist has the ability to identify color trends that evolve from such external influences as major art exhibitions, timely couturiers, and popular travel destinations.

Career Challenges

The colorist is part chemist, part artist, and part fashion forecaster. It takes a wealth of skills in many areas. This person must maintain extremely high standards and pay careful attention to detail. It is critical that the colorist be an effective communicator. Think about describing a specific color to someone and explaining it so effectively that this person can actually mix the paint for the exact color. It is not an easy task. Colorists most often work standard hours, but they need to be flexible to meet deadlines, especially prior to market week or production deadlines.

TEXTILE TECHNICAL DESIGNER

A **textile technical designer** creates new textile designs or modifies existing textile goods, altering patterns or prints that have been successful on the retail floor to turn them into fresh, new products. The textile technical designer will develop color alternatives for a modified fabric print or pattern or work with a colorist to accomplish this task. Most textile technical designers work on computers to create or modify designs. An example of a popular fashion product and textile design software program is Kaledo by Lectra, as shown in Figures 6.10a and b. Technical textile designers can work in several specialized areas, including wovens, knits, or prints. For example, a technical textile designer may work primarily with either sweater knits or woven shirtings. The textile technical designer who specializes in prints often uses a computer-aided design program to create a croquis.

design, textiles, or a related discipline is a minimum requirement.

- *Experience.* Technical designers, particularly those with experience in textiles, may move into the position of colorist. An understanding of how a textile will be used, what properties it needs in order to function optimally, and how the addition of color dyes or surface treatments will affect these properties is critical to the colorist's work. Two to five years' experience in design is often a prerequisite for this position. One of the paths to move into the position of colorist is to work as an assistant to the colorist. Some fortunate college students are able to secure internships in the color department of a product development division.

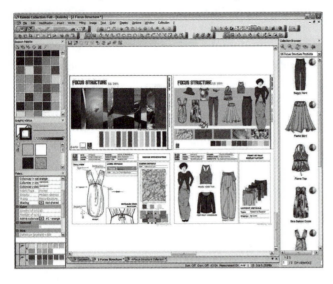

Qualifications

The following is a list of qualifications for the career path of a textile technical designer:

- *Education.* A bachelor's degree in textiles, textile technology, fashion design, computer-aided design, graphic design, fine arts, or a related discipline is a minimum requirement.
- *Experience.* Many textile technical designers begin in this position after college graduation. An internship in the technical design division of a retail corporation is an ideal way to open the door to this field.
- *Personal characteristics.* A textile technical designer has knowledge of textiles and their applications and usage, computer-aided design, and technical considerations as they relate to textile applications. An awareness of

consumer wants and needs and an eye for color and patterns are essentials. The successful textile technical designer is simultaneously creative and technologically savvy.

Career Challenges

Textile technical designers live in a high-touch, high-tech world. They must understand the technical features of CAD and the production aspects of knit, woven, print, and textured fabrics. In addition, they must understand the feel, or hand, of a diverse array of fabrics and the application of each. Which types of fabrics are best suited for which products? How do these fabrics wear? What are the care factors for each? There is much to know in this field, in which new fabrics, computer technology, and manufacturing techniques arrive daily.

PRODUCT DEVELOPMENT PATTERNMAKER

The **product development patternmaker** takes accurate measurements and develops a pattern, using either draping or flat pattern methods, which, if correctly developed, ensure that the designer's vision will be implemented. Specification lists, commonly referred to as **spec sheets**, typically provide detailed measurements and construction guidelines. Designers may give patternmakers sketches and a few measurement specifications for guidance or may actually drape a garment to get the exact form they envisioned. Following the designers' approval, patternmakers develop detailed spec sheets. A spec sheet includes a technical sketch, all of the measurements and tolerances, type and yardage of fabrication, and trim information. Different companies have their own spec sheet formats, but all of them have similar components. Each item on the spec sheet can have a critical impact on cost and on production of the item. The components of a spec sheet are illustrated in Figure 6.11.

Some retail product developers have additional challenges. They often do not employ in-house patternmakers and do much of the manufacturing in faraway factories, where the factories' patternmakers do the work. They frequently have to complete whole spec packages to send overseas that tell factories every detail of what will be required to engineer a style. Spec sheets are often used to calculate estimated costing, so that items can be adjusted

Figure 6.11

Example of a spec sheet for a basic woven shirt.

SPEC SHEET: Basic woven shirt	STYLE	
SEASON:	DESCRIPTION:	
LABEL: (SIZE CATEGORY)		
DATE:		
TECHNICAL SKETCH Basic woven shirt	SKETCH/PHOTO	

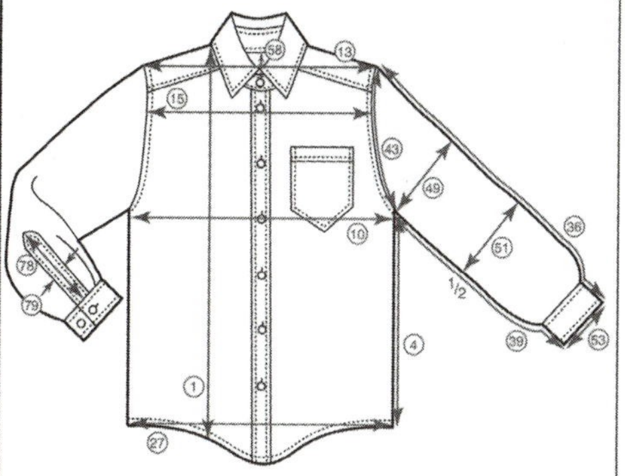

CODE	POINT OF MEASURE	TOL. +/−	4	S/6	8	M/10	12	L/14	16	XL/18
1.	Front length	1/2								
2.	Center front length	1/2								
3.	Center back length	1/2								
4.	Side length	1/4								
10.	Chest width circumference	1/2								
13.	Across shoulder	1/4								
15.	Across chest	1/4								
16.	Across back	1/4								
27.	Bottom opening/sweep width circumference	1/2-3/4								
32.	Yoke width front	1/4								
33.	Yoke width back	1/4								
34.	Yoke depth front	1/8								
35.	Yoke depth back	1/8								
36.	Sleeve length top armhole	3/8								
39.	Sleeve length underarm	3/8								
43.	Curved armhole width circumference	3/8								
49.	Muscle width circumference	1/4								
51.	Elbow width circumference	1/4								

(Tolerance 1/4-3/8 S, M, L, XL = 3/8" 4-18 = 1/4")

The measured garment spec sheets are for *illustrative purposes only* and should not be used as industry standards

or canceled before a costly sample is made. If the company does not employ the technical staff to write specifications, it can contract with patternmaking and CAD companies that will write specs and prepare detailed spec sheets.

Qualifications

Following are the qualifications for a patternmaker on a product development team:

- *Education.* A bachelor's degree in fashion design, product development, or a related field is often required.

- *Experience.* If a position as a patternmaker's assistant is available, this position is often an entry for college graduates. Some technical designers and sample makers move into the patternmaker slot. Two to five years' experience is usually required for a key pattern-maker position. Effective skills in draping, flat pattern making, and CAD are necessary.

- *Personal characteristics.* The product development patternmaker is, in essence, an engineer. A keen attention to detail, the ability to construct almost every type of garment, and a passion for accuracy are necessary characteristics of successful patternmakers.

Career Challenges

In addition to the challenges faced by a professional patternmaker discussed in Chapter 5, patternmakers must work with accuracy and speed on details. If a pattern piece is one-eighth inch smaller than it should be, the entire garment may not be able to be produced. Even if it can be manufactured, it may not fit, or it may have a design flaw. That is a large responsibility to bear. Many of the people who are interested in pattern making enjoy methodical and detailed work—engineering of sorts. What they often do not enjoy is the pressure of deadlines. With the influx of computerized pattern making, some patternmakers are finding full-time employment difficult to secure and are working in freelance capacities.

QUALITY CONTROL MANAGER

The **quality control manager** of a product development team is responsible for the initial inspection of sample garments and the final inspection of stock garments from the manufacturer. The quality control manager checks fabric, fit, and construction for quality and adherence to product specification guidelines. In a large company, this person is responsible for training the quality control staff and for developing specific guidelines and standards for the department.

Qualifications

The background and characteristics of a successful quality control manager in the retail setting are as follows:

- *Education.* An associate of arts degree in fashion design, product development, or a similar field is required. A bachelor's degree is preferred.
- *Experience.* Knowledge of textiles and clothing construction is required. Two to four years of experience in quality control are expected as a prerequisite for this supervisory position. The quality control manager must have a solid understanding of garment construction, garment specifications, and spec sheets.
- *Personal characteristics.* The quality control manager should possess an excellent eye for detail and a commitment to high standards. Bilingual skills may be necessary, depending on the location of the manufacturing facilities. Excellent communication and people skills are important.

Career Challenges

The quality control manager must maintain excellent standards and oversee every detail of production from beginning to conclusion. It can be a high-pressure job with little recognition. The product development team, the retail personnel, and the customers assume that products will be made correctly and will perform well. When this is not the case, the white-hot spotlight shines on the quality control manager.

Summary

Product development describes the processes needed to bring a product, or product line, from conception and manufacturing to marketing and sales. In this chapter, product development conducted by both the manufacturer and the retailer is examined. The three main reasons retailers moved into the business of developing their own product lines include satisfying specific merchandise needs of their customers, creating exclusive products unique to their particular companies, and generating higher profit margins. Several product development classifications have evolved as retailers and manufacturers increasingly engage in the customizing of product lines. These classifications include retail label, private label, private brand, direct market brand, and licenses.

As a result of this move into product development, large manufacturing and retail companies are major employers of product development staffs. The careers in this field include director of product development, merchandiser, sourcing staff, designer, colorist, textile technical designer, patternmaker, and quality control manager. The director of product development is ultimately responsible for the strategic planning of the division, specifying exactly what the company will make and market, as well as when it will do this. The merchandiser collaborates with the director of product development in deciding what to produce and then organizes and manages the entire product development process. The sourcing staff of a product development team is responsible for finding the best possible fabrics, findings, trims, and manufacturers to make the designers' lines a reality. The product development designer is the creator of the merchandise lines. The colorist chooses the color combinations that will be used in creating the product lines. Using this color direction, the textile technical designer creates new fabric designs or modifies existing textile goods by altering patterns or prints that have been successful on the retail floor to turn them into fresh, new products. The patternmaker uses draping, flat pattern, or computer-aided patternmaking methods to develop a pattern that uses these textile options and implements the designers' vision.

Endnotes

1. Macy's, Inc., "A Premier omnichannel retailer with iconic brands," https://www.macysinc.com/about
2. Kirsteen Buchanan, Stephens College, Columbia, Missouri, 2013.

Key Terms

brick-and-click store
brick-and-mortar store
carryover
color palette
colorist
colorway
contractor
croquis
cross-shopping
decentralized buying
design-driven brand
design process
direct competition
direct market brand
director of product
   development
exclusive
fashion exclusivity
fast fashion
knockoff

labdip
line plan
merchandiser
merchandising calendar
merchandising-driven brand
private brand
private label
product development
product development
   designer
product development
   patternmaker
production authorization
quality control manager
retail label
retailer
sales forecast
spec sheet
strike-off
textile technical designer

Online Resources

retailinginfocus.wordpress.com/tag/forever-21/
corporate.target.com/careers/career-areas/product-design-development
wwd.com/business-news/business-features/think-tank-npd-1202663219/

The quality control manager reviews the final product for fit, durability, and overall quality. Together, the product development team brings exclusive merchandise developed specifically to appeal to an exclusive target market from conception to reality.

www.retaildive.com/news/8-target-private-label-brands-that-launched-this-year/541814/
www.forbes.com/sites/kirimasters/2018/11/09/apparel-brands-amazon-puts-fashion-forward/#56d6f5477c8f
digiday.com/social/brands-using-private-label-fashion-lines-compete-amazon/
www.businessoffashion.com/articles/news-analysis/walmart-launches-new-private-label-clothing-brands
www.entrepreneur.com/article/319368
www.wwd.com/fashion-news/fashion-features/first-lady-michelle-obamas-lesson-in-fashion-7973141
ca.hellomagazine.com/royalty/02017081638037/kate-middleton-effect-designers-talk-boost-in-business
www.independent.co.uk/life-style/fashion/meghan-markle-prince-harry-royal-wedding-clothes-fashion-a8320526.html

Discussion Questions

1. What are your predictions for the future of private-label merchandise by retailers? Will it increase, decrease, or remain the same, and why?

2. This chapter mentions that a few of the product categories retailers place in product development include basic apparel, jeans, and product categories that have a lower level of competition from major brands. Provide specific examples of brands in the latter product categories (those with less competition from national brands) and identify retailers that have succeeded in these merchandise classifications.

3. Develop a line plan for a small private-label jean line. Specify the season of the line, then identify the number of styles, colors, size ranges, and price points that are in your line. Provide word descriptions and visuals for the line, such as magazine clippings, Internet images, or sketches.

CHAPTER 7
PROMOTION FOR THE DESIGNER AND MANUFACTURER

Picture a new fashion designer who has recently been featured in magazines, in blogs, on Twitter, and on television. The former Mr. Unknown becomes a significant name and face to fashion industry professionals and fashion followers. When you peruse a fashion magazine, such as *Vogue*, *In Style*, or *W*, you are inundated by promotion in the forms of glossy and, sometimes, eyebrow-raising advertisements of fashion brands such as Louis Vuitton, Cynthia Rowley, Versace, and Gucci. You may also see editorial pieces on celebrities who wear these designs or about the designe0rs themselves. Examples of fashion promotion include the home decor article about the pink Manhattan apartment designed by Betsey Johnson and the one featuring her custom-made Kentucky Derby hat (Figure 7.1).

Through a major television series like *Game of Thrones*, costume designer Michele Clapton has placed the spotlight on a fictionalized and highly stylized medieval world. Sweeping capes, lush fur-trimmed collars, rich tapestries, embroideries, and loose, flowing silhouettes are not just fodder for cosplay events. With over ten million viewers worldwide, designers are inspired—subliminally or directly—and hints of these details have made their way into their collections and on into mainstream fashions (Figures 7.2a, b and c). As the popularity of the show and its lush costumes inspires magazine articles, advertisements, and editorial pieces, all of these forms of promotion result in *GOT* fashion trend. **Promotion** refers to the endorsement of a person, a product, an idea or cause, or an organization. The ultimate goal of promotion is to encourage the growth, exposure, and development of an individual, product, idea, or company by advancing it to a higher position in the public's mind.

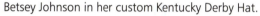

Figure 7.1

Betsey Johnson in her custom Kentucky Derby Hat.

Let's take a look at how the promotional process might have helped inspire fashions based on costumes from *Game of Thrones*. The much-anticipated television series based on the novels by George R.R. Martin goes into development. Because the place and time are imaginary fantasy with a nod to ancient Europe, Greece and Asia, the costumes are fantastic, bold, and otherworldly. Fans of the novels go to social media with speculation about the show—who will play each of the characters, where will it be filmed? Early promotion of the show focuses on

Figure 7.2a

In *Game of Thrones*, costume designer Michele Clapton places a spotlight on rich, lush fabrics, embroideries, and dramatic silhouettes to help define the characters of this Medieval fantasy drama.

Figures 7.2b and c

The dramatic sleeves, lush textiles, and wide belt translated into modern women's fashions.

the scale of the production, lavish sets to be built to recreate the author's imaginary world, CGI technology and how it is used. There is a nod to the costumes that help define the characters and this world they live in and to the designer. Fans search for images online, photographs and stories appear in blogs, and designers who mine popular culture for inspiration and the latest trends find themselves drawn to the embroideries, fabrics, and details—so unique and visually lush. The promotion director of the public relations firm for the production company hopes to build on this social media buzz and contacts a magazine and pitches a story to the editor about the costumes, the team of highly skilled craftspeople who have been assembled to develop the garments with such intricate detail, how fabrics are found, how flea markets are scoured, and what inspirational sources the designer mines to create the unique looks and themes for each character. As the popularity of the show grows, numerous print and Internet articles feature the designer, retail stores begin to carry and promote garments that are *GOT*-inspired—oversized sleeves, wide leather belts, capes, and sweeping silhouettes. All of these activities are part of fashion promotion. The major tasks for a director or manager in promotion involve (1) understanding the significance of public relations; (2) recognizing the costs and uses of various advertising vehicles; (3) never underestimating the importance of selling; (4) creating a network of contacts in the field of promotion; (5) finding hooks, or topics of interest, for each media source; and (6) organizing sponsorships and partnerships, especially via the Internet, for fashion businesses and events. **Promotion directors** work diligently to find themes or topics that the media will want to cover and to tie these into the businesses of their clients. For example, a promotion director may work for a major apparel manufacturer/designer, such as Nicole Miller. When Nicole Miller introduces her new home accessories lines of bed linens, pillows, photograph frames, and dinnerware, the public relations director may schedule her to appear at some key retail stores around the country. In conjunction with these retail partner arrangements, the promotion director will contact the media and fashion organizations in each city to generate news coverage of the designer's appearances in the retail stores.

The interrelationship between these promotional tasks illustrates the teamwork and versatility required by the industry: glossy magazines with advertising and feature stories, visual media with videos of backstage happenings before shows and events, front-of-house press dossiers and seating plans. The term **promotion product** can refer to an item, such as a press release or an advertisement, or an event, such as a fashion show or music video.

Career opportunities in fashion promotion exist in the industry sectors of apparel and accessories; home furnishings and accessories; publishing, art, and music; image and style consultancy; photography, illustration, and digital visual imagery; and styling of all kinds, from music groups to television and theater celebrities, broadcast media and DVDs, to the Internet. General areas of study provide a strong foundation for future employees in all career tracks within the fashion promotion industry. An understanding of merchandising and marketing will be used consistently in all fashion promotion career options. Knowledge of computer-aided design and graphics provides an employee in this area of the industry with the skills to communicate a design concept through drawings and board presentations. Knowledge of public relations and advertising is a key component of all promotional careers. Journalism skills prepare the fashion promotion candidate for fashion writing, whether in commentary scripts, advertising copy, press releases, or editorial features in consumer or trade publications.

CONSUMER AND TRADE PUBLICATIONS

What is the difference between consumer and trade publications? A **consumer publication** is readily available to the layperson, the general customer. The consumer may subscribe to the periodical, online or in print, or purchase it at a store. Nearly all consumer lifestyle publications feature some type of fashion content (e.g., *People*, *Town & Country*, and *Travel*); some are devoted exclusively to fashion and interior design. Examples of fashion consumer publications include *Vogue*, *In Style*, *House & Garden*, *W*, and *Elle*; the list goes on and on (Figure 7.3). Most magazines with a nationwide readership are headquartered in New York City.

In contrast, **trade publications** are designed for readers who are interested in or employed in specific professions or vocations. These magazines and newspapers are promoted to people in a specific career field. Other publications provide information about a wide range of merchandise classifications to retailers, designers, manufacturers, and buyers. The top publication in women's apparel and accessories is *Women's Wear Daily*, a print

Figure 7.3
A spread of consumer fashion magazines.

and Web news source that focuses on different merchandise types each day of the week and often features broad-scope fashion news, such as general retail trends in sales or mergers and acquisitions in the fashion industry.

FASHION STYLIST

A **fashion stylist** is the person who does most of the work before the cameras start shooting, whether for a magazine, film, television series, fashion show, or a personal client. **Fashion photostylist** is the term used to specify the stylist who works with photography. Whether styling for a photograph or a fashion show, a stylist must be aware of the latest trends and bring great resources and a strong personal style to every event. **Fashion shoots**, photography sessions of models and fashions, are a team effort, and the stylist's role is critical to its success. Stylists are responsible for selecting and assembling the garments and accessories needed for the event and preparing the people involved in the event, such as the models, dressers, makeup artists, hairstylists, and lighting designers. Box 7.1 features an interview with free-lance wardrobe stylist, Lauren Schugar. Stylists must make decisions in minutes, quickly determining, for example, how various items of apparel are to be combined and accessorized to show each off to the best features. Stylists also handle a myriad of details, ensuring that the right sizes and colors are available for each model. If the models are celebrities, the appropriateness of the apparel to each of their images becomes an additional factor. Stylists must be diplomats to win the cooperation of everyone involved in an event. In addition to magazine work, stylists may find employment with advertising agencies, working on print ads or television commercials. Figure 7.4 features a fashion stylist working on a fashion shoot in a photography studio.

Qualifications

Do you have what it takes to pursue a career in fashion styling? Following is a list of qualifications for a fashion stylist:

- *Education.* A bachelor's degree in fashion design, fashion merchandising, fashion journalism, fashion communication, photography, visual arts, or a related field is preferred.
- *Experience.* An internship with a photographer or stylist is an excellent way to build one's résumé for employment in this industry. Some fashion stylists begin in visual merchandising or as an assistant to a

CASE STUDIES IN CAREER EXPLORATION

BOX 7.1 The Fashion Stylist

Do you enjoy putting looks together for yourself and others? Have you considered what it might take to do this sort of work as a career? Lauren Schugar talks about her career as a professional wardrobe stylist.

As a freelance stylist, she describes the primary part of her job is "getting work!" She does have an agent who helps her book assignments, but she puts a considerable amount of time herself finding work, spending time following up with former clients to develop repeat business, running down leads, and making contacts with other creative professionals who she might align services with.

In her current role, she creates images for ad campaigns, works with individuals to develop personal or professional wardrobes, or works for retailers to develop e-commerce product photography. With experience and exposure, she has added speaking engagements to her resume.

A typical day varies by project; however, once she has collaborated with the client and determined the look and theme of the job, she shops—sometimes up to ten hours a day—to find the right merchandise. She steams and prepares, fits the garments on the models, accessorizes each outfit, and works with makeup and hair professionals to complete each look. Most of the merchandise is returned to the stores when the job is finished.

As a freelance stylist, Lauren stresses that while it is fun to be creative and be around clothes, it is a business, and it's not a business for everyone. Her advice to young people seeking a career in this field is to be realistic about how much income you need to survive, write a business plan, and be diligent. The biggest misconception, she feels, is that people think this profession is easy and glamorous, and she warns that it is anything but—when the work is booked, the hours are often long and busy, often without time to eat! When work is not booked, there is no income. And it's not instant success. It takes years to build a clientele and establish professional credibility. But she does get a thrill from seeing her work on billboards and in magazines and on TV, being around other creative people, and meeting new talent and making friends.

Her start in the business came as a favor for a friend who was doing public relations for a firm and did not have a budget for a stylist. She did that first job for free and used it to build her portfolio and make contacts. Most commercial work is for photo shoots—static images. She would like to add film and television to her resume; she says that styling for moving talent is a different type of challenge.

Talent is just the beginning. For success in this field, it takes accountability—showing up and being on time is essential! Become a good business manager and be diligent.

Source:

Schugar, L., "Interview with a wardrobe stylist," Jobshadow, Jobshadow.com/interview-with-a-wardrobe-stylist/

---

stylist. Fashion stylists are often chosen based on the look of their "books," large volumes of tearsheets, or samples of work, from published print or Internet work to Polaroid or digital images that illustrate work they have done with different photographers and/or models. Digital portfolios and computer-aided design skills are beneficial.

- *Personal characteristics.* The attributes of successful fashion stylists include having a network of professionals in photography, hair and makeup design, and the modeling industry; a keen eye for detail; the ability to apply visual art principles to print work and photographs; effective verbal, written, and visual communication skills; strong time-management skills; and the ability to work well under pressure, whether with deadlines or uncontrollable factors, such as poor lighting during an outdoor shoot or models who miss their flights.

Career Challenges

Fashion stylist positions are often only available with large companies or as freelance work. It is a growing, exciting, and potentially profitable career track. Fashion stylists face many challenges, including quick decision making and coordinating a multitude of details. Because stylists

Figure 7.4

A stylist works with models and photographers, selecting garments on a fashion photography set.

must ensure that the correct apparel is available for the right models, they must do a great deal of preplanning for the expected and the unexpected, such as broken zippers, a late hairstylist, or models with attitude. "Plan ahead and be prepared for anything" is a motto for successful fashion stylists. Stylists must also work with all types of people and be able to motivate everyone involved in the shoot. It is not enough to have the vision; it is as important to have the skills to implement the vision.

PUBLIC RELATIONS AND ADVERTISING DIRECTORS

Public relations directors are responsible for finding minimal or no-cost ways to effectively promote the designer or company they represent. They develop proposals that will put their clients in a favorable spotlight and persuade media outlets to feature press about the client. Public relations directors work with all types of media

representatives, from television and radio producers to newspaper, magazine, Web site, and blog publishers. Some public relations companies specialize in fashion and represent designer and manufacturer clients. In addition, many of the designer firms, such as Gucci, Salvatore Ferragamo, and Tod's, have in-house public relations staffs.

Some of the activities that public relations directors develop include social events such as fashion shows, book signings, and parties; events that raise awareness for a fashion company or designer while generating funds and appreciation for a philanthropic cause; press coverage for designers who are presenting new collections; and competitions for fashion students to submit original designs that will be produced by a major manufacturer (Figure 7.5).

While the public relations director is seeking out nonpaid ways to promote his or her company, the advertising director is determining how and where to spend money on promotional activities that will generate business and brand-loyal customers. **Advertising directors** develop and implement a company's paid promotional strategy for

Figure 7.5

A fashion student works on an original design for the Vogue Knitting Magic of Mohair competition.

the purpose of increasing visibility, image, and, ultimately, sales. **Advertising** refers to a type of promotion that is a paid, nonpersonal communication delivered through mass media. Public relations and advertising directors generally work under the supervision of the promotion or marketing director.

Qualifications

Public relations and advertising directors should meet the following criteria:

- *Education.* A bachelor's degree in marketing, public relations, promotion, advertising, business administration, fashion merchandising, fashion design, or a related field is a minimum requirement.
- *Experience.* To move into the director position, one usually needs a minimum of eight to ten years of fashion public relations or advertising experience and must have an array of excellent contacts within the fashion and lifestyle media fields. Additionally, prospective public relations and advertising directors must compile portfolios of work samples to present at job interviews.
- *Personal characteristics.* Exceptional writing and oral communication skills are essential for public relations and advertising directors. They need to be creative, with a specialty in finding new ways to look at what may be perceived by others as old topics. They are described as possessing "excellent pitching skills," the ability to sell one's ideas in a persuasive and articulate manner. Budget management skills are also essential.

Career Challenges

Successful public relations and advertising directors are great salespeople, frequently selling (and reselling) a person's or company's image, ideas, and products. This person must have the ability to stay positive and enthusiastic in a world of repeated rejection. With so much going on in the fashion world, public relations and advertising directors are competing in a world of many vying for the attention of newspaper and magazine publishers, online publishers, and television producers. Finding creative ways to pitch stories and build relationships with ever-changing media representatives are challenges these directors face.

This career path is not all about selling, creating, and networking though. Public relations and advertising directors must have a head for numbers to meet the responsibility for finding cost-effective ways to promote the company. At some point in their careers, public relations directors will likely be confronted with countering negative publicity. In such cases, they must have the skills to work under the pressures of time and stress, quickly developing plans that will put the company in a favorable spotlight and persuading the media to feature positive press about the company.

ADVERTISING RESEARCH AND PROMOTION POSITIONS

The major source of revenue for a Web and print publication is the sale of advertising space. Those who like to sell may find their niche as **advertising sales representatives**, the people who sell advertising for consumer and trade publications, such as *Glamour, Women's Wear Daily,* or *Lucky.* Other positions in fashion publications include those in advertising research and promotion. Many publications offer positions for those who prefer research. An **advertising research assistant** helps sell advertising space in a publication by supplying facts that advertisers will want to know, such as the number of issues sold, the top locations in terms of sales volume, and the profile and buying power of the publication's readers. These facts indicate the publication's ability to reach potential customers for the advertiser. The **advertising promotion staff**, yet another source of job opportunities, develops presentations to help sell advertising space to new and existing accounts. These people often have skills in persuasive writing and creative projects.

A related job option in advertising is that of **media planner**. Media planning is a statistical and mathematical process through which planners determine prices, including quantity discounts, for a media buy that may include several venues, such as radio, television, Internet, and newspaper. They determine how advertising budgets are best spent to generate the most exposure and sales.

Qualifications

Following is a list of qualifications for a career in advertising research and promotion:

- *Education.* A bachelor's degree in advertising, journalism, business administration, marketing, fashion merchandising, or a related field is required.
- *Experience.* Working in retail sales is a great way to get started while still in school. Selling is selling, whether it is for an apparel retailer or a newspaper publisher. Some students gain direct sales experience selling advertisements for college publications, such as the yearbook and programs for athletic events and theatrical performances. Some enter the advertising industry through copywriting and/or research jobs with newspapers or publishing firms and then move into the advertising sales representative position. Others gain experience at the retail level through a position in a store's advertising department, writing copy for advertised items, or laying out the actual advertisement.
- *Personal characteristics.* The ability to sell one's ideas is key to success in advertising. An understanding of budgets and accounting is necessary. With a high level of attention to detail, successful advertising professionals are focused on accuracy and fact checking.

Career Challenges

Advertising research and promotion personnel must gather data from all types of sources and then compile this research to tell a story—why their media vehicle is the best choice for advertisers to spend their promotional dollars. This job is not an easy one, because it combines the abilities of acquiring and interpreting data with strong writing skills. Advertising is a creative, numbers-based, and fast-paced field. Advertising research and promotion staff members need to stay up to date on all facets of the competition: their target markets, companies that

advertise in their publications, and their advertising rates. As competition in this industry is constantly evolving, this is a time-consuming task.

SOCIAL MEDIA DIRECTOR

With the high-speed growth of Internet marketing, fashion public relations is jumping into social media with both feet, and a new career path has evolved—that of the social media director. **Social media** refers to the tools and social Web sites of the Internet that are used to communicate online with others. **Social Web sites**, such as Facebook, LinkedIn, Twitter, Pinterest, Vine, and Polyvore, function as online communities of Internet users. **Social networking** is the grouping of individuals into factions with similar interests. The Internet is filled with millions of individuals who are looking to develop friendships or professional alliances, to gather and share firsthand information and experiences about fashion and news, to find employment, and to market products. Twitter.com indicates that, in 2018, it had 100 million active daily users sending 500 million tweets per day. To say that Twitter has a global reach is an understatement, as 79 percent of these accounts are outside of the United States.

The integration of Facebook, Twitter, Instagram, and the like into our daily lives has led to the development of the career position of social media director. The **social media director** develops, manages, and oversees the implementation of public relations programs in the social media venue (Box 7.2). This includes creating content and generating coverage for social media efforts in all forms. Primary responsibilities of the social media director include the following:

- Managing and initiating strategic and creative planning of public relations campaigns through social media projects
- Integrating projects with marketing, advertising, and promotional divisions
- Managing public relations agencies contracted by the company, if applicable
- Cultivating and developing productive relationships with social media contacts
- Managing press interviews with company executives
- Working to innovate and integrate the use of technology/social media into all public relations efforts
- Managing department resources—personnel and fiscal

SOCIAL MEDIA STRIKES
BOX 7.2 Sustainability and Social Media

Gucci's sales growth in recent years is phenomenal—in 2017 sales grew by over 44 percent over the previous year, with revenues reaching $2.2 billion in 2018, up over 48 percent compared the same period during the prior year.

What is behind this? One reason is millennials. The brand appeals to their core values: personal satisfaction and purpose.

Traditionally, luxury brands have established themselves through two key elements: high-quality craftsmanship with superior quality and exclusivity. But millennials do not necessarily buy into these traditional selling points. Consumers in this generation crave purpose, authenticity, and passion. And they are attracted to companies that behave in a committed and ethical way. In short, luxury brands must embrace a higher purpose in order to win over millennial shoppers.

As issues like sustainability, transparency, and ethical manufacturing practices receive greater attention in the media,

Gucci has responded with a progressive program, Gucci Equilibrium (http://equilibrium.gucci.com), which is an online communication platform outlining the brand's corporate social responsibility policies, environmental impact, employee satisfaction, and other innovations. This level of transparency and communication grants the Gucci brand the level of authenticity, transparency, and accountability that consumers now seek.

Sources:

Bezamat, B., "Gucci launches online platform to promote sustainable purpose," The Current Daily, June 6, 2018, https://thecurrentdaily.com/2018/06/06/gucci-equilibrium-platform-sustainable-purpose/

Primo, D., "What can luxury brands learn from Gucci about millennials?" Forbes, November 2, 2018, www.forbes.com/sites/forbesagencycouncil/2018/11/02/what-can-luxury-brands-learn-from-gucci-about-millennials/#3a9ce5c5e5ba

Qualifications

Future social media directors should work to acquire the following qualifications:

- *Education.* A bachelor's degree in marketing, computer information systems, public relations, advertising, business administration, fashion merchandising, or a related field is a minimum requirement.
- *Experience.* To move into the director position, one usually needs a minimum of five to seven years of fashion public relations experience with an emphasis on social media. Broad knowledge of social media tools, current and future, is expected, as is a knowledge of traditional fashion press. A comprehensive understanding of competitors and their social networking outreach is a plus. Additionally, the candidate for a social media director position must present a portfolio of proposals.
- *Personal characteristics.* Excellent leadership and management skills are necessary tools. Successful social media directors are described as possessing excellent "futuring" skills, the ability to anticipate the next big thing in social networking. Budget management and human resource skills are also essential.

Career Challenges

The social media director is faced with the challenges of updating the social networking efforts of the company by the minute, hour, or day. The work must be ever-changing yet consistent. Conveying the company's image accurately and person-to-person through an online presence is critical. In addition, new online communities and media vehicles for people to connect to one another are popping up constantly. Anticipating which new social media will be the latest universal tie-in and which current one is the next to go out of favor are critical decisions for the social media director. Finding new topics and interesting ways to engage social media views is yet another significant challenge for the social media director.

FASHION EVENT PRODUCER

Have you ever visited a pop-up shop? Viewed a fashion show production? Attended a trunk show? Participated in a bridal show extravaganza? If so, you have seen the handiwork of a **fashion event producer**, or *fashion event planner*, also referred to as a *special events coordinator*. Fashion event producers increase the visibility of design houses, brands, products, or fabrics by coordinating fashion events that provide positive exposure for the company.

Fashion Events

Fashion event producers coordinate and implement many occasions to promote an image, an idea, an organization, or a product (Box 7.3). As discussed in the next section of this chapter, trunk shows in the designer salon of a department store, for example, may spotlight a new designer line.

BOX 7.3 FASHION EVENT PRODUCER

Job Title: Production Assistant
Location: New York City
Education: Bachelor Degree

A fashion event company currently seeks a Production Assistant, responsible for providing support to the global event production team. The ideal candidate will exercise discretion and independent judgment, as well as the ability to interface and work with senior level business leaders and their teams. The ideal candidate will have the ability to effectively provide support through all stages of the event production business.

Roles and Responsibilities:

- Prepare correspondence for executives and route accordingly.
- Research industry related items for presentations and proposals.
- Weekly updates of client database.
- Manage email activity, calendar appointments, and meetings.
- Coordinate and manage VP's meeting and travel schedule.
- Assist with execution of projects or specific stages of projects as assigned; track progress and results when necessary.

- Prepare expense reports.
- Lead, manage and coordinate NYFW Venue Assistants program.
- Support Production Teams during NYFW and all client related events onsite and in back office.
- Additional ad-hoc projects as assigned.

Qualifications:

- Bachelor's degree.
- Minimum 1–2 years' experience assisting a senior level executive.
- Previous event production experience preferred.
- Interest in fashion industry.
- High proficiency with MS Office (Word, Excel, PowerPoint and Outlook). CRM and Concur experience is a plus.
- Ability to work with all levels of management.
- Ability to handle multiple assignments and deadlines with accuracy.
- Detail-oriented and proactive.
- Exceptional interpersonal skills.
- Professional demeanor and communication skills.

Another way to create exposure is through tearoom modeling for a women's organization or a community group at a country club or restaurant. A newer development in the fashion event sector, one that takes the fashion show or trunk show a step further, is the pop-up shop.

Whether you call them **pop-up shops** or pop-up stores, these projects are like hide-and-seek boutiques that pop up within other retail locations or at vacant retail spaces with few preliminary announcements. They quickly draw crowds, are open for a limited period, and then disappear or morph into something else. The designer's or manufacturer's goals for the pop-up stores are to add freshness, exclusivity, and surprise to their images and product lines, and to sell merchandise. Some brands now use them to do real-time consumer research, observing consumers and gathering data to generate meaningful learning. Whether it is tagged mass exclusivity or planned spontaneity, it is working. Figure 7.6 shows an example of a pop-up shop.

Figure 7.6
The Armani Box beauty pop-up store in West Hollywood, California.

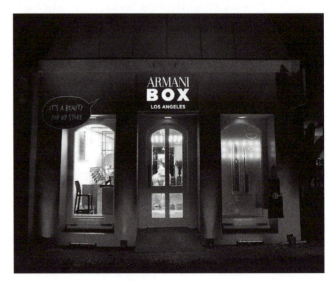

Some of the fashion experiences that fashion event producers develop and participate in are discussed in the following sections.

Bridal Shows

Through **bridal shows**, or bridal markets, wedding product or service manufacturer's reps and retail buyers are able to get together to review the new season's offerings. The bridal market is often organized in a convention center with booths that feature each of the vendors and with a fashion show as the main event. These are usually staged in the Fall before the Spring wedding season.

Informal Fashion Show

An **informal fashion show** is one without extravagant staging and technical assistance, often taking place in a conference center, hotel, or restaurant, in which models circulate among the tables as refreshments are served. The apparel manufacturer may team up with another organization and use this activity as a drawing card for an internal sales meeting or as an external fundraiser for a philanthropic cause. Instead of commentary, printed programs are often left at the place settings or on chairs to enable guests to read descriptions, prices, and size ranges of the featured garments and accessories at their leisure.

Trunk Shows

Through a **trunk show**, a fashion event producer or a manufacturer's representative brings the vendor's full seasonal line to a retail store that carries that particular manufacturer (Figure 7.7). The planner or representative works with individual customers, educating them about the line and providing personal fashion consultations. The customers can then place special orders. Sometimes, a trunk show in an upscale department or specialty store may feature a well-known designer, as well as the designer's latest collection and be hosted by a well-known celebrity (Figure 7.8).

Party Planning

In some instances, fashion event producers can literally be paid to party—prepare and manage the party, that is. **Party planning** can involve a manufacturer, a designer, a PR director, or an organization hiring a fashion event producer to put together a celebratory event (Figure 7.9). For example, a textile manufacturer may employ a fashion event producer to coordinate such an event during

Figure 7.7
Through a trunk show, a fashion event producer or a manufacturer's representative brings the vendor's full seasonal line to a retail store that carries that particular manufacturer.

Figure 7.8
Designer Gail Elliot's Trunk Show hosted by model and celebrity Cindy Crawford.

Fashion Week for retail buyers—potential and existing clients. The event producer arranges to have the showroom open after hours for the party and sends out invitations to the retail buyers who registered to attend the show, offering them a private showing of the new product line during the party. He or she works with the sales manager of the textile production firm to schedule sales

Figure 7.9

The fashion event or party planner coordinates parties for new products and stores, like this launch party for the Showpo Pop-up store.

associates for this evening event and locates a new restaurant and wine shop to serve complimentary appetizers and drinks in exchange for publicity. The event producer decorates the showroom and locates a desk and hostess at the entrance of the showroom to greet and sign in guests and to secure their contact information for future emails. Door prizes provided by the manufacturer are incentives for guests to stay for the entire length of the party. The cost of the event is minimal; the visibility is great, as the textile producer showcases its business to the retail buyers. The freelance fashion event producer is then paid well for a job well done.

Educational Events

A fashion event producer or an employee hired by a fashion event producer may stage an **educational event** to inform an audience about a product. For example, depending on the manufacturer's product line, the presenter may demonstrate different ways to wear jewelry, sportswear, or evening wear. In home furnishings, a demonstrator may educate an audience of sales reps by showing how to configure a new sectional sofa for a number of different looks and space needs. The presenter hired by a manufacturer may have an audience of sales reps, retail buyers, or ultimate consumers; it depends on the company's objectives for the event.

Partnership Events

A **partnership event** is one in which a fashion firm collaborates with another company outside of the fashion industry, with the intent of drawing in more customers. For example, an apparel manufacturer and an airline may get together and hire a fashion event planner to conduct workshops on how to pack for travel and what to wear on an African safari. The fashion event producer plans and implements the events, which are part of a larger promotional plan that showcases both the manufacturer and the airline. Collaborating with companies outside of the fashion industry allows the fashion event planner to generate new contacts and, possibly, additional revenue.

Philanthropic Fashion Show

A fashion event planner may execute a fashion show that benefits a nonprofit or charitable organization through its ticket sales or donations. This is referred to as a **philanthropic fashion show**, or *charity fashion show*. Community leaders, local celebrities, or executives of the philanthropic organization often model the apparel and accessories, acting as a drawing card for the show. The fashion event planner may also solicit door prizes or auction items from benefactors to generate additional funds for the cause.

Fashion Shows and Technology

Technology has impacted the world of fashion shows. Designers are streaming their fashion shows online so that their fans from anywhere in the world can see their newest collections as soon as they hit the runway. Some fashion firms are combining digital media in promotion with technology in fashion shows. At the Badgley Mischka fall 2018 show at New York Fashion Week, guests were invited to download an app onto their smartphones or tablets, allowing them to rate the runway looks in real-time as the models moved down the runway. Audience members were able to rate each outfit "like it," or "love it" while also accessing additional information about the fashion on their device. During the fifteen-minute show, 1,396 votes were cast by 179 guests, representing seventeen countries, while designers Mark Badgley and James Mischka watched the feedback on an iPad. The feedback is instant for the brand, instead of having to wait six months when the numbers and comments come in from the retailers.

Technology in fashion shows is helping designers connect with potential and current customers around the globe. New York Fashion Week used to be closed to the exclusive buyers and other fashion executives, but with social media, anyone can stream a runway show from their smartphone or tablet. It makes the event bigger and more effective for brands in terms of reach and inclusiveness. For example, Maybelline partners with designers for NYFW, and uses the event to focus on a specific branding message, celebrating inclusive beauty through the wide variety of makeup shades that they offer. In addition to branding messages, designers and brands maximize the runway moment for its worldwide streaming potential. Through holograms, extreme graphics, and even a rhinestone-clad robot, the visuals are designed to help generate maximum social media posts, and meant to be shared and enjoyed by an enthusiastic global audience.

Whether the fashion event producer uses holograms, projected imagery, or a traditional stage, his or her basic responsibilities in fashion show production are the same.

Duties of a Fashion Event Producer

There are many ways to generate interest through fashion events. Because there is much work involved and, in many cases, a great deal of expertise needed, some manufacturers and designers hire freelance fashion event producers to execute them, whereas others have part- or full-time staffs to do this. So, what kinds of activities do fashion event producers perform? Here is a sampling:

- Locate and reserve the place after negotiating the price, terms, and dates for the event—to fit the client's needs and desires and to fit within the budget
- Determine staging, lighting, music, sound system, and technology needs
- Assemble merchandise to be featured
- Hire and fit models, arrange lineup, and supervise rehearsals
- Compile commentary, if appropriate, and recruit commentator
- Arrange for printing needs (e.g., tickets, signage, invitations, and programs)
- Arrange for seating, to include setup and breakdown of seats, tables, and staging
- Recruit backstage help, such as hairstylists, makeup artists, and dressers

- Recruit front-of-stage help, such as ticket sales, concessions, and ushers
- Locate caterers or sponsors for refreshments, if needed
- Handle publicity, which may include invitations, press releases, advertisements, television and/or radio interviews, social media, and other media-related activities

The job of fashion event producer is one of those "chief cook and bottle washer" positions that may have the planner initially doing a little bit of everything to pull the event together. Once the producer becomes more established in the industry, then he or she is able to hire others to handle parts of the larger projects.

Qualifications

This career requires the following qualifications:

- *Education.* A bachelor's degree in fashion merchandising, fashion design, promotion, special events planning, or a related field is required.
- *Experience.* Fashion event planners come from a wide range of industry sectors: retail, design, and manufacturing. Many work as assistants to fashion directors or coordinators in retail operations or manufacturer's showrooms before branching out on their own. Others initially work as assistants to established fashion event planners. Some large retail stores have special events departments through which starting, or assistant, fashion event planners can learn the ropes of fashion event planning and production. Through the positions leading up to becoming a fashion event planner, a large and useful network of contacts related to the fashion industry can be developed.
- *Personal characteristics.* Successful fashion event planners have the following skills and knowledge: an enthusiastic and creative personality, the ability to sell one's ideas and vision, accounting skills to develop and manage budgets, strong organizational and communication skills, and effective time-management abilities.

Career Challenges

The job tasks of fashion event planning require endless attention to detail to ensure trouble-free events. Fashion event planners need a strong sense of fashion, organizational skills, the ability to work well in stressful situations, and the communication skills to work with a wide range of people. Managing a major fashion event can be compared to coordinating a three-ring circus. Frequently, many people are involved and myriad details need to be considered. When combining these stresses with the need to keep events on budget and on time, fashion event planners must have the skills to remain calm and collected under pressure. This person needs nerves of steel and iron-clad organization skills.

Summary

Promotion refers to the endorsement of a person, a product, a cause, an idea, or an organization. The ultimate goal of promotion for the designer or manufacturer is to encourage the growth, exposure, and development of the designer, company, its lines, and its image by advancing it to a higher position with a greater number of consumers. The ultimate goal is increased visibility in positive ways that motivate consumers to buy, resulting in increased sales. Promotion career opportunities in the primary level of the fashion industry include fashion stylist, public relations director, advertising director, advertising sales representative and related positions, social media director, and fashion event planner. Although the public relations director, social media director, and advertising representative are usually employed by a large firm, fashion stylists and fashion events planners may choose a career with a retail company, manufacturer, or public relations firm, or decide to open their own companies. In all of these promotion careers, the goal is to sell an idea, an image, or a product—directly or indirectly. It is marketing in its truest form; it is creative, thought provoking, and profitable at its best.

Key Terms

advertising
advertising director
advertising promotion staff
advertising research assistant
advertising sales
   representative
bridal show
consumer publication
educational event
fashion event producer
fashion photostylist
fashion shoot
fashion stylist
informal fashion show
media planner

partnership event
party planning
philanthropic fashion show
pop-up shop
promotion
promotion director
promotion product
public relations director
social media
social media director
social networking
social Web site
trade publication
trunk show

Online Resources

www.lyst.com
www.forbes.com/sites/robertwynne/2015/07/22/top-10-pr-
   blogs-you-should-be-reading/#25004f98a4e0www.fashion-
   tweets.com/
www.huffpost.com/entry/instagram-accounts-fashion-month_
   l_5c59a99ce4b00187b5553834

www.prcouture.com
www.harpersbazaar.com/fashion/fashion-week/g2933/new-
   designers-to-know-0913/https://www.themuse.com/
   advice/20-power-pr-women-to-follow-on-twitter
www.prnewsonline.com/2017-top-women-pr-winners/

Discussion Questions

1. How does your favorite designer promote his or her products? Determine the promotional activities coordinated by the company's public relations director. Is the public relations director contracted from an outside firm? If so, what other companies does this firm promote? Are there similarities among its clients?

2. Which do you read more regularly—consumer or trade publications? Read an article from each type of publication and analyze the value of each as it relates to your future career goals.

3. Go online to locate three recent examples each of fashion designers' and manufacturers' use of digital media in promotion. Set up a spreadsheet to compare and contrast these examples. What are the similarities and differences among these?

CAREERS IN FASHION RETAILING

Unit 3 examines the retail level of the fashion industry in three function areas: marketing, management, and merchandising. In Chapter 7, promotion activities used by the manufacturer/designer to inform potential consumers (i.e., retail buyers and end users) about the company and its products were examined. The more a business can integrate advertising, publicity, sales promotion, and personal selling, the more promotion will be effective. Retailers use additional promotional efforts, such as window and in-store displays, Web sites, product labeling and packaging, and store signage, as other ways of promoting the product. Regardless of the type of promotion, the reason for choosing and constructing all promotional messages in all media venues is based on (1) the principles of marketing and (2) in-depth knowledge of the company and its consumer. In Chapter 8, "Marketing for the Retailer," the marketing mix and marketing plans are explored, and career tracks that focus on marketing and promotion are introduced: marketing director and manager, product marketing manager, brand marketing manager, digital marketing manager, art director, and copywriter.

Chapter 9, "Merchandising for the Retailer," illustrates the tremendous impact retail merchandisers, or buyers, have on their fashion retailing businesses in terms of exclusivity, image, and pricing. The major activities of the buyer in merchandising include locating and purchasing products, with the preferences of the consumer in mind, and then selling these products at a profit. Merchandising also includes extensive research on the department's or store's customers, trying to predict which types of merchandise customers will want to buy for upcoming seasons. There are a variety of positions available in the merchandising division of retailing operation, depending on its size and channels of distribution. The career options discussed in Chapter 9 include the general merchandising manager, divisional merchandising manager, buyer/

fashion merchandiser, assistant buyer, planner, distribution manager/allocator, and merchandising trainee. The varied career tracks in merchandising for the retailer have several challenges in common—locating products that (1) appeal to the customer, (2) are priced right, (3) arrive at the right place when needed, and (4) sell to the retailers' customers.

In Chapter 10, "Management for the Retailer," career opportunities in retail management—the division in charge of organizing and controlling of the affairs of the business as a whole or a particular department—are explored. This chapter focuses on management careers in fashion retailing that include a wide variety of retail venues, such as manager of an apparel store, manager of an Internet fashion operation, or assistant manager of a factory outlet. The specific career tracks in retail management examined in Chapter 10 include the following positions: regional manager; operations manager; retail store manager; manager-in-training (MIT); assistant and associate store manager; department manager; customer service manager; and retail operation entrepreneur, or store owner.

The 3 Ms of retailing—marketing, merchandising, and management—interrelate to facilitate a successful fashion retail operation. If one of the three is weak, then the company will likely have issues. For example, the buyers can purchase the top-selling, best-priced, and most customer-centered merchandise, and the store management team can be skilled and ready to sell it, but, if the store and the merchandise are not marketed well, the sales may not happen. Alternately, if the merchandise and the marketing are top-notch and ready to roll out, but the store management and staff are not motivated and customer service oriented, then the customers may not come to the retailer. It is a balancing act to keep this triangle upright, and one that pays off when it is done well.

CHAPTER 8
MARKETING FOR THE RETAILER

In the previous chapter, promotion was examined from the perspectives of designers and manufacturers of fashion products. In this chapter, we examine how retailers penetrate their markets and use promotion. Take, for example, H&M and how it communicates its business model of "fashion and quality at the best price" through the various advertising campaigns. H&M's promotions are produced internally at its headquarters in Stockholm, Sweden, by the marketing department, in cooperation with creative professionals located in the major fashion hubs of the world. The campaigns are designed to be clear and simple and to inform customers of what is new at H&M; the focus is on product, not celebrity models or a corporate message. H&M's advertising images do not aim to communicate any specific ideal, but rather a range of styles and attitudes. H&M goes one step further by featuring models with different looks, styles, and cultural backgrounds to advertise its products for women, men, teenagers, and children. The models "must portray the current fashion in a positive and healthy manner," H&M declares.

In contrast, Zara has grown with very little advertising and much word-of-mouth promotion. It is intentional and part of the retailer's business model, which has a mini-marketing department that does not engage in showy campaigns, as its competitors do. Instead, Zara saves on the expense of traditional advertising, relying on word-of-mouth and free media coverage of celebrities wearing its clothes, such as the Spanish Queen Letizia and Prince George's mother Kate Middleton, Her Royal Highness, the Duchess of Cambridge. Instead of promotion, Zara's Spanish parent company, Inditex, is well-known for its focus on real estate. The company invests heavily in the aesthetics, historical appeal, and locations of its shops.

Although its buildings may be expansive, Inditex is famously an introverted company when it comes to press. Despite being one of the world's three richest men and the primary owner of Zara, Mr. Amancio Ortego refuses to do press interviews. *Fortune* describes him in this way: "He's difficult to know, impossible to interview, and incredibly secretive."[1] With its marketing strategy built on "un-promotion" (i.e., without advertising and almost all forms of mainstream marketing), ultimate locations, and its exclusive, ever-changing lines, Zara is exploding. Zara owns 2,220 stores in 88 countries.[2] You can read more about Zara in Box 8.1.

In Chapter 7, promotion career opportunities in the primary level of the fashion industry were explored, to include fashion stylist, public relations director, advertising director, advertising sales representative and related positions, social media director, and fashion event planner. The majority of these positions are also available at the retail level of the industry, with many of the same position requirements and similar career challenges. In this chapter, other career tracks that focus on marketing and promotion are introduced: marketing director and manager, product marketing manager, brand marketing manager, digital marketing manager, art director, and copywriter.

As stated in the previous chapter, promotion involves the activities used to inform the potential consumer (i.e., retail buyers and end users) about the company and its products. The more a business can integrate advertising, publicity, sales promotion, and personal selling, the more promotion will be effective. Retailers use additional promotional efforts, such as window displays and in-store displays, Web sites, product labeling and packaging, and store signage, as other ways of promoting the product. Regardless of the type of promotion, the reason for choosing and constructing all promotional messages in all media venues is based on (1) the principles of marketing and (2) in-depth knowledge of the company and its consumer. Next is an examination of the foundation for retailers' marketing plans, the marketing mix.

BOX 8.1 Product: Zara's Customer Is Always Right and Wants It Right Away

For the press, the face of Inditex is its quiet public relations director, Jesus Echevarría, who may be the only PR director in the world who tries hard not to apologize when he must answer questions about Inditex's skyrocketing success. In discussing the number of stores in different countries, Echevarría states, "When we open a market, everyone asks, 'How many stores will you open?'" he said. "Honestly, I didn't know. It depends on the customer and how big the demand is. We must have the dialogue with the customers and learn from them. It's not us saying you must have this. It's you saying it."

Store managers monitor customers' reactions on the basis of what they buy and don't buy and what they say to a sales associate, such as "I like this scooped collar" or "I hate zippers at the ankles." The sales staff is trained to draw out these sorts of comments from their customers. The store managers report this information to headquarters daily, where it is then transmitted to Zara's creative team of more than 200 professionals. The team receives constant feedback on the decisions its customers are making at every Zara store and quickly develops new designs to send to factories to be made into apparel.

Zara's designers and customers are inextricably linked. The company believes that the customer is always determining production—not the other way around. Every unit of apparel and accessories Zara produces has, in a way, been requested. Its business model is *that* closely attuned to the customer.

Source:

www.nytimes.com/2012/11/11/magazine/how-zara-grew-into-the-worlds-largest-fashion-retailer.html?pagewanted=all&_r=0 (March 2019)

THE MARKETING MIX: THE FOUR, MAKE THAT FIVE, PS OF MARKETING

Retailers look at methods of differentiating their business from those of competitors through the four Ps of marketing: price, product, placement, and promotion. A fifth P of marketing can be added—the people or consumers who are targeted as potential customers or product users, referred to as the **target market**. These market variables, referred to as the **marketing mix**, when combined, must reinforce the image of the company and its products to the potential and active customer. All five elements should complement one another in order to achieve the firm's marketing objectives. The best marketing plan for a company is one that directs resources or dollars toward products, place, promotion, and pricing, with the highest potential to increase revenue and profits among the people who are targeted as product buyers. Next, we examine how the components of the marketing mix are integrated into a strategic marketing plan and which career track manages each part of the plan.

THE MARKETING PLAN

Determining a successful marketing plan, or marketing strategy, is key to directing the retail fashion business on implementation of the five Ps of the marketing mix and, ultimately, leading the retail fashion business to success. The effective marketing plan reaches customers and motivates them to buy. The **marketing plan** helps define and quantify user benefits, establishes the market size as well as potential customer interest, and addresses the competition. The marketing plan serves several purposes. First, it helps the retailer determine how potential customers can become aware of the product or service. Second, it helps define the message the retailer wishes to convey about the product, service, or company. Third, it helps identify the methods that will best deliver and reinforce that message, and how sales will be achieved. Finally, the marketing plan addresses how the company positions itself relative to the competition. Now, imagine that you are writing a marketing plan for a boutique you plan to open in your community. Then, imagine developing a marketing plan for a company with 2,200 stores located all around the world. Zara has done just this and is successfully getting to know and compare its customers globally, as illustrated in Box 8.2.

MARKETING DIRECTOR

Although a higher executive position of **chief marketing officer (CMO)** exists in some large companies of the fashion industry, the **marketing director** often develops, implements, and facilitates the marketing plan in fashion retailing. The key job responsibilities of a marketing director are as follows:

- *Develop the marketing plan.* Translate company objectives to brand portfolio objectives, strategies, and plans to facilitate company growth.
- *Monitor the marketing budget.* Plan and administer the firm's marketing operations budget.
- *Manage marketing suppliers.* Negotiate with media agents to secure agreements for translation of materials into other media. Develop and edit promotional materials according to specific market or customer requirements.
- *Oversee business development and corporate communications activities.* Coordinate external and internal communications and systems, as well as public relations efforts.
- *Oversee the marketing database.* Gather financial and traffic results of promotions, plus consumer demographics, to include spending patterns, patronage motives, and shopping incentives, etc.
- *Manage the marketing department.* Build and develop a successful marketing team. Manage day-to-day activity with PR and press.

Depending on the company, the marketing director may be promoted to the position of vice president of marketing or CMO. In some firms, a **marketing manager** position is just below that of marketing director in the executive hierarchy and has qualifications similar to those of marketing director.

Qualifications

If director of marketing is your career goal, certain educational goals, work experiences, and personal characteristics will help you open the door and then move upward in this career path.

- *Education.* A bachelor of science in marketing, fashion merchandising, or a related business administration or fashion field is required.
- *Experience.* A minimum of five to eight years of executive-level marketing experience in a fashion organization is required, as is experience with new media and Internet advertising.

- *Personal Characteristics.* The marketing director is detail-oriented and has the skills to manage projects from conception through execution. He or she must have excellent communication skills—verbal, visual, and written. Successful marketing directors have a hunger to learn and the ability to flourish in a dynamic, high-growth, and entrepreneurial environment. The effective marketing director is a self-starter with a hands-on approach to problem solving.

Career Challenges

The marketing director needs to maintain a high energy level despite long hours and frequent meetings with a wide variety of staff members and administrators. Marketing directors need exceptional skills in multitasking and prioritizing, because they are often managing several projects simultaneously, with different deadlines, budgets, and objectives for each. Their responsibilities require excellent time management and negotiation abilities. Picture the marketing director walking a high wire while balancing a tray of drinks, and you will have an idea of the possible stress level involved in the position. Finally, the marketing director must be both creative and analytical, coming up with innovative and unique concepts while managing people and processes.

Fashion resides in a competitive, revolving marketplace. Retailers must be open to innovation and change in their product lines and, subsequently, the marketing plan.

Next, the marketing position that focuses on the product, or the product line, is introduced—that of the product marketing manager.

PRODUCT MARKETING MANAGER

The product life cycle must be understood in order for the retailer, and in particular the product marketing manager, to determine if and when to introduce new products into the existing product line. There are four stages in the product life cycle: introduction, acceleration, peak, and decline (Figure 8.1). There are no predictable time periods for products to reside in any one of the phases. In fact, the product life cycle of a fad item may last as little as four to six weeks. Fashion trend items can last for a season or a decade. The challenge for the **product marketing manager** is to anticipate when to get into a fashion style, color, or theme and when to get out. The time to introduce a new product is during the early life cycle of the current product when sales are strong and profit margins are higher.

Product Placement and the Product Marketing Manager

The P in the marketing mix called "place" is referred to as **distribution** and involves the product marketing manager in making sure that the product is available where

Figure 8.1

The product life cycle should be understood by the product marketing manager in order to determine when to introduce new products into the existing product line.

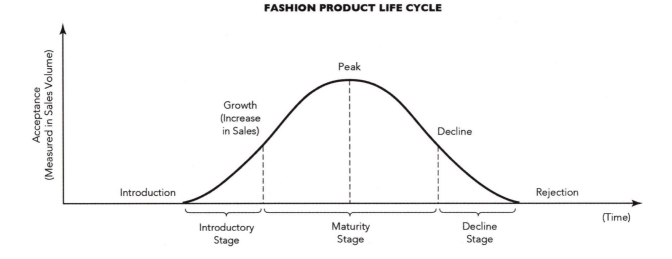

FASHION PRODUCT LIFE CYCLE

and when it is wanted. Marketers can choose among many ways of moving products to consumers. They may choose among different types of outlets and store locations (Box 8.3). In contrast, with today's online access, many retailers are reducing investments in locations and turning to an online presence, not only to promote the business, but also to offer the sale of products to consumers on a global scale. Distribution also involves decisions such as how much inventory to hold, how to transport goods, and where to locate warehouses.

Consumers are looking for products and services that are convenient for them to acquire exactly when they want or need them. In selecting the **channel of distribution**—the method selected for moving goods from producer to consumer—the product marketing manager gives careful consideration to using distributors that can provide good service at a reasonable price. The primary channel of distribution for the fashion retail industry moves from manufacturer to retailer to consumer. Some manufacturers, however, sell directly to the consumer

THE JOB SEARCH

BOX 8.3 RETAIL MARKETING MANAGER

An international brand is always interested in hearing from talented, globally-minded individuals with a passion for fashion.

If you enjoy working in a creative, fast-paced environment, then we would love to hear from you!

Position Overview:

In collaboration with the Retail Marketing Senior Director, the Retail Marketing Manager will execute seasonal plans & strategies that support U.S. Lifestyle & Collection stores. Responsibilities include the development and implementation of local marketing opportunities, tourism partnerships, and in-store & advertising initiatives that drive in-store traffic, client acquisition and client retention. Critical to the role is creativity, innovation and success executing drive to store partnerships / initiatives and in-store activations. The ideal candidate will also possess a deep understanding and experience in leveraging Mall Marketing channels.

Main Responsibilities include but are not limited to:

Maintain strong relationships with Mall Partners and leverage and test new marketing opportunities.

- Create and implement in-store activations to promote increased traffic during key selling moments throughout the year.
- Build tourism initiatives through marketing partnerships (ex. Alipay, WeChat, CLA) driving key tourist groups to stores.
- Identify partnership opportunities in local markets to drive new in-store traffic and client experiences.
- Collaborate with Digital Marketing to implement digital drive to store campaigns.

- Partner with Global Media team to brief strategy and approach to execute impactful Advertising placements that support priority U.S. stores.
- Work cross-functionally with Global Events and Social media teams to execute impactful in-store events and media support that increase traffic, ROI, and brand loyalty.
- Ensure clear and concise store communications are developed through Retail Communications for all retail marketing initiatives in a timely manner.
- Work with Retail Marketing Coordinator to maintain overall Lifestyle & Collection budget and brand appropriate store support as requested.
- Assist in the creation and enhancement of the clientele program and support the platform roll-out as needed.
- Collaborate with Retail Marketing Coordinator to partner with Analytics and Training teams to provide strategic clientele lists, results and analysis.

Qualifications:

- Bachelors' Degree is required
- Minimum of 5 years Marketing experience, preferably in a retail environment
- Mall Marketing relationships preferred
- Experience with developing client-centric strategies within a retail environment
- Exceptional problem-solving skills
- Power Point and Excel
- Ability to prioritize and multitask effectively
- Thrive in a fast paced on-time deliverable environment
- Strong analytic and project management skills
- Critical thinking and analytical problem-solving skills

through catalogs, Web sites, or factory outlets. An alternative, and less frequently used, channel of distribution in the fashion industry is the wholesaler. In this case, the manufacturer sells merchandise to a **wholesale** company, one that sells the goods to the retailer for subsequent resale to the consumer.

Price and the Product Marketing Manager

Pricing decisions impact almost every aspect of a business—the product's image, the company's sales, and the retailer's success. Pricing is a component of the marketing strategy. Covering expenses and making a profit are crucial, but pricing is also an issue of relationship to competitor's pricing, the product's positioning, and supply and demand—what the customer is willing to pay. Pricing is not just about numbers. The price of the merchandise sends a message about the perceived value of the product to customers regarding the product or service they

are buying. For example, using the fast fashion business model of H&M or Zara, customers know that they will find new merchandise in the stores almost weekly, and they are confident that they can afford it. The retailers control its price structure through spin-offs of successful products with low or nonexistent start-up expenses (e.g., pattern development, sample construction, and fit perfection), as well as production in its own factories, which saves costs.

High-end designers and brands, such as Victoria Beckham, the iconic British boot brand Hunter, and Vera Wang, have had success by introducing **diffusion labels** (secondary lines) at lower prices exclusively to mass merchandisers in an attempt to increase market share. These designers are offering less-expensive labels and distributing those labels through discount stores, such as Target or Kohl's. Popular style and trend site Popsugar built on this practice of using brand and name recognition to extend its brand to a wider audience, with a data-driven curated collection for Kohl's (Figure 8.2).

Figure 8.2
POPSUGAR partners with Kohl's on a mixable collection of wardrobe pieces, curated and designed based on search data from the popular site.

In some retail firms, the product marketing manager may be in charge of brand marketing; however, more companies are adding the position of brand marketing manager to focus on the importance of creating and managing the brand of the product.

BRAND MARKETING MANAGER

Branding is defined as the sum of all the associations, feelings, beliefs, attitudes, and perceptions customers have with a company and/or its products. The American Marketing Association defines a *brand* as "a name, term, design, symbol, or any other feature that identifies one seller's good or service as distinct from those of other sellers."[3] Fashion icons such as Louis Vuitton, Nike, and Gucci have brands that are recognizable and unmistakable. The brand is reflected in the name, logo (i.e., its color, font, and tag lines), and trademarks.

Reporting to the marketing director or CMO, the **brand marketing manager** strategically develops and executes multichannel brand marketing and promotional programs in order to drive brand awareness, support and reinforce the brand's character, and ultimately generate increased revenue. The brand manager monitors and measures customer activity that he or she works to create. Brand marketing managers use a variety of communication tools to send the messages of their brands, including PR, direct marketing, visual merchandising, and print.

Because of the need for a consistent message and a variety of ways to spread that message, the brand marketing manager and team often work with other departments, such as digital marketing and PR. Following is a listing of the key responsibilities of the brand marketing manager:

1. *Develop a vision for the brand.* What does the business aspire to be? The vision should focus on a longer-term perspective. Brands take time to build and become recognized in the marketplace. The more solid the brand vision, the greater the chance the customer will understand and relate to the vision.

2. *Position the brand in relationship to the competition.* The brand should differentiate the business from the competition. Successful brands focus on what separates them from the competition. Brands are multidimensional in that they carry with them images and associations in the minds of the consumer.

3. *Create a personality.* Each brand has a distinct personality. Some take on a more comical approach, whereas others lend themselves to a more serious product or service. Desigual, a retailer and manufacturer, brands with humor, open-mindedness, and a free spirit (Figure 8.3), whereas Chanel conveys sophistication, luxury, glamour, and beauty. The more emotion a brand can communicate, the more memorable it will be in the mind of the market. TOMs shoes—with its "buy one to give one to a needy child" business model—provides an example of an emotional and memorable message that tells a story.

Figure 8.3

Managing a brand includes creating a personality for it. Desigual, a retailer and manufacturer, uses the following description for its brand: humor, open-mindedness, and a free spirit.

4. *Articulate the benefits.* The brand represents a set of benefits and value to the customer.
5. *Define the values the brand represents.* The brand represents a defined set of values established by the retailer. Clearly defining the value of the business can create long-term customers.

The message of the brand is then conveyed through the sum of its marketing materials—from its logo, business cards, and brochures to its signage, Web site, and advertisements.

The qualifications of the product and brand marketing managers are very similar to those of the digital marketing manager and will follow the discussion of this career path.

DIGITAL MARKETING MANAGER

The **digital marketing manager** works to further develop and manage a company's digital marketing presence and oversees the digital marketing strategy for the brand. This person is responsible for managing online brand and product campaigns to raise brand awareness. One of the digital marketing director's main goals is to devise strategies to drive online traffic to the company's Web site, blog, Pinterest boards, or whatever media the company uses to connect with customers. In addition, he or she evaluates customer research, market conditions, and competitor data, especially the ways competitors are using their Web sites and social media.

The digital marketing manager collaborates with the company's product and brand managers, as well as the social media director. Digital marketing managers work closely with the Web master to improve the usability, design, content, and conversion of the company's Web site.

Web Site Marketing

Web sites have become standard equipment for fashion retailers and their customers. The Web site can serve as an online retail store, a means to communicate information about the business, a promotional tool, a direct line to each current and prospective customer, and the hardest-working salesperson in the company. With 24/7 availability, most Web sites work to build the brand and customer list, while selling products any time of the day or night.

Following are questions digital marketing directors and Web developers ask when developing or redesigning a Web site:

1. What is the purpose of the Web site? Is the purpose to generate customer interest? Serve as an animated and informational brochure? Or function as an online retail store?
2. Who is the target audience?
3. How will customers find the Web site? Offline strategies, such as advertising, can drive traffic.
4. What do customers expect to find on the site? The ability to purchase? Pricing? Hours of operation? Location? Arrivals of new merchandise?
5. What can be done to cause customers to linger longer at the site?
6. How does the Web site compare to that of the competition? Just as brick-and-mortar stores compete for customers, Web sites compete as well. How are they designed? What are the messages?
7. How will the Web site be monitored? A good Web site host will provide a set of statistics that disclose number of visitors, when they visited, how they found the site, what they viewed, and whether they made a purchase.

Next, qualifications for product, brand, and digital marketing managers are presented.

Qualifications

- *Education.* A bachelor's degree in digital media or computer information systems is required for the digital marketing manager. A bachelor's degree in fashion merchandising, fashion design, product development, marketing, advertising, retailing, or a related field is required for the product or brand marketing manager.
- *Experience.* For the product, brand, and digital marketing managers, on-the-job experience in fashion retailing is necessary to develop a strong understanding of current brick-and-mortar and online marketing concepts, strategies, and best practices. Substantial digital marketing experience within a retail company is often required for the digital marketing manager. Students can gain work experience in their area of interest through an internship and/or part-time employment or volunteer work while attending college.
- *Personal Characteristics.* Effective visual, verbal, and written communication abilities are necessary for these positions. Organization and time management are also needed skills. The ability to sell the company and its image, as well as yourself and your work, is essential and is a critical component of the networking that all of

these positions require. An understanding of the numbers, from budgets to consumer data, is required.

Career Challenges

One brand manager put it this way: "In marketing, there is no such thing as consensus." That is one of the digital, brand, and product marketing managers' greatest obstacles. They must work to bring the CEO, CMO, marketing director, and interdepartmental colleagues together in support of the marketing concept before the development of the marketing campaign can get off the ground. Multiple projects driven by time and funding constraints, long hours and late nights when projects are due, and negotiating with co-workers (repeatedly) are some of the challenges the digital, brand, and product marketing managers regularly face.

CREATIVE DIRECTOR

In some large retail companies, there are both a creative director and an art director. The differences are often internal to a specific company, but there are some general distinctions. In most cases, **creative directors** oversee art directors and other in-house art staff. The creative director often works directly with the marketing director (and, in some companies, the creative director *is* the marketing director) to ensure that the strategy, marketing goals, and branding expectations are being met. A creative director position is more managerial and reports to the CMO, while an art director position is more hands-on in the design process and reports to the creative director. The creative director conceptualizes and works on the visual components and production of a campaign, and the art director manages and oversees the visual design and production of projects. The creative director articulates the vision and selects and directs the talent (e.g., graphic designers, Web developers, and photographers), while the art director designs a project with a direction that is already set. The creative director usually goes into this position with at least twelve years of experience, while the art director can start with three to five years of experience.

ART DIRECTOR

The **art director** produces or oversees production of artwork for advertising campaigns, magazines, television shows, films, Web sites, or products, often working with the other marketing divisions and reporting to the creative director. Art directors lead creative sessions for project kick-offs and, later, collaborate with product designers, graphic designers, copywriters, photographers, and others to discuss project requirements and concepts. They review and approve proofs of printed copy and art materials developed by creative department members. They may also coordinate and attend photo shoots and printing sessions to ensure that the images needed are obtained. All of these tasks are completed by the art director in line with the budget planned for the art department.

COPYWRITER

A **copywriter** is responsible for writing the words, slogans, and audio scripts that accompany promotional visuals—online and in print. A typical copywriting project includes the following activities:

- Discussing the core message and target audience
- Brainstorming visual and copy ideas with other members of the creative team
- Writing and presenting a few options to management
- Modifying copy to meet management's expectations
- Overseeing the production phase

The art director and copywriter are accountable for checking that all of the content being advertised is appealing, clear, reflective of the brand, truthful, and in compliance with codes of advertising practice.

Qualifications

- *Education.* For the art director, a bachelor's degree in art, fine arts, graphic design, and computer-aided design is commonly required. For the copywriter, a degree in journalism, English, writing, advertising, or a related field is mandatory.
- *Experience.* The art director should have a thorough understanding of art, photography, typography, and printing. The art director needs a broad range of art expertise, from the ability to sketch to computer-aided design. Excellent computer skills in relevant art and design software packages are must-haves for the art director. The copywriter should have a keen understanding of journalism, advertising, promotion, and publicity.

- *Personal Characteristics.* Both the art director and the copywriter should be highly creative and have excellent interpersonal and communication skills. They need to work well as part of a team with a range of people. Having an interest in social and cultural trends helps encourage creativity. The successful copywriter must have not only excellent writing skills but strong interpersonal skills as well. Both must be able to work under the pressure of deadlines and quantitative goals (e.g., how many sales the copy in banner advertisements or the images on billboards have generated). Both must also have a keen eye for aesthetics, detail, and accuracy.

Career Challenges

The art director and copywriter face two primary challenges: time and money. There is substantial pressure to be creative on demand, to be constrained by budget parameters, and to declare a product finished in order to be on time. In addition, the art director and copywriter need to be able to see other people's points of view and cope with criticism. This can be difficult when significant time and effort went into a copywriting assignment or a graphic design for an advertisement. It is also challenging to be highly motivated and creative on every project. Finally, positions in these two creative marketing areas are limited, and starting salaries are often low.

CUSTOMER SERVICE AND CUSTOMER RELATIONSHIP MANAGEMENT

Rooted in understanding and quantifying consumer behavior, **client/customer relationship management (CRM)** marketing encompasses the ability to analyze significant amounts of data to understand consumer demographics, key market segments, and best practices for recruiting or retaining those customers. This information helps the marketing divisions of a fashion company leverage the brand to accomplish the following goals:

- To reach the most qualified customers
- To develop loyalty programs
- To determine the best media forms to reach the consumer
- To understand online consumer behavior to drive sales at the brick-and-mortar stores

As a result, the CRM department works closely with other members of the other marketing divisions. CRM team members know that promotion alone will not generate all of a company's sales. Customer service is an important element of most successful retail operations. As we communicate via e-mail, text messages, Web sites, Facebook, LinkedIn, Instagram, Twitter, and the like, face-to-face interaction between retailers and their customers becomes scarcer. With this shift in communication, retailers must find new and better ways to stay in touch with their most valuable assets: their customers.

One of the ways fashion retail businesses differentiate from each other and compete with larger companies is by providing exceptional customer service. Working closely with customers to build lasting relationships is important in retaining lifelong customers. Nordstrom, for example, is committed to exceptional customer service. It implements a culture of motivated and empowered employees, each with an entrepreneurial retailing spirit. Nordstrom encourages sales associates to do all they can to make sure a shopper leaves the store a satisfied customer. Nordstrom's Web site includes a live chat room, which allows customers to chat online in real time with personal shoppers. In addition, Nordstrom has a hassle-free online return policy, and customers can return merchandise to any Nordstrom store.

Some retailers are making it a point to work on attracting, training, and retaining good sales associates who will provide quality customer service. When asked, most customers state they decided to buy from a particular fashion retailer because of the company's reputation, the level of customer service, the manner in which the retailer responded to complaints and requests, and the relationship they have with the salespeople.

Summary

Developing a marketing strategy, as well as constructing and implementing a marketing plan, is key to the successful penetration of the market. Analyzing the marketing mix includes an examination of the interrelationship of product, price, placement, promotion, and people (i.e., customers—past, present, and future) in a cohesive marketing plan. Thoughtfully pricing the product and placing it can help define and differentiate the marketing strategy and play a crucial role in the success of the business. As marketing and promotion gain importance, several career options designed to transmit messages to the target market about the company's image, product lines, and services have also gained importance. These career tracks include marketing director and manager, product marketing manager, brand marketing manager, digital marketing manager, art director, and copywriter. All work, autonomously and collaboratively, to determine the target market, select the right medium, and clarify promotional goals to reach and penetrate the market. Effective customer relationship management (CRM) is also part of the marketing plan.

Successful marketing identifies the reasons consumers choose to buy products from one company over another. Several global companies have accomplished this objective—from H&M, Forever21, and Zara to Nordstrom, Saks Fifth Avenue, and Macy's. They may be part of the reason why Americans are the world's largest consumer market, with each person purchasing an average of 60 garments per year."[4]

Endnotes

1. Berfield, S., and Baigorri, M., "Zara's Fast-Fashion Edge," *Bloomberg Businessweek*, November 14, 2013.
2. Business of Fashion, "Zara," https://www.businessoffashion.com/organisations/zara
3. The Branding Journal, https://www.thebrandingjournal.com/2015/10/what-is-branding-definition/
4. Bain, M., "Americans have stopped trying to stuff more clothes into their closets," Quartz, February 26, 2018, https://qz.com/1212305/americans-have-stopped-trying-to-stuff-more-clothes-into-their-closets/

Online Resources

www.hoovers.com
www.fortune.com/2013/01/08/meet-amancio-ortega
  -the-third-richest-man-in-the-world/
www.businessweek.com/articles/2013-11-14/2014
  -outlook-zaras-fashion-supply-chain-edge
www.thefashionlaw.com/home/is-fast-fashion-dying
  -or-is-it-just-hm
wwd.com/business-news/marketing-promotion/gallery
  /the-best-fashion-ad-campaigns-spring-2018
  -11083452/

Key Terms

art director
brand marketing manager
branding
channel of distribution
client/customer relationship
  management (CRM)
chief marketing officer
  (CMO)
copywriter
creative director

diffusion labels
digital marketing manager
distribution
marketing director
marketing manager
marketing mix
marketing plan
product marketing manager
target market
wholesale

Discussion Questions

1. Evaluate the five Ps of marketing and assess why each is important to the company's marketing strategy. Rank them in order of importance, in your perspective, and explain why one is more important than another.

2. Construct a two-column chart and identify the differences and similarities between *marketing* and *promotion*.

3. Outline the advantages and disadvantages of the various advertising media. Consider newspapers, magazines, online advertising, radio, television, mailers, billboards, etc.

4. Discuss the importance of customer service. What constitutes good or valuable customer service—in-store and online? Examine each separately.

CHAPTER 9
MERCHANDISING FOR THE RETAILER

How simple is it to find a new pair of jeans to buy? All you have to do is go to the nearest discount, department, or specialty store, or order the jeans online at your favorite apparel Web site. Have you ever wondered how the dozens or even hundreds of pairs of blue jeans ended up at the retail store or Web site in the first place (Figures 9.1a–c)? Who decided which brands and styles of jeans the retailer would sell and which ones it would not? Chances are, a buyer indirectly influenced your wardrobe. Effective retail buying is so important to the success of retailers that they are finding innovative ways to include their customers in buying decisions.

Modcloth.com knows this and invites its customers to be part of its buying process. Sometimes, Modcloth's retail buyers adore certain designs and want to buy them for their customers, but the manufacturer/designer can only put them into production with a large quantity order in hand. For a retail company like Modcloth, it is difficult to make these big inventory commitments without knowing if customers will love the designs as much as the buyers do. Both the manufacturing and retailing sides of the business are looking for ways to minimize their risks.

Rather than looking into a crystal ball, Modcloth created "Be the Buyer," a program that invites the customer to be a virtual member of the ModCloth buying team. Potential designs are posted online, and using the "Pick It" button, customers can vote for their favorites. If a style gets enough votes, it will be manufactured by the designer and sold by ModCloth. When the item a majority of customers selects is produced and becomes available for purchase, the "Pick It" voters will receive an email inviting them to be among the first to buy the design. "Be the Buyer" participants can spread the word about the pieces they chose that won the vote-off by sharing links with their friends via Facebook, Twitter, or email.

Modcloth exemplifies how customers can be included in buying decisions, but the merchandise found in a fashion retail operation is ultimately selected and purchased either by the business owner or a buyer who is employed by the business owner. A buyer can work for a specialty chain (e.g., Gap, The Limited, or Charming Charlie), a department store (e.g., Nordstrom, Macy's, or Saks Fifth Avenue), a privately owned store or boutique, or an online retailer (e.g., Nasty Gal, Zappos, or Zuilily). In large operations, the buying tasks are performed by a team of merchandising specialists who have acquired in-depth knowledge of buying for a specific department or a group of related departments. In small operations, the buying function may be one of many carried out by the company's owner. Alternatively, the small business owner may employ a buyer to purchase merchandise for all of the departments in the retail operation.

Merchandising refers to all of the activities involved in the buying and selling of the retailer's products. The major activities in merchandising are locating and purchasing products, with the preferences of the consumer in mind, and then selling these products at a profit. Merchandising includes extensive research on the department's or store's customers, trying to predict which types of merchandise customers will want to buy for upcoming seasons. Box 9.1 discusses new innovations to help retailers distinguish themselves with personalization of goods, services, and the shopping environment. The selection of products available for sale in a fashion operation is commonly called its **inventory**, or *merchandise assortment*. Who are the people involved in selecting the merchandise assortment, and how do they do it?

Figures 9.1a–c

Have you ever wondered how the dozens or even hundreds of pairs of blue jeans ended up at the retail store or Web site for your selection?

In this chapter, merchandising positions for the retailer are explored. The career options that are discussed include the general merchandising manager, divisional merchandising manager, buyer/fashion merchandiser, assistant buyer, planner, distribution manager/allocator, and merchandising trainee.

GENERAL MERCHANDISING MANAGER

A **general merchandising manager (GMM)** is the boss of the buyers' boss. The GMM leads and manages the buyers of all divisions in a retail operation. This key administrator is responsible for setting the overall strategy and merchandise direction of the retail operation. The GMM develops the buying and selling strategies that will, hopefully, maximize business performance and profitability. The GMM ensures that pricing decisions, promotional strategies, and marketing activities support the financial objectives of the merchandising team. To accomplish this, the GMM must understand not only the competitors' strengths, weaknesses, and strategies, but also the customers' demographics, wants, and needs, as well as merchandise trends in all departments.

GMMs set the merchandise direction to ensure a focused continuity on the selling floor. They work with the divisional merchandising managers and buyers to develop competitive merchandise assortments that appeal to customers at the right prices and at the right fashion level. They also assist the buying staff with securing the best merchandise exclusives, product launches, and deliveries available in the market, as illustrated with Fenty Beauty, a beauty brand collaboration with singer Rihanna and LVHM, and sold through the LVMH subsidiary, Sephora (Figure 9.2). The GMM collaborates with the buying team on which manufacturers or designers, fashion items, and merchandise categories will be carried in depth by the retail organization.

GMMs manage, coach, and develop the buying staff, creating an environment that promotes the professional development of the divisional merchandising managers

SOCIAL MEDIA STRIKES
BOX 9.1   Trends in Merchandising – Personalization Is the New Black

In what seems to many shoppers like a sea of merchandise where everything looks the same – same colors, same quality, same design—retailers at all merchandise levels find success by amping up their personalization efforts, and making their customers feel like their own unique, personal style or need is at the forefront of their shopping experience.

Shoppers want individualized service and products that help them express themselves and help them stand out from the crowd. According to a study by Deloitte, one in four customers are willing to pay more for a personalized product or service, and more retailers are using brick-and-mortar to help bring this to customers. Using data and technology, retailers curate an experience for the in-store shopper and provide them options based on that data to ensure that whatever they purchase is truly their own. And the personalization pays back! When products and services are more personalized, customers are happier. And happy customers like to post their product or experience on social media.

"Due to leaps forward in technology, the products for sale are able to be customized and personalized as well, often while you watch," explains Sterling Plenert, SVP and Sector Leader for Luxury Retail at Callison RTKL. "In-store fabrication facilities are becoming more common and allow everyone to be able to purchase one-of-a-kind products from their favorite brands. This kind of individualized experience is what is making brick-and-mortar retail more exciting than it has ever been. The smart retailer has learned how to keep the environment fresh so that it's new and engaging every visit . . . spaces that make the customer feel special and enhance the experience of making a purchase."

Some retailers are improving on existing products through personalized services:

- De Beers uses blockchain to authenticate its diamonds as conflict-free for shoppers
- L'Oreal is using augmented reality (AR), artificial intelligence (AI) and facial recognition to go beyond simulating make-overs on a screen, adding skin health diagnostics to their capabilities

- Burberry is empowering associates with data and iPads to provide sales associates access to shoppers' purchase histories in order to enable meaningful conversations with customers
- Dr. Scholl's kiosks offer on-the-spot scanning of the foot, noting the areas that receive the most pressure, and recommendation of the appropriate orthotic based on that specific data
- Chanel sales associates change it up by going old school, and send hand-written, personal thank-you notes to customers
- Retailers use former purchase data gleaned from loyalty programs or other data gathering sources to personalize targeted advertising based on prior purchases
- Dresden lets in-store shoppers create their own pair of eyeglasses or sunglasses
- Levi's Taylor Shops allow customers to personalize their Levi's purchases with stenciling, monograms, embroidery, distressing, and more
- Enfagrow uses birth data to tailor messages and sales pushes to moms about products based on the growing baby's age and stage of development

Now it's your turn! What ideas do you have about how to personalize products and services at the places you like to shop?

Sources:

DeLoitte, "The Deloitte consumer review: Made-to-order," 2019, https://www2.deloitte.com/content/dam/Deloitte/ch/Documents/consumer-business/ch-en-consumer-business-made-to-order-consumer-review.pdf

Nicasio, F., "9 examples of personalization to try in your retail store," Vend Blog, January 1, 2019, https://www.vendhq.com/blog/examples-of-personalization-retail/

Roberts, J.J., "The diamond industry is obsessed with the blockchain," Fortune, September 12, 2017, http://fortune.com/2017/09/12/diamond-blockchain-everledger/

Tekscan, Dr. Scholl's kiosks," https://www.tekscan.com/applications/dr-scholls-kiosks

Wassel, B., "The evolving luxury industry embraces social media and personalization," Retail Touchpoints, September 13, 2018, https://www.retailtouchpoints.com/features/trend-watch/the-evolving-luxury-industry-embraces-social-media-and-personalization

Figure 9.2

In collaboration with LVMH, singer Rihanna developed FENTY, an inclusive beauty line, for distribution through Sephora stores worldwide.

and buyers and enhancing morale among the entire buying team. While collaborating with the divisional merchandising managers in developing merchandise assortments that support the needs of the customers and the financial objectives of each merchandise division, GMMs are ultimately responsible for overseeing merchandise selection and procurement of goods by the buyers.

The number of GMM positions is limited, as these are top leadership slots available in midsize and large retail operations. Some companies offer GMMs supplementary packages, such as bonuses or stock options, based on increases in the company's sales volume and gross margin.

DIVISIONAL MERCHANDISING MANAGER

Once you have mastered the buying side of the fashion world as a fashion merchandiser, you may be ready for advancement. Before a buyer becomes a GMM, the next step up the career ladder is to the divisional merchandising manager position. A **divisional merchandising manager (DMM)** works under the GMM and provides leadership for the buying staff of a division, or a related group of departments, such as menswear, women's wear, or home furnishings. DMMs coordinate teamwork among the buyers and delegate responsibilities to the buyers, assistant buyers, and planners. They collaborate with the buyers on future purchases, marketing and promotional efforts, merchandise expenditures, and inventory management. The main objective of the DMM is to keep profits up and losses down by maximizing sales and minimizing markdowns. They also study the fashion industry through shopping the competition, forecasting trends, attending markets, and working with buyers on the right fashion directions for the upcoming season.

In general, DMMs oversee the work of the buyers in a particular department of the business. Specifically, their job responsibilities include the following:

- Developing merchandise strategies in support of the total company
- Managing, coaching, and developing the buying staff, to include assistant buyers
- Mentoring and fostering an environment that promotes the development of buyers and their businesses as a divisional buying team
- Setting the overall strategy and merchandise direction for the division
- Directing buyers to develop assortments that support the needs of the customer and the financial objectives of the merchandise division
- Ensuring that pricing, promotional strategies, and marketing support the financial objectives of the merchandise division
- Working with the planning organization to develop by-store assortment plans that support the overall plan for positioning key merchandise categories, selected trends, items, and vendors

- Working with the buyers to strengthen market relationships and knowledge of market trends
- Understanding competitors' strengths, weaknesses, and strategies
- Facilitating and promoting timely communication and cooperation between branch stores, merchandising functions, and resources

Are you looking for a leadership role in the buying division? What does it take to be at the highest levels of the merchandising career ladder? While it takes intelligence, perseverance, and a high level of energy, the retail employer will expect a high level of qualifications as well. Because the GMM and DMM positions have similar education requirements, experience expectations, characteristics, and challenges, a list of the qualifications and discussion of career challenges for a top-notch GMM or DMM follows.

Qualifications

- *Education.* A bachelor's degree in fashion merchandising, retailing, retail merchandising, management, marketing, business administration, or a related field is necessary. A master's degree in these fields may be required.
- *Experience.* A minimum of ten years of retail management, divisional merchandise management, or extensive buying experience is often required for the GMM. Five to seven years of retail buying experience is typically required for the DMM position. For both, administrative experience in a full-line department store, specialty store chain, or e-commerce site is usually required for this key administrative position. Experience in multi-location retail stores as a merchandiser or with multiple delivery systems (e.g., brick-and-mortar, Internet, and catalogue) and product development is preferred.
- *Personal characteristics.* Strong leadership, organizational, and financial skills are necessary. The ability to change priorities and work topics quickly is a needed personal quality. Being able to manage teams and relate to all levels of employees is important. Excellent communication and negotiation skills are critical for the successful DMM and GMM, as are being able to plan

ahead and be an analytical problem solver. In terms of personality, the best GMMs and DMMs are articulate, enthusiastic, and charismatic.

Career Challenges

As leaders of the merchandising staff, the GMM and DMM must understand the team of merchandising personnel and all of their merchandise classifications. Leading a group of diverse buyers working in a wide range of departments requires a great deal of multitasking and prioritizing. It is critical to be able to move quickly between buyers and their respective departments and be up to date on each of their areas. As leaders, the GMM and DMM are challenged to keep all merchandisers on the same path in terms of merchandise selection, price ranges, fashion trends, and similar variables. They need to know when to push or pull back buyers who are not meeting sales goals or buying into the designated fashion trend statements.

The GMM and DMM are often held accountable for the accuracy of the numbers the buyers submit, such as planned sales and inventories. In summary, these executives must specialize in a variety of areas—fashion, merchandising retail mathematics, vendor negotiations, and personnel management.

BUYER OR FASHION MERCHANDISER

Are you someone who enjoys the thrill of the shopping hunt? Do you enjoy trend forecasting and being involved in product development? Are attending markets and purchasing the newest trends to sell to customers enticing job tasks for you? Do you have, or can you acquire, skills in retail mathematics? Then you may want to pursue a career as a buyer/fashion merchandiser. **Buyers**, or *fashion merchandisers* or *retail buyers*, are typically responsible for all of the product purchases for a company or particular department of a company within a certain budget. Buyers monitor the fashion trends and determine which seasonal items their customers will buy. They search for the items (often traveling to do so) that best fit the seasonal theme and their customers' preferences, primarily during market weeks at apparel markets. They locate the right merchandise suppliers and negotiate prices, shipping, and discounts. They sometimes work with other departments in the retail operation, such as advertising and visual merchandising, on promotions and product placement. Read the interview in Box 9.2 with the Women's Contemporary Apparel Buyer of Zappo's.

The ultimate goal of a buyer is to recognize trends that fit with the target market in terms of taste and price, procure merchandise that reflects these trends, and translate them into a profitable business plan for the retailer. Buyers select and purchase products from designers, manufacturers, or wholesalers for retail sale to their customers.

CASE STUDIES IN CAREER EXPLORATION

BOX 9.2   Interview with Women's Contemporary Apparel Buyer for Zappos.com, Mandy Raines-Cordia

Interviewed by Michele M. Granger

When did you realize you wanted to work in fashion merchandising?

I knew from a young age that I wanted to work in the fashion industry. A family friend introduced me to the business when he was buying children's clothing and asked me what I would want to wear. When I discovered the job required traveling and shopping, I knew it was for me. If only I had known then that buying is a little more complicated than just traveling and shopping.

What was your path to where you are today?

I grew up in a small city where my passion for shopping and fashion led me to major in fashion merchandising and minor in business at a local university. Once I graduated college, I started out in the industry as a Merchandise Assistant for a television retailer. Since then, I've been lucky enough to hold a few different positions in the industry, including working on the wholesale side in sales and product development, buying for a small boutique, and working as an assistant buyer for a department store before landing my current buying role for a major online retailer. I learned along the way that my passion is for the nontraditional retailer, and the online space is where I feel the most at home. Growing up in a small town, my shopping options were limited. I love the Internet because it put anything and everything at my fingertips. I have bought several different categories over the years, from handbags to footwear, jewelry to housewares, and accessories to beauty, before arriving in apparel. I feel like a good buyer can buy anything, but it helps to be passionate about the category you are buying.

Figure Box 9.2
Buyer for Zappos, Mandy Raines-Cordia.

What are your position responsibilities?

Simply put, my job as a buyer is to have the right product, at the right time, at the right price. Buying is a lot of numbers and analysis (which is ironic because I never liked a single math class I took in school). I create sales plans and budgets for a group of brands, travel to market to select product based on customer demand (not my own personal demand), negotiate with suppliers, track sales and performance for these suppliers, manage inventory levels based on sales, research trends, report selling history and trends, strategize to optimize business, and the list goes on. As a buyer, you routinely collaborate with other divisions within your organization. I work very closely with marketing, legal, planning, and accounting, just to name a few.

Do you use social media in your work? If so, for what purposes?

As an e-commerce buyer, social media has become an important part of my job. Social media has bridged the gap between brands/designers/businesses and the end consumer like never before. We use social media to increase site traffic, generate brand awareness, engage consumers, and build customer loyalty. I personally have more interaction with Pinterest and Instagram as a way to share trends and outfit inspiration through product placement.

What do you love most about what you do?

I have always been entrepreneurial minded and have wanted to run my own business. As a buyer, I have that feeling of running my own business without the personal financial commitment. I have the power to make the decisions I feel will grow and support the business. I am responsible for my successes, as well as the failures. I am held accountable for my decisions but encouraged to take risks. It's exciting to see the product you selected do well and see a risk pay off. I love taking a struggling brand, growing it, and taking it to the next level.

What have been your toughest challenges?

Life is full of challenges, and the fashion industry is no exception. I personally struggle with the fact that there will always be factors beyond my control that will affect my business no matter how prepared I think I am. I cannot control the weather, the economy, a supplier's manufacturing capabilities, company directives, or shipping mishaps—all impact my business. As a buyer, sometimes all you can do is adapt and adjust going forward. I work very hard to achieve my sales goals and have a hard time not taking lackluster sales personally. I have to remind myself to breathe and let it go. If I've done everything I can do, I have no choice but to let it go, learn from it, and be prepared for the next time.

What kind of skills have you learned from your experiences, and/or what skills do successful fashion buyers have?

I started out in the industry young and naïve, but I had a willingness to learn. I have learned so much through a wide variety of experiences, but here are a few things that have benefitted me the most:

1. Never stop learning. Learn from your mistakes, learn about the industry, learn about new innovations, and learn about current events as they will all impact your buying decisions
2. Be able to build relationships through honesty and trust
3. If you don't already have it, invest in some thick skin. It will pay dividends
4. Communication skills are a must. You have to be able to effectively communicate the needs, strategy, and results of your business
5. Never settle for the status quo. There will always be opportunity for improvement
6. Never take a job for the money. The money will come and experience is priceless

What advice would you give to aspiring fashion buyers?

Someone once told me that if you do a job you are passionate about, you will never work a day in your life. This is so true. My job is not a 9 to 5 job, and it's rare that I ever get to disconnect from email. It doesn't feel so glamorous when you are trekking New York City with a laptop and line sheets in a foot of snow in February when it's 20 degrees, and you realize your favorite designer boots are not waterproof in a puddle of slush. It's not glamorous, though it has its moments. You really have to love the industry and job to be a buyer, or you will feel like you are working every single day.

Second, as with anything in life, stay determined to reach your goals and dreams. You will encounter bumps along the way. You might get fired from your first job, you might work for a difficult boss, you might get passed up for a promotion, you might make the wrong decision on product a few times, and you will probably encounter situations where you will have to make difficult decisions. Never let a job, a boss, a missed opportunity, or the fear of change keep you from your goals. Everything happens for a reason, every challenge is a chance to learn, and every closed door is a new opportunity. Trust me on this one.

Source:

Courtesy of Mandy Raines-Cordia.

They use their fashion sense, knowledge of trends, and understanding of their target customers' wants to purchase desirable merchandise assortments at markets for their retail businesses (Figure 9.3). Due to the length of time it takes for a designer or manufacturer to fill orders, buyers often make their purchases three to six months in advance, or longer if they are high-fashion goods. Buyers must be effective at budgeting and planning their assortments so that a good selection of products is always available to the consumer. Buyers for larger retail operations usually specialize in a merchandise classification, such as men's tailored apparel or home tabletop fashions.

To get started, a buyer begins with an analysis of the numbers—sales, markdowns, and inventories by month for the past year or a few years. Next, the buyer develops a buying plan, usually six months to one year before the merchandise can be purchased by customers. The six-month **buying plan**, or six-month plan, is a financial plan that takes into account past and projected sales, inventory, markups and markdowns by department, and profit, or **gross margin**. After developing the buying plan, the buyer tracks and analyzes market trends, calculates how much will be spent on new products, and then goes to markets and meets with manufacturers to preview apparel that will be produced (Figure 9.4). Once the manufacturers' lines are reviewed, the buyer places orders for merchandise to

arrive in the future, from one month for reorders to as much as one year in advance for new merchandise.

Being a fashion merchandiser or buyer is like being a product developer, with a twist. Instead of reinventing the wheel every season, the buyer takes the retailer's bestsellers from the previous season or year and finds the item with slight changes. The buyer may locate an item that was a bestseller with an updated color or new styling detail. The result is a new item with a good sales history for the upcoming selling season. A fashion merchandiser also makes decisions on new, fashion-forward merchandise. The buyer always wants fresh, trendy looks to welcome customers into the department.

This career path, however, is not all about shopping. The fashion merchandiser is accountable for the bottom line. The company wants to know whether the merchandise selected for customers to buy has made a profit. Fashion merchandisers are responsible for the financials of their departments and the resulting profit or loss. It is a daily task for fashion merchandisers to track the sales of merchandise and decide whether items need to be reordered or put on sale. They also spend time talking with vendors and negotiating the best wholesale prices so that higher profits can be achieved. Because most fashion merchandisers have worked their way through the ranks, they also know how important it is to communicate with

Figure 9.3
Collaborating with the visual merchandising department, the buyer plans visual presentation strategies for the stores to support seasonal trends.

Figure 9.4
After developing the buying plan, the buyer analyzes market trends, calculates how much will be spent on new products, and then attends markets to preview apparel lines.

the department and store managers and solicit feedback about what customers are seeking, buying, and rejecting. A career as a fashion merchandiser is a very exciting and rewarding one for a high-energy person, as shown in Box 9.3, which features a classified advertisement for the shoe buyer position with a luxury retailer.

The most important task performed by the buyer is selecting merchandise for the retail operation. This responsibility encompasses determining which goods are needed, calculating the size of purchases and from which vendors the goods should be bought, recognizing when merchandise should be ordered for timely delivery, and negotiating the prices and terms of a sale. From a planning perspective, the buyer projects sales and inventory levels by month for each department and, subsequently, determines the amount of funding to be spent on inventory. Another part of the planning process is determining merchandise assortments in terms of color, size, and style. The amount of money allocated for new merchandise purchases each month is referred to as **open-to-buy**. With open-to-buy as the lead factor, the buyer determines which lines will be carried in large quantities and which ones will be stocked in smaller quantities. Those manufacturers' lines featured as the greatest proportion of a retailer's inventory are called **key vendors**. Lines carried in smaller quantities are referred to as **secondary vendors**.

Buyers have a great number of responsibilities in addition to locating the vendors, selecting and purchasing the right amount of the right merchandise, and setting prices on the merchandise, primarily depending on the size of the retail operation. In addition to purchasing goods, buyers often handle tasks that relate to merchandising in other departments in the company. For example, they may assign floor space for items or lines, select specific merchandise for visual displays and advertisements, and manage or collaborate with personnel in various areas of the business. A buyer may hold training seminars to educate management and sales staffs on the newest trends and product lines. In multi-unit retail operations, the buyer advises receiving or warehouse personnel on how many units, sizes, and/or colors of a style should be shipped to or transferred from one branch store or another. With the advertising department, the buyer determines marketing plans and promotional calendars for each month. Collaborating with the visual merchandising department, the buyer plans visual presentation strategies for the stores, to support seasonal trends (Figure 9.5). For example, the buyer may meet with the director of visual merchandising to discuss color trends, specific manufacturers' lines, and key fashion items that should be featured in windows and interior displays to give the retail operation a strong, fashion-forward look and, ultimately, sell products.

BOX 9.3 SHOE BUYER FOR A LUXURY FASHION RETAILER

Job Responsibilities:

- Manage, update, and review open-to-buy
- Extensive data analysis, financial, and retail data modeling
- Evaluate competitive market trends within the luxury environment
- Partner with Global Merchandising team, Retail Performance Manager, Visual Merchandising Manager, and Press Team to effectively collaborate and communicate goals and objectives
- Select/place seasonal market orders
- Project seasonal sales
- Review weekly sales reports, ensuring planned sales and inventory levels are achieved
- Place and confirm reorders as needed
- Manage return-to-vendors
- Review and follow up with deliveries
- Manage stock placement for new merchandise
- Update and manage purchase orders
- Place and confirm special orders as needed
- Manage inventory for store events
- Recap show and incentive results
- Monitor product performance; make stock projections, review sales and net receipts

- Oversee stock balances
- Review sales results on advertising campaigns and catalogue styles
- Prepare and review fast/slow sellers report
- Prepare and review sell-through report
- Provide end of season (EOS) product analysis and final sales report
- Provide EOS final sale reports

Skills and Competencies:

- Ability to effectively manage merchandise coordinator
- Strategic agility
- Excellent organizational skills and drive for results
- Ability to train, manage, and inspire a growing team

Job Requirements:

- Four to six years prior merchandising experience; luxury retail preferred
- Availability for frequent travel; national and international
- Strong knowledge of Microsoft Office programs (e.g., Excel, PivotTable, and Word)

Figure 9.5

Buyers use their fashion sense, knowledge of trends, and understanding of their target customers to purchase desirable merchandise for their retail businesses.

Qualifications

Do you love to travel, enjoy searching for a specific item, and have proficient mathematical and analytical skills? You may consider the career path of buyer. What are the education and work experiences you will need to secure a position in this field? Which personal characteristics are significant to the success of a buyer? The answers to these questions are as follows:

- *Education.* A bachelor's degree in fashion merchandising, retailing, retail merchandising, or a related field is required. A minor or additional coursework in business administration and fashion design is very helpful.
- *Experience.* Two to five years of work in the apparel industry is required for a buyer, including retail or sales experience. Retail sales experience is very helpful, because understanding customer buying behavior is a

key part of being a successful buyer. The common step into a buyer position is from assistant buyer. To move up the career ladder, buyers gain experience buying for a variety of departments, usually moving from one department to another of higher sales volume.

- *Personal characteristics.* Successful buyers love fashion and have knowledge of fashion history and trends, as well as an understanding of the fashion industry as a whole. They have good analytical, mathematical, and computer skills (e.g., Microsoft Excel), particularly in budgeting, planning, and inventory management. Successful buyers are good negotiators, possess excellent communication and organizational skills, are detail oriented, and are able to deal well with deadlines and stress.

The outlook for career opportunities in buying is very good to excellent. The number of new buyer positions available is expected to remain stable, and existing positions will become available because of internal promotions or transitions. One can grow on the job by being promoted to the buyer's position in a larger department with greater sales volume.

Career Challenges

There are many buyer positions available in the fashion industry; however, buyers excel by showing maintained profitability and growth within their departments and by making good buying decisions for their particular target markets. Because the numbers tell the story, buyers are under pressure to reach or surpass sales-volume goals while maintaining the planned inventory levels—every single month. If a line does not sell, the buyer is expected to negotiate with the vendor for returns, exchanges, or a reduced price to cover the cost of markdowns. Items planned for advertising can be a source of stress if they are not delivered as planned. The buyer has a multitude of tasks to juggle, and all of them require high attention to detail and quick turnarounds.

ASSISTANT BUYER

An **assistant buyer** works directly for the buyer of a department or group of related departments. Assistant buyers primarily work with the six-month plan, open-to-buy, and inventory, taking cues from buyers. In some companies, they will accompany buyers to markets. They often work hands-on with the merchandise assortment, transferring items from one retail location to another as needed, and placing special orders. In most companies, the assistant buyer is in training for a buying position in the future.

Qualifications

Following are the education and work experience requirements for the assistant buyer, as well as necessary personal characteristics:

- *Education.* A bachelor's degree in fashion merchandising, retailing, retail merchandising, or a related field is usually required. Some companies will accept an associate's degree in these disciplines. Additional coursework in business administration and fashion design is very helpful.
- *Experience.* Two to three years of apparel industry experience, including retail or sales experience, is required. Experience in accounting and budgeting is extremely helpful. Some companies have an executive training program to prepare entry-level employees for a merchandising career, often beginning as an assistant buyer.
- *Personal characteristics.* Assistant buyers understand the fashion of today and yesterday—its history and current trends. To move up the career ladder, they must have both a sense of what is fashionable and of who the customer is. Additionally, they should have knowledge of retailing and sales and strong analytical, mathematical, and computer skills, particularly Excel, because their responsibilities include extensive work in budgeting, planning, and inventory management. Assistant buyers who are self-directed and motivated will advance quickly. Effective communication and organizational skills, attention to detail, an eye for accuracy, and the ability to work well under pressure are significant attributes.

College graduates who begin at the assistant buyer level and have the right skills, personal qualities, and ambition have a good chance of becoming full-fledged buyers within three to five years.

Career Challenges

Many assistant buyers describe their job responsibilities as "doing what the buyer does not want to do, or does not have time to do." The key word in the job title is "assistant," as this person is employed to help the buyer accomplish all merchandising tasks. Some buyers believe it is a part of their responsibilities to educate assistant buyers on all it takes to become a buyer; others do not. Some buyers do not want to retrain a new assistant and, consequently, prefer to keep their assistant buyers in this position. It can be a challenge for the assistant buyer to learn all of the ropes of merchandising and earn the support of the buyer to move into a buying position, but it can be accomplished. Anticipating what needs to be done and doing it well and independently are keys to succeeding in this position.

PLANNER

In large companies, a **planner** works in collaboration with a buyer to develop sales forecasts, inventory plans, and spending budgets for merchandise to minimize markdowns and achieve the retailer's sales and profit objectives. Using past sales data and sales projections based on fashion trends, planners construct merchandise assortments for specific departments. The merchandise assortment plan can include sizes, colors, styles, price ranges, and classifications. For example, a planner in a junior sportswear department may construct a chart, referred to as a planning module, for top-to-bottom ratios. In this **planning module**, the planner will project how many blouses, T-shirts, and tank tops to purchase and how many pants, shorts, or skirts need to be purchased for a given season. Today's junior customer, for instance, buys two to four times as many tops as she does bottoms. The merchandise assortment needs to reflect this proportion to be profitable. Using the planning module, planners recommend product flow (e.g., tanks, tees, and long-sleeved shirts) by department and by month or season. They also project markdown dollar budgets by month or season, based on actual markdowns during prior seasons, and assist buyers in determining how much money will be available to spend on new merchandise by providing seasonal buying budgets and monthly open-to-buy dollars by department and by season.

In addition to planning at the start of a season, planners in multi-unit retail firms review sales and stock performance by retail location as it compares to plans. They also ensure that key vendor plans are in place and that there is adequate inventory for the sales of major lines. Throughout each season, the planner coordinates communication to and from stores with regard to merchandise performance and sales plans. A department manager in the retail store may, for example, contact a planner for additional types of items that have sold out in the store. The planner will transfer the preferred merchandise into this store from a branch store that has not sold the items as well.

In partnership with the buying staff, the planner's main goal is to accurately anticipate and control inventories at the retail locations to maximize sales, inventory, and profit. The planner works to keep all store locations in stock of key items by directing the distribution of goods through reorders and transfers of merchandise. If you enjoy working with numbers, are accurate, and want to move into buying, the position of planner is a great place to begin.

Qualifications

A listing of the educational background, experience, and personal characteristics needed for the job of merchandise planner follows:

- *Education.* A bachelor's degree in fashion merchandising, retailing, accounting, finance, or a related field is a prerequisite. Some companies hire candidates who have completed a two-year associate degree in one of these fields for the position of assistant planner.
- *Experience.* Gaining retail sales experience is an excellent way for the future planner to start. The person who understands the customer's desires as they pertain to sales and inventory is a step ahead of job candidates without this work experience.
- *Personal characteristics.* Planners must be detail oriented with strong analytical skills. They must be quick, accurate, and able to work with advanced spreadsheet applications. Effective interpersonal and communication skills are important in this position, as is the ability to work well with all levels of employees of the organization.

Some larger retail organizations offer the position of planning manager. A **planning manager** provides leadership, direction, and support at the merchandise-division level to plan, distribute, and monitor inventory appropriately within the company's various retail locations to maximize sales. The planning manager supervises the planners and supports the buyer and DMM in the financial planning process.

Career Challenges

The planner is a number cruncher, and this may be a challenging job for the fashion graduate entering the merchandising field. Although being a planner is an excellent entry-level position for the future assistant buyer or buyer, it can be a tough tour of duty for those who are interested in working with the actual merchandise. The important thing to remember is that those numbers represent the merchandise, and there is much to be learned in the planner's position. Accuracy is a critical part of this job, as one decimal point off can equal thousands of the company's dollars.

DISTRIBUTION MANAGER/ ALLOCATOR

Have you ever thought about how merchandise gets to the retail floor for customers to purchase? A **distribution manager**, or *allocator*, is responsible for planning and managing merchandise deliveries received from vendors, as ordered by buyers, to the retail locations. In some companies, this position is referred to as *replenishment analyst*. The merchandise is held in a central distribution warehouse to be allotted to the right store, at the right time, and in the right quantities to meet customer demands and maximize sales for the retail stores. Figure 9.6 depicts an allocator assessing the inventory of merchandise of each store unit prior to distribution of the shipment.

Distribution managers oversee merchandise receipts from manufacturers, shipments to the retail stores from the distribution center, and shipments from one store to another via the distribution center. They arrange for the transportation of merchandise to the retail outlet locations and may work for catalog and Internet distribution centers, where they are responsible for keeping items in stock in the warehouse. Their main job is to be certain that merchandise is available when a customer stops by a store or orders an item over the phone, by mail, or via the Internet. Distribution managers have some of the responsibilities of buyers. They must study sales and inventory reports and then analyze the needs of each individual retail store to determine the correct quantities to distribute to the stores.

Qualifications

If you are detail oriented and organized, and enjoy working with merchandise and numbers (while not on a sales floor), this career path may be ideal for you, if you meet the following criteria:

Figure 9.6
An allocator assesses the merchandise inventory of each store unit prior to distribution of the shipment of soft goods.

- *Education.* A bachelor's degree in fashion merchandising, retailing, business administration, or a related field is usually required. Some firms hire employees with associate's degrees in these fields.
- *Experience.* One of the most important backgrounds for the distribution manager may be surprising. It is retail experience. Working on the sales floor, observing the flow of merchandise, and getting to know the customer provide a future distribution manager with a solid foundation for this career. An internship in a distribution department is an ideal door-opener. Merchandising experience, such as being an assistant buyer, is another way of going into distribution management.
- *Personal characteristics.* Good problem-solving skills, detail and deadline orientation, the ability to coordinate scheduling, and strong math skills are important personal characteristics for distribution managers. Effective communication skills are important as well.

Opportunities for distribution manager positions can be found throughout the industry with major retailers of all kinds.

Career Challenges

If merchandise is not on the selling floor, then it will not sell. A distribution manager, or allocator, is under pressure to push products out of the distribution warehouse to the correct retail store quickly and in the right amounts, after it is tagged correctly. During pre-holiday times, when there are huge amounts of merchandise receipts and many buyers calling to check on the distribution of their orders, this is particularly challenging. Speed, organization, and accuracy must go hand in hand in this career track.

MERCHANDISING TRAINEE

One avenue by which college graduates often choose to move into a merchandising career track is through an executive training program. Many retailers, particularly larger ones, offer these programs, which help graduates work their way up to buying positions. For example, the executive training programs at Neiman Marcus, Saks Fifth Avenue, Macy's, Nordstrom, and Bloomingdale's prepare participants for jobs as assistant buyers and, ultimately, buyers for the company.

A **merchandising executive training program** is designed for new hires, former interns, college recruits, or current employees who have shown skills in merchandising, to prepare them for their first assignments as assistant buyers. Through on-the-job and classroom training, trainees gain the necessary skills needed for analyzing financial data, planning assortment selections, and developing vendor relationships to achieve business goals. The executive training program is a structured development program of classes, guest speakers, and projects. The trainee must show active participation and successfully complete all of the training assignments within the time frame of the program, which can range from six weeks to twelve months.

Qualifications

What do you need to know to become a merchandising trainee?

- *Education.* A bachelor's degree in fashion merchandising, retail merchandising, retailing, business administration, or a related field is often required.
- *Experience.* Retail sales experience and, possibly, an internship with a retail organization are work experiences that make a potential merchandising executive trainee appealing to a retailer. Many companies require trainee candidates to complete tests that reveal proficiency in the areas of mathematics, case study analysis, writing, and presentation skills.
- *Personal characteristics.* Merchandising trainees exhibit strong analytical abilities, effective computer skills, organizational skills, and excellent communication skills—written, oral, and visual. Effective time management, flexibility, and the ability to react quickly and calmly to change are also important attributes. Successful merchandise trainees are self-motivated, self-directed, and able to work effectively as part of a team.

Career Challenges

There are very few career disadvantages when starting as a merchandising trainee with a major company. You select the company of your choice, secure the trainee position, and the company prepares you for an entry-level executive position. These training programs are often referred to as a form of graduate education without the price tag. Although you do not earn college credits or pay tuition, you do receive additional education that can be applied directly to the company. Frequently, the tough part is making the cut or securing the position. Company recruiters often interview 1,000 candidates for fewer than 100 trainee openings. In some firms, trainees complete a general company training program and then are assigned to either the merchandising or management track, based on their performance in the program. For those trainees who have their hearts set on one track or the other, this may be a difficult assignment if it does not match their preference.

Summary

Merchandising encompasses all of the activities involved in the buying and selling of a retailer's products. The major responsibilities of merchandising personnel are to locate and purchase products, with the consumer's preferences in mind, and then sell these products at a profit. Merchandising career opportunities include the following positions: general merchandising manager, divisional merchandising manager, buyer/fashion merchandiser, assistant buyer, planner, distribution manager or allocator, and merchandising trainee.

General merchandising managers (GMMs) lead and manage the buyers of all divisions in the retail operation. They are the key administrators responsible for setting the overall strategy and merchandise direction of their retail operations. The divisional merchandising manager (DMM) works under the GMM and provides leadership for the buying staff of a division or a related group of departments. Buyers, or fashion merchandisers, are typically responsible for all of the product purchases for a company or particular segment of the company within a certain budget. Buyers monitor fashion trends and determine which seasonal items their customers will purchase. They search for the items at trade marts that best fit the seasonal theme and their customers' preferences and negotiate prices, shipping, and discounts. They then monitor sales and inventory, adjusting the prices of merchandise and the amount of money they spend on new items accordingly. The assistant buyer works directly for the buyer of a department or group of related departments (e.g., handbags, jewelry, and scarves). The assistant buyer helps the buyer with updating the six-month plan, open-to-buy, and inventory. The planner works in collaboration with the buyer and assistant buyer to develop sales forecasts, inventory plans, and spending budgets for merchandise to achieve sales and profit objectives. The distribution manager, or allocator, is responsible for planning and managing the deliveries of goods received from the vendors, as ordered by the buyers, to retail locations. A merchandising, or merchant, executive training program is designed to prepare new hires, former interns, college recruits, or current employees who have shown skills in merchandising for their first assignment in the merchandising division of the retail operation. There are many career tracks in merchandising for the retailer, and they have several challenges in common—locating products that appeal to the customer, are priced right, arrive at the right place when needed, and sell!

Key Terms

assistant buyer
buyer
buying plan
distribution manager
divisional merchandising
    manager (DMM)
general merchandising
    manager (GMM)
gross margin
inventory

key vendor
merchandising
merchandising executive
    training program
open-to-buy
planner
planning manager
planning module
secondary vendor

Online Resources

Discussion Questions

1. Consider a major department store and construct a diagram separating the departments into divisions that would be headed by three separate divisional merchandise managers. Bracket together the departments that would be covered by an individual buyer.

2. Visit a menswear store or the men's department in a large retail operation to study how the merchandise may be segmented into classifications. Develop the categories for the merchandise plan of a men's sportswear department, including merchandise classifications, styles, sizes, colors, and price ranges.

3. Assume that you are the buyer for a large home accessories department. How will you divide the responsibilities of the planner and the assistant buyer assigned to your department? Compare and contrast the duties of each.

CHAPTER 10

MANAGEMENT FOR THE RETAILER

If you are a person who loves the retail experience, you may envision yourself running a specialty store, an exclusive boutique, a designer outlet, a Web site, or a large department store. You may be someone who thrives in a retail environment and craves the excitement of getting new merchandise onto the sales floor, assisting customers with purchases, motivating sales associates, and challenging yourself and your team to surpass last year's sales figures. If this describes you, a career in retail management may be your path to profit and pleasure.

Management refers to the organizing and controlling of the affairs of a business or a particular sector of a business. This chapter focuses on management careers in the retail sector of the fashion industry, such as manager of an apparel store, manager of an Internet fashion operation, or assistant manager of a factory outlet. There are several career tracks in retail management, including the following positions: regional manager, operations manager, retail store manager, manager-in-training (MIT), assistant and associate store manager, department manager, customer service manager, and retail operation entrepreneur or store owner.

REGIONAL MANAGER

Regional store managers, also known as *area* or *district managers*, are responsible for directing the retail stores of a particular company that are located in a particular area of the country. An **international store manager** supervises store sales and staff performance in a different country, or group of countries, not in the company's country of residence. Whether in the United States or abroad, these regional managers are responsible for the smooth operation and profitability of the company, as well as the success of employees in the retail outlets located within a specific geographic area (often referred to as an area, district, region, or territory). They are the liaisons between the corporate office and the retail stores in their territories. They collaborate with their store managers and other employees by making store visits, communicating through e-mail or telephone, and facilitating conferences, in person or electronically.

During these meetings, store managers share their current sales, markdowns, and returns; point out items that are selling well and those that are not; and identify promotional programs or incentives for employees that are increasing sales or traffic flow into the store. If sales are declining, regional managers work with store managers to stimulate sales by implementing in-store promotions or working with the retail organization's headquarters on promotional campaigns. The four main goals of the regional store manager are to (1) maximize sales at a profit, (2) motivate store employees, (3) share successes from one store with another, and (4) communicate with the corporate office. Box 10.1 provides descriptions of L Brands retail store management positions—the parent company of Victoria's Secret, Bath & Bodyworks, and Pink.

Qualifications

If regional store management is your career choice, the following educational goals, work experiences, and personal characteristics will help you get a foot in the door:

- *Education.* A bachelor's degree in fashion merchandising, fashion retailing, business administration, retailing, management, or a related field is a requirement.

CASE STUDIES IN CAREER EXPLORATION

BOX 10.1   Management Career Track with L Brands

L Brands is the parent company for three successful retail brands—Victoria's Secret, PINK, and Bath & Bodyworks. Victoria's Secret has more than 1,600 retail stores and more than $7.3 million in sales. Bath & Bodyworks has sales reaching $4.5 million and operates more than 1,800 stores worldwide with eighty stores in twenty different countries under franchise, licensing, and wholesale arrangements. PINK nets over $7.3 million with over 150 stores and outlets worldwide. With more than 88,000 associates worldwide, this global powerhouse is a company offering opportunity.

L Brands goal is to make every moment for the customer special. This often means that associates at every level of the management and sales team wear many hats to ensure the brand is well represented and the customer's desires are fulfilled. Opportunities in retail management with L Brands include:

Regional Manager: A seasoned leader, the Regional Manager is a coach and mentor with ten-plus years of retail management experience. Someone with demonstrated success leading strategic and operational initiatives that drive sales profitability, improve sales ROI (return-on-investment), drive field enthusiasm around new programs, and optimize sales efficiencies across their districts. This is achieved through establishing creative yet focused direction setting and coaching and developmental activities of their teams. Responsibility also resides in building top talent sales succession strategies and influencing home office decisions.

District Manager: A capable, self-directed leader, who holds a Bachelor's degree or equivalent experience, and with five to seven years of retail management experience. The District Manager (DM) ensures consistent execution of the customer service and operational execution in all district stores. An L Brands DM is responsible for brand and relationship building, recruiting and developing a talented and diverse workforce that will drive profitable top-line sales growth. The District Manager is the linchpin to execution in the stores and market growth within the district.

Store Manager: The Store Manager is an outgoing and engaging leader who is creative, dynamic, and possesses an independent spirit for people and fashion. These leaders embody the day-to-day principles and values of the brand. They coach and develop store associates to consistently provide a positive customer experience by offering products, information, and a shopping experience that will build brand loyalty. Store managers handle the operational execution of the stores through positive service experiences that will drive profitable top-line sales growth. Enjoy the best of both worlds: operate like an independent store owner with the support of the top "best in class" specialty retailer.

Co-Manager: This professional will assist the Store Manager in managing the operational execution of the store to ensure positive customer experiences and to drive profitable top-line sales growth. L Brands look for candidates who take ownership of a unique division of responsibility in areas such as driving the store's visual execution; attracting, hiring, training, and developing all levels of associates; or managing the backroom process and reducing shrinkage.

Sources:

L Brands, "Job areas," https://careers.lb.com/job-areas/

L Brands, "FAQ," https://careers.lb.com/faq/

Zaczkiewicz, A., "L Brands seen as top specialty retail player," WWD, January 27, 2016, https://wwd.com/business-news/financial/victoria-secret-parent-lbrands-retail-performance-10332336/

- *Experience.* Retail sales and store management experience are mandatory work experiences. Buying, advertising, visual merchandising, human resource development, marketing, inventory control, and customer service knowledge are areas of experience that will move a regional manager candidate to the top of the list. Previous work success as an assistant store manager and store manager gives the job candidate an edge over the competition.

- *Personal characteristics.* Strong communication and leadership skills are required. The ability to speak effectively to individuals and groups is important. Accounting skills, human resources knowledge, motivation and conflict skills, and an understanding of retail law are important. Organization, cognitive thinking, and time management are personal skills that support the regional manager's tasks in coordinating stores in a wide geographic area.

Career Challenges

Because they are responsible for several retail locations, regional managers may find their work to be stressful and without time constraints. Regional managers are responsible for not just one store, but a significant number of retail units in the operation. This means they oversee all of the employees who take care of the customers shopping in each store. It takes a person with abundant fashion and retail knowledge, excellent communication skills, and business savvy to succeed in this career choice. Long hours and frequent travel are realities of the job.

OPERATIONS MANAGER

In major companies, an operations manager reports to the regional manager or, in a very large company, the national operations director of stores. The **operations manager** works with other administrators and store managers in developing marketing strategies and funding plans for merchandising and management personnel, as well as supervising stock replenishment, equipment and supply needs, and inventory control procedures. The primary objective of the operations manager is to develop and maintain effective programs to operate and control all of the retail units in the company, with a focus on superior customer service and cost control. For example, the operations manager may work to find a faster, less expensive way to move merchandise from the central distribution warehouse to store units.

Developing a company-wide training program to help all employees identify and report theft may be another activity of the operations manager, because another area of responsibility for the operations manager is security. Security can have tremendous impact on the bottom line—profit. **Security** refers to safekeeping of merchandise in the store, as well as the safety of employees and customers. Because inadequate lighting, unsafe equipment, and poorly placed fixtures can prove to be safety hazards for people in the store, this is an important focus for the operations manager. In large stores, a **security manager** may be employed to work directly for the operations manager,

overseeing the safekeeping of merchandise in the retail operation and minimizing theft.

The security manager works with the operations manager to determine which equipment will be used to deter theft, such as tags, security cameras, or perhaps a security employee disguised as a shopper. Security not only protects the physical inventory from outside theft but also monitors against internal theft or pilferage. **Physical inventory** refers to the actual merchandise within the retail operation, whether on the sales floor, on trucks for delivery to the stores, or in the warehouse waiting to be transported to the store units. **Internal theft** refers to merchandise or money stolen by employees within the company. To minimize internal theft opportunities, employees may be required to have personal purchases processed through the cash terminal by a store manager, rather than on their own. They may be required to store their handbags and packages in lockers and use a clear bag on the sales floor. Advanced technology also helps minimize internal theft. Surveillance cameras are very discreet and can capture activity in front of and behind the cash register. Cash register terminals can video and store individual transactions numerically for swift information retrieval, and encouraging the use of debit and credit cards limits access to cash. Additionally, security management covers loss training for employees of the company (Figure 10.1). Seminars on how to spot a shoplifter, who to contact, and where to go for assistance when identifying a thief assist employees in safely combating **shrinkage**, or merchandise losses resulting from theft (Figure 10.2).

Figure 10.1
Security decisions include determining which equipment will be used to deter theft.

Figure 10.2

Seminars on how to spot a shoplifter, who to contact, and where to go for assistance when identifying a thief assist employees in safely combating theft.

Qualifications

Next are the educational background, work experience, and personal characteristics needed to succeed in the position of operations manager:

- *Education.* A bachelor's degree in business administration, merchandising, operations management, retail management, retailing, project management, or a related discipline is required. In some larger retail operations, a master's degree is required.
- *Experience.* A minimum of five years' experience in the operations field is required. Operations managers must have experience in project management, logistics, system analysis and budgets, and forecasts. Experience in Microsoft Excel and other programs used within the retail operation is necessary.
- *Personal characteristics.* Excellent organization, communication, and leadership skills are necessary for this position, as are superior analytical and technical skills. Good decision-making and problem-solving abilities are required. The operations manager may be expected to travel extensively to store unit locations.

Career Challenges

The challenges for an operations manager are similar to those of the regional store manager. Being responsible for the operations and employee performance in a significant

number of store units is a large workload. Extensive travel and long hours are common requirements for this position. The operations manager spends much time analyzing the costs associated with the stores and developing ways to save money and improve sales without compromising quality. This requires much attention to detail, strong analytical skills, and the ability to see the big picture that will result when changes are implemented.

RETAIL STORE MANAGER

A **retail store manager** oversees the activities of a retail store's operation, from sales transactions and advertising to special events and the store's people—the customers and employees, including assistant managers, department managers, sales associates, and other staff. The retail manager is responsible for implementing the firm's retail marketing and sales plans, while ensuring the efficient operation of sales, operations, and security within a retail location. Store managers' primary responsibilities are overseeing sales promotions, transitioning merchandise from receiving to the sales floor, monitoring sales and inventory levels, managing personnel, and generating profits. They oversee the inventory, ensuring that the store has the right quality, type, and amount of merchandise available. They also make sure supplies are reordered on time.

Depending on the store's size, the store manager may be involved in some manner with all of the store's departments, from displays and advertising to merchandising and human resources. Store managers may have hundreds of employees or just a few sales associates to lead. Either way, they set a tone for the store and share a vision of success and expectations about customer service, promotions, and store goals with all employees. They work with a wide variety of individuals, from executives in the corporate office to the customer who has a complaint. The main objectives of the store manager include the following:

- Ensuring that the sales targets are reached and profits increased
- Handling customer service issues and complaints
- Implementing health, safety, and security regulations
- Assuring that the store is attractive, organized, and well-maintained
- Overseeing that strong employees are recruited, interviewed, trained, supervised, motivated, and retained

Qualifications

Following are the educational goals, work experiences, and personal qualities that enhance one's opportunities to secure a store manager position:

- *Education.* A bachelor's degree in fashion merchandising, fashion retailing, business administration, management, retailing, or a related discipline is a requirement.
- *Experience.* Several years of retail sales and management experience are needed to become a store manager. Most candidates are promoted after successfully working as an assistant store manager. Additional work experience in buying, advertising, store planning and visual merchandising, human resources management, marketing, inventory control, and customer service areas are helpful in securing prime positions.
- *Personal characteristics.* Store managers must be good team leaders who are self-motivated, adaptable, quick thinking, and prepared to make and be accountable for decisions. They must enjoy a fast-moving, high-pressure environment. On an interpersonal level, store managers must be able to communicate clearly with a variety of people at all levels and be committed to the needs of the customer. They must understand relevant retailing and human resources laws, business accounting, and computer programs in word processing, spreadsheet development, and inventory control.

Career Challenges

Store managers should anticipate a lengthy work schedule, which includes weekends, nights, and holidays. Working six days a week is not uncommon. The position includes office work, but managers are expected to spend much of their time on the sales floor. The store manager is head of the day-to-day business in the store, with the support of and responsibility to higher management. This means that the store manager must respond to the requests of the regional manager. The store manager who aspires to become a regional manager—the next step up the career ladder—should anticipate relocating several times to gain experience in various stores within the company. Moving from one location to another with little advance notice can be a difficult process for some people.

Box 10.2 is a classified advertisement for the store manager.

MANAGER-IN-TRAINING

A **manager-in-training** (MIT) is just that: an employee who is being trained to move into a management position. Some large retail organizations offer an MIT program through which prospective management employees are trained for assistant manager or store manager positions within the company (Figure 10.3). The main difference

---

Figure 10.3

Some large retail organizations offer an MIT program through which prospective management employees are trained for assistant manager or store manager positions within the company.

BOX 10.2 STORE MANAGER

Here's what's possible for our STORE MANAGERS:

Yes, we are seeking Store Managers, but don't be fooled by the word "manager." Truth is, the rest of the world is just more familiar with the word. And while managing is part of the job, we're really looking for leaders. Leaders who can drive profitability by maximizing sales. Leaders who can also shape the store according to our shared values, standards, policies, and procedures along with the District Team. And sometimes, these leaders will take on multiple roles, such as the manager on duty or department manager or leader on the floor. You know, being whatever is necessary at any given moment so our customers can find what's possible for their personal style, and our team members can find what's possible for their careers.

Responsibilities:

- Responsible for sales and profit performance in store; responsible for achieving store shrinkage goals and for the establishment and implementation of both new and existing loss-prevention procedures
- Works with the general manager to establish and achieve sales and margin goals, develop operating budgets, and monitor employee and store performance
- Partners with visual merchandising team to develop merchandise presentation and ensure visual standards. This includes maintenance and upkeep of the departments

- Responsible for training and supervision of store staff to maximize sales and profit performance and provide succession planning for all staff and management team in the store
- Directs the execution of promotional strategies and programs, ensuring that they support retail sales, marketing, and profit objectives
- Regularly visits relevant competition to maintain an awareness of store-performance issues and market trends

Job Requirements:

- Four-year college degree or High School graduate with appropriate experience
- 2–3 years of retail management experience
- Ability to lift 20 pounds, stand long periods of time, bend, stretch, engage in repetitive motions, and carry items such as mannequins and display items short distances
- Strong business acumen and skill set that enables the management and development of staff
- Exceptional customer service skills, strong communication and interpersonal skills

About 5% travel required as necessary for district meetings, workshops, and other local or regional activities. We are an equal opportunity employer offering dynamic career opportunities with growth potential and a generous company discount.

---

between an executive training program and an MIT program is that most companies train the MIT on the job in one of the branch store locations, rather than in a training facility at company headquarters. L.L. Bean, Nordstrom, Inc., Burberry, Brooks Brothers, and Sephora, Nike, Macy's, and Dillard's are examples of fashion companies with management training programs for new and/or existing employees.

Qualifications

Here are the qualifications often required for admittance into a manager-in-training program.

- *Education.* A bachelor's degree in fashion merchandising, fashion retailing, business administration, management, retailing, or a related field is usually required. Some MIT programs require the candidate to have a minimum cumulative, or major, grade point average, such as a 3.0 or 3.5 (on a scale of 4.0).
- *Experience.* One to three years' experience retailing is often required for this position. Many MIT candidates obtain this experience through part-time employment and/or an internship in retailing during their college years. A college graduate can apply directly for placement in an MIT program, or a company employee may decide to apply for admission into the program.

- *Personal characteristics.* Excellent interpersonal skills that support a team environment are required. Effective oral and written communication skills are needed to work with a wide range of employees. Strong planning and organizational skills with a sense of priority for deadlines and attention to detail are necessary for the successful MIT. Most important, the best MIT candidates are dedicated to high levels of customer service and sales productivity.

Career Challenges

As with the executive training program, one of the toughest parts of the MIT position is securing the job. As many as 100 candidates inside and outside of the retail operation may apply for as few as ten positions. Of those selected for the MIT openings, only a few are promoted to the position of manager. The job is challenging in that it is "trial by fire," learning how to do the job well, while on the job. Long hours, which are often scheduled on weekends, holidays, and nights, are required for this job. The MIT is often on call and must be ready to go to work if the manager or another key employee is unavailable.

ASSISTANT AND ASSOCIATE STORE MANAGER

An **assistant store manager** helps the store manager in all of the daily responsibilities of successfully operating a store. The assistant manager takes direction from the store manager and works closely with all of the other departments in ensuring that the store's mission and financial goals are met. In some companies, assistant store managers have specified responsibilities, such as scheduling employees, supervising sales floor moves, and monitoring sales and inventory levels. In other companies, they may support store managers in all store management duties. Figure 10.4 shows an assistant store manager assessing inventory plans for the store manager.

Some companies with large individual store units hire for a position that lies between the assistant store manager and the store manager. This position is called **associate store manager**.

Qualifications

There are several prerequisites in education and experience for assistant or associate store managers, as follows:

Figure 10.4
The assistant store manager helps the store manager by planning strategies for employees to take the store inventory.

- *Education.* A bachelor's degree in fashion merchandising, fashion retailing, business administration, management, retailing, or a related field is usually required.
- *Experience.* Retail sales experience, managerial experience, or in-house management training is usually required. Work experience with a variety of departments—from buying, advertising, and human resources management to marketing, inventory control, and customer service—make the job candidate more appealing to the employer.
- *Personal characteristics.* Effective interpersonal and communication skills are significant attributes for this position. Assistant store managers also must have knowledge of business accounting, personnel, and marketing. They are detail oriented, have strong organizational skills, and are flexible. They must be able to adapt to constantly changing work schedules. Most important, the assistant manager must be a strong team player, anticipating the needs of the store and, in particular, those of the store manager.

DEPARTMENT MANAGER

A **department manager** oversees a specific area, or department, within a store. For example, a department manager may be responsible for men's clothing, junior sportswear, or women's accessories. For their assigned departments, department managers coordinate the sales associates in their areas, assisting with employee hires, scheduling weekly work hours, handling employee and customer complaints, and monitoring the performance of employees. They schedule regular meetings with the store managers, assistant store managers, and other department managers. During these meetings, department managers report on weekly sales, discuss promotions, and talk about concerns or opportunities in their respective areas. They also stay in close contact with the buying office, as they relay employee and customer feedback on merchandise and advise buyers on reorders or possible voids in stock to help generate sales.

Department managers also maintain the sales floor by setting out new merchandise, adding signage for promotions, recording markdowns, and executing floor sets. Changing **floor sets** refers to moving fixtures and merchandise on the sales floor of the department to create a fresh look and to highlight new or undersold merchandise. Department managers work with sales associates in keeping the department neat and organized so that customers can easily find exactly what they are seeking.

Qualifications

What does it take to become a department manager? It is an excellent starting place for the college graduate. A list of qualifications follows:

- *Education.* A bachelor's degree in fashion merchandising, fashion retailing, an area of business administration, or a related degree is often required. Some companies accept an associate's degree in these disciplines.
- *Experience.* Successful retail sales experience is the top requirement for a department manager position. The sales associate who has gained experience in floor sets, exceptional customer service, and visual displays is well qualified for a promotion to department manager.
- *Personal characteristics.* The department manager is detail oriented, well organized, and an effective problem solver with good interpersonal skills. This position often demands a flexible work schedule, including weekends, nights, and holidays.

Career Challenges

The department manager often works long hours for fairly low pay. The department manager reports to several people, including the assistant or associate store manager, store manager, and buyer. Each may have a different perspective on how to run the department. The department manager is challenged with satisfying several bosses, who may have dissimilar priorities.

CUSTOMER SERVICE MANAGER

It is likely that you have heard the saying "The customer is always right," but is this really true? Most retailers have specific policies concerning merchandise returns and exchanges, out-of-stock advertised merchandise, and returned bank checks. With the Internet as an emerging retail channel, e-retailers need another set of policies concerning returns, shipping costs, payment, and security. All retailers want to keep their customers satisfied to establish a loyal customer base, yet customer care policies often have to be implemented to ensure a profitable bottom line. A **customer service manager** assists a customer with an issue or complaint and implements the retail operation's policies and procedures for returns, exchanges, out-of-stock merchandise, product warranties, and the like (Figure 10.5). It is the customer service manager's responsibility to maintain company policies, while assuring that customers feel their problems are being heard and taken care of in a professional and timely manner. The customer service manager often trains the sales staff to effectively assist customers with concerns and teaches them the people skills needed to calm irate customers and find win-win solutions for all involved.

Figure 10.5
A customer service manager assists clients and implements store policies.

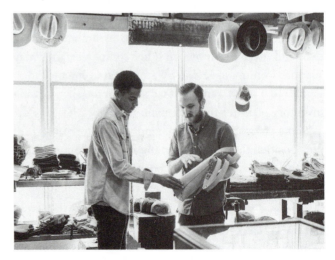

Some large business operations have a separate department organized under the customer service manager that has the sole function of servicing the customer. In addition, some retail organizations handle the customer service responsibilities informally through management or personnel who have direct contact with the customer. Which types of services are coordinated by the customer service manager? Businesses offer varying types of services, often reflecting the price ranges of their products. For example, a high-fashion boutique carrying expensive designer garments will usually offer a wide range of customer services from alterations to home delivery. However, discount retail operations, such as Sam's Wholesale Club, provide minimal customer services in an effort to maintain retail prices that are below those of its competitors. At Sam's, for example, the customer is not provided with dressing-room facilities, packaging, or delivery. Innovative ways that companies use social media to connect with their customers are discussed in Box 10.3.

SOCIAL MEDIA STRIKES
BOX 10.3 Trends in Communicating with the Customer

Customer experience is a top priority for companies, and customers tend to base their preference for a product or brand based on meaningful and authentic experiences. As a result, companies and brands do not just rely on speedy checkout and easy navigation of a site to ensure customer satisfaction and loyalty—they are using social media more and more to build relationships and employ 360-degree communication with their customers. Social media is designed to share, and sharing is a proven way to make a friend and build a relationship.

Used effectively, social media is more than free product promotion, or a way to respond to complaints; it offers real power to build customer connections and brand loyalty.

According to a report by Sprout Social, a social media marketing firm, customers believe in the power of social media to connect communities, and 76 percent of the respondents said they were more likely to buy from a brand they felt connected to on a social media platform than a competitor.

Developing a rich customer relationship through social media is more than just being entertaining and putting out content. It's also about listening. In what is referred to as "call-out culture," customers who use social media to complain want to be heard, and it's important for brands to listen. In 360-degree communication through social media, companies receive an abundance of feedback. The hope is that most of it is positive. But the negative feedback and comments are helpful too. This type of feedback provides a learning opportunity for the company. In a study on why consumers "call-out" companies, 70 percent wanted to raise awareness of an issue among other consumers, 55 percent wanted an apology or a solution, 51 percent wanted to get the word out to a larger, traditional, or mainstream media audience, 38 percent wanted a refund, 19 percent hoped for a discount, and only 3 percent just wanted to complain.

Responding quickly is the next step. 32 percent of customers expect a response within thirty minutes, and 42 percent expect a response within an hour. Rapid response builds trust.

The human touch is essential. It is important to embrace personalization and authentic human connection. Things like staff photos, bios, and stories go a long distance in creating that human connection through social media and the customer.

Look for ways to go the extra mile by treating customers with something fun, like a surprise discount, or an invitation to promotion just for active followers. Customers love a good deal, and when it feels exclusive and personal, it helps build trust and lasting connections.

Embracing user content is a way to tell customers that they matter and that the company values their point of view. According to Photoslurp, user-generated photos are five times more likely to generate sales and convert customers. By asking followers to share ideas about product, or post images of them with the product in use, brands gain greater insight about how people use the product and what they want from the company. When a follower's idea comes to life, then they feel more invested in the brand.

Sources:

Baer, J., "42 percent of customers complaining in social media expect 60 minute response time," Convince & Convert, https://www.convinceandconvert.com/social-media-research/42-percent-of-consumers-complaining-in-social-media-expect-60-minute-response-time/

Carter, R., "8 tips to build customer relationships with social media," Sprout Social, February 26, 2019, https://sproutsocial.com/insights/build-customer-relationships/

Photoslurp, "Converting customers: User-generated content vs professional content," https://info.photoslurp.com/hubfs/Converting%20Customers%20-%20Photoslurp%20Research.pdf

Sprout Social, "The Sprout social index, edition XII: Call-out culture," https://sproutsocial.com/insights/data/q3-2017/

Qualifications

Are you an individual who remains calm in any situation? Are you an active listener? Do people find you to be an effective negotiator and a fair decision maker? If so, then the position of customer service manager may be the career option for you. The qualifications of a customer service manager include the following:

- *Education.* A bachelor's degree in fashion merchandising, fashion retailing, business administration, management, human resources, or a related field is a common requirement.
- *Experience.* Three to five years of experience in retail sales, preferably management, are required. Evidence of superior customer service through sales awards and positive customer feedback is a plus.
- *Personal characteristics.* The effective customer service manager has exceptional interpersonal and communication skills and is trustworthy, personable, and outgoing. Being a capable negotiator and a good listener are also important skills. The customer service manager must have a thorough understanding of the company and its policies.

Career Challenges

The customer service manager works with all kinds of people. If you have ever stood in line waiting to return a purchase, you may have seen a few of the types. They can be demanding to the point of unreasonable and rude to the point of unbearable. Regardless of the customer's state of mind, the customer service manager has to remain calm, polite, and helpful. The hours can be long, and the starting pay can be low.

RETAIL OPERATION OWNER

Perhaps you dream of owning your own retail business, as many fashion students and graduates do. Maybe you love the fashion industry and seek the challenge and freedom of working for yourself. The good news is that a great number of people open their own businesses each year. The bad news is that you must, as a store owner, do everything discussed in this chapter (and several other tasks as well).

The retail **entrepreneur**, or *store owner*, is financially responsible for the company and oversees all aspects of the retail business. There are three types of business ownership: sole proprietorship, partnership, and corporation. A business owned by an individual is referred to as a **sole proprietorship**. A **partnership** is owned by two or more people. In a **corporation**, stockholders own the company, which may be run by an individual or a group.

Before opening a business, the prospective owner or ownership group must develop a **business plan**, a document that details plans for the business concept and target market, location and space needs (i.e., facility or Web site), growth and exit strategies, sales and inventory, and financing needs, among others. Whether the prospective entrepreneur is purchasing an existing business or opening a new one, securing funding to own the business is often a critical first step. **Funders**, financing sources such as banks and the Small Business Administration, require a well-written business plan that justifies financing because of a good potential for profit, minimal risk, and long-range potential.

Once the business loan is approved and after a location is secured, the owner often attends to the merchandise selection for the business by identifying the trends customers will want and then buying, or overseeing the buying, of the merchandise that fits the target market. The retail owner is responsible for developing a budget for seasonal purchases to make certain that the company's finances are not overextended. Once merchandise is received, the store owner and employees inventory, price, and tag the merchandise, and place it on the sales floor. The entrepreneur or an employee will take on the responsibility of creating and installing window and in-store displays (Figure 10.6). Straightening the inventory, cleaning the store, and restocking fixtures and shelves are all tasks the entrepreneur handles personally or assigns to employees.

A retail entrepreneur often locates, hires, trains, motivates, and evaluates all employees. In a small business, the entrepreneur is a one-person human resources department. Scheduling employees to meet the needs of fluctuating customer traffic and fit within the payroll budget is often a challenge for small business entrepreneurs. In many small operations, the customer prefers to work with the entrepreneur, valuing the personal attention and expertise. Rather than leaving it to employees, the retail entrepreneur often functions as customer service manager, handling customer returns, exchanges, and complaints. The retail entrepreneur is also responsible for making promotion, technology, and social media decisions for the fashion retail operation.

Qualifications

Are you ready to take on the ultimate challenge of owning your own business? Consider the following list of educational background, work experience, and personal characteristics needed for successful business entrepreneurship:

- *Education.* A bachelor's degree in fashion merchandising, fashion retailing, business administration, marketing, management, retailing, entrepreneurship, or a related field is beneficial.
- *Experience.* Three to ten years of experience in the fashion industry, working in as many areas of a fashion business as possible, are critical to the future retail operation owner. An internship with an entrepreneur provides ideal on-the-job education. Many entrepreneurs recommend that future business owners gain experience in the type of business that they intend to open in the future. For example, if you dream of owning a bridal boutique, working in this type of specialty store will provide knowledge and experience you will need in the long term.
- *Personal characteristics.* Successful business owners are calculated risk takers. They are well organized, financially savvy, respectful of money, flexible, responsible, and willing to ask for and accept help.

Career Challenges

Each month, the retail business owner faces the pressure of paying employees, vendors, the landlord, utility companies, and more. It can be a huge burden for some people. Because there is no way to accurately determine how much profit the business will generate, it is a risky profession in which one must constantly search for ways to maintain or grow the business. The retail business owner is ultimately responsible for all facets of the business. In most cases, a store owner does everything, including taking the trash out! Being a store owner can be one of the most gratifying experiences, although it can be very stressful at times. Being solely responsible for all of the expenses incurred by the business can be overwhelming.

Summary

This chapter explores management career options in fashion retailing. It is difficult to envision how many people are required to get a single product from the retail sales floor into the customers' shopping bags. The administrative employees in this industry sector are referred to as retail management. Management is the organization and control of the affairs of a business or a particular sector of a business. There are several career tracks in retail management, including the following positions: regional manager, operations manager, retail store manager, manager-in-training, assistant and associate store managers, department manager, customer service manager, and retail operation owner.

The regional store manager is responsible for the smooth running and profit of the operation and the success of employees in the retail store outlets located within a specific geographic area. Working with the regional store manager, the operations manager analyzes sales and inventory performance and procedures for general business practices, such as customer service and store security. A store manager oversees all aspects of a retail store unit's operation, from advertising and special events to the customers and employees. Some large retail organizations offer a manager-in-training program in which prospective management employees train for assistant manager or store manager positions within the company. The assistant store manager supports the store manager in all of the daily responsibilities of operating a store successfully. In some companies, there is a step between the assistant store manager and the store manager: the associate store manager. A department manager oversees a specific area, or department, within a store. The customer service manager assists consumers with their needs and concerns. Finally, retail operation owners are financially responsible for their own companies and oversee all aspects of the retail business. They are the managers of all managers.

Key Terms

assistant store manager	management
associate store manager	manager-in-training (MIT)
business plan	operations manager
corporation	partnership
customer service manager	physical inventory
department manager	regional store manager
entrepreneur	retail store manager
floor set	security
funder	security manager
internal theft	shrinkage
international store manager	sole proprietorship

Online Resources

about.nordstrom.com/careers/#/student-center/main
www.hbc.monstermediaworks.ca/
www.fashion.net/jobs/
www.macysjobs.com
www.stylecareers.com/
www.businessinsider.com/best-fashion-retail-companies-to-work-for-2013-11?op=1
www.payscale.com/research/US/Job=Retail_Store_Manager/Salary
www.forbes.com/sites/walterloeb/2018/08/06/who-are-the-top-10-u-s-online-retailers/#33dd94213401

Discussion Questions

1. Using the Internet and/or by interviewing a professional in a regional manager position, investigate the advantages and disadvantages of this career. Find out about the size of the regional manager's territory, the number of management personnel with whom the regional manager interacts, and the prospects for promotion in this field.

2. Investigate one of the job responsibilities of operations and security managers by exploring the types of security systems that are available to deter theft. Compare and contrast both technological devices and common-sense techniques, such as placing small, easily pocketed items at the cash counter to minimize theft.

3. Using the Internet or your college's career services department, locate four companies with MIT programs and compare them. What are the requirements to enter each of the programs? What is the length of each MIT program? How many participants are in each program? What types of training and projects are included in the programs? Which types of positions can one expect to work in after successfully completing MIT training?

4. Assume that you plan to open your own retail business in several years. First, conduct research to identify the type of fashion business that will have the best opportunity for success by identifying market voids and consumer shifts in the location where you would like to work. Next, develop a list of the work experiences that will prepare you for ownership of this retail operation. Finally, construct a chart of the general steps you will need to take to get ready for the business opening.

CAREERS IN THE ANCILLARY BUSINESSES: DIGITAL COMMUNICATIONS, STYLING, EDUCATION, AND COSTUME DESIGN

Unit 4 presents ancillary businesses that promote, educate, house, and generally provide support to the producers, retailers, future employees, and consumers of fashion goods. Some of these businesses focus on digital communication. Digital communication incorporates technology in Web sites and promotion. Fashion visuals include such activities as fashion shows, photography shoots, and films or videos wardrobed by costume designers or stylists. Whether working as freelancers or within a company, these ancillary businesspeople primarily offer services rather than tangible products.

In a new Chapter 11, "Digital Communication," the ever-growing career opportunities in fashion journalism and blogging are explored. Breaking into these career paths requires not only skills in writing and technology but also great persistence and patience. With the increase of technology, these industries are evolving rapidly. Inspiration, creativity, hard work, and mastery of necessary technical skills are keys to breaking into journalism and blogging. As fashion moves further to the online platform and blogging becomes mainstream, careers in the fashion digital media and visual communication industry are not only attractive but attainable.

In Chapter 12, "Fashion Styling, Photography, and Costume Design," career options are presented as fashion services and examined from the career path perspectives of the fashion show and event producer, modeling and talent agency director, fashion photographer, fashion stylist, and costume designer.

In Chapter 13, "Fashion Curatorship and Scholarship," career opportunities in education, to include museums, schools, and universities, are explored. Opportunities in the fashion or historical costume division of a museum discussed in this chapter include museum director, museum curator, collections manager, museum archivist, and museum conservator. Within the fashion scholarship segment of the industry, the fashion educator may instruct and/or conduct research in historical costume or many other facets of the fashion industry, from production to design and product development to merchandising and entrepreneurship, among other areas of study.

Chapter 14, "Visual Merchandising and Retail Design," presents another segment of fashion ancillary businesses with its focus on environments—visual merchandising and retail design—both of which work with physical spaces where fashion businesses may be located, whether in the production, retail, or ancillary levels of the industry. The primary career tracks discussed in Chapter 14 include visual merchandiser, store planning director, and mall manager.

CHAPTER 11
DIGITAL COMMUNICATION

Viewing the latest collections from Paris used to require airfare, a hotel, and a coveted invitation. Now, access is at your fingertips! Any number of fashion Web sites, bloggers, and live streaming from the creators themselves can take us backstage or to the runway. The digital communication industries bring us right to the front row.

Careers in digital communication—journalism and writing, as well as blogging—are all areas of growth in relation to technology and the online medium. Fashion magazines and books are transforming into online blogs and collections. Web sites provide a platform for designers and retailers to brand themselves and showcase their products. The retail industry no longer depends on brick-and-mortar stores for its sales. Retailers can be just as successful, if not more, by providing online commerce. Trend boards are no longer prepared by hand but are, instead, crafted and shared online. The globalization and digitization of the fashion industry has not only helped the fashion industry to become seamless in operation, but it has also opened up numerous fashion industry jobs that incorporate software mastery, computer expertise, and Web-based design skills. This chapter discusses the particular types of career paths within the digital sectors of the industry and gives an overview of what it takes to be successful in such a promising area for future job seekers.

FASHION JOURNALIST

Overall, **fashion journalists**, or *fashion writers*, develop stories and materials, such as articles, advertisements, and product descriptions, for books, magazines, newspapers, and online Web sites and blogs. Job titles for fashion writers can vary from fashion journalist or fashion writer to technical writer or copywriter to, simply, writer. Although these titles are similar, there are differences among positions and within differing businesses.

The journalist in the fashion industry has expertise in fashion and advanced writing skills, combined with the ability to communicate ideas and facts in interesting ways. You might imagine reporting on the latest fashion trends from the red carpet at The Oscars (Figure 11.1). Yes, journalism can be a fast-paced and prestigious career, but when you picture it, envision a little glamour and much hard work. A typical day may include writing or editing articles or stories; dealing with photographers, public relations specialists, and designers; and researching the next big designer, retailer, or fashion trend. A journalist needs the skills to write and report for various media, including news publications, magazines, television, blogs, and Web sites. The top journalists build a network of fashion who's who to secure the best, most exclusive interviews. Fashion journalism often focuses on design trends, beauty products, and marketing strategies, written to appeal to

Figure 11.1

A fashion journalist reporting on the red carpet fashions at The Oscars has expertise in fashion and advanced writing skills, combined with the ability to communicate ideas and facts in interesting ways.

consumers. Journalists often begin a career path as an assistant to a journalist, editor, or reporter and work their way to becoming an actual journalist or reporter; they may then become editors, analysts, or professors.

Technical writers translate highly technical information into easy-to-understand text. They may work with textile manufacturers, museums, beauty product developers, and similar companies to prepare informational and educational documents. **Writers** work on blogs, stories, books, and the like—fiction and nonfiction. Some writers focus on creative writing. There is some debate about the difference between a journalist and a writer. Often, journalists focus on investigating and news reporting, whereas writers have more freedom in creating stories beyond the researched facts. To add to the ambiguity, some fashion firms and professionals use the terms **writer** and **journalist** interchangeably.

The Job Market for Fashion Journalists and Writers

Unfortunately, the job market for writers is a tough one because of strong competition within the field. However, a career in writing often spans several decades, and there is room to move around among different types of writing positions. With the meteoric rise of online publications, there are tremendous opportunities for writers with multimedia experience. According to the U.S. Bureau of Labor Statistics (2018), the median salary for a writer in 2017 was $61,820 per year, with an annual range of $30,520 to $118,760. Increasing numbers—currently about two-thirds of the writing population—are self-employed freelance writers or full-time bloggers, which are discussed in the next section. No matter what kind of writer you want to be, a love for writing and working well under pressure are imperative personal traits. Box 11.1 provides a glimpse into the world of a fashion journalist through an interview with Robin Givhan, an author and fashion critic and writer for *The Washington Post*.

Qualifications

The qualifications for a fashion journalist, technical writer, and writer are similar and are presented as follows:

- *Education.* Many journalists and writers hold bachelor's degrees in journalism, fashion journalism, communications, creative writing, literature, or English. Fashion,

marketing, and business are also viable options, particularly as support areas. Technical writers need a degree or a support area in writing, but they also need a firm grasp of the industry they are writing about.

- *Experience.* Being involved in writing before college graduation is advantageous, whether it is for the high school or college paper or the local community paper or radio station. Recently, the popularity of writing is rising, with freelance blogging as a way to get your foot in the door to full-time writing positions. It is essential to include a portfolio of examples of writing when applying for jobs and interviewing. If you do not have these, write some sample pieces before applying for an internship or some sort of freelance experience. Journalists often begin as an assistant to a journalist, editor, or reporter and work towards becoming an actual journalist or reporter, with some moving on to becoming an editor or analyst. Writers generally start with a position as an intern and then move to editorial assistant, proofreader, or fact checker.

- *Personal Characteristics.* Writers must be able to communicate ideas effectively and efficiently. A love of language is very helpful in keeping an interest in a career such as this. Attention to detail, grammar, sentence structure, and punctuation are also necessary. Knowledge of when to break the rules of language and grammar is also necessary. Writers must be able to sell stories, and those stories can vary among specializations. For example, some writers sell a brand, journalists sell a story, business writers sell a company, or PR professionals give concise information to the media and public. Journalists and writers must not only be able to tell stories, but they also must be master researchers and proofreaders. Graphic design and page layout skills are increasingly necessary as more writing jobs move to online platforms.

Career Challenges

Journalists and writers often deal with long, varying hours and an uncertain schedule. The work revolves around the writing project. Many must pay their dues before becoming a full-time writer; this includes working as a proofreader, fact checker, or research assistant for several years before advancing to a full-time writing job. Writers are often assigned their stories by their editors. They have to prove themselves through strong writing and research, using correct sources and citations to build solid

CASE STUDIES IN CAREER EXPLORATION

BOX 11.1   Fashion Journalist Robin Givhan, "The Best Fashion Journalist in the World"

Robin Givhan is perhaps one of the most well-known fashion journalists in the world today. Being the only fashion categorical journalist to win a Pulitzer Prize for Criticism in 2006, Robin Givhan has made her mark not only in the fashion world, but also within the sphere of high-end journalism. Robin graduated from Princeton in 1986 with a bachelor's degree in journalism, and she later received a master's degree also in journalism from the University of Michigan. After graduation, Givhan went on to work for the Detroit Free Press, Vogue, and the San Francisco Chronicle. Starting in 1995, she worked on and off as Fashion Editor at the Washington Post for 10 years, until her departure in 2010. She worked as style and culture correspondent for Newsweek, The Daily Beast, and fashion critic for

The Cut, as well as being named one of Time magazine's "All Time" 100 Fashion Icons. She returned to The Washington Post in 2014 as its Fashion Critic and Writer.

Some of her most notable contributions include her coverage of First Lady Obama's first year in office, Dick Cheney's parka in 2005, and L'Wren Scott's abrupt and tragic suicide. In addition to her writing, Givhan has appeared as a guest on the Colbert Report and CBS News interviews, and she has contributed to various pieces of literature work, including *Runway Madness*, *No Sweat: Fashion, Free Trade and the Rights of Garment Workers* and *Michelle: Her First Year as First Lady*. Givhan is known for her opinionated understanding of the fashion culture and dress as it relates to business and culture. Her strong arguments and command of the English language has set her apart from the rest. In addition to acute fashion editorial work, Givhan is the author of three books; *The Battle of Versailles: The Night American Fashion Stumbled Into the Spotlight (2015)*, *Michelle: Her First Year As First Lady (2010)*, and *Everyday Beauty (2018)*.

Excerpts of Robin's work include the following:

> The best collections this season have been those in which the designer's voice is akin to that of Van Noten: clear and honest. Those such as Haider Ackermann, Junya Watanabe, Céline's Phoebe Philo, Chitose Abe at Sacai, and Jun Takahashi of Undercover do not stray from their philosophy. They are lucky; they don't have to balance house codes not of their making with their own vision. They are not single-minded, but they have an underlying aesthetic— a passion—that doesn't waiver. For them, each new season doesn't negate the past (March 2014).

> Fashion is built on desire. It thrives on change. But it is only memorable when it has a soul.

Figure Box 11.1 Fashion journalist Robin Givhan.

Source:

Courtesy of Robin Givhan/The Cut

For the entire article and more examples of Robin Givhan's work for The Cut, go to http://nymag.com/thecut/2014/03/read-all-robin-givhans-fashion-month-reviews.html. For examples on The Daily Beast, go to: www.thedailybeast.com/contributors/robin-givhan.html.

credibility in the industry before they can choose their own material. Full-time jobs in writing are often located in larger metropolitan areas, but it is possible through freelancing to have a career in writing almost anywhere, given the use of technology. Approximately one in four jobs as a writer is part-time, and writers are often paid by the story and not an annual salary. Many writers move on to become authors of books.

THE FASHION BLOGGER

Fashion bloggers are much like fashion writers, but with a definitive online presence, a distinct personality, and an informal writing style (Figure 11.2). Fashion bloggers possess unique creativity in the telling of a story, the curating of an idea, the teaching of a skill, or the inventing of something new. Whereas a journalist must be matter of fact and tell a story based on those facts, a blogger uses a more conversational tone and often shares his or her personal messages. The blogger must catch the reader's attention in seconds, usually with the title of the blog post. The competition for bloggers is intense; all have the same goal in mind—to become a viral hit on the Web. Box 11.2 features some of social media's top-ranked fashion bloggers and how they reach their audience with their unique fashion perspectives. Most bloggers are self-employed or freelance for several blogs. One commonality among bloggers is their overwhelming passion for a certain topic—in this case, fashion. In the world of fashion, there are three different types of blogs: the street style blog, the fashion blog, and the micro blog.

SOCIAL MEDIA STRIKES
BOX 11.2   Spreading the Word as Fashion Bloggers

Once the domain of just the elite and select few who fit into a very limited set of size and height requirements, and who paid their dues and worked their way up the fashion ranks, fashion modeling, styling, opinion, and reporting is now held tightly in the hand of the fashion blogger!

Part model, part scribe, part trend-setter, part designer, part photographer, part influencer—fashion bloggers have harnessed the power of social media to get their own ideas about fashion and beauty out to an astounding number of enthusiastic followers. Here are a few top bloggers and how they use social media to reach their audiences with their own unique fashion perspectives.

MODESTMIRA Instagram – 59K followers
Based in Manchester, England, Amira shows her followers how to dress modestly and stylishly.
http://modestmira.blogspot.com

GABIFRESH Instagram – 680K followers
Based in Detroit, Michigan, Gabrielle Gregg started blogging about 2007, but things really took off when a photo of her showing off her curves in a striped bikini went viral in 2012. She launched Premme, a plus-size apparel line, with Nicolette Mason in 2017.
http://gabifresh.com

THE BLONDE SALAD Instagram – 10.4M followers
Italian-based blogger Chiara Ferragni and her fashion blog The Blonde Salad is the stuff of blogging legend. She turned her blog into a high-end brand and business employing 20 staff. She's moved from a blog in 2009 to what some describe as a digital empire, turning blogging into designing, netting an estimated $20 million in 2016 through her footwear and accessories line.
https://www.theblondesalad.com/en-US

GAL MEETS GLAM Instagram – 1.2M followers
Based in South Carolina, Julia Engle started her fashion and lifestyle blog in 2011. Mixing upscale, casual, feminine, and traditional, she has parlayed her style and popularity into promotions with brands like Coach, Club Monaco, and Tory Burch.
https://galmeetsglam.com/category/style/julias-style/

MANREPELLER Instagram – 2.1 M followers
Not even the shortest list of top fashion bloggers would be complete without including Leandra Medine and her fashion blog MANREPELLER. Witty, funny, and sharply observant writing on fashion, lifestyle, and popular culture sets Medine apart. Her fashion brand collaborations include Topshop and Outdoor Voices, and in 2016 she launched her own line of shoes, MR.
https://www.manrepeller.com

Sources:

Blalock, M., "Find out which fashion bloggers are making millions," WhoWhatWear, October 10, 2016, https://www.whowhatwear.com/how-do-bloggers-make-money

Chandra, J., "These are the top 10 fashion influencers in the world, according to Forbes," Bazaar, October 3, 2017, https://www.harpersbazaar.com.au/fashion/top-10-fashion-influencers-forbes-14532

Figure 11.2

You can see the results of digital artists' work in products, technical manuals, publications, film, and videos.

Street style blogs encompass fashion trends, environments, and styles seen on the streets. Whether featuring an object, a group, or an individual, they can use action shots or posed ones, usually taken in the middle of a city. These shots are often accompanied by a quote or explanation of location of where the photo was taken and/or which designer the subject was wearing. One of the most famous fashion street style blogs is www.thesartorialist.com.

The traditional **fashion blog** covers all areas of fashion and focuses on designers at all levels. It discusses and shares information about products, retailers, designers, and anything else related to clothing and accessories. One of the most successful fashion bloggers in this category is Leandra Medine, creator and director of fashion and lifestyle blog MAN REPELLER (https://www.manrepeller.com/) as featured in Figure 11.3.

Micro blogs provide shorter stories that are easy to read and are accompanied by video clips and links that

Figure 11.3

Fashion bloggers share information about products, retailers, designers, and anything else related to clothing and accessories; one of the most successful bloggers in this category is www.manrepeller.com.

Figure 11.4
Five-year-old Zooey Miyashi hosts a popular kids' fashion blog, Zooey In The City, with her mother. Its short fashion stories and specific focus on children's urban fashion make it a successful micro blog.

are smaller in size and easy for readers to share with one another. A good example of this format is Zooey In The City, (zooeyinthecity.com), run by 5-year-old Zooey and her mom (Figure 11.4).

The Job Market for Fashion Bloggers

It is fairly easy to become an independent fashion blogger. However, pay is not guaranteed and can vary greatly. Blogging is a fast-growing art form, but it can often take years to become a profitable venture. Finding a full-time job as or with a blogger can be tricky. Some tips to set you apart from the competition include the following:

- Establish yourself as highly knowledgeable in the area in which you want to blog
- Make sure you know the ins and outs of blogging (i.e., software, coding, permission rights, ethical implications, how to publish content, and how to track traffic)
- Establish your own blog and build an online presence. The best time to start your own blog is in college, when you can build a presence and be prepared to enter the blogging workforce upon graduation
- Prove that you can bring something to the site you hope to work for
- Bring a portfolio of writing samples of blog posts to an interview

Independent bloggers are generally not paid until they can start making money through advertisers who pay to be featured on their blogs. This happens once a blog has become so popular that it is driving high numbers of consistent traffic, or followers. Several tools are available online to help bloggers build up the necessary traffic. Important tools for successful blogging include templates, headers, RSS feeds, plug-ins and add-ons (such as spam blockers), editors, and analytic tools that provide services (such as traffic statistics). In addition, other forms of social media, such as Twitter, Instagram, Pinterest, Facebook, and YouTube, should be tied into the blog to maximize repeat viewers and spread the word of the blog.

Qualifications

Some of you are managing your own blogs now; most of you are reading a few, or quite a few, blogs regularly. Can you actually make a living doing something you absolutely love as fun and leisure? You can, but it is important to recognize that it takes time, perseverance, and a focus on differentiating your blog from the masses of others. In addition to managing your own blog, there are three other options to consider: (1) contributing to another blog, eventually for a fee per story; (2) running your blog while working a paying job and building blog traffic and sponsors; and (3) applying to work as an intern or employee on the blogs of digital media teams of designers and retailers (e.g., Nike, Zara, Adidas, Louis Vuitton, H&M—if it is a fashion firm, it likely has a blog).

Whatever career path you choose, the following education, work experience, and personal characteristics will help you prepare to be a blogging professional:

- *Education.* In order to be a fashion blogger, you need to be a general expert in the fashion field and a specialist in distinctive areas of the field (e.g., a category such as bespoke men's suiting, vintage designer costume jewelry, or Birkin handbags). A bachelor's degree in fashion marketing or fashion design will set you on the right track to understanding the industry. Marketing, social media, and computer technology are excellent support areas of study for the future blogger.
- *Experience.* It is important for bloggers to not only be good writers and to be creative, but they must also be very software savvy. It is helpful if bloggers understand HTML, XHTML, and CSS languages to help them

better manage their blog sites. Many online tutorials and programming classes are offered within universities that provide these services. It is a fact: Many bloggers have a day job that supports their blogging. Be sure to incorporate skills mastered in that day job and translate them to directly relate to blogging skills. For example, communication, writing, idea creation, editing, and so on are all imperative skills to be a successful blogger. An aspiring blogger for a fashion firm should maintain a personal blog and include that Web address in his or her résumé and cover letter.

- *Personal Characteristics.* Bloggers must possess a marathon mindset in order to be successful, which does not happen overnight. It takes much patience, hard work, and perseverance. Bloggers must also be considerate of those around them. Sources of content, images, and photos should be cited, and most content (always photos) must be granted permission. It is vital to remember that whatever is said is available to the entire Internet world. It is critical to not use slander and to fully understand the repercussions of the possible backlash of the Internet populace. If you are a full-time blogger who has been hired for a specific company, then the company will often have specific rules and regulations for how the blog is to be run. In addition, the company may have an editing and approval process of content before publishing.

Key Terms

fashion blog
fashion blogger
fashion journalist
micro blog

street style blog
technical writer
writer

Online Resources

www.99designs.com
www.nowfashion.com
www.bloggerfreelance.com/10-things-a-blogger-resume-must-include/
www.condenast.com
www.indeed.com/q-Fashion-Journalism-jobs.html
www.intraligi.com
www.manrepeller.com
www.nymag.com/thecut
www.pinterest.com
www.refinery29.com
www.thesartorialist.com
www.stylecareers.com

Career Challenges

Starting a fashion blog can be tricky. With so much competition, setting yourself apart from the rest can be very difficult. Being a full-time blogger can come with much freedom, but income is unpredictable, and there are also often costs associated with the start-up phase of a blog. Another caveat relates to the matter of ethics. Bloggers have the freedom to write in an informal and conversational way, but a code of ethics must still be upheld in the business.

Summary

There are many career opportunities in the world of digital communication, including journalism/writing and blogging. Breaking into these career paths requires not only skills in writing and technology but also great persistence and patience. With the increase of technology, these industries are evolving rapidly. Inspiration, creativity, hard work, and mastery of necessary technical skills are keys to breaking into them. As fashion moves further to the online platform and blogging becomes mainstream, careers in the fashion digital communication industry are not only attractive but also attainable.

Discussion Questions

1. In order to be a part of the digital communication industry, what core skills and tools are needed to be successful? How are they applied on the job for each sector?

2. All of the digital communication industries hold the ability to freelance or become self-employed. What are the most common and most important traits of a freelancer in this area?

3. Fashion blogging has become a digital mainstay. What specific qualities do you find in bloggers you follow that make them successful and stand out? What are some ideas you may have for fashion blogging that you feel might be yet untapped?

Claire Fraser
18th century interpretation of the Dior Bar Suit

CHAPTER 12

FASHION STYLING, PHOTOGRAPHY, AND COSTUME DESIGN

If you have ever watched a visually opulent film such as Sofia Coppola's *Marie Antoinette* or television's breathtaking *Game of Thrones*, then you have experienced the art of the costume designer. Costume designers play a critical role in the story telling process. They read the script for fashion cues, research the period for accuracy, and build a significant list of resources to create and source costumes. Whether the performance takes place during the Italian Renaissance, or in England during World War II, the right wardrobe helps bring the character to life for actors and audience before the first word is spoken.

If you have ever been to a fashion show, trunk show, or retailer's grand opening, you have seen the work of a fashion show and event producer and, perhaps, a modeling and talent agency director, a stylist, and a fashion photographer. The models, caterers, entertainers, and workers did not simply arrive and know just what to do and where to be on their own. Fashion show and event producers, modeling and talent agency directors, stylists, and fashion photographers work with a wide range of activities, from small boutique and megastore openings to product launches, celebrity appearances, and trade shows. Lesser-known activities, including trunk shows, sample sales, and conferences, are also arranged and implemented by event planners. No matter what type of event is being held, it takes a huge amount of advance planning and on-the-job management to make that event a success.

In this chapter, companies or persons producing **fashion visuals** (e.g., fashion shows, photographs, films, costumes, and wardrobes) are examined as ancillary businesses. Some retail organizations, for example, hire a fashion show coordinator and a fashion photographer as employees. Many, however, contract these activities from outside companies or individuals. The companies and people who provide these fashion styling services are what this chapter is all about. In addition to the costume designer, the following career paths, as independent businesses, are explored: fashion show and event producer, modeling and talent agency director, fashion photographer, and stylist.

FASHION SHOW AND EVENT PRODUCER

A retailer, manufacturer, designer, or organization may contract an independent firm, the fashion show and event planning company, to do all or part of this work for a fee. In general, the **fashion show and event producer** manages fashion shows and special events for its clients. The company works with each client to determine the type of event, intended purpose, designated audience, and the budget. The company may be contracted to handle part or all of the advertising and public relations, which can include contacting the media and writing press kits, biographies, and letters. Fashion show and event producers are reaping press by supplementing, or even replacing, the traditional fashion show or special event with technology. Digital mapping, holograms, and video projection are launching the technology component of fashion productions. What is next? Only the imaginations of current and future fashion creators can tell.

In addition, the fashion show and event firm may be responsible for the selection process for products and models. For example, a jury of selection may be configured to review fashion products for acceptance into a show. For the apparel industry, the planner may also recruit and select models, fit them in garments, and then choreograph and rehearse the presentation (Figure 12.1). The fashion event producer is often responsible not only for the site selection but also for the design and installation of staging, dressing rooms, seating, lighting, and music. Preparing and handling a reception following the show may be part of the fashion event company's contract as well.

Many fashion show and event companies do not solely produce fashion shows for their clients. Some of them design, organize, and coordinate other types of events, such as conventions, conferences, corporate meetings, and exhibitions for corporations and organizations. Fashion show and event producers may be responsible for every aspect of these functions, from marketing, catering, preparing, signage, and displays to locating audiovisual equipment, printing sources, and providing security. They may also be contracted to coordinate participants' registration, accommodations, and travel. Most significantly, they are often responsible for the financial side of events by working with clients to establish realistic budgets and then monitoring expenses and income for the ventures.

What types of activities are assigned to a fashion show and event firm? Although conferences and conventions, trade shows, and company training seminars are common events for the manufacturing and retail sectors of the fashion industry, the fashion show and event firm may also be contracted to coordinate company social gatherings and meetings, organize charity fundraisers, and direct the grand openings of new retail locations or the launches of new product lines.

One area of growth in event planning is the wedding planning field. Today, engaged couples are spending thousands of dollars to hire someone to plan, implement, and manage the wedding event, from the engagement party to the honeymoon. Most major cities hold one or more wedding expos each year so that couples can explore venues, products, and services for the big event. As more and more companies vie for a share of this $72 billion industry, a wedding planner can help couples plan their weddings efficiently and on budget (Figure 12.2).

What are the typical tasks for a fashion show and event producer? In many ways, event management is similar to

Figure 12.1
The fashion event planner may audition and select models, fit them in garments, and then choreograph and rehearse the presentation.

Figure 12.2
An area of growth in event planning is the wedding planning field. A wedding planner can help a couple navigate the ever-growing field of options, plan their wedding efficiently, and help them stay on budget.

advertising and marketing. The fashion show and event producer views the event as a product or brand and then develops and promotes it in creative ways. The ultimate goal is to ensure that the attendees (the consumers) have a positive experience that leaves them feeling good about purchasing the product and supporting its sponsors, whether the sponsor is a business, a charity, or a club. Organization is critical in the planning process, especially when dealing with the management and coordination of services and supplies. Every physical detail needs to be considered, from the layout and design of the venue to lighting, sound, communications, videography, and other technical concerns. Catering services must be organized, along with less glamorous concerns, such as security, parking, and restroom facilities. Promotion, public relations, and advertising must also be planned and executed. Last, but not least, the performers, speakers, or participants need to be located, terms negotiated, and plans confirmed.

The fashion show and event producer must anticipate the costs of all of these aspects in advance, continually checking that the budget balances. Finally, management of the event is an organizational challenge in itself. The degree of the event's success is often a result of the level of planning and organization before the event. Following the conclusion of the event, the fashion show and event producer is responsible for formally thanking participants, ensuring that all income and expenses are reconciled, and evaluating the success of the event, noting corrections of errors to implement in the next event.

Qualifications

Is a career in fashion show and event producing for you? If so, you may want to work toward achieving the following educational goals, work experiences, and personal characteristics:

- *Education.* Top event planners typically have bachelor's degrees in fashion merchandising, business administration, marketing, event management, tourism or hospitality administration, or a similar field.
- *Experience.* Knowledge of marketing and press relations is invaluable. Work experience as an assistant or an intern in fashion show production or event planning is critical.
- *Personal characteristics.* An excellent understanding of fashion marketing, a great amount of energy and flexibility, and a high level of organizational and logistical skills are required for successful fashion show and event producers. Their presentation and communication skills should be excellent. Fashion show and event producers need the skills to motivate other people, along with the creative abilities to solve problems and make things happen. If you aspire to become a fashion show and event producer, be prepared to put in extra hours to ensure that the job gets done within its budget and on time. This work requires perfection, so the event planner must pay attention to every detail and be capable of handling last-minute disasters that may happen despite superb planning.

The event planning industry continues to grow rapidly, particularly in the areas of weddings, international conferences, and hospitality. Marketing and public relations are becoming even more important facets of the event planning business.

Career Challenges

The fashion show and event planner works in a high-stress environment. Lack of attention to a detail or two, a narrowly missed deadline, or an unexpected emergency can literally annihilate a major fashion show, trade show, or charity ball. If, for example, an event planner remembered everything but forgot to confirm catering arrangements, there may not be food and drinks at a charity ball. Another pressure for fashion show and event companies or freelancers comes with generating regular business events with repeat clientele to ensure consistent income.

MODELING AND TALENT AGENCY DIRECTOR

Most models are recruited by modeling scouts or modeling and talent agency directors, who travel around the world in a tireless search for fresh faces. Models are often discovered in shopping malls, schools, clubs, concerts, or other obvious places where young people hang out. Some agencies also locate models through photographs sent by model hopefuls; another way is through an agency's open casting calls. Some prestigious agencies do not charge upfront fees to join the agency; rather, these agencies are profitable by taking a percentage of the models' earnings.

Fees for administration and training are often deducted after the model has found paid assignments. Training can consist of full- or part-time courses that last for a few days to a few months. Topics for courses may include diet, health, image, grooming, runway turns and movements, photographic modeling techniques, and professional conduct with clients. Individual guidance on such areas as skin care, hairstyling, makeup, and overall appearance may be provided when the model first joins the agency. The **modeling and talent agency director** is ultimately responsible for locating and contracting new models, training them, and securing modeling jobs for them.

Modeling agency directors are often very involved with their models at the start of their careers. They will often find newly signed models an apartment and help them get settled into their new lives. Many modeling and talent agency directors have found that the beginning of a modeling career is a very difficult time for a young person. Most models are young, inexperienced, and far away from home. The agency director tries to support them through difficult times while teaching them to be safe and disciplined, show up to meetings on time, and treat modeling as a real job.

Modeling agencies hire for a variety of modeling positions. **Fit models** are used as live models to test how garments fit and for designers to drape, cut, and pin fabric and garments. Most companies rely on fit models, also referred to as *fashion house models*, to give them feedback on how a garment fits and feels, as well as where it needs adjustments. They may also model the finished garments for retail buyers in the company showroom and, in the case of couture, for individual customers. Box 12.1 provides information on the work and requirements of fit models.

CASE STUDIES IN CAREER EXPLORATION

BOX 12.1   The Fit Model

After Fashion Week in New York City has officially ended, the amazing looks on the runway models will eventually trickle their way onto the sales floors and Web sites of retailers around the country. How does a runway-model size 0 translate into an average-person size 12? The fit models of the fashion world are the heroes who help make sure the new designs can actually be worn by the rest of us. Fit models are the behind-the-scenes fashion lifesavers

for most of the consumer world, those who care about how clothes fit.

There are few experiences more satisfying for a woman than finally finding "the one"—that one pair of jeans that actually fits like a glove and flatters her body. The perfect pair gently hugs but isn't too snug, isn't too short in the stride, and has room in the thighs. The cut and fabric have enough give for walking or climbing stairs without the circulation being cut off in her legs. She can comfortably sit down without the back waistline opening into an embarrassing gap. Who does she thank for this masterpiece of perfect clothing? The department store buyer? The manufacturer? The designer? The person to thank is a fit model. Fit models are rarely seen outside of the design studio, but their presence is felt by anyone who is wearing a comfortable and flattering fit. A fit model helps make the customer happy and, as such, can make or break a manufacturer's line.

Expert fit models recognize the problems in a garment before they happen, prior to production. They know how a sleeve should fit, where the buttons should be located, how the stitching should be, where the hem of the jacket should hit—qualities that sell a garment. It is the fit model's job to try on each piece to show the designer and the technical designer how it moves on a real person, instead of a mannequin. They discuss fit, comfort, and how the garment moves with the body. Wearing the sample garment, can the fit model comfortably hug a friend without the shoulders pulling? Can he or she reach for a box on a shelf without ripping an armhole? Do the buttons need to be moved so the blouse does not gap at the bustline? All of these questions and more must be answered before a garment goes into production. The manufacturer's bottom line depends on it. Poor-fitting clothes can cost a small retailer thousands of dollars and a national chain tens of thousands of dollars.

Each manufacturer dictates sizing standards for fit models; however, in general, sizes for female fit models are juniors' (size 5), misses' (size 8), contemporary (size 8), plus (usually around a size 18), and petite (size 8). Many large retailers and manufacturers prefer fit models who wear sizes in the middle of their lines, such as a size 12 for a line that runs from a 0 to a 20. Unfortunately for the consumer, not all companies use the same fit models, or even fit models with the same measurements, resulting in size variations among manufacturers. The two following classified advertisements for fit models were posted on the same day by fashion manufacturers:

"Size 8 fit model needed with these exact measurements: 33", 26", 36". Must be 5'6" to 5'8" tall and have a flexible schedule."

"Wanted: Size 8 fit model. Applicants must be at least 5'8". Measurements: bust-36", waist-29", high hip-35", lower hip-39"."

This isn't your average woman. According to a *Women's Wear Daily* 2011 report, since 2005, the average dress size in America has grown to size 14 from size 12. For size 14 and above, sizing is a whole different ball game. Sometimes, manufacturers have an existing style that sold well in small sizes that they want to produce as size 14 and above. The style that sold well in small sizes, however, doesn't always accommodate or flatter a larger size (e.g., strapless, one-shoulder, or inset waistline styles). While working with the fit model, the designer may add wide shoulder straps (to make it more bra friendly), raise the neckline (to ensure appropriate décolleté), and remove an inset waistline (to add comfort and a flattering shape). Throughout the restyling sessions, the fit model is there to help and guide the designer.

Fit models must know the slope of their shoulders, the placement of their waists, and every possible measurement. Male fit models should be aware of their chest, arm, shoulder, waist, inseam, and thigh measurements. A fit model must maintain his or her measurements within a half-inch to an inch or risk losing a job. Fit modeling is one of the few areas in the modeling world that allows for a long career if the fit models maintain their sizes and shapes.

One of the large retailers relying heavily on a team of fit models to size its apparel is New York & Company. It conducted a fit model study on backsides, for example, and revealed that there are several different types of bottoms on women: curvy, modified curvy, and rectangular. The company determined that it would be remiss not to fit those three distinct derriere categories, because they clearly exist in the customer base. A New York & Company fitting can include up to 50 people discussing how a garment fits the fit model. Once the sample garment has been fitted and approved, the specs for all sizes are determined, and the information is sent to a factory overseas. The garments are produced and shipped back to the stores. Welcome, perfect pair of jeans, and thank you, fit model.

Sources:

Flanagan, J., "Fashion fit models," WNYC, February 18, 2011, https://www.wnyc.org/story/115002-behind-stage-fashion-week-fit-models/

Krupnick, E., "'Plus-size' models are more popular than ever," Life, January 23, 2014, http://www.huffingtonpost.com/2014/01/05/plus-size-models_n_4544777.html

Monget, K., "The Oprah effect," WWD, January 24, 2011, http://www.wwd.com/markets-news/intimates-activewear/more-choices-for-plus-sizes-3443993

Show models, or *runway models*, present merchandise in fashion shows, whereas **photographic models**, also known as *print models*, are those hired for photographs to be used in promotional and selling materials, such as catalogues, brochures, or magazine advertisements. The modeling agency takes bookings from clients who need models to work at fashion exhibitions, trade markets, product launches, and so on.

What is the talent part of the modeling and talent agency director's job? In addition to locating and booking models, the modeling and talent agency director also finds and hires talent for film and media companies. For example, a movie producer from Los Angeles may choose Seattle as the location for filming. The casting director for the film may contact a modeling and talent agency to locate actors, extras, costumers, or hair and makeup professionals in the Seattle area. The modeling and talent agency director may also commission entertainment for special events, such as conferences, galas, benefits, parties, management and sales meetings, weddings, designer appearances, book signings, and so on.

Qualifications

What are the educational, experiential, and personal characteristics of a successful modeling and talent agency director? The list is as follows:

- *Education.* A bachelor's degree in fashion merchandising, marketing, business administration, visual arts, or a related field is a common requirement.
- *Experience.* Some modeling and talent agency directors once worked in the field, either as models or actors. Others gained work experience through employment with this type of company. Employment with a retailer in the fashion coordinator's office provides excellent opportunities to work with print and runway events. An internship with a modeling and talent agency is an excellent way to determine whether this business is for you and to get your foot in the door.
- *Personal characteristics.* Modeling and talent agency directors are constantly observing those around them, networking with industry professionals, and building relationships. The successful director is truly a people person. Business skills are critical, as this person often owns the company and must hire the right people to maintain a positive reputation and encourage repeat business.

Career Challenges

The modeling and talent agency is only as lucrative as the people employed by the firm. If the modeling agency and talent director discovers and hires a new model who becomes a supermodel, then the director benefits financially from all of the model's jobs. Training, guiding, and managing new and often young talent can be challenging, as is maintaining a positive reputation in a field that is not always viewed as having high integrity.

FASHION PHOTOGRAPHER

Thanks to our fashion-conscious society and the Internet, a fashion photographer can live just about anywhere. Fashion photographers used to locate to Paris, Milan, New York, or Los Angeles to earn a good living. Today, with the help of technology, this career dream is a possibility in almost any location. Successful fashion photographers are more than people who take good pictures. They can make products and their models look their best artistically. To succeed, a fashion photographer must possess the technical and artistic skills to ensure a professional, eye-catching, and distinctive photograph. Photographers work to develop an individual style of photography to differentiate themselves from their competition.

Fashion photography can be a highly creative and well-paid career, but it is a career path with limited opportunities and a focus on freelance work. A **fashion photographer** is in the business of taking pictures of models wearing the latest apparel, accessories, hairstyles, and makeup, or highlighting the newest home furnishings and other fashion products, primarily for commercial use. The photographs are used in a variety of media, including advertisements, catalogs, billboards, television, Web sites, and art venues. Often working to meet a client's requests, the photographers control lighting, tone, and perspective in their work, using a range of photographic equipment, accessories, and imaging software. Photographers must have a technical understanding of the medium, as well as an artistic vision. Key tasks of the fashion photographer include choosing and preparing locations; setting up lighting; selecting the appropriate cameras, lenses, film, and accessories; composing shots; positioning subjects; and instructing assistants. After shooting, they may process and print images or view and manipulate digital images using software such as Adobe Photoshop.

Some fashion photographers choose exclusive employment with a retailer, a publication (e.g., a magazine or a newspaper), a designer, an advertising company, a manufacturer, or a direct-mail company. Others may choose to freelance, with or without an agent, or open their own studios. These independent photographers make up the ancillary segment of the fashion industry. Most successful independent photographers develop positive reputations by accumulating considerable work experience in mail-order, editorial, or advertising work. Some photographers enter the field by submitting unsolicited photographs to magazines. There are many avenues for a fashion photographer to break into this business: freelance without an agent, freelance with an agent, or through one's own studio.

Photographers usually specialize in one of the following six areas: general practice, advertising or editorial, fashion, press, corporate, and technical. General practice, or social, photography refers to photographic services for local communities or businesses, with the majority of work in wedding and family photography. **Advertising photography**, or *editorial photography*, expresses a product's personality or illustrates a magazine story. It is usually classified as still life, food, transportation, portraiture, or landscape photography. Fashion photographers work with models and art directors in the apparel, accessories, or home products industries. They are often commissioned by art directors of catalogues and magazines. **Press photography**, also known as *photojournalism*, focuses on images directly related to news stories, both events and personalities. Corporate, also referred to as industrial or commercial, photographers produce images for promotional materials or annual reports. The **technical photographer** produces photographs for reports or research papers, such as textile durability analyses. Figure 12.3 is an example of technical photography.

In all areas of specialization in photography, the successful photographer has several work objectives:

- Maintaining a technical knowledge of cameras and related rapidly changing technologies, as photographers increasingly need to know how to use computer software programs and applications that allow them to prepare and edit images
- Developing an artistic understanding of light, distance, and perspective
- Cultivating a keen eye for aesthetic detail and inventive ways to communicate moods and ideas

Figure 12.3
An illustration of technical photography in the textile sector of the fashion industry.

- Building strong interpersonal skills to work with models and be sensitive to their moods so that they are comfortable in front of the camera
- Understanding studio lighting to bring out the best in skin tones and textures and colors of different fabrics
- Working well with natural light (or a lack of) for on-location shoots
- Establishing good relationships with stylists, art directors, modeling agents, and fashion editors
- Identifying and securing future assignments and clients
- Understanding the roles and responsibilities of an entrepreneur

Professional photographers often employ assistants to help the business run smoothly. **Assistant photographers** may deal with clients and suppliers; organize estimates, invoices, and payments; arrange props and assist with lighting; communicate with photographic labs and stylists; work with the photographer on shoots; and maintain the photographer's Web site and portfolio.

What are the benefits of a career in fashion photography? The attractions of fashion photography are obvious: exotic locations, plenty of foreign travel, and personal publicity in fashion journals and other magazines. There is also the chance to work within the world of fashion and design and to associate with the glamorous people who live there.

Qualifications

What do you need to know and do to secure a position in this field? Following are the qualifications required of a fashion photographer:

- *Education.* A bachelor's degree in photography or visual arts and a strong portfolio are usually essential. Freelance photographers need continuing education in technical proficiency, whether gained through a degree program, vocational training, or extensive work experience.
- *Experience.* Because entry-level positions for a fashion photography firm are rare, gaining a position as a photographer's studio assistant is a common way to enter the field. Some of the entry career paths for fashion photographers who are interested in freelance work or business ownership include working for periodicals, advertising agencies, retail operations, fashion designers, modeling agencies, catalogues, galleries, or stock photography agencies.
- *Personal characteristics.* Those fashion photographers who succeed in attracting enough work to earn a living are likely to be the most creative and adept at operating a business. They are also excellent at building and retaining relationships with other professionals. The independent fashion photographer needs to be extremely confident and have the persistence to solicit consistent work. Stamina is needed for working long hours, sometimes in uncomfortable conditions. Excellent communication skills and a flexible personality are needed, as the photographer must often have patience: it can take a long time to get the right shot.

The Portfolio

A photographer's most important tool is the portfolio, particularly for beginners who have not established a reputation. A **portfolio**, or *book*, is a collection of work that illustrates the job candidate's range of skills and outcomes. Many photographers find that Web sites offer an inexpensive way to showcase a relatively large number of their images, but most industry clients will still need to see a traditional portfolio before they hire a photographer. Because magazine editors regularly receive many unsolicited portfolios, the fashion photographer must develop a portfolio that stands out in a crowd. Many fashion photographers find that at least twenty images and several tearsheets, if available, should be included in the portfolio. A **tearsheet** is a page that has been pulled from a newspaper, model book, or magazine, showing the work in its final use with the publication. Tearsheets are an excellent way to show and verify publication. The candidate for a photography job should be prepared to leave a copy of the portfolio with a potential client for at least a week (and include a self-addressed and stamped envelope if the photographer wants the portfolio copy returned). As technology progresses, more photographers are creating digital formats such as Web sites and electronic files for prospective employers to view their portfolios.

Career Challenges

This is a tough field to enter, as it can take many years of experience at low pay to find opportunities to build a portfolio of work. Fashion photographers often pay their dues before establishing a strong reputation in the field. Some photographers find it frustrating to be directed by the retailer or designer on who will model or how and where to shoot print work. The individual's aesthetic sometimes must take a backseat to the employer's vision. Photographers are also challenged to constantly update software and related skills on the computer in order to alter or edit imagery.

STYLIST

There are two types of stylists in the ancillary level of the fashion industry—the photo stylist and the fashion, or wardrobe, stylist. **Photography stylists** work with teams of people, such as photographers, designers, lighting technicians, and set builders. They set up the shoot for the photographer, scouting locations and selecting appropriate props, fashions, accessories, and, perhaps, the models to enhance the shoot. The photo stylist often prepares backdrops, lighting, and equipment for the photographer. **Fashion stylists**, or *wardrobe stylists*, pull together outfits or wardrobes for their clients, to include executives, celebrities, fashion designer clients, and everyday people, from a new graduate entering the workforce to a new retiree moving into a more casual lifestyle.

Both types of stylists are responsible for bringing to life a photographer's, director's, or individual's vision and fashion image. For the photography stylist, this work shows up in magazines, catalogues, and Web site or newspaper advertisements. The fashion stylist's work may be seen in the wardrobes of clients—from sports celebrities to the cast of a television series to the new manager of the local bank, depending on the image, reputation, and skills of the stylist. Companies such as magazines, newspapers, retailers, advertising agencies, and music production companies often employ fashion stylists. Many stylists also choose to run their own businesses.

Typical work activities for the stylist are varied, from the shopping time to shooting the photograph or film. **Assistant stylists** are often responsible for contacting public relations companies, manufacturers, and retailers to locate the best assortment of merchandise to be used in a shoot. Next, they will borrow, lease, or purchase garments and props, and then they arrange to transport the selections to the studio or location to determine which combinations work best. Before the shoot begins, stylists work with hair and makeup personnel and dress the people featured in the shoot, adjusting the fit of apparel and accessories as needed.

Interning or apprenticing with a well-known stylist is an ideal way to learn the business, including inside information such as where the best military uniforms or 1940s evening wear is available, which tailor can do overnight alterations, and who can design and sew a sailor suit for a Chihuahua. Occasionally, a stylist has to deal with big egos, as well as big time constraints; it simply goes with the territory. Stylists have to avoid allowing their egos and tastes to interfere with a director's vision or a client's image. Box 12.2 features a classified advertisement for an Internet stylist.

THE JOB SEARCH

BOX 12.2 Internet Stylist

Full-time employee for large retail/product development company
San Francisco, California

Major Responsibilities
- Manage styling direction
- Execute each Web site's styling point of view for all in-house photography to include product lay-down and on-figure photography, and special lay-down and marketing photography
- Understand the marketing and merchandising seasonal objectives and executing site features based on those objectives
- Establish partnership with brand-styling team to promote styling and product consistency from the stores to the Web sites
- Obtain appropriate approvals from cross-functional partners to ensure consistency and translate the brand point of view appropriately for each Web site
- Create/manage a product style guide of all e-commerce sites
- Partner with creative team to co-lead and drive the styling direction for all e-commerce sites
- Create a relationship between the photography, stylist, and assistant stylist team to provide team synergy
- Manage operating practices
- Drive photography work flow by assessing the volume and photography set requirements
- Identify/document/present process efficiencies within the photography floor

Minimum Qualifications
- Minimum four years of experience with fashion styling and/or visual fashion retail experience
- Bachelor's of art or science degree in a related field
- Ability to balance creative with strategic deliverables
- Strong collaboration skills and ability to form effective partnerships across cross-functional team: photo studio, creative, merchandising, and marketing teams
- Extremely flexible, detail oriented, organized, and self-motivated with leadership skills
- Comfortable in a fast-paced environment
- Comfortable working with Excel, Photoshop, and related software, and databases in general
- Experienced in managing others

Qualifications

If the vision of searching for the right look, pulling together wardrobes, and creating strong visual images sounds ideal to you, then the career of stylist is one to consider. It requires the following education and work experiences, as well as personal characteristics:

- *Education.* An associate's or bachelor's degree in fashion design, fashion merchandising, visual arts, photography, visual merchandising, or a related field is often required.
- *Experience.* Retail sales or management experience is helpful, as are internships with fashion publications or fashion stylists. Stylists may progress from editorial assistant work on fashion magazines, where there is constant contact with public relations companies, manufacturers, and retailers. The career path for a stylist may also begin with an internship or apprenticeship with an experienced stylist before moving into an assistant stylist position, and then to a staff fashion stylist.
- *Personal characteristics.* The fashion stylist has an eye for style and upcoming fashion trends, as well as a broad knowledge of historical fashions. Technical knowledge for creating sets and using lighting effectively is important. One needs to be creative, resourceful, persistent, and self-motivated. The fashion stylist should have good interpersonal, presentation, and communication skills. The ability to market one's self is critical. Aspiring fashion stylists should have the perseverance to work their way to the top. The most successful fashion stylists have extensive networks of contacts within the fashion industry to get the job done quickly and within budget.

With the influence of movies, television, and the Internet on the consumer, it is no surprise that stylists are often credited with setting fashion trends around the globe. A stylist may dress an actress in a funky retro gown or an amazing necklace to wear to a premiere. Once the image is splashed across the pages of fashion magazines and featured on television and the Internet, it can become a trend and put the stylist's name in the spotlight around the world.

Career Challenges

The stylist may find this career filled with irregular work, long hours, limited budgets, and clients with conflicting personal tastes. It can be difficult to work for several bosses, from the client to the photographer or film director. This is a career track in which there is growing interest and strong competition for the minimal number of jobs that currently exist. It is challenging to get your foot in the door, and when you do, you have to be great. For those who are great, excellent remuneration, job satisfaction, and the opportunity to build a reputation are quite possible.

COSTUME DESIGNER

A **costume designer** collaborates with film and video directors to design, consign, or construct apparel and accessories that fit with the mood, time frame, and image of the visual. Depending on style and complexity, costumes may be rented, made, bought, or revamped out of existing stock. The costumer's designs need to faithfully reflect the personalities of the characters in the script. Stage costumes can provide audiences with information about a character's occupation, social status, gender, age, sense of style, and personality. Costumes have the ability to reinforce the mood and style of a production and distinguish between major and minor characters. Costumes may also be used to change an actor's appearance or be objects of beauty in their own right.

The shapes, colors, and textures that a costumer chooses can make an immediate and powerful visual statement to the audience. Creative collaboration among the costumer, production director, and set and lighting designers ensures that the costumes are smoothly integrated into a production as a whole. Costuming also includes any accessories needed to project a character, such as canes, hats, gloves, shoes, jewelry, or masks. These costume props add a great deal of visual interest to the overall costume design. The costumer may also collaborate with a hair and wig master, hairstylist, and makeup artist. In European theater productions, these are often the items that truly distinguish one character from another.

Costumers begin their work by reading the script to be produced. If the production is set in a specific historical era, the fashions of this period need to be researched. To stimulate the flow of ideas at the first meeting with the director and design team (i.e., set, costume, lighting, and sound designers), the costumer may choose to present a few rough costume sketches. This is also an appropriate time to check with the director on the exact number of characters who need costumes, because any nonspeaking characters the director plans to include may not have been listed in the script.

It is the costumer's responsibility to draw up the costume plot. The **costume plot** is a list or chart that shows which characters appear in each scene, what they are wearing, and what their overall movements are throughout the play. This helps track the specific costume needs of every single character. It can also identify any potential costume challenges, such as very quick changes between scenes. Following the director and production team's approval of the preliminary sketches, the costumer draws up the final costume designs. The final designs are done in full color and show the style, silhouette, textures, accessories, and unique features of each costume. A summary of the responsibilities of the theater, film, video, and television costume designer follows:

- Research and utilize a broad range of cinematic, social, and historical references
- Read and analyze scripts
- Source costumes and materials
- Conceptualize, illustrate, and create costumes
- Oversee fittings

Colleen Atwood (Box 12.3) has received four Academy Awards in the category of Best Achievement in Costume Design for *Chicago* (2002), *Memoir of a Geisha* (2005), *Alice in Wonderland* (2010), and *Fantastic Beasts and Where to Find Them* (2016). Figure 12.4 shows her with sketches of her Oscar-nominated costumes for *Into the Woods* (2014). For Atwood, it is not just about the creative process, but the technical one as well. For example, *Into the Woods* (2014), which earned Atwood her eleventh Oscar nomination, the costume for the witch (played by Meryl Streep) had to lift and float. To achieve the desired effect, Atwood observed Streep's specific movements in the action of the scene, determined the best combination of fabrics, and worked through choreography of the wind movements and placement with the technical set team. This is just one of many examples of how Atwood strives to build authentic costuming into the film narrative.

Costuming may also include creating masks, makeup, or other unusual forms, such as Atwood's chilling mask for Hannibal Lecter (played by Anthony Hopkins) in *Silence of the Lambs* (1991) and one her most iconic costume creations—Johnny Depp's scissor hands for his title role in *Edward Scissorhands* (1990).

Costume designers typically work to enhance a character's personality through the way that character is dressed, while allowing the actor to move freely and perform actions as required by the script. The designer needs to possess strong artistic capabilities, a thorough familiarity with fashion history, as well as knowledge of clothing construction and fit. Professional costumers generally fall into three classifications: freelance, residential, and academic.

Figure 12.4
Costume designer Colleen Atwood (right) with sketches of Oscar-nominated costumes for *Into the Woods* (2014).

CASE STUDIES IN CAREER EXPLORATION

BOX 12.3 Academy Award–Winning Designer Colleen Atwood

The description "living legend" has never been truer than for stage and screen costume designer Colleen Atwood. With twelve Academy Award nominations for Best Achievement in Costume Design, and four wins, for *Chicago* (2002), *Memoir of a Geisha* (2005), *Alice in Wonderland* (2010), and *Fantastic Beasts and Where to Find Them* (2016), Colleen Atwood is truly legendary in the world of filmmaking.

One of the most prolific designers in modern film, Atwood is credited as designer in over fifty films, as well as recipient of a Council of Fashion Designers of America (CFDA) award, a television Emmy, three BAFTA awards, and three Academy of Science Fiction, Fantasy & Horror Films. In addition to screen work, her resume includes work on a number of stage productions, including Sting's "Bring on the Night" world tour, and costumes for the 2005 and 2006 seasons of the Ringling Bros. Barnum & Bailey Circus.

Atwood began her fashion career in the 1970s after studying painting at the Cornish College of Arts in Seattle, Washington. She moved to New York in 1980 with $800 to her name and secured her first job sewing labels into the custom creations of Soho designers. From there, she landed a job as a production assistant on the film *Ragtime* (1981), and her career in film grew from that point.

Her creations range from contemporary to historical to fantastical, with a reputation for elaborate and highly skilled work. But her creative process begins with the character and the actor cast in the role and moves outward from there. Then, once she has formulated an idea of what she wants, Atwood visits places she has discovered for materials, inspiration, and point of view. And she's not a fan of online shopping—she likes to touch and see things to really get inspired. Among her particular favorites she includes several of the little shops on Portobello Road in the Notting Hill neighborhood in London, and B&J Fabrics in New York.

One of the most prolific relationships in her design career has been her many collaborations with director Tim Burton, beginning with *Edward Scissorhands* (1990), which led her to create one of her most iconic costumes: Johnny Depp's scissors for hands. She embraces not only

Figure Box 12.3 Academy Award–Winning Designer Colleen Atwood attends the World Premiere of Disney's *Dumbo*.

the creative role she has as a designer, but her technical one as well. She observes the actor's movements in the action of the scene and the best combination of fabrics to achieve the desired result, and she works with the technical stage team to determine things like chorography of wind movements, lighting, or other visual film effects. Costumes are part of the film narrative, helping the actor tell the story and play the character. It is creative, technical, and, according to Atwood, it doesn't just magically happen. It is hard work.

In her recent collaboration with Tim Burton, Atwood returns to the circus world and helps bring Disney's beloved

Dumbo to life in the live-action revival of the animated classic. *Dumbo* is not only a fantasy circus film but also a period piece, so there was a great deal of consideration to color and aging of the textiles as well as historical research into vintage circus costumes. She reported a total of over 2,000 costumes designed and manufactured for this film. This included period costumes for 500 to 600 extras, 120 circus performers, and the wardrobes for the principal cast. The 4:30 a.m. calls for hair, make-up, and wardrobe were typical to get the extras camera-ready. A team of dressers had the cast prepared and dressed by 8:00 a.m.

The key to success for a cast this large was an organized system. Atwood explained the importance of a great team to execute the costumes for a major film production. "You have a lot of people working under you, so you have to be able to manage people, in a way that's wise and kind and inspirational for people, so that they enjoy doing what they do. It's really important that they love it, too. You have to share it. It's not just yours. That, as a designer, is a really important lesson." To Atwood, it's important to say, "Wow, you did a great job on that. That wasn't my idea, that was your idea, and that's really great."

Sources:

Abrams, B., "Three-time Academy Award winning costume designer Colleen Atwood talks shop," The Credits, November 4, 2014, https://www.mpaa .org/2014/11/three-time-academy-award-winning-costume-designer -colleen-atwood-talks-shop/

Blair, E., "Colleen Atwood: To design the costume, understand the character," NPR, September 30, 2016, https://www.npr.org/2016/09/30 /496119928/costume-designer-colleen-atwood-took-unlikely-path-to -hollywood-royalty

Galas, M., "Colleen Atwood on designing *Into the Woods* costumes," Variety, February 13, 2015, https://variety.com/2015/artisans/production /colleen-atwood-on-designing-into-the-woods-costumes-1201432677/

Kilcooley-O'Halloran, S., "Colleen's costume change," Vogue, June 17, 2014, https://www.vogue.co.uk/gallery/colleen-atwood-costume-designer -bag-collection-interview

Murphy, D., "*Dumbo* costume designer Colleen Atwood reveals the secrets behind her circus creations," ET, March 29, 2019, https://www.etonline .com/dumbo-costume-designer-colleen-atwood-reveals-the-secrets-behind -her-circus-creations-exclusive

Norman, T., "Tag: Colleen Atwood," Citizens of Humanity, February 27, 2018, https://mag.citizensofhumanity.com/blog/tag/colleen-atwood/

Radish, C., "*Dumbo* costume designer Colleen Atwood on helping Tim Burton create Disney magic," Collider, March 30, 2019, http://collider.com /colleen-atwood-interview-dumbo/

Thilman, J., "Oscar winning costume designer Colleeen Atwood vies for yet another nomination," HuffPost, December 24, 2014, https://www.huffpost .com/entry/colleen-atwood-interview_n_6142646

Vanity Fair, "A few of Colleen Atwood's, costume designer for *Into the Woods*, favorite things," February 20, 2015, https://www.vanityfair.com /hollywood/2015/02/into-the-woods-costumes-colleen-atwood-my-stuff

Freelance costumers are hired for a specific production by theater companies or production studios. A freelance costumer is traditionally paid in three installments: at hiring, on the delivery of final renderings, and on the opening night of the production. Freelancers are usually not obligated to any exclusivity in projects they are working on and may be designing for several theaters concurrently. A **residential costumer** is hired by a specific film company or theater for an extended series of productions. This can be as short as a summer stock contract or as long as several years. A residential costumer's contract may limit the amount of freelance work the costumer is permitted to accept. Unlike the freelancer, a residential costumer is consistently on location at the filming site or theater and is readily at hand to work with the costume studio and other collaborators. Residential costumers are more likely than freelancers to be associated with a union, as most theaters that can retain such a position have agreements with such organizations as the Actors' Equity Association.

Qualifications

If the career of a costumer appeals to you, following is a list of educational credentials and work experiences that will contribute to your success, and the personal characteristics you should acquire:

- *Education.* A bachelor's degree in theater costuming, historical costume, visual arts, fashion design, or a similar field is required.
- *Experience.* Some successful costumers begin in the career field through an internship with an experienced costume designer. Others gain work experience as assistant fashion designers or fashion stylists before moving into the film and theater industry. Interning in summer stock productions, volunteering to assist in off-Broadway or local theater productions, and working or volunteering at a costume rental agency are excellent ways for college students to acquire work experience. High school and college students can gain

experience through costume, hair, or makeup work in school theater productions.

- *Personal characteristics*. A creative and resourceful personality is a plus. An understanding of historical fashion, clothing construction, and fit are necessities. Many costume designers find that the ability to sketch well is essential to communicating their ideas to directors and producers.

Career Challenges

The costumer is challenged with accurately interpreting the words and vision of the writer, director, or producer. In some cases, such as productions set in a different time or unique location, this takes a great deal of research. The costumer often works on a tight budget and an even tighter timeline. Costumes may require alterations, repairs, or replacement during the production. As costumers often work on several projects simultaneously, this career fits a person who can effectively multitask. Low pay and long hours should be expected at the start of this career track.

Summary

Fashion visuals include such activities as fashion shows, photography shoots, and films or videos wardrobed by costume designers or stylists. Some of these career tracks are examined as ancillary fashion businesses; others are viewed as company positions; all are viewed as offering fashion services. Some retail organizations, for example, hire fashion show coordinators and fashion photographers as employees. Many, however, contract these activities from outside companies. These career paths include the fashion show and event producer, modeling and talent agency director, fashion photographer, fashion stylist, and costume designer.

The fashion show and event producer manages fashion shows and special events for his or her clients for a fee. Special events include, but are not limited to, trunk shows, sample sales, weddings, meetings, conferences, training seminars, and trade markets. The modeling and talent agency director is ultimately responsible for locating and contracting new models, training them, and securing modeling jobs for them. Fashion photographers take photographs of models wearing the latest apparel, accessories, hairstyles, and makeup, or highlighting the newest home furnishings and other fashion products, primarily for commercial use. The photographs are used in a variety of media, including advertisements, catalogues, billboards, television, Web sites, and art galleries. Fashion stylists are responsible for bringing to life a photographer or director's vision for a fashion shoot, magazine layout, music video or film, television commercial, or print advertisement (Figure 12.5). The costume designer collaborates with stage, film, and video

Figure 12.5
Fashion, or wardrobe, stylists pull together outfits or complete closets of clothing and accessories for their clients, to include executives, celebrities, fashion designer clients, and everyday people.

directors to design, consign, or construct costumes that fit with the mood, time frame, and image of the visual.

All in all, fashion media and visual career options are creative and growing entrepreneurial paths. As diverse as the careers of the freelance fashion show and event planner, modeling and talent agency director, photographer, stylist, and costumer are, those who follow them have something major in common. They are all entrepreneurs—owners of their own futures. As such, they require the business skills needed to estimate expenses and labor accurately, sell and market their services, and maintain and grow a client base. It is a creative, independent, and self-directed lifestyle that combines creativity with passion.

Key Terms

advertising photography
assistant photographer
assistant stylist
costume designer
costume plot
fashion photographer
fashion show and event
    producer
fashion stylist
fashion visual
fit model
freelance costumer
modeling and talent agency
    director
photographic model
photography stylist
portfolio
press photography
residential costumer
show model
tearsheet
technical photographer

Online Resources

www.anothermag.com/current/view/332/Costume
    _Designer_Antonella_Cannarozzi
http://collider.com/colleen-atwood-interview-dumbo/
https://eventplannersassociation.com/
http://www.nationalassociationofeventplanners.com/
twitter.com/ChinaShopMag
www.clothesonfilm.com
www.fashion.net
https://www.nytimes.com/2015/04/19/arts/television
    /behind-outlander-on-starz-true-hearts-in-the
    -highlands.html
http://tyrannyofstyle.com/outlander-costume-design
    -terry-dresbach
http://taramaginnis.com/manifesto/
https://bandjfabrics.com/

Discussion Questions

1. By perusing trade publications and the Internet, develop a list of fashion show and event planning firms that are available to fashion retailers and manufacturers for contract. In what areas do these firms specialize? What career opportunities are available?

2. What are the requirements for a costume designer who wants to secure clients in the entertainment industry? Compare and contrast the licenses, union memberships, or other credentials that are required or are helpful.

3. What are the sign-on requirements for a major modeling agency? How does the director determine who receives a contract and who does not?

4. Select a costume designer for a well-known period film and describe this costumer's research and outcomes for the film's characters' costumes.

5. Compare and contrast the careers of the fashion stylist and the costumer. Clarify the differences and similarities. Can a person be both?

CHAPTER 13

FASHION CURATORSHIP AND SCHOLARSHIP

In this chapter, we are looking at fashion through new lenses, which are focused on the education of fashion. **Fashion scholars** study, research, write, and teach students in a classroom or online about the industry (past, present, and future), its careers, and the skills needed to succeed in it. Fashion is an intersection of art (from impressionism to self-expressionism), history, and culture. Coco Chanel said it well: "Fashion is not something that exists in dresses only. Fashion is in the sky, in the street, fashion has to do with ideas, the way we live, what is happening."[1] **Fashion curators** contextualize fashion works within their historical and socioeconomic frameworks. Curators educate people about fashion through accessing and archiving fashion artifacts and sharing many of these with the public. Fashion curators are often part of a team responsible for preserving, researching, documenting, and displaying collections of fashion, textiles, and furniture. We begin our study of careers in fashion curation and scholarship with an examination of fashion careers available in museums and foundations.

There are many different sizes and types of fashion and interior-related museums and foundations throughout the world, and they hold a vast treasure trove of history. Museums can be large or small, public or private, and operated by colleges or universities, communities, the government, or a foundation. For example, many colleges and universities, such as Kent State University and the Fashion Institute of Technology (FIT), present design exhibitions in their museum facilities. Community or city museums feature collections and exhibits on fashion or topics related to soft goods associated with their locales, such as quilts, costumes, or apparel and accessories. **Foundations**, institutions formally set up with endowment funds, present costume exhibitions, such as the Guggenheim Foundation in New York and the Foundation Pierre Bergé-Yves Saint Laurent in Paris. And some world-renowned museums have costume collections, such as The Costume Institute of the Metropolitan Museum in New York City, Musée des Arts Décoratifs and Musée de la Mode et du Textile in Paris (Box 13.1), and the Victoria and Albert Museum in London (Box 13.2).

Museums are not only sites of exhibitions for public view, but they are also centers of research and conservation. Within museums around the world, there is also a variety of career options, many that are lesser known to the general public. The work is interdisciplinary, combining the study of fashion and textile history with hands-on skills in analysis, conservation, storage, and exhibition of textile and costume materials. Most towns and cities have museums, and staffing of the museums depends on their size. Larger museums employ a director and a team of curators, assistants, and technicians. In a small museum, the curator may take on the responsibilities of a museum director. Large or small, museums offer many career opportunities that fill the needs of a fashion student who enjoys learning about and preserving cultural references in history through costumes and interiors and sharing them with others.

The following fashion careers in museums are examined in this chapter: museum director, museum curator, assistant curator, collections manager, museum archivist, and museum conservator. Additional museum positions are not examined in this chapter, because these positions are often limited to very large museums. These include the museum technician, who works in restoration and conservation; the development associate, who is in charge of generating revenue for the museum; the membership associate, who is responsible for increasing the number

BOX 13.1   The Museum Trio: Foundation Pierre Bergé-Yves Saint Laurent, Costume Institute of the Metropolitan Museum, and Musée des Arts Decoratifs-Musée de la Mode et du Textile

What makes an outstanding fashion museum? Online searches glean dozens of lists posted by a wide variety of publications and groups, and these three consistently make the cut. Collections that show the full range of artistry and industry of a single creator such as the Foundation Pierre Bergé-Yves Saint Laurent, and carefully curated collections of key artifacts spanning many cultures over many centuries like the Costume Institute of the Metropolitan Museum or the Musée de la Mode et du Textile. Excellent collections help archive and illustrate art, industry, trade, culture, gender, class, politics, technology, and more.

Foundation Pierre Bergé-Yves Saint Laurent

Yves Saint Laurent and Pierre Bergé opened their haute couture house in 1962. During FORTY years of creating fashion, Yves Saint Laurent used what was considered traditional masculine styling to bring women self-assurance and power, while preserving their femininity. His designs are part of twentieth-century history, reflecting women's emancipation in every domain, from personal to social to political. Yves Saint Laurent invented the modern woman's wardrobe: the pea jacket, trench coat, the first women's tuxedo (Le Smoking), the safari jacket, transparent blouses, and the jumpsuit.

Figure Box 13.1a Monsieur Yves Saint Laurent in Paris.

The Pierre Bergé-Yves Saint Laurent entity is not a museum but a foundation. The foundation has established three primary goals: (1) to conserve the 5,000 haute couture garments, 1,000 rive gauche styles and the 15,000 accessories, 35,000 sketches, patterns, and other objects associated with the four decades of Yves Saint Laurent's creativity; (2) to organize exhibitions of fashion, paintings, photographs, and drawings; and (3) to support cultural and educational projects. The Foundation Pierre Bergé-Yves Saint Laurent includes three types of space: public rooms for exhibitions, appointment rooms (for students, researchers, and journalists), and private rooms, such as the studio, which is open on occasion for tours. Rooms used for conservation of clothes, accessories, and sketches are also accessible by appointment.

The Foundation Pierre Bergé-Yves Saint Laurent opened its doors in 2004 with its debut exhibition: "Yves Saint Laurent, Dialogue with Art." In this exhibition, the relationship between art and fashion designer was visually communicated. Forty-two different haute couture outfits created by YSL between 1965 and 1988 were displayed, in conjunction with five paintings that inspired YSL. The artists included Picasso, Mondrian, Matisse, and Warhol.

Online at www.fondation-pb-ysl.net, you can view the production boards for each of St. Laurent's collections, sketches, an overview of the design process by Berge, St. Laurent's biography, and photographs of his studio.

Costume Institute of the Metropolitan Museum

The Costume Institute houses a collection of more than 35,000 costumes and accessories spanning seven centuries, from the fifteenth century to the present. The Costume Institute's curators organize one or more special exhibitions annually. In addition, two fashion-focused tours are available year round: "Fashion in Art," a tour led by Costume Institute docents that discusses costume history within the context of the Museum's collections of textiles, paintings, sculpture, and decorative arts, and

"Costume: The Art of Dress," a tour that highlights historical costume throughout the Museum's galleries. Past thematic exhibitions have included "Jacqueline Kennedy: The White House Years," "Extreme Beauty: The Body Transformed," "Death Becomes Her: A Century of Mourning Attire," "Superheroes: Fashion and Fantasy," "The Model as Muse: Embodying Fashion," and "Heavenly Bodies: Fashion and the Catholic Imagination," which is the most visited exhibit in the museum's history, with attendance reaching over 1.65 million. Monographic exhibitions have featured prestigious designers, such as Alexander McQueen, Yves Saint Laurent, Madame Grès, Christian Dior, Gianni Versace, Chanel, Paul Poiret, Charles James, and Rei Kawakubo/Comme des Garcons.

Redesigned Costume Institute space was opened in 2014 after a two-year renovation as the Anna Wintour Costume Center with the exhibition "Charles James: Beyond Fashion." The fashion industry provides strong support for the work of the Costume Institute, including its exhibitions, acquisitions, and capital improvements. Each May, the annual Metropolitan Costume Institute Gala Benefit, its primary fundraising event, celebrates the opening of the spring exhibition. The benefit was introduced in 1948 and has been dubbed "the party of the year." The gala has become one of the most visible and successful charity events, drawing a stellar list of attendees from the fashion, film, society, business, and music industries.

Figure Box 13.1c Hussein Chalayan creations at the Musée des Arts Décoratif's Musée de la Mode et du Textile in Paris.

Musée des Arts Décoratifs-Musée de la Mode et du Textile

The Musée des Arts Décoratifs was created after the success of the historic *Expositions Universelles*, and the Musée de la Mode et du Textile opened in the Marsan wing of the Louvre in 1905, moving in 1997 to over two levels in the Rohan wing. Located at 107 rue de Rivoli, its collections now contain some 16,000 costumes, 35,000 fashion accessories, and 30,000 pieces of textile. The artifacts total more than 81,000 works that trace the history of costume from the Regency period to the present day and innovations in textiles since the seventh century. These collections are regularly enriched by generous gifts made by private donors, designers, and manufacturers. The museum presents theme exhibitions that change every year, such as costumes and accessories from the seventeenth century to the twenty-first century, textiles and embroideries, and important works by renowned couturiers, such as Paul Poiret, Madeleine Vionnet, André Courrèges, Christian Dior, Coco Chanel, Elsa Schiaparelli, Christian Lacroix, Yves Saint Laurent, and Alexander McQueen.

Sources:

The Met, www.metmuseum.org

Musée des Arts Décoratifs, https://madparis.fr/francais/musees/musee-des-arts-decoratifs/

Musée Yves Saint Laurent Paris, www.fondation-pb-ysl.net/en/Accueil-Foundation-Pierre-Berge-Yves-Saint-Laurent-575.html

Page, T., "Musée des Arts Décoratifs – Musée de la Mode et du Textile," Travelsignposts, www.travelsignposts.com/Paris/sightseeing/musee-des-arts-decoratifs-musee-de-la-mode-et-du-textile

Figure Box 13.1b An exhibit at the Costume Institute of the Metropolitan Museum in New York City.

CASE STUDIES IN CAREER EXPLORATION

BOX 13.2   The Victoria and Albert Museum

An example of a large and prestigious museum with a significant fashion collection is the Victoria and Albert Museum (V&A) in London, which has collected both dress and textiles since its earliest days. The collections cover fashionable dress from the seventeenth century to the present day, with an emphasis on progressive and influential designs from the major fashion centers of Europe. The V&A collections also include accessories such as jewelry, gloves, millinery, and handbags.

Research is a core activity of the V&A and is carried out in all of its departments. Some research concerns the identification and interpretation of individual objects, whereas other studies contribute to systematic research.

This helps develop the public understanding of the art and artifacts of many of the great cultures of the world, past and present.

The conservation department of the V&A is primarily responsible for the long-term preservation of its collections. At the core of the V&A conservator's work is the development and implementation of storage, mounting, and handling procedures that reduce the risk of damage during movement and display.

Source:
Victoria and Albert Museum (V&A), www.vam.ac.uk

Figure Box 13.2
The Victoria and Albert Museum in London.

of members; the education specialist, who develops educational programs for visitors; the docent, who presents lectures or conducts educational tours of exhibitions; and the exhibit designer, who creates and installs displays.

MUSEUM DIRECTOR

Museum directors are responsible for managing collections of artistic, historical, and general-interest artifacts. In large facilities, museum directors manage the general operations and staffing of the institution and coordinate the public service mission of the museum. They literally run the business of the museum, with responsibilities for the human resources, public relations, budget development, and management of the facility. They work closely with assistants, curators, and staff to fulfill the mission of the organization. Foremost, the museum director is a steward of the artifacts held by the museum.

Increasing areas of focus for the museum director include public affairs, marketing, and development. **Public affairs** work includes collaborating with the community, the government, industry, and social and academic organizations to develop exhibitions and collections that appeal to and educate the community and its visitors. The museum director often acts as a guide for groups viewing the exhibitions, answering visitors' questions and giving talks in the museum to local organizations or school groups. Making the museum user-friendly and accessible by as much of the public as possible is a key objective of most museum directors. As a result, technology, including social media, has become an important marketing tool for the museum, as illustrated in Box 13.3. Outside of the museum, directors may also be invited speakers at clubs or universities to present on the museum's collections or a specific installation. They may be asked to co-chair a gala or work with an outside sponsor on a public event planned to raise awareness or funds for the institution.

A leading museum cannot only influence the educational and civic well-being of a community, but it can also affect its fiscal health through revenue generated by tourists coming to see the museum. When visitors travel to a city to view its museum, they often spend money in the local restaurants, hotels, and stores, in addition to paying the museum admission fee and, possibly, patronizing its gift shop. Although directors work to attract visitors to a museum, they may also be asked to seek out and secure funding for the museum through national and state grants. Today, a significant part of a director's duties, perhaps shared by assistants, involves fundraising and promotion, which may include researching, writing, and reviewing grant proposals, journal articles, and publicity materials. Fundraising and promotional activities may also include attending meetings, conventions, and civic events.

SOCIAL MEDIA STRIKES
BOX 13.3   Pinterest for Those with Museum Interest

Pinterest is known as *the* social media channel for food and fashion. It's a visual delight and a treasure trove of information, with businesses, educators, and publishers using Pinterest to complement their other online material. Many museums have jumped on the Pinterest bandwagon. The Museum at the Fashion Institute of Technology is a perfect match for Pinterest. "The most fashionable museum in New York City" offers a rare level of expertise for Pinterest pinners. There are more than 100 boards featuring historical costumes sorted by century or decade, designer or inspiration, categories from handbags to hats, fashion illustrations and photographs, and much more. These images allow viewers to see artifacts of the collection that are rarely, if ever, exhibited. It's a peek behind the scenes and under the muslin covers of priceless fashion pieces from fashion icons like Charles Worth, Paul Poiret, Coco Chanel, and Elsa Schiaparelli. Check it out at www.pinterest.com/museumatfit/boards. You don't have to leave your apartment, stand in line, and pay admission—just sit back, relax, and start pinning your very own fashion archive.

Sources:

Museum at FIT, www.fitnyc.edu/museum.asp

Pinterest, Museum at FIT, www.pinterest.com/museumatfit/boards

Syms, C., "The art of the pin," Museum Hack, June 23, 2016, https://museumhack.com/museums-pinterest-accounts/

Washenko, A., "8 incredible museums sharing on Pinterest," Mashable, January 29, 2014, www.mashable.com/2014/01/29/pinterest-museums/

Qualifications

The position of museum director requires knowledge and experience in diverse areas: museum studies, public relations, marketing, and human resources, to name a few. Following is a list of the educational qualifications, work experience, and personal characteristics that are needed for a museum director:

- *Education.* A bachelor's degree in fashion design, textiles, historical costume, museum curatorship, museum studies, heritage studies, art history, history, archaeology, or a related field is expected. Many museums require that the director have a master of arts or fine arts or a master of science degree in one of these fields. Candidates with a doctoral degree in a related discipline have an edge in the job search.
- *Experience.* Applicants for the position of director must have experience in museum work, preferably as a museum curator or the director of a smaller museum. Management experience is essential, particularly in the areas of human resources and budget development and control. Many museums require that the prospective museum director have public relations and marketing experience; some view experience in the tourism and hospitality industries as a plus. Fundraising experience may be required or preferred. Computer skills are needed for information retrieval, maintaining the inventory of artifacts, and imaging of collection items.
- *Personal characteristics.* Museum directors are often passionate about history, community affairs, and education. The effective museum director is a strong leader and a visionary who is committed to generating public interest, and possibly funding, for the museum. The work requires a range of skills, including organizational abilities, time-management skills, and a high level of attention to detail. The successful director has strong oral and written communication skills, a heightened aesthetic sense, and excellent presentation skills.

Career Challenges

The museum director carries the weight of many responsibilities, from budget development and management of the facility to human resources and public relations. In human resources, the director supervises assistants, curators, and all other staff in the museum, as well as teams of unpaid volunteers. In public relations, the director must find innovative and inexpensive ways to promote the museum and generate funding through events and programs. It is challenging to sell an institution and its services, rather than a tangible product. The museum director has the role of being a jack-of-all-trades in a leadership role that often takes long hours and much multitasking.

MUSEUM CURATOR

In large museums, **museum curators**, referred to as *museum keepers* in some countries, work under the supervision of the museum director. Curators direct the accession, deaccession, storage, and exhibition of collections (Figure 13.1). **Accession** refers to receiving new items and adding them to the collection; **deaccession** is the removal of items from a collection because of repetition of artifacts, the receipt of better examples, loss, or decay. Sometimes, when building collections, museums sell valuable pieces (often, duplicates in the collection) to raise money to buy items that they want more than the deaccessioned pieces. Curators negotiate and authorize the purchase, sale, exchange, or loan of collection items. They may be responsible for authenticating, evaluating, and categorizing the items in a collection. Curators also oversee and help conduct the museum's research projects and related educational programs.

Figure 13.1
Curators direct the accession, deaccession, storage, and exhibition of collections.

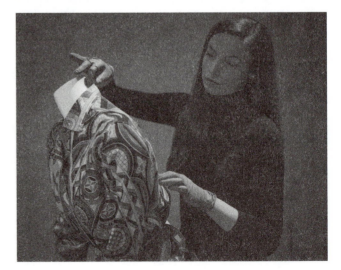

In a large museum where there are teams of curators, each may be involved in one area of specialization, such as 18th-century fashions or Gothic furnishings. A large historical costume museum, for example, may employ different curators for its collections of textiles, accessories, menswear garments, and women's apparel. Some curators maintain their collections, some conduct research, and others perform administrative tasks. In small institutions with only one or a few curators, a curator may be responsible for many varied tasks, from maintaining collections to directing the affairs of the museum. The main role of the curator is to acquire objects and research, identify, and catalogue them, usually on a computer. Curators in large and small museums are also responsible for ensuring correct storage conditions. Other duties that they may be assigned include overseeing security and insurance and developing policies and procedures for the collections in collaboration with the museum director, if there is one.

Providing information to the public is an important part of the museum curator's job. This is accomplished through written reports, presentations, and exhibitions to the public. When assigned the task of a public exhibition, the curator either identifies or assists the museum director in identifying topics for public exhibitions (e.g., wedding gowns through the ages, 1940s costumes of women in film, Amish quilts, or menswear of the 18th century). After the subject of the exhibition is determined, the curator plans and designs the exhibition and selects the items to be displayed. In selecting items for display, the delicacy and rarity of some items will keep them from being included. If a museum collection does not contain all of the artifacts needed to implement the theme of the exhibition, then the curator may decide to borrow items from other establishments, companies, or private individuals. After the items to be displayed are confirmed, the artifacts are installed and correctly labeled, and related publications are developed. The curator may be responsible for writing signage copy, working with other departments in the museum to publicize the showing, and writing a program for viewers to follow. A trend in museum exhibitions is the **interactive display**, in which viewers can press a button to run a video or actively participate in the exhibition's subject matter. For example, a textile exhibition may include an instructional video and a work area where the viewer can weave a piece of fabric. Museums have added entertainment to their educational goals to engage the public. With such large undertakings, the curator often works with a staff of assistants and technicians.

Although the range of museums has expanded enormously, from large museums with full-scale models being prepared for the public to visit and recapture past ages and small museums specializing in specific artifact categories (e.g., Victorian decor or nineteenth-century apparel and accessories), the curator's role has also expanded. Granted, most curators have the primary responsibility of collecting and displaying objects of historical, cultural, and scientific interest in order to inform and instruct. However, the majority of curators' work also includes regularly establishing policies and procedures to protect artifacts in their care. Most curators are called on to talk to museum visitors and answer their questions and to give lectures and visual presentations to local groups. Now, there is a new addition to the curator's job: fundraising and development. Writing grants and other publications, soliciting donors for gifts, locating sponsors for exhibitions, and attending conferences—with or without a museum director—help stretch limited museum budgets.

Training for museum curators covers three main areas: academic, museological, and managerial. **Academic curator training** refers to how to study and understand collections. **Museological training** for the museum curator covers how to care for and interpret collections. **Museum managerial training** for the curator focuses on how to run a museum, from personnel to finances to operations. Some large museums offer a type of internship or apprenticeship for the prospective curator, often referred to as the **curatorial traineeship**. If you do not secure one of these prestigious and limited positions, how can you open the door to a career as a museum curator?

Qualifications

Here is a list of educational goals, work experience, and personal characteristics you will need to become a museum curator:

- *Education.* A bachelor's degree in fashion design, textiles, historical costume, museum curatorship, museum studies, heritage studies, art history, history, archaeology, or a related field is required. Many top museums require that the curator have a master of art or fine arts or a master of science degree in one of these fields.

Candidates with a doctoral degree have an advantage, particularly in museums with a widespread reputation for their collections or exhibitions.

- *Experience.* Preference is usually given to applicants with experience in museum work, which may be obtained on a voluntary basis. An internship in a museum, usually unpaid, is an excellent way to gain experience and, perhaps, college credit. Computer skills are needed for information retrieval, inventory of artifacts, and imaging of collection items. Promotion will probably be from a small museum to a larger one that will be more specialized. From there, curators can progress to directors. There are career opportunities for curators within private or national collections.

- *Personal characteristics.* Curators show a deep interest in the past and heritage and a commitment to education. In addition to an intellectual curiosity, they often have high levels of sensitivity and patience. The work is often time consuming and methodical, requiring strong organizational skills and attention to detail. The successful curator has strong oral and written communication skills, an eye for aesthetically pleasing displays, and managerial abilities that include human resources, as well as budget development and management.

Curators work closely with technicians, conservation officers, and restoration personnel who care for a wide range of artifacts and exhibits, from Egyptian jewelry to centuries-old pictures and wallpaper to costumes and accessories. The curator may work with assistants, as well as the conservation and restoration staff, to research and identify the source, material, and time period of artifacts. Establishing authenticity, providing as much information as possible about museum artifacts, soliciting new items, and clearing out unwanted items are key parts of the curator's job.

COLLECTIONS MANAGER

Collections managers provide front-line supervision of specific museum collections. A collections manager usually takes one of two tracks to move up in the museum world: the curator or conservator track. Occasionally, the collections manager may prefer to take the archivist track. **Collections managers** are responsible for preparing, managing, and supervising the collections records; processing and cataloguing items in the museum collections; and maintaining and entering data into a computerized collections management system. They maintain and supervise the organization of artifacts in storage, making sure everything possible is being done to keep items safely preserved. They also supervise artifact cataloguing, keeping in mind that systems must provide access to the collections by the public, staff, researchers, and other museums. Collections managers may work with volunteers in the collections department by preparing instructions, assembling needed materials, training them in tasks, and reviewing their work. Additional duties may include overseeing the photography of the collection, handling the preservation of the collection, conducting research, and participating in exhibit development.

Qualifications

In the job search, the collections manager candidate is expected to have certain educational requirements, work experiences, and personal characteristics. An overview of these expectations follows:

- *Education.* A bachelor's degree in fashion, textiles, museum studies, archaeology, history, art history, or a related field is required. Some museums require or prefer the candidate with a master's degree in fine arts or museum studies for this position.

- *Experience.* Work experience, volunteer or paid, in museum activities is required. College students may want to secure an internship in a museum to gain experience. Some collections managers gain paid work experience in a starting position, such as a museum technician. Computer skills are needed for information retrieval, cataloguing of acquisitions, and imaging of collection inventory.

- *Personal characteristics.* Strong written, oral, and visual communication skills are needed. Collections managers must be organized and effective managers who are capable of leading and motivating a staff or team of volunteers. They must have strong attention to detail and accuracy, as well as knowledge of history, for cataloguing artifacts. An eye for effective displays and exhibitions is also needed.

Career Challenges

Working with volunteers requires the abilities to schedule, train, and motivate workers who are not being paid for the jobs they do. This can be a tough way to acquire the workforce that you need to get the job done. The collections manager is also challenged with maintaining high levels of accuracy and organization when dealing with collection artifacts. At any time, the collections manager should be able to quickly locate a single item in the collection.

MUSEUM ARCHIVIST

With the curator's busy roles in accessing and displaying historical artifacts, public relations, and marketing, the position of museum archivist has become more important and prevalent in today's museums. Although some duties of archivists and curators are similar, the types of items they deal with are different. Curators usually handle objects with cultural, biological, or historical significance, such as sculptures, textiles and textile-related items, and paintings. **Archivists** mainly handle records and documents that are retained because of their importance and potential value in the future. Archivists analyze, describe, catalogue, and exhibit these important records for the benefit of researchers and the public. They preserve important records and photographs that document the conception, history, use, and ownership of artifacts.

Archivists are responsible for collecting and maintaining control over a wide range of information deemed important enough for permanent safekeeping. This information takes many forms: photographs, films, video and sound recordings, computer tapes, and video and image disks, as well as more traditional paper records, illustrations, letters, and documents. Archivists also solicit, inventory, and save records and reports generated by corporations, government agencies, and educational institutions that may be of great potential value to researchers, exhibitors, genealogists, and others who would benefit from having access to original source material.

Archivists maintain and save records according to standards and practices that ensure the long-term preservation and easy retrieval of the documents. Records may be saved on any medium, including paper, film, videotape, audiotape, or computerized disk. They also may be copied onto some other format to protect the original and make the records more accessible to researchers who use them. Some archivists work with the originals of specialized forms of records, such as manuscripts, electronic records, photographs, motion pictures, and sound recordings, and they determine the best ways of creating copies

and saving the originals of these works. As various storage media evolve, archivists must keep abreast of technological advances in electronic information storage. **Archive technicians** help archivists organize, maintain, and provide access to historical documentary materials.

Qualifications

If working with history and preserving it for the future sounds like a fascinating and fulfilling career to you, here is what you need to do and know to become a museum archivist:

- *Education.* A bachelor's degree in textiles; museum studies; costume and textiles; fashion and textile studies; history, theory, and museum practice; art history; or a related discipline is required.
- *Experience.* Archivists may gain work experience in a variety of organizations, including government agencies, museums, historical societies, and educational institutions. An internship or work experience as an archive technician is an ideal way to open the door to this career path. Experience in computer imaging, including photographs, illustrations, and films, is a plus.
- *Personal characteristics.* Archivists are methodical, detail oriented, and well organized. They often have inquisitive natures. They work to stay up to date on evolving restoration and preservation techniques.

Career Challenges

Education is never-ending for the museum archivist. Technological advances and new types of cleaning and restoration equipment help the archivist maintain collection items for longer periods of time, and the person in this position must constantly learn about the latest preservation techniques. The archivist is always working with details and must work methodically and with focus.

MUSEUM CONSERVATOR

Museum conservators manage, care for, preserve, treat, and document works of art, artifacts, and specimens (Figure 13.2). Museum conservators are also referred to as *restoration and preservation specialists*. With regard to fashions or costumes, conservators acquire and preserve important visuals (e.g., photographs, illustrations, or

Figure 13.2
This image shows how historic textile items are stored for proper conservation and safe-keeping and tagged for identification and easy retrieval.

sketches), costumes, accessories, furnishings, and other valuable items for permanent storage or display. Much of their work requires substantial historical, scientific, and archaeological research. Conservators use X-rays, chemical testing, microscopes, special lights, and other laboratory equipment and techniques to examine objects. Conservators' objectives are to determine the artifacts' conditions, their need for treatment or restoration, the best way to repair worn or damaged items, and the appropriate methods for preserving items. Many institutions prefer not to repair but to effectively maintain and preserve artifacts to minimize damage and deterioration. The conservator's work is performed under close supervision with an emphasis on saving and maintaining, or **stabilizing**, artifacts while developing the studies of historical preservation. Conservators may specialize in a particular material or group of objects, such as documents and books, paintings, decorative arts, textiles, metals, or architectural materials.

Qualifications

Qualifications for the museum conservator include the following educational goals, work experiences, and personal characteristics:

- *Education.* A bachelor's degree in museum studies, archaeology, textile science, art history, or a related field is a requirement. Larger, more prestigious museums require a master's degree in one of these areas.
- *Experience.* Museum conservators must have the knowledge, skills, and abilities required to perform basic preservation maintenance, repair, and treatment of historical artifacts. Consequently, training, coursework, or an internship with a museum or educational institution can provide the opportunity to learn these skills and remain up to date on the latest technology and restoration techniques.
- *Personal characteristics.* Museum conservators must have the patience and organizational skills to work methodically. They have the curiosity and ability of an investigator to piece information together. They are interested in science and keep current with restoration and preservation techniques.

Career Challenges

The challenges of a museum conservator's career are similar to those of the archivist. He or she is challenged to come up with the techniques, products, and equipment to restore and preserve artifacts. Although an interest in fashion is a plus, it is more important to have an understanding of chemistry, textile science, and technology. These museum employees are challenged to work methodically and accurately with safety and preservation of artifacts as key pressures. Next, an examination of the career opportunities in fashion scholarship is presented.

FASHION EDUCATOR

Starting with pre-college education, middle and high school teachers in the area of apparel and textiles often graduate from college and university programs with a bachelor's or master's degree in **Family and Consumer Science Education (FCSEd)**. They may be asked to teach courses in textiles, fashion, clothing selection and apparel care, clothing construction, interior design, consumer education, personal financial literacy, and careers in the fashion industry. Some FCSEd graduates choose employment with community colleges or **vocational schools**, providing training for students who elect not to participate in a four-year college degree program after high school graduation. In these programs, they teach a range of courses, such as commercial clothing construction, apparel alterations, pattern making, and retailing. Upon completion of these programs, the student may earn an associate's degree. There is also the opportunity for employment as a teacher in **trade schools**, those institutions offering fashion programs and providing certificates, rather than degrees, once the student completes the program. Trade schools offer programs in such areas as fashion design, illustration, retailing, and fashion merchandising.

Regardless of the type of school, educators in fashion programs are professionals who have many roles in addition to classroom instruction. Many develop and change curriculum, upgrading technology, make purchasing decisions about textbooks, supplies, software and equipment, such as sewing machines, sergers, and dress forms. Some conduct research, write about their findings, and submit their reports for publication. Others seek out funding sources for their programs in the schools, sourcing and writing grants, and soliciting sponsors from the government or industry. Many participate in organizations and on committees that focus on pedagogical issues, curricula in schools and colleges, instructional methods, and job outlooks in fashion industry professions, among other topics.

Many fashion educators include **professional development** on their to-do lists. This includes continuing education, often toward a higher degree; internships in the field; conference participation; and memberships in trade and educational organizations. Educators in colleges and universities often have the **terminal degree**, or highest degree available (or its equivalent) in fashion, business administration, higher education, or a related field—with specializations in their areas of instruction. For example, a fashion design professor may have a doctorate in the field, industry experience as a designer, and a broad knowledge of fashion design. In addition to a general knowledge of the field, this professor is expected to have technical expertise in specialized areas such as computer-aided design, draping, pattern making, or garment construction. In addition, many universities require college-level teaching experience, often not only in the classroom but also through other delivery methods, such as guided studies and online courses.

If the college-level teaching position includes responsibilities for advising and instructing graduate students, the faculty member must hold a terminal degree and be approved as a member of the graduate faculty. Experience in research and publication is preferred to demonstrate professional potential in scholarly work. Terms of appointment for college faculty range between nine and twelve months. They may be tenure track, instructor, or lecturer positions. With prior experience, tenure track positions can be secured at the levels of assistant or associate professor, primarily. Many colleges and universities specify the proportion of teaching and research that a position will hold, such as 50 percent research and 50 percent teaching.

Qualifications

The following is a list of the educational goals, work experiences, and personal characteristics that will assist the person seeking a career in fashion education:

- *Education.* Fashion teachers in middle and high schools need at least a bachelor's degree and teaching certification. Their majors in college may include FCSEd, education, fashion design, textiles, interior design, fashion merchandising, and similar degree programs. Many of these teachers choose to complete a master's degree in the field to attain a higher knowledge level and a higher salary. For the college or university educator, a master's degree in an appropriate discipline (e.g., fashion design, fashion merchandising, education, or business administration) is required as a minimum. Most colleges and universities prefer a teaching candidate with a doctoral degree in a related field; many require this.

- *Experience.* For some college and university teaching positions, the candidate must have a minimum of five years of professional industry experience. College teaching experience in specific areas (e.g., fashion design, fashion merchandising, or product development) may also be required by certain colleges or universities. In some cases, a record of juried, scholarly publications is either required or preferred. Prospective employers may require a portfolio that includes examples of one's own work and examples of students' work.

- *Personal characteristics.* Flexibility, creativity, and a passion for lifelong learning are qualities of the successful educator. The ability to work as a team member is critical, as is the ability to develop and maintain collegial and industry relationships. The effective teacher is often a constant student, participating in professional development activities to stay abreast of industry trends and career opportunities.

Career Challenges

Staying up to date on industry trends while staying on top of teaching responsibilities, such as preparing lectures and grading assignments, is a challenge. Many universities also require faculty to maintain a program of research, one that results in creative exhibits or publications, and to serve on college or community committees. This requires time management, organization, balance, and devotion to one's profession. Many fashion educators must wear several hats, from teacher and author to advisor and recruiter.

Summary

Museums offer a wide range of career opportunities, including museum director, curator, assistant curator, collections manager, archivist, and conservator. Curators administer the affairs of museum centers and historic sites. The head curator of a museum is usually called the museum director. Depending on the size of the museum, the curator may supervise one or more assistants. Whereas curators usually handle objects of historical significance, archivists handle mainly records and documents that are retained because of their importance and potential value in the future. The collections manager is responsible for preparing, managing, and supervising one or more specific groupings of artifacts in the museum. Museum conservators manage, preserve, treat, and document works of art and artifacts. On a related yet different career track, fashion educators teach, research, and contribute greatly to the fashion industry through career instruction and further studies.

Endnote

1. Gould, Hallie, "11 of Coco Chanel's Best Quotes: Because she spoke the stuff of legend," *Marie Claire*, July 23, 2014. https://www.marieclaire.com/fashion/news/a9366/coco-chanel-quotes/

Key Terms

academic curator training	interactive display
accession	museological training
archive technician	museum conservator
archivist	museum curator
collections manager	museum director
curatorial traineeship	museum managerial training
deaccession	professional development
Family and Consumer Science Education (FCSEd)	public affairs
	stabilizing
	terminal degree
fashion curators	trade school
fashion scholar foundations	vocational school

Online Resources

www.fitnyc.edu/museum.asp
www.aafcs.org/about/about-us/what-is-fcs
www.vam.ac.uk/collections/fashion
www.fondation-pb-ysl.net
www.guggenheim.org/new-york
www.itaaonline.org
costumesocietyamerica.com/
textilesocietyofamerica.org/
www.aeshm.hs.iastate.edu/tc-museum/
www.stephens.edu/stephens-news/stephens-college
   -to-open-teaching-from-the-collections-fashion
   -exhibition/
www.tam.missouri.edu/MHCTC/
www.kent.edu/museum
www.metmuseum.org
www.fitnyc.edu/museum/about/links/online
   -collections.php
www.imls.gov/
www.metmuseum.org/about-the-met/curatorial
   -departments/the-costume-institute
madparis.fr/en/about-us/collections/nouvelle
   -traduction-20-mode-et
researchguides.library.tufts.edu/c.php?g=502251
   &p=3560727
palaisgalliera.paris.fr/en
www.cntraveler.com/galleries/2013-10-12/fashion
   -designer-museums-italy-spain-south-korea
www.nytimes.com/2012/10/11/arts/11iht-rartcurating
   11.html?_r=0
tmagazine.blogs.nytimes.com/2014/06/27/duro-olowu
   -curate-art-show-more-material/
www.vogue.co.uk/article/met-gala-2019

Discussion Questions

1. Compare and contrast the work responsibilities of the museum conservator with those of the archivist. Using the Internet, research and report on the types of technological advances that may affect conservation and restoration of historic textiles.

2. After perusing classified advertisements online (e.g., chroniclevitae.com and itaaonline.org) for clothing and textile educators in colleges and universities, list the differences in education and work experience requirements for the following types of educator positions: tenure track, lecturer, and instructor.

3. Locate and list descriptions of six lesser-known museums around the world that specialize in decorative arts, apparel, accessories, and interior furnishing and accessories. What are their missions, educational programs, and preservation strategies?

4. Many fashion designers visit museums for design inspiration, construction ideas, and color ideas. Identify three well-known designers who use historical costume as a source of inspiration. Provide illustrations, such as magazine clippings, of current garments the designers have created that were inspired by historical costumes. Identify the time periods and designers of these historical costumes.

CHAPTER 14
VISUAL MERCHANDISING AND RETAIL DESIGN

Envision a fashion business as a Tiffany necklace; think of its environment as the turquoise suede jewelry pouch encased in the signature blue box embossed with a beautiful logo and tied up with white ribbon (Figure 14.1). The building housing a retail store, a kiosk in a mall, a boutique in a strip center, and a Web site's landing page can function as the boxes that house various types of fashion businesses.

Think about fashion retailers focusing on the business environment for new brick-and-mortar stores. The visual merchandiser or store planning director may select the fixtures and mannequins, then set up the sales floor to entice consumers to come into the store and buy. If the retailer is in e-commerce, the Digital Marketing Manager, discussed in Chapter 8, is responsible for the visual look of the store through Web site design. All of these career professionals are responsible for creating the most attractive and functional box possible for the business within the space and budget allocated by the retailer.

The fashion industry is a visual one. As a result, the way a fashion business's building and interior look can affect the business's profitability and image. The mall manager works to keep the interior environment looking fresh and appealing for consumers. Careers involved in developing the environments of fashion businesses examined in this chapter are visual merchandising professional, store planning director, mall manager, and assistant mall manager.

Figure 14.1
The exterior and interior of a brick-and-mortar store can be related to the wrappings of a Tiffany product—with the box being comparable to the store exterior.

VISUAL MERCHANDISING PROFESSIONALS

What is visual merchandising? Often called the "silent salesperson," **visual merchandising** refers to the design, development, procurement, and installation of merchandise displays that enhance the ambiance of the environment in which the displays are shown. Effective visual merchandising aims to create an image that reflects the company and, most important, sells the company's product lines. Some visual merchandising efforts are institutional, such as Macy's large boulevard windows that feature holiday extravaganzas of mechanical dolls and a twelve-foot tree made of glass lollipops. Others are product-driven, such as Tiffany's shadow-box windows that highlight new jewelry pieces.

Visual merchandisers are the people responsible for window installations, in-store displays (Figures 14.2a and b), signage, fixtures, mannequins, and decorations that give a retail operation aesthetic appeal and a distinct image. Visual merchandisers are stylists of sorts; they have the ability to look at the merchandise selected by the buyers and, through their creativity and expertise, create an image of the store that entices customers to enter the store or Web site and purchase merchandise. Think about an outfit displayed in a retail window or on a mannequin. As a result of seeing the presentation of the garment and accessories, you may have decided to buy the items on display. This purchase can be attributed, at least in part, to the successful work of a visual merchandiser.

The field of visual merchandising has grown as a career area and as a spin-off of the tremendous growth of interiors businesses and e-retailing, as well as the value consumers place on image and branding. Promoting the image of a product line, store, or service through visual merchandising is an effective way for fashion firms to market their products to prospective customers.

The visual merchandiser is responsible for several key tasks:

- Designing an aesthetically appealing environment that reflects the company's image
- Creating exciting visual displays to educate customers and to sell merchandise
- Presenting the merchandise in ways that will maximize sales, such as displaying the full range of colors of a new handbag and matching footwear

Frequently, the visual merchandiser consults with the retail operation's buyers to determine which merchandise should be featured. Because one of the main goals of visual merchandising is to increase revenue, merchandisers will ask the visual merchandiser to create displays for new, fashion-forward key items that have been purchased in depth, as in Figure 14.3, at Lord & Taylor in New York. Alternatively, the buyer may ask the visual merchandiser to feature products that are not selling well to increase sales on the items so that the merchandiser will not have to mark them down, thereby decreasing the retailer's profit. Some visual merchandisers have numerous job responsibilities in addition to designing and installing window displays. They may set up new stores for openings, locate and purchase props and fixtures for installations, create in-store displays and department floor arrangements, and produce signage for display windows and the sales floor.

Growing Visual Merchandising Career Opportunities

Many auxiliary businesses have developed from the increasing emphasis on the importance of visual merchandising; all hire visual merchandising professionals. A growing area of visual merchandising is the **prop house**, or prop company. These firms rent furniture, fixtures, mannequins, and décor accessories to visual merchandisers, saving the company money on limited-use display pieces while reducing the amount of warehouse space and labor needed to inventory and store visual merchandising props. Other areas of employment in visual merchandising are with mannequin, equipment, and fixture suppliers. These companies sell all that one needs to outfit a store. Fixtures, such as T-stands, rounders, and four-ways, are offered; wall slats and hanging bars provide additional merchandising space. The visual merchandising professional working for one of these interior-related firms is, in essence, responsible for in-house promotion that will be seen by the company's clients.

Some fixture and equipment companies hire visual merchandising professionals to work with their clients, retailers, and manufacturers on efficient and attractive space usage. Often using a computer-aided design system, the visual merchandising professional develops plan-o-grams. A **plan-o-gram** is a floor plan on which the placement and types of racks, fixtures, display units,

Figure 14.2a
Lord & Taylor, New York.

Figure 14.2b
Bergdorf Goodman, New York.

Figure 14.3
Lord & Taylor, New York.

and merchandise is laid out in order to create an easy flow of traffic and to present the merchandise most effectively. The plan-o-gram is used as an effective interior design tool to show the retailer or manufacturer how many different types of fixtures will be needed and what the interior of the business will look like when it is furnished. It is also an essential tool for corporate retailers wanting to ensure that stores, particularly chains, have a uniform appearance so that customers will know where the merchandise they want can be found quickly, no matter where the location is. The store managers and staff can see exactly how their stores should look by following the plan. MockShop software program allows visual merchandisers to develop their vision digitally. This video details this program and its multiple features (https://vimeo.com/68773786).

Yet another employer of the visual merchandiser (commonly freelance, in this case) is the designer or manufacturer of apparel and accessories. Take, for example, a

manufacturer's showroom on Broadway in the Fashion District of Manhattan. The manufacturer may hire a visual merchandising professional to design and install displays in the showroom and its windows with every market week, just as retailers around the world do with every new fashion season (shown in Figures 14.4a–c).

Qualifications

Are you a person who is artistic, resourceful, and loves creating visual displays? If so, this may be the career path for you. Successful visual merchandising professionals are likely to possess the following qualities:

- *Education.* A two- or four-year college degree in fashion merchandising, fashion design, interior design, retail planning and design, fine arts, visual arts, or visual merchandising is often a minimum requirement.

Figure 14.4a
Larusmiani, Milan.

Figure 14.4b
Galeries Lafayette, Paris.

Figure 14.4c
Macy's, New York.

- *Experience.* Many visual display professionals begin as a member of the visual merchandising team for a retailer, installing window and interior displays. Others may come from the fields of interior design, fashion styling, or store planning. With all of these backgrounds, employers expect job candidates to have a variety of visual merchandising work experiences, sales training, and a solid portfolio of work. One of the best ways to prepare for the job search is to build a portfolio of work: photographs of displays created for local merchants, class projects, or internships in visual merchandising. Most visual merchandisers have experience in drafting, either computer-generated or sketched, which allows them to visualize concepts before executing them.

- *Personal characteristics.* The visual merchandising professional must understand design, marketing, and merchandising. An excellent aesthetic sensibility, computer-aided design skills, and an understanding of visual art principles are keys to securing a position in this area. The ability to create effective displays using props, mannequins, and other display components is critical. The successful visual merchandiser requires a breadth of skills and knowledge: an understanding of fashion marketing and merchandising; an eye for color, line, balance, and proportion; a theatrical vision; a strong sense of fashion; the ability to develop and follow time and budget schedules; computer-aided design skills to develop schematics of displays; and the ability to rethink and reuse props, mannequins, and other display components. The effective visual merchandiser is not only self-motivated but also able to take directions to execute work as a team member. This position requires one to be able to work well under pressure.

Career Challenges

People interested in pursuing a visual merchandising career often start at the first rung of the career ladder as a display associate, paid a fairly low hourly wage. Beginning a career in visual merchandising is not easy. The jobs are available in many sectors of the fashion industry, including retail stores, manufacturers' showrooms, and visual merchandising companies; however, not everyone is interested in making the sacrifices that are often required to get started in this field. Low pay, hard work, and long hours, including nights and weekends, describe the start of many visual merchandising careers.

In addition, the job of visual merchandiser does not consist solely of selecting beautiful merchandise and designing attractive displays. It includes vacuuming the floors of the store windows, cleaning the glass, refurbishing props to stay within budget, and working evenings to install displays when customers are not in the store. After paying their dues in this position, display associates may move into assistant visual merchandising director positions and upward to the position of director.

Future Outlook for Visual Merchandisers

Career opportunities in this field are increasing, because the retail industry understands how important visual image is to the consumer. It is significant to note that the job of visual display can be accomplished at all levels of the fashion industry—from the manufacturer/designer to the retailer to ancillary service providers, such as special event producers. Many companies outside of the retail industry hire visual merchandisers as part of their staffs. These include home furnishings and accessories manufacturers, beauty and cosmetics firms, trend-forecasting firms, fabric and notions representatives, and online visual merchandising trend Web sites, as illustrated in Box 14.1. There are also opportunities to work as either a self-employed or company-employed visual merchandiser in all levels of the fashion industry.

STORE PLANNING DIRECTOR

A store planning director develops a plan that details fixture placement, lighting, dressing rooms, restrooms, windows, aisles, and cash and wrap areas of a store. Store planning directors keep several goals in mind when laying out store floor plans. Aesthetic appeal, image consistency, visibility and security of merchandise, comfort and ease of staff and consumers, and merchandising flexibility are among these objectives. Once a floor plan is finalized, all of the supplies (e.g., hangers, bags, and tissue) are purchased, along with the equipment (e.g., four-way fixtures, T-stands, slat walls, mirrors, and computer registers) to set up the retail floor. All of this must be accomplished within a predetermined budget.

The store planning director often works with the visual merchandising director to design the store layout. Window and interior display areas and cases to exhibit small

CASE STUDIES IN CAREER EXPLORATION

BOX 14.1   Visual Merchandiser for an International Retailer

Yes, we are seeking Visual Merchandisers, but only those who refuse to settle. Those who are fearless of pressure. You see, Visual Merchandisers here do more than just style our fashion according to our store guidelines; they also work with the Store Manager and Management team to maximize sales. They also coach the Sales Advisors, identifying and teaching new talent. Most importantly, they are charged with helping our stores make a great first impression every day. Because at the end of the day, we can only sell what inspires our customers and it's up to our Visual Merchandisers to show them what's possible.

Title: Visual Merchandiser
Function: Sales
Department: Store
Reports to: Store Manager – dotted line to Store Visual Manager if applicable
Direct Reports: None

Overall Job Function: Responsible for presenting the garments according to the store guidelines in order to maximize sales with guidance and direction of Store Manager and management team.

Job Responsibilities (including but not limited to):

Customer Service: Provide excellent direct and indirect customer service according to our standards and meet the five basic demands on the selling floor (Smile, Eye Contact, Say Hello, Say Goodbye, and Wear Name Badge), in the fitting room and at the cash point.

Job Knowledge: Ensure garment presentation and garment care are executed per store guidelines:

- Use resources provided by leadership to maintain consistent visual standards. These include the Commercial Handbook, Visual Merchandising Book, Technical Book, Sales Tools, Store Information guidelines, and seasonal plan-o-grams.
- Plan and implement all store campaigns and activities together with the store team. Plan and coordinate a kick-off for management and sales teams.
- Ensure consistent garment care throughout the entire store.

Efficiency:

- Actively work in a commercial way to maximize sales, focusing on priority products, point-of-purchase items as well as ensuring a visual story and theme is clearly demonstrated through the store.
- Order display materials and supplies and maintain displays.
- Keep the visual room clean and organized, minimizing safety risks.
- Plan and work with sales and operation goals to drive growth.
- Support in-store routines when necessary.

Team Player:

- Train, coach and give daily feedback on garment presentation to the store staff.
- Plan and conduct the training together with the Department Manager.

Minimum Candidate Qualifications:

- Associate's degree in a fashion industry specialty preferred.
- 2 years of retail visual merchandising experience.
- Ability to lift in excess of 20 pounds.
- Ability to stand for long periods of time, bend, stretch, engage in repetitive motions, push, pull and carry items (mannequins, clothing, totes, torsos, etc.) for a short distance.
- Ability to climb a ladder and use a step stool.

Competencies:

- Strong visual merchandising skills and the ability to drive business through creativity, fashion consciousness and commerciality.
- Knowledge of basic computer skills.
- Ability to provide day-to-day visual training and guidance.
- Ability to work in a fast-paced, deadline-driven environment.
- Exceptional customer service and interpersonal skills.
- Strong organizational, communication and time management skills.
- Able to work independently while still working within a team environment.
- Must be able to work with hand-and-power operated tools and lift in order to execute display setups.
- Ability to work flexible hours and extended hours at times.
- May be required to travel to support other stores.

Job Status: Nonexempt, Hourly (Part-Time or Full-Time)

goods, fixtures, and mannequins are of interest to both. The store planner who has work experience in visual merchandising often has an edge over one who does not.

Qualifications

What else does it take to have a successful career in store planning? Education, experience, and personal qualifications are the following:

- *Education*. A bachelor's degree in fashion merchandising, interior design, retailing, or a related field is a minimum requirement.
- *Experience*. Between two and five years of experience in retail management, visual merchandising, interior design, or buying are preferred.
- *Personal characteristics*. Store planners are detail oriented, computer literate (CAD), and task oriented. They have effective communication skills—oral, written, and visual. Additionally, they have strong quantitative skills, as space allocation and budgeting are core responsibilities of someone on this career path.

The job outlook for this field is good. Most large retail operations rely on store planning directors for updating facilities, setting up new departments or stores, and keeping the equipment and supplies for the retail floor in stock, up to date, and safe.

Career Challenges

The store planner has a great deal to consider when designing or remodeling a retail operation. Store managers, buyers, sales associates, customers, receiving clerks, and maintenance staff have specific space needs and desires. While working under the control of a budget, the store planner must consider the comfort and safety of all constituencies, while keeping in mind the main goal of the retailer—selling merchandise. Designing a space to meet all of these objectives takes observation, patience, and perseverance.

MALL MANAGER

A **mall manager** is responsible for everything in the mall, from planning its budget and promotional activities to developing its mix of tenants and building community relations. On a given day, the mall manager is involved

with marketing; tenant leasing; increasing capital; building improvements; construction; and tenant, customer, and staff security. What makes a mall successful is often the mix of stores available to the customer (Figure 14.5). The mall manager examines the mall's retail mix to determine its strengths and weaknesses. Incorporating interesting stores and concepts that are unique to the area, as well as balancing the number of apparel, home, service, and food retailers, is key to a mall's success.

Mall managers calculate customer demand into the equation, striving to meet the needs of the current demographic segment and anticipate through research what the future demographics may be. They look at home ownership, income, and customer profiles within the community to understand what the customer is looking for and

Figure 14.5
The image and aesthetics of the mall reflect the type of tenants that mall management will seek out—from restaurants to retailers.

BOX 14.2 MALL MANAGER

Position: Mall Manager
Company: Mall Property Development Group
Location: Columbus, Ohio

Description:

Managers are responsible for leasing (long-term and temporary), negotiation of contracts, staff supervision, office management, budgeting and monthly financial analysis and reporting, tenant and public relations, and operational issues, all with the goal of maximizing the asset value of the property.

Position Requirements:

- Bachelor's degree in the areas of marketing, merchandising, business administration, real estate (leasing), property management and/or retail management, or related field
- Understanding of business administration principles
- Minimum of five years professional management experience; preference given for shopping center management
- Excellent communication and organizational skills
- Temporary and/or permanent leasing experience
- Must possess superior communication and interpersonal skills with a high degree of human relations skills
- Strong management skills

who that customer is. The ultimate goals of the mall manager are to grow the value of the property while improving tenant listings and leasing capacity. To be 100 percent filled is the objective, as is finding ways to complement an already integrated mix of stores. A classified advertisement for a mall manager is featured in Box 14.2.

ASSISTANT MALL MANAGER

In larger malls, the mall manager may supervise one or more assistants. An **assistant mall manager** is responsible for administering mall programs under the supervision of the property's mall manager. This person is critical in communicating operational issues to tenants, contractors, and staff.

Qualifications

A list of the educational requirements, work experiences, and personal characteristics for the successful mall manager and assistant mall manager follows:

- *Education.* A bachelor's degree in management, merchandising, marketing, retailing, business administration, real estate (leasing), property management and/or retail management, or a related field is a minimum requirement.

- *Experience.* Retail sales experience with a variety of retail operations provides an excellent background, including summer or part-time employment during college. An internship with a mall management firm is an excellent way to gain experience in this career path. Many mall managers also secure store management experience, so they can understand the needs and concerns of their mall tenants. Assistant mall managers usually work a minimum of three to five years before moving up to the position of mall manager.

- *Personal characteristics.* The mall manager must be a strong leader who knows what needs to be done. Because multiple tasks arise daily, the mall manager must be a self-motivated individual who is able to work independently. Working in a mall with staff, tenants, and consumers demands being a good listener and an effective problem solver. The assistant mall manager must be able to adapt to a changing work environment and be an ambassador with staff and tenants in representing the mall manager.

Career Challenges

The mall manager and assistant mall manager have a team of bosses: all of the tenants in the mall. It is not easy to please a group of employers with different needs, expectations, and lease costs. Communicating with a group of this size is another challenge. Mall management reports to yet another audience: the mall's customers. It can be stressful to strive for a leasing level of full capacity, particularly when existing tenants and customers have specific ideas on which retailers will complement the current tenant mix. For example, the owner of an athletic footwear store that has made its home in the mall for years may be extremely dissatisfied to find that the mall manager has leased space to a similar retail operation. Keeping both tenants and customers happy and encouraging growth in the mall are two key objectives that may be tough for mall management to accomplish.

Summary

Exterior, interior, and visual merchandising environments profoundly influence image and profitability of all types of businesses in the fashion industry. Pursuit of a career in environments demands both technical and aesthetic know-how. Visual merchandising professionals work with retailers (online and brick-and-mortar); fashion manufacturers and designers; and ancillary companies, such as mannequin manufacturers, prop houses, home furnishings manufacturers, and equipment and fixture vendors. They are responsible for presenting an aesthetically appealing environment that reflects the company's image and sells merchandise. The mall manager and assistant mall manager are responsible for everything in the mall, from planning its budget and creating promotional activities to developing its mix of tenants and building community relations.

Physical and virtual spaces are continually expected to create, buy, sell, and transform. As with many careers, the key to success in these fields is satisfying the client. If you have strong technical, visual, and communication skills, consider a future in environments.

Key Terms

assistant mall manager
mall manager
plan-o-gram

prop house
visual merchandisers
visual merchandising

Online Resources

www.1stdibs.com
www.dirtt.net
fashionbrainacademy.com/trade-show-booths-things
 -you-need-to-know-to-make-great-visual-displays/
www.globalshop.org/
www.houzz.com
www.icsc.org/
www.interiordesign.net/
www.sfd.co.uk/
vimeo.com/68773786 (MockShop)
www.vmsd.com

Discussion Questions

1. Consider a shopping district in the area where you live. What types of businesses stand out? How do the exteriors, interiors, and visual merchandising strategies relate to one another within each business? Evaluate how the sum of the business's environments can create a successful entity.

2. Visit a mall or other type of shopping center and record some of the major tenants (i.e., types of businesses, including retail, restaurant, and entertainment), their adjacencies, and any voids in types of tenants that would draw customers to the facility. Describe the lifestyle approach the shopping facility represents. Identify the most desirable location in the facility based on customer traffic, proximity to parking, and nearness to the best neighboring stores.

3. Take a tour of the mall and note and/or photograph the visual merchandising themes you are seeing in window and in-store displays there. Review your notes and develop a list of the top three fashion retail trends you identify as being repeated in the displays of these retailers.

4. Visit major discount retailer such as Target or Walmart. Carefully examine how the store is laid out, how shoppers move through the merchandise, how signage is used. Examine how things like flooring, colors, lighting, and other visual elements are used. Review your notes and develop a list of techniques you observed to organize the store and help guide customers.

APPENDIX A
CAREER TRACKS AND SALARIES CHART

Below is a list of online resources for those interested in exploring employment opportunities in the fashion industry. Following the online resources, there is a chart of the fashion career positions discussed in the book. They are sorted by career area, with Web links to salary and benefit information.

- https://jobs.wwd.com/   Browse jobs by category; read about featured employers and jobs; check out the student center and internships; and much more.
- www.payscale.com   Here, you can enter a job title and location to find an annual salary, as well as an average salary.
- https://www.bls.gov/spotlight/2012/fashion/home .htm The Bureau of Labor Statistics provides an informative overview of the fashion industry here.
- https://fashionista.com/2018/04/fashion-jobs-aver-age-salary-2018 Three thousand fashion professionals responded to this survey. Browse through the Web pages to get an idea of average salaries in more than forty different fashion-related job tracks, including retail and sales, marketing, publicity, design, social media, and creative tracks, such as art departments.
- www.careerbuilder.com   Lots of good information on job descriptions and salaries at this site. There is an interesting section entitled "8 Jobs for Fashionistas."
- www.indeed.com   A place to find actual fashion jobs by location. This is a good resource for checking out salaries by company and geography. It also provides prerequisites for hiring.
- www.stylecareers.com   This site provides a detailed listing of positions available by employer, location, and type of job. It is updated regularly and used by a great number of key employers in fashion manufacturing, wholesaling, and retailing.

The list below provides links to salary and wage information for the key career areas highlighted in this text. Sources vary based on the position and include bls.gov, salary.com, careerexplorer.com, glassdoor.com, ziprecruiter.com, chron.com, simplyhired.com, and payscale.com. For all positions, a bachelor's degree is a prerequisite for employment.

Account Executive (see Manufacturer's Representative)
(Ch 2)

Advertising/Promotions Director
https://www.bls.gov/ooh/management/advertising -promotions-and-marketing-managers.htm
(Ch 7)

Archivist/Technician, Museum
https://www.bls.gov/ooh/education-training -and-library/curators-museum-technicians-and -conservators.htm
(Ch 13)

Art Director
https://www.bls.gov/ooh/arts-and-design/art -directors.htm
(Ch 8)

Assistant Buyer, Retail
https://www1.salary.com/Merchandise-Buyer -Assistant-salary.html
(Ch 9)

Assistant/Associate Fashion Designer
https://www.glassdoor.com/Salaries/assistant-fashion -designer-salary-SRCH_KO0,26.htm
(Ch 5)

Assistant Importer/Agent
https://www.glassdoor.com/Salaries/import-agent-salary-SRCH_KO0,12.htm
(Ch 3)

Assistant Museum Curator
https://www.glassdoor.com/Salaries/assistant-curator-salary-SRCH_KO0,17.htm
(Ch 13)

Assistant Store Manager
https://www.glassdoor.com/Salaries/associate-store-manager-salary-SRCH_KO0,23.htm
(Ch 10)

Blogger
https://www.ziprecruiter.com/Salaries/Fashion-Blogger-Salary
(Ch 11)

Buyer/Fashion Merchandiser
https://work.chron.com/much-fashion-buyer-make-per-year-starting-23595.html
(Ch 3, 9)

Chief Marketing Officer, Retail
https://www.glassdoor.com/Salaries/chief-marketing-officer-salary-SRCH_KO0,23.htm
(Ch 8)

Colorist, Textiles
https://www.simplyhired.com/salaries-k-textile-colorist-jobs.html
(Ch 2, 6)

Company Salesperson/Representative
https://www.ziprecruiter.com/Salaries/Fashion-Sales-Representative-Salary
(Ch 4)

Copywriter, Corporate
https://www.glassdoor.com/Salaries/copywriter-salary-SRCH_KO0,10.htm
(Ch 8)

Costume Designer
https://www.glassdoor.com/Salaries/costume-designer-salary-SRCH_KO0,16.htm
(Ch 12)

Creative Fashion Director
https://www.glassdoor.com/Salaries/new-york-city-creative-director-fashion-director-salary-SRCH_IL.0,13_IM615_KO14,48.htm
(Ch 2)

Customer Service Manager
https://www.glassdoor.com/Salaries/customer-service-manager-salary-SRCH_KO0,24.htm
(Ch 8, 10)

Department Manager
https://www1.salary.com/Retail-Store-Manager-Salary.html
(Ch 10)

Digital Media Director, Corporate
https://www.glassdoor.com/Salaries/director-digital-media-salary-SRCH_KO0,22.htm
(Ch 11)

Digital Media Artist
https://www.glassdoor.com/Salaries/digital-artist-salary-SRCH_KO0,14.htm
(Ch 11)

Distribution Manager/Allocator
https://www.glassdoor.com/Salaries/distribution-manager-salary-SRCH_KO0,20.htm
(Ch 9)

Divisional Merchandising Manager
https://www.glassdoor.com/Salaries/divisional-merchandise-manager-salary-SRCH_KO0,30.htm
(Ch 9)

Fashion Designer
https://www1.salary.com/Fashion-Designer-I-Salary.html
(Ch 5)

Fashion Photostylist, Entry Level
https://www.glassdoor.com/Salaries/photo-stylist-salary-SRCH_KO0,13.htm
(Ch 7)

Fashion Show/Special Events Planner
https://www.glassdoor.com/Salaries/fashion-event-coordinator-salary-SRCH_KO0,25.htm
(Ch 7, 12)

Fashion Stylist for Television/Film/Video
https://www.payscale.com/research/US/
Job=Fashion_Stylist/Hourly_Rate
(Ch 7, 11)

Fashion/Trend Forecaster
https://www.simplyhired.com/salaries-k-trend
-forecasting-jobs.html
(Ch 1)

Fashion Photographer, Retail
https://www.glassdoor.com/Salaries/fashion
-photographer-salary-SRCH_KO0,20.htm
(Ch 12)

Fashion Stylist/Personal Shopper, Retail
https://www.glassdoor.com/Salaries/personal
-shopper-salary-SRCH_KO0,16.htm
(Ch 7, 12)

General Merchandising Manager
https://www.glassdoor.com/Salaries/general
-merchandise-manager-salary-SRCH_KO0,27.htm
(Ch 9)

Import Production Coordinator
https://www.glassdoor.com/Salaries/import
-production-coordinator-salary-SRCH_KO0,29.htm
(Ch 3)

Import Manager
https://www.glassdoor.com/Salaries/import-manager
-salary-SRCH_KO0,14.htm
(Ch 3)

Licensing Director, Corporate
https://www.indeed.com/salaries/Licensing
-Director-Salaries
(Ch 3)

Mall Manager
https://www.glassdoor.com/Salaries/mall-general
-manager-salary-SRCH_KO0,20.htm
(Ch 14)

Manufacturer's Representative
https://www.bls.gov/ooh/sales/wholesale-and
-manufacturing-sales-representatives.htm
https://careertrend.com/average-salary-sales
-representative-wholesale-apparel-28474.html
(Ch 3, 5)

Merchandise Coordinator
https://www.glassdoor.com/Salaries/merchandise
-coordinator-salary-SRCH_KO0,23.htm
(Ch 4)

Merchandise Planner
https://www.payscale.com/research/US/Job
=Merchandise_Planner/Salary
(Ch 3, 10)

Merchandising/Management Trainee
https://www.glassdoor.com/Salaries/merchandising
-trainee-salary-SRCH_KO0,21.htm
(Ch 9)

Marketing Manager/Director
https://www.bls.gov/ooh/management/advertising
-promotions-and-marketing-managers.htm
(Ch 8)

Model
https://www.bls.gov/ooh/sales/models.htm
(Ch 11)

Model /Talent Agency Director
https://www.ziprecruiter.com/Salaries/Model-Agency
-Salary
(Ch 12)

Museum Conservator
https://www.bls.gov/oes/2017/may/oes254013.htm
(Ch 13)

Museum Director
https://www.payscale.com/research/US/Job=Museum
_Director/Salary
(Ch 13)

Museum Curator
https://www.glassdoor.com/Salaries/museum-curator
-salary-SRCH_KO0,14.htm
(Ch 13)

Operations Manager
https://www.bls.gov/oes/current/oes111021.htm
(Ch 10)

Patternmaker
https://www.bls.gov/oes/2017/may/oes516092.htm
(Ch 4)

Stylist, Retail
https://www.payscale.com/research/US/Job
=Retail_Stylist/Salary
(Ch 12)

Wholesale/Manufacturing
https://www.payscale.com/research/US/Industry
=Apparel_Manufacturing/Salary
(Ch 6)

Product Development Manager/Director, Retail
https://www.payscale.com/research/US/Job
=Product_Development_Manager/Salary
(Ch 6)

Production Assistant
https://www.glassdoor.com/Salaries/fashion
-production-assistant-salary-SRCH_KO0,28.htm
(Ch 4)

Production Manager
https://www.payscale.com/research/US/Job
=Production_Manager%2c_Manufacturing/Salary
(Ch 4)

Production Planner
https://www.payscale.com/research/US/Job
=Production_Planner%2C_Manufacturing/Salary
(Ch 3, 4)

Promotion Director/Manager
https://www.payscale.com/research/US/Job
=Promotion_Director/Salary
(Ch 7 and 9)

Public Relations Manager
https://www1.salary.com/Public-Relations-Manager
-Salary.html
(Ch 7)

Quality Control Manager
https://www.payscale.com/research/US/Job
=Quality_Control_Manager/Salary
(Ch 4, 6)

Regional (District) Store Manager https://www
.payscale.com/research/US/Job=Regional
_Manager%2C_Retail/Salary
(Ch 10)

Resource Room Director/Reference Librarian
https://www.payscale.com/research/US/Job
=Reference_Librarian/Salary
(Ch 2)

Retail Store Owner/Entrepreneur
https://www.payscale.com/research/US/Job
=Retail_Store_Owner/Salary
(Ch 10)

Security Manager, Retail Store
https://www.ziprecruiter.com/Salaries/Retail
-Security-Salary
(Ch 9)

Showroom Manager/Sales
https://www.indeed.com/salaries/Fashion-Showroom
-Manager-Salaries
(Ch 4)

Social Media Manager, Midlevel
https://www.payscale.com/research/US/Job
=Social_Media_Manager/Salary
(Ch 7)

Sourcing Manager
https://www.payscale.com/research/US/Job
=Strategic_Sourcing_Manager/Salary
(Ch 3)

Specification Technician
https://neuvoo.ca/salary/?job=Fit%20Technician
(Ch 5)

Store Manager
https://www.payscale.com/research/US/Job
=Retail_Store_Manager/Salary
(Ch 10)

Store Planning Director
https://www.payscale.com/research/US/Job
=Store_Planning_Director/Salary
(Ch 14)

Sustainability Officer
https://www.payscale.com/research/US/Job
=Sustainability_Officer/Salary
(Ch 4)

Technical Designer
https://www.payscale.com/research/US/Job
=Fashion_Technical_Designer/Salary
(Ch 5, 6)

Textile/Apparel Cutter
https://www.payscale.com/research/US/Job
=Fabric_Cutter/Hourly_Rate
(Ch 4)

Textile Designer
https://www.payscale.com/research/US/Job
=Textile_Designer/Salary
(Ch 2)

Textile Engineer
https://www.ziprecruiter.com/Salaries/
Textile-Engineer-Salary
(Ch 2)

Traffic Manager
https://www.payscale.com/research/US/Job
=Traffic_Manager/Salary
(Ch 4)

Transparency Officer
https://www.payscale.com/research/US/Job
=Risk_Officer/Salary
(Ch 4)

Visual Merchandising Assistant, Entry Level
https://www.ziprecruiter.com/Salaries/Visual
-Merchandising-Assistant-Salary
(Ch 14)

Visual Merchandising Director/Manager
https://www1.salary.com/Visual-Merchandising-
Director-Salaries.html
(Ch 14)

Web Site Designer/Developer
https://www.payscale.com/research/US/Job
=Web_Designer/Salary
(Ch 11)

Writer/Journalist
https://work.chron.com/average-wage-fashion-writer
-19099.html
(Ch 11)

APPENDIX B
RÉSUMÉ TIPS, INTERVIEW GUIDELINES, EMPLOYER RESEARCH, AND RÉSUMÉ SAMPLES

The Résumé

Your résumé should:

- *Be more an outline than a narrative.* Think of it as a calling card or an offering to a prospective buyer. Keep it simple and to the point. Tried-and-true résumé tips and sample résumés follow to assist you in making your calling card a memorable one that spurs the employer to contact you immediately.

- *Be specific, particularly in the Objective section.* Most interviewers do not want to conduct career counseling. Know what types of career positions you are prepared for and want to pursue before you send your résumé and indicate this under the *Objective* heading. If you are interested in more than one type of position, develop different objectives and design separate résumés for each type of position, focusing on the needs of the employer and the specific career track.

- *Be factual.* Tell the truth and nothing but the truth. Do not get caught having to explain a point that is not clear and does not have support.

- *Read like the trailer for a great movie.* The résumé should help you get through the door without telling the whole story. You need to be ready to jump in and to fill in the gaps during phone or online screenings and personal interviews.

Support your résumé with:

- *A good letter of application* (often referred to as a cover letter). It should be short and to the point. It should show that you have done your homework and know a thing or two about the company you are pursuing. Make sure the recipient knows what you want (e.g., a full-time job, an internship, an informational interview, a contact, etc.) and how you have prepared to succeed.

- *A good listing of references.* Ask references for permission before including them on your reference listing. Include the job title and complete contact information (e.g., postal mailing address, e-mail address, and telephone number) of each reference. Some job seekers add a brief description of their relationship and work experiences with the reference (e.g., intern, part-time sales associate, etc.).

- *Excellent target employers provided by your contacts.* Ask alumni (graduates of your institution); they want to help if they can. Ask family, friends, faculty, guest speakers, internship contacts, former employers, and hometown contacts. This is how you develop your network, one that you build throughout your career.

- *The informational interview.* Identify key professionals within your target career path and schedule meetings to learn more about the business or the career path.

Contact people in both human resources and other areas. The more people in support of you, the better your opportunity for success.

- *Positive social media presence.* Clean up your social media before launching your job search. Make your accounts private, hide or delete any inappropriate posts, deactivate old accounts, add professional photos and delete anything that might compromise your professional image. Add a professional bio, edit your handles and URLs, make it a point to post industry-related news, and follow inspiring people and companies.

Tried-and-True Résumé Tips

No matter if your résumé is scanned and e-mailed, sent through the postal system, or hand-delivered, its content is most important. Follow these tried-and-true résumé tips as you work toward résumé perfection.

- Always use spellcheck.
- Begin with a goal or an objective. It should include key words that are pulled from the position description and/or job advertisement.
- For *Education*, include your major, minor, and month and year of graduation. You may include your grade point average. Some employment professionals suggest listing the grade point average only if it is 3.0 or above on a 4.0 scale. Most professionals also recommend that you do not include high school information if you are a college student or graduate.
- *Work Experience* should include internships and part-time jobs (within reason).
- If you are lacking relevant employment experience, include information about college projects that would relate to the position for which you are applying.
- Include extracurricular activities, keeping in mind these tips:
  - Identify the skills and experiences you will need in your target field and look for organizations on campus where you will get these.
  - If you hold an officer position within the organization, or head up various committees within the organization, mention these.
  - Have a variety of extracurricular experiences to demonstrate your ability to work with a range of people.

- Be involved throughout your college career, not just during your final year in school.
- Many companies place a high value on service activities, such as volunteer work on campus, in your community, or in the world community.
- List specific skills related to your career goals, such as computer skills, language fluency, international experiences, etc.
- List outcomes whenever possible. For example, if you led a fundraising project for a philanthropic organization, state the amount of money raised and the name and a brief description of the charity.
- You may choose to list highlights of your coursework (courses that relate to the position) under the *Education* section, if you do not have adequate experience to fill a one-page résumé. If you do have enough experiences to effectively fill a one-page résumé, courses can be listed on a separate sheet of paper, along with a brief description if the course titles do not adequately explain them. You may want to have this list in case the interviewer asks for this information.
- Keep the résumé to one page. Although you may have many great experiences in college, you likely have not had enough yet to warrant more than a one-page résumé.
- For hard copies, use light-colored, standard size (8 1/2" x 11") paper. Use high-quality paper and a good printer. Choose white, eggshell, beige, or light gray paper. Avoid grainy paper.
- Place your name and contact information at the top (in the header) of each page after the first one, such as a reference listing.
- If you are sending your résumé via postal mail, do not fold the résumé; send it in a flat envelope. Do not use staples.

INTERVIEW GUIDELINES
Planning for the Interview

- Be prepared. Research the company *and* the industry *before* the interview. Know exactly when and where to go for the interview well ahead of time.
- Come prepared with good questions to ask and know the good questions the interviewer will likely ask (it's even better if you know the answers).

- Be polite and courteous. You are building your professional reputation.
- Think of the interview in the following segments:

The Time Breakdown of an Interview by Minutes

0–5   Size it up.
Be impressive. You are both evaluating each other and first impressions count.

5–20   Sell yourself.
This is the part when you explain your résumé. Know which parts of your background to stress. Do not be shy about your accomplishments—specifically, outcomes. Describe yourself and your experiences but remember the time. You will be judged on how well you organize your thoughts. If the interviewer asks you a yes or no question, answer it that way. Watch and listen to know if he or she wants you to elaborate.

20–25   Let the interviewer sell you.
Ask questions about the organization. Why is it such a great place to work? Remember, this is an important decision for you.

25–30   Wrap it up.
Determine what will happen next. Will the interviewer call you, or should you contact him or her? When?

- A well-written thank-you letter is essential after the interview.

Points to Keep in Mind for the Interview

1. Be strategic and focused.
2. Even if you do not know exactly what you want, sound like you at least have an idea.
3. Really understand the reality of the workplace and the reality of really working.
4. Service businesses in the fashion industry are good places to look. Be creative.
5. New industries and businesses are often the ones seeking new employees with fresh ideas.
6. Think about the environments in which you would like to work (e.g., a large company, a big-city location, a formal structure, etc.).

7. Find a good training program. Down the road you will benefit greatly from a good foundation. Sales and retail management often have the best programs. Internships can also provide excellent training.
8. Consider the merits of graduate school. Then, consider working first. Evaluate the pros and cons of each. More and more young professionals have advanced degrees. They are likely the people you will compete with on the career ladder. In contrast, you may want to gain some experience in the workplace in order to add personal and professional value to further education. You may even find an employer who will pay for graduate coursework.
9. Whether you are completing or have completed a bachelor's or master's degree, consider yourself fortunate to have a solid education. Your college or university has provided you with a strong foundation for lifelong learning and diverse exposure. Recruiters appreciate that.
10. Enjoy yourself. Have fun! Sell yourself; you are your most important and valued resource. Many doors can be opened for you, but it is up to you to sell yourself in order to walk through them.
11. Be realistic. Send out many more letters of application and résumés than you believe you will need. There is much competition in the job market. The more opportunities you have, the higher your chances of having several positions offered, giving you the chance to choose from among them.

RESEARCHING EMPLOYERS

Why Research Employers?

Researching prospective employers is—surprisingly—a frequently overlooked step when applying for a job. It is easy to get excited when you believe you have found the perfect opportunity; however, not digging deep into an employer's current and past situations and its reputation can prove to be a costly mistake. You can be certain that employers are checking your references, online profiles, and college credentials before extending an offer. You would be remiss not to do the same with any prospective hiring organization. The more you know about a company, the better you will be able to communicate your value to this employer during your interview. The hard work that you put into your research will pay off by reflecting your interest, confidence, and enthusiasm to employers, and providing you with the confidence that this is a secure employment opportunity. Taking the time to learn about a company and then sharing what you learned about it is a form of flattery to company representatives. Before you complete your letter of application and send out your résumé, we will take a closer look at why you should research employers, what to look for, and how to investigate like a detective.

The majority of college graduates have held some type of employment; some have had wonderful experiences on these jobs, whereas others may have been wondering what the employer was thinking, how bad it could get, and when it would be over. In the latter case, they learned the hard way to spend dedicated time learning about an employer before applying for a job. Why should you do some investigative work on prospective employers?

- *To determine if the company is a fit for you.* You may find you do not particularly like a specific career path in the industry. You may dig up unfortunate corporate digital dirt or uncover information on poor employee relations.
- *To decide if you are right for the company.* Some companies or industries may not be the right fit for your skill sets, values, or corporate culture preferences. It is also possible to find that you are not really interested in the company's products or services. Be sure to consider your goals, desires, and ethics to see how they fit given the information you have revealed.
- *To help tailor your résumé and letter of application to the position.* Knowing specifically what makes the company successful can turn your application into the winning ticket.
- *To give you the information required to effectively address the organization's needs.* Knowing why the company needs to hire is key to addressing how you can help the company.
- *To help you prepare effective interview questions.* Knowing specific industry information or advanced product knowledge can get you closer to an offer as you impress the interviewer with insightful questions and answers.
- *To demonstrate sincere interest in the company.* A common interview question is "Why do you want to work for us?" Having an educated answer puts you ahead of the competition. One of the most important ways to distinguish yourself in an interview is to speak knowledgeably about the organization.

- *To educate yourself about a particular career path in the industry.* Perhaps this job is in a new sector of the industry for you. Get in the know before writing your résumé and shopping for an interview.

When to Research Employers

The best time to research employers is before you prepare your résumé and letter of application to request an interview with a company. By doing some due diligence early, you can quickly rule out firms and positions that do not match your personal needs, academic requirements, or desired career path.

Where to Conduct Employer Research

Conducting employer research is much like preparing a college assignment or project. The idea is to develop two lists: one of companies for which you are interested in working and another of resources for researching businesses. Next are examples of a few good places to start your list of resources to help your investigation of prospective employers:

- *Corporate Web site.* Look for industry information, product or service details, and management information. Most corporate sites indicate company age, size, ownership, locations, and leadership or management details, often in the "About the Company" or "About us" link at the top or bottom of the Web site's landing page. Check the Web site to see if the company is public or private. A review of annual reports may reveal interesting corporate details, such as the firm's financial situation, health of the industry, mission statement, and number of employees.
- *Google.* Search forums, Web sites, blogs, and online articles that will enable you to see what others have to say about the company's products, services, and employee relations. You may be surprised. Take these as they are—opinions and comments. Make a decision that is based on facts yet allows room for majority opinion.
- *Better Business Bureau.* This organization can alert you to complaints against companies in specific geographic areas or cities. You may want to contact them to see if your prospective employer is on the list.

- *Consumer and trade publications.* Research the employer's industry activity through print, in addition to Internet sources. Read magazines, newspapers, trade publications, and journals related to the field and organization.
- *Trade associations.* Is the company affiliated with an association? Consult association Web sites to see if the prospective employing organization is in good standing and how it contributes to the profession.
- *Chambers of Commerce.* You may want to begin by contacting the Chambers of Commerce in the communities where the companies you are interested in are located. You will often find a searchable comprehensive directory online.
- *Public relations and promotions.* Check out any product or service advertisements the company runs in the media. Locate press releases about the company. Many companies have these at their Web sites; however, keep in mind that these are usually positive reflections of the firm. Employer recruitment brochures are a great marketing tool for the company and provide a good overview for the prospective employee. Brochures and sales flyers also offer a good look at the company.
- *Former or current employee references.* Do you know any current or former employees? Ask them why they left, who supervised them, and if they would ever work there again.

Types of Information to Uncover Through Employer Research

Begin by locating general information about each company in which you are interested. Keep an accurate record of what you learn. If you are ready to go onto the Internet to begin your research, keep the following in mind:

1. Know what you are looking for before you go online. Keep a list beside you so that you can check off items as you locate them. An electronic spreadsheet is ideal to post information as you find it. It is easy to get frustrated or disinterested in the research phase when you don't keep organized records.
2. Bookmark major Web sites as you come across them. Create folders to organize the sites.
3. Although the Internet is an invaluable research tool, the library is still one of the best places to locate information. The reference librarian at your college, university, or local library should be able to point you in the direction of many useful directories and indexes. Examples of resources that you will find in the library are *Dunn and Bradstreet* reports, *Standard & Poor's* corporation records and rating services, *World Business Directory*, *Hoovers*, and *Ward's Business Directory*. Now that you know where to look for general information, you may want to format a spreadsheet of which details to uncover.
4. Consider these variables when researching an employer:

- Mission, philosophy, and objectives of the company
- Source(s) of funding, including assets, earnings, and losses
- Company ownership (e.g., private or public, sole proprietorship or partnership, foreign or domestic ownership, etc.)
- Company divisions or subsidiaries and their locations
- Board of directors or advisory board
- Reputation of the company
- History or background and age of company
- Products (to include services) that the company sells or provides
- Target market or clientele list
- Strategies and goals
- Market positioning or repositioning efforts
- Areas of specialization
- New projects and major achievements
- Size of the company and number of employees
- Patterns of growth or decline
- Forecast of future growth
- Recent issues or events (e.g., layoffs or hiring, closings or expansion, etc.)
- Number of employees
- Location of the company headquarters and length of time it has been established there
- Office/facility environment
- Personnel policies
- Types of people employed and from where employees are recruited
- Corporate culture
- Health of the industry
- Compensation and benefits for entry-level employees
- Career path or promotion opportunities within the company

Be sure to consider other details specific to the types of positions in which you are most interested. It is important not to be slow, vague, or inaccurate about this process, as any employer worth your time and effort on the job is well worth your time and effort now.

The Final Word on Researching Before Sending Out Your Résumés

Finding the right job is work. Researching a prospective employer is work, but the results can be very rewarding, especially if you find the ideal positions based on your findings. It just makes sense to do some homework on a company before sending out résumés and letters of application to just any firm you hear about or stumble across. You are not simply applying for any job. This is the start of your career, and you are determining who will be the provider of your paycheck in the future. You are your most important investment of time and energy. Next, samples of résumés for a range of fashion careers are presented.

SAMPLE RÉSUMÉS

The résumé of a product developer needs to illustrate abilities in trend forecasting, knowledge of various target markets, and strong analytical, negotiation, and leadership skills. In addition, the product developer must show a detail orientation, which is important when communicating with factories, tracking sample status, calculating costs, and communicating details to the merchandising/design team and/or factories. Creative and business skills are required, with problem-solving abilities in both areas. The ability to work under pressure is essential. (See the résumé example for a product developer position.)

A résumé for a digital media artist or graphic designer should be eyecatching and creative. A résumé in this field is viewed as an extension of a candidate's work. Social media should be highlighted, and the résumé writer's own social media should be representative of the image/brand she or he is intending to convey. Social media fluency and incorporating a three-dimensional presence through the

résumé will help the prepared candidate secure an interview. The résumé will open the interviewer's door, but the portfolio (online, more frequently) often lands a job in this field. It is okay to be different, but be certain to show familiarity with a wide array of techniques and software skills within your portfolio, as well as branding your own unique design style. (See the résumé example for a digital media artist or graphic designer in fashion.)

A resume for a theatrical designer should illustrate the applicant's design ability—both creative and technical. The theatrical designer needs to be able to design and direct the visual aspects of a production, with attention to the elements of the story, technical requirements, and historic accuracy. The résumé needs to show that the applicant has the necessary range of education and experience to design and execute the physical elements of a production, while also working collaboratively with the director and actors, as well as manage a budget and supervise the production crew.

An effective résumé for a buyer or merchandiser should highlight the following qualities: an eye for fashion and an understanding of the target market, the ability to keep up with the latest trends, skills in organization and interpersonal relationships, the ability to work under pressure, and strong mathematical abilities. (See the two examples of résumés for a merchandiser.)

The résumé for a fashion writer is almost as important as an interview because it reflects the essence of the position—communicating through writing. The writer who actively bridges the gap between print and digital media has what it takes to be a twenty-first-century journalist. In fact, many employers will investigate the number of followers a journalism candidate has on Facebook, Instagram, Twitter, and other relevant social media. Of course, you need to show that you can write well, but personal qualities to illustrate in the writer's résumé include a curious and positive attitude, a proactive approach, the ability to multitask effectively, and a generalist's knowledge of the fashion industry. An excellent article for fashion writer candidates to review is located at www.huffington post.com/2014/05/27/fashion-editor-career-advice -eva-chen-_n_5372007.html. (See the sample résumé for a fashion journalist.)

JORDAN L. BAJKOWSKI
(bei-kau-ski)

Objective
To secure an internship in product development and trend forecasting in which I can test and apply skills in a way that allows continued development and benefits the firm.

Employment
Intern
Cotton, Inc., May 17 – Aug. 2, 2019; New York, NY

- Created a 20-page spring/summer 2021 menswear forecast for the Product Trend Analysis (PTA) team that consisted of macro trend, color, silhouette, fabric, and print/pattern analysis.
- Researched, analyzed, and synthesized over 50 text sources and over 400 runway and street style images from spring 2019 shows in Milan, Paris, and London.
- Explored the New York City streets, taking street style and art exhibit photos to inspire the PTA team.

Intern
BridgeBlue Sourcing Partners, Jan. – May 2019, Springfield, MO

- Developed social media and video marketing strategies for home products line.
- Created trend forecasting and analysis materials through visual media.
- Collaborated with teammates through entire creative theming and product development process by editing/revising blog post copy and writing copy of my own.

Intern
Baldwin Denim, Standard Style, LLC., Jun. 2018 – Aug. 2018; Kansas City, MO

- Cultivated relationships with clients to create a community dynamic around brand and product.
- Conveyed unique selling points of brand to clients through superior product knowledge.
- Developed styling expertise through exercise and practical application for clientele.

Education
University of Kentucky, GPA 3.38, 4.0 scale
Fall 2016 – Present
Anticipated Graduation: May 2020
Bachelor of Science – Entrepreneurship

Awards, Honors, Community Experience
Inter-Fraternity Council
President, Fall 2018 – Present

- Administrate and govern student community of over 1,000 members
- Coordinate executive council of 10 vice-presidents and $30,000 budget
- Increased annual IFC membership by 12%, exceeding a goal of 10% (422 to 472)

Pi Kappa Phi
President, Fall 2017 – Fall 2018

- Applied for and won the Fraternity and Sorority Life Chapter of the Year Award for 2018
- Oversaw 27 officers and committee chairs and a budget of $20,000
- Increased chapter membership from 40 to 70 over one year
- Fraternity and Sorority Life Outstanding Male Sophomore of the Year, 2017

Skills
Microsoft Office and Adobe Creative Suite

Coty Beagle
Graphic Designer
& Web Developer

 Email
 Telephone
 Address

 LinkedIn
 Facebook
 Twitter

I am currently looking for freelance and consultant work.

My Work:

For more info and examples of my work, please visit

beaglecreative.com

Personal Statement:

> Well-rounded designer with extensive experience in multimedia. Enthusiastic, intuitive, insightful, and hardworking.
>
> Views technology as an incredible tool for improving communication between people and understands that, above all, the user experience is key.
>
> Great in a pinch and knowledgeable in current industry shifts and trends.

References:

Brent Morgan – CEO
reference@domain.com
Brent managed me directly at MIS Technologies.

Joan Varney – Accountant
reference@domain.com
Joan managed me directly at The Bobblehead.

Jorge Cruz – Account Manager
reference@domain.com
Jorge is a colleague that works for Ikros.

Ashley Stevenson– System Admin
reference@domain.com
Ashley is a friend who works for the USDA.

Education and Work

○ Education ◉ Work Experience

Fort Osage – High School Diploma
2013
Took advanced coursework in desktop publishing, photography, and biosciences.

MIS Technologies – Webmaster, Creative Manager & Consultant
September 2015 – Present
As webmaster and creative manager, I maintained the company's server, designed marketing graphics, maintained websites, and created an internet presence. I also created flash animations, optimized web graphics, and programmed UIs for control units.

M.C.C. – Associate of Arts
2013 – 2015
Additional coursework in graphic design, marketing, and web design.

The Bobblehead LLC – Webmaster & Creative Manager
September 2015 – Present
I maintained company servers, created promotional artwork, designed web content, managed the company's website, and oversaw all internet marketing including SEO and SMO. We rose from page ten on Google to page one in a year.

Beagle Creative – CEO/Owner
July 2015 – Present
Specialization in UI design for web, mobile, and applications, always keeping UX in mind. Best-practice knowledge leads to groundbreaking presentations. Understanding the implications of the web and its medium and its ability to reach very targeted audiences.

U.M.K.C. – B.A. Communications (Emph, Film & Media Arts)
2017 – 2019
Additional coursework in graphic design, marketing, and web development.

Ikros / Crossover Graphics – Technical Account Manager
July 2019 – October 2019
I was responsible for maintaining client relationships, overseeing web projects, developing detailed project mockups and wireframes, reinforcing and furthering industry-standard UX practices, and building department processes for an online presence and an intranet.

Technical Expertise

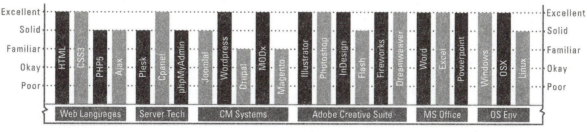

Carrie Von Kleig

Education

Smithsonian National Museum of Design
Parons, The New School
M.A. History of Design and Curatorial Studies

New Jersey Institute of Technology
B.S. Industrial Design (2015)
B.A. Technical Theater (2015)
Magna Cum Laude

Licensed Tour Guide of New York City
Department of Consumer Affairs, May 2014

Experience

Educational Fellow
Cooper Hewitt Museum (New York, NY) / Sep 2015 – Ongoing
Smithsonian Design Museum under director Caroline Payson /
Managing Docents, curriculum fortours, Overseeing Docent Program.

Studio Manager / Sales Rep
American Design Club (Brooklyn, NY) / Jan 2014 – Ongoing
Under principal Kiel Mead / Manager of Kiel Mead Design Studio.

Historian Intern
Society of Architectural Historian / May 2012 – August 2013
Managing "tags" (internet database) / Under Editor G. Esperdy

Tour Guide
Bike and Roll, NYC / May 2013 – Ongoing
Guided Biking tours of Central Park / Licensed NYC Tour Guide

Archivist
Jim Wise Archiving Center / May 2012 – May 2015
Organizing rare and special materials / Art and document handling

Industrial Design Intern
Pod Design (Brooklyn, NY) / May 2013 – August 2013
Under principal Brooks Atwood / Product families, packaging,
and graphic design

Production Design Intern
Workhorse Design (Brooklyn, NY) / Sep 2013 – Dec 2013
Under principal Austin Swister / Production Design Process

Assistant to the Theater Director
NJIT – Rutgers Theater Department / February 2011 – May 2015

Office assistant / Graphic Design work / Backstage Managing

Skills

Adobe Creative Suite
Excellent: Photoshop, Illustrator, InDesign
Proficient: Premier, After Effects

3-D Modeling / Rendering
Excellent: Solidworks, Rhino
Proficient: 3dS Max, Autodesk Revit

Awards

NADA Scholarship Recipient 2016
Smithsonian Institutions
Scholarship reward for academic pursuits abroad, application
reviewed by NADA Committee

Senior Class President
New Jersey Institute of Technology
Senior class president for the year 2014 – 2015. Responsible for
representing senior class in student government, event planner for
multiple trips including international, graduation speaker.

School of Art & Design Medal
College of Architecture of Design
The highest honor from the school of Art and Design, given to one
graduating senior who exemplifies all four years of excellence,
consistency, leadership and involvement with the community.

Best in Show: ICFF 2014
International Contemporary Furniture Fair
Named as one of Design Milk's "Best in Shows" for 2014 for Rubber
Ottoman.

Industrial Design Distinguished Designer
College of Architecture and Design:
Named top industrial Design Student 2013 – 2014.

Designer's Director Scholarship
College of Architecture and Design:
Top Student entering their senior year in Design School.

Design Showcase 2015 / 2014 / 2013
College of Architecture and Design:
Selected student projects to be put on display.

Highlander Achievement Award
New Jersey Institute of Technology
Two senior students picked out of undergraduates as most
contributing to student body through campus involvement, academic
excellence, and leadership.

NATHAN GREGORY COATES

<u>Objective</u>
Obtain a position in a growth-oriented firm where I can contribute to the bottom line.

<u>Related Industry Experience</u>   **June 2018 – Present**
Bombfell, Inc. New York, NY
> ***E-Commerce Merchandise Assistant*** – Assist Head Buyer (HB) with all necessary tasks, manage calendar, schedule appointments for Market week both locally and nationally; partner with HB to procure buying selections and assortments for improved sales performance; coordinate assortment to enable best merchandising for multiple brands and classification pairing with HB; execute and manage purchase order process from entry to maintenance and receiving logistics; mediate logistics between vendor and 3rd party warehouse, resolving all discrepancies; continually update vendor guidelines and ensure follow through.
> ***E-Commerce Coordinator and Stylist*** – Created and maintained digital and physical filling system/library for financials, line sheets, and all essential buying materials enhancing workplace efficiency; excelled in vendor relations and new brand procurement; delivered repeat and referral business while increasing projected revenue by over 2x in less than 6 months; directed commercial and editorial photo shoots focusing on web strategy and execution; assisted developers to increase programming effectiveness by sourcing glitches and creating web enhancements; strategized with marketing team to implement ideas for user acquisition, increased over 3x.
> ***E-Commerce Intern*** – Met daily styling goals for extensively growing clientele base; handled daily customer service requests promptly and accurately; maintained stock room organization; increased social media presence by over 2.2x in 3 months, achieved through planned content distribution, search optimization, and strategic user interaction.

                                                                                   March 2017 – May 2018
Aldo Group, Springfield, MO
> ***Senior Sales Lead/Key Holder*** – Excelled in training both new managers and brand associates; aided in the merchandise planning and set EOD/EOW/EOY financial objectives; ensured brand associates met sales quotas and followed corporate regulations; coordinated frequent communications with regional and district management; conducted store opening and closing procedures directly under management.
> ***Brand Representative*** – During the six months before promotion to Sales Lead, accomplished personal and corporate initiatives resulting in consistently performing with some of the highest numbers within our district and nationally, maintaining excellent customer relations as noted by consumer feedback; addressed customer concerns/queries regarding purchases, returns and repairs; stimulated sales via visual merchandising and extensive brand/product quality knowledge.

                                                                                   August 2014 – Present
Freelance Stylist/Personal Shopper
> Style experience led to TV spot on KOLR 10 News as a style consultant; produced multiple fashion shows, raised over $10,000 to effectively execute senior fashion show; assisted the Dean of the College of Business to educate business students about appropriate industry attire. Success led to evaluating the Dean's personal image/wardrobe issues, worked as her Personal Shopper/Stylist; developed costumes for theatrical stage and film productions.

<u>Education</u>
Bachelor of Science, Fashion Merchandising/Design and Minor Advertising and Promotion
College of Business, Missouri State University, Springfield, MO   **Graduation August 2018**
> Dean's List Honors 2015 – 2018; graduated as Merchandiser of the Year.

<u>Related Volunteer Experience</u>   **September 2018**
Couture Fashion Week, New York, NY
> Worked as assistant to the director, completing all tasks in a timely and efficient manner.   **April 2016**
The Plaid Door Resale Boutique – The Junior League of Springfield
> ***Visual Merchandising Volunteer*** – Supports abused women and children. Incorporated knowledge of visual merchandising and retail planning by redesigning/merchandising entire floor layout and window displays to increase sales/engage traffic; provided comprehensive plan for continued implementation.

<u>Skills and Proficiencies</u>
> ***Computer*** – Extensive knowledge of Microsoft Excel, Word and Power Point; equivalent Macintosh programs; Adobe Photoshop and Illustrator; Lectra Knit, Print, Weave and Style.
> ***Talents*** – Working proficiency in French language; Can toe touch, landing in a split for comedic value or a needed distraction.

Carly E. Minis

[contact information redacted]

EDUCATION

Indiana University   May 2018
School of Art and Design   Bloomington, IN
Bachelor of Science: Major: Apparel Merchandising, Minor: Business
Honors: Ruth Mary Griswold Scholarship, BRAG Scholarship, Leah Weidman Scholarship

APPAREL MERCHANDISING AND RETAIL EXPERIENCE

Macy's Inc   Oct 2018 – Present
Assistant Buyer – Junior Dresses   New York, NY
- Support buying team to drive sales by devising and recommending assortment strategies and supporting assortment optimization Coordinate executive council of 10 vice-presidents and $30,000 budget
- Run daily, weekly, and seasonal sales reports to analyze business
- Maintain vendor database, contact list and vendor order logs to keep track of product and timely shipments
- Analyze business trends to identify growth opportunities

Foot Locker, Inc.   May 2017 – Aug 2017
Summer Intern - Allocations   New York, NY
- Assisted in the management of inventory
- Analyzed product needs across all stores nationally
- Maintained Excel Spreadsheets for merchandising systems
- Assisted with the development and distribution of reports
- Collaborated with a team for consistent and strategic alignment

My Sister's Closet   Oct 2016 – Dec 2016
Retail Fashion Intern   Bloomington, IN
- Created and advertised compelling looks for women entering the job market
- Posted fashion trends and events on social media
- Recruited and photographed models and wrote fashion scripts

Cole Haan   May 2016 – Aug 2016
Retail Sales Associate   Kansas City, MO
- Achieved and exceeded sales goals
- Provided a world class shopping experience
- Responsible for visual merchandising standards consistent with brand strategies
- Partnered with management ream on implementation of monthly directives

Nordstrom Rack   May 2015 – Jan 2016
Sales Associate – Women's Department   Overland Park, KS
- Ensured high levels of customer satisfaction through excellent sales service
- Collaborated with coworkers to provide exceptional customer service
- Assessed customer needs and provided assistance and information on product features
- Assisted in display of merchandise
- Quoted prices, discounts and accepted payment at the register and on mobile devices

GLOSSARY

academic curator training Instruction for the prospective museum curator on how to direct the accession, deaccession, storage, and exhibition of collections; the study of managing museum collections. (Chapter 13)

accession The addition of an artifact to a museum collection. (Chapter 13)

account executive Sells to a manufacturer and manages accounts. May also be called *manufacturer's representative* or *sales representative*. (Chapter 2)

advertising A type of promotion that is paid, nonpersonal communication delivered through mass media. (Chapter 7)

advertising director Develops and implements a company's paid promotional strategy for the purpose of increasing visibility, image, and, ultimately, sales. (Chapter 7)

advertising photography Expresses a product's personality or illustrates a magazine story and is usually classified as still life, food, transportation, portraiture, or landscape. Also known as *editorial photography*. (Chapter 12)

advertising promotion staff Develops presentations to help the sales representatives of print and electronic media firms sell advertising to new and existing accounts. (Chapter 7)

advertising research assistant Helps sales representatives sell advertising space, in a publication for example, by supplying facts that an advertiser will want to know, such as the number of issues sold and top locations in terms of sales volume, or the profile and buying power of the publication's readers. (Chapter 8)

advertising sales representative Sells advertising for consumer and trade publications. (Chapter 7)

archive technician In a museum, this person helps archivists organize, maintain, and provide access to historical documentary materials. (Chapter 13)

archivist Analyzes, describes, catalogues, and exhibits records and documents that are retained by museums because of their importance and potential value, benefiting researchers and the public. (Chapter 13)

art director Develops and implements the creative concepts for advertising, catalogues, mailers, and signage; this person provides an overall and consistent visual view of the manufacturing or retailing company, including signage, photography, direct mail, and packaging. (Chapter 8)

assistant buyer Supports the buyer, often working with the six-month plan, open-to-buy, inventory, and vendor follow-up; takes direction from the buyer. (Chapter 9)

assistant fashion designer Supports designers by helping them create, modify, and locate new materials, styles, colors, and patterns for fashion brands and labels. (Chapter 5)

assistant importer Works for the import production coordinator and follows up on orders with overseas suppliers. He or she also communicates with freight companies and customs agents, processes documents, and checks pricing agreements. (Chapter 3)

assistant mall manager Responsible for administering mall programs under the supervision of the property's general manager (mall manager). This position is critical in communication among tenants, contractors, consumers, and mall staff. (Chapter 14)

assistant photographer Supports the photographer and works with clients and suppliers; organizes estimates, invoices, and payments; arranges props and assists with lighting; communicates with photographic labs and stylists; helps the photographer on shoots; and maintains the photographer's Web site and portfolio. (Chapter 12)

assistant piece goods buyer Often works with the piece goods buyer to calculate quantities of fabrics needed, to follow up on deliveries, and to locate fabric sources, while training for a buying position in the future. (Chapter 3)

assistant store manager Assists the store manager in scheduling employees, overseeing sales performance in the store, planning promotions, etc.—all of the daily responsibilities of operating a store successfully. (Chapter 10)

assistant stylist Supports the stylist; responsible for contacting public relations companies, manufacturers, and retailers to locate the best assortment of merchandise to be used in a shoot. (Chapter 12)

assistant textile designer Works under the direction of the textile designer in developing new fabric prints and colorways, sourcing new patterns for fabrics, and modifying successful fabric prints and patterns. (Chapter 2)

associate store manager This position lies between the assistant store manager and the store manager; assists with employee hires, personnel scheduling, promotional activities, employee training, and other responsibilities assigned by the store manager. (Chapter 10)

block A basic flat pattern that is used as a starting place for pattern modifications. Also called a *sloper*. (Chapter 5)

body scanning Use of light beams to accurately measure the human body. (Chapter 4)

brand marketing manager Strategically develops and executes multichannel brand marketing and promotional programs in order to drive brand awareness, support and reinforce the brand's character, and ultimately generate increased revenue. (Chapter 8)

branding The sum of all the associations, feelings, beliefs, attitudes, and perceptions customers have with a company and/or its products. (Chapter 8)

brick-and-click store A retail business that offers its products to consumers through a store facility and through the Internet. (Chapter 6)

brick-and-mortar-store A retail business that has a physical appearance, as opposed to an Internet-based company. This includes department stores, mass merchants, specialty stores, boutiques, discount stores, and outlet stores located in buildings. (Chapter 6)

bridal show Event also called a *bridal fair*, where bridal wear manufacturers and retailers team up with auxiliary businesses, such as wedding planners, caterers, florists, and travel agents, to offer a fashion presentation of the season's offerings for brides-to-be, their friends, and their families. (Chapter 7)

broad-spectrum firm A company that provides forecasting services for a wide range of target markets and product categories or industries. (Chapter 1)

business plan A document used to solicit business funding that details strategies for the business concept and target market, location and space needs (i.e., building lease, facility purchase, or Web site requirements), growth and exit strategies, sales and inventory levels, and financing needs. (Chapter 10)

buyer Typically responsible for all of the product purchases and inventories for a company or particular department of a company, within a certain budget; this position is also referred to as *fashion merchandiser*. (Chapter 9)

buying plan A financial plan that takes into account past and projected sales, inventory, markups, and markdowns by department; it is also referred to as a *six-month plan*. (Chapter 9)

carryover A best-selling item from one season that is featured again with minor modifications in the next season. (Chapter 7)

channel of distribution The method(s) selected for moving goods from producer to consumer. (Chapter 8)

chargebacks Credits to a vendor for damaged merchandise and returns on defective goods. (Chapter 3)

chief marketing officer (CMO) A higher executive position to the marketing director; develops, implements, and facilitates the marketing plan in fashion retailing. (Chapter 8)

client/customer relationship management (CRM) Marketing that encompasses the analysis of significant amounts of data to understand consumer demographics, key market segments, and best practices for recruiting or retaining those customers. (Chapter 8)

collection Grouping of related styles. (Chapter 3)

collections manager Supervises museum personnel working in a specific area within a museum classification, such as historical textiles, eighteenth-century millinery, or Egyptian jewelry. (Chapter 13)

color palette The specific color selections for a particular pattern, print, or a collection or season of apparel or accessories. (Chapter 6)

colorist Chooses the color palette or color combinations that will be used in creating product lines. (Chapter 6)

colorway Color selections for a particular pattern or print. (Chapter 2, Chapter 6)

company salesperson Sales representative employed directly by a particular firm. (Chapter 4)

computer-aided design (CAD) The process of developing garments, prints, and patterns on a computer screen; this is an important trend in textile design. (Chapter 2, Chapter 5)

computer-aided patternmaking Manipulation of the components of pattern pieces on a computer screen. (Chapter 5)

computer-integrated manufacturing (CIM) Computers are tied together to communicate throughout the entire product development and manufacturing processes, from design to distribution. (Chapter 4)

consumer publication Magazine or newsletter that is written for and made readily available to the general consumer. (Chapter 7)

consumer tracking information Findings gathered from sales data and credit card applications that are interpreted as customer demographics and psychographics. (Chapter 1)

contractor Can either be a factory that makes and finishes goods or a firm that is hired to manufacture a product line domestically or abroad. (Chapter 2, Chapter 3, Chapter 6)

copywriter The person responsible for writing the words (e.g., slogans, promotions, and scripts) that accompany promotional visuals—online and in print. (Chapter 8)

corporation Company that is owned by stockholders, and may be run by an individual or a group. (Chapter 10)

cost price (*cost*) Wholesale price. (Chapter 4)

costume designer This person collaborates with film and video directors to design, consign, or construct apparel and accessories that fit with the mood, time frame, and image of the visual; also referred to as *fashion costumer*. (Chapter 12)

costume plot A list or chart that shows characters as they appear in each scene, what they are wearing, and what their overall movements are throughout a play. (Chapter 12)

country of origin The nation in which goods are primarily manufactured. (Chapter 3)

creative director Determines the primary fashion trend for upcoming seasons (Chapter 1); oversees art directors and other in-house art staff. (Chapter 8)

croquis A rendering or miniature visual of a textile pattern or print. (Chapter 2, Chapter 6)

cross-shopping A customer's inclination to purchase a wide variety of products in an array of brands and prices from any number of providers—directly from the manufacturer, in a resale store, at a flea market, or through a couturier. (Chapter 6)

curatorial traineeship Internship or apprenticeship for the prospective museum curator. (Chapter 13)

customer service manager Assists customers with issues or complaints and implements the retail operation's policies and procedures for returns, exchanges, out-of-stock merchandise, product warranties, and the like. (Chapter 10)

cut-to-order Considered the safest method of projecting manufacturing needs, this refers to producing the quantity of products specified on orders received. (Chapter 4)

cut-to-stock Involves purchasing fabrics and other product components before orders are secured. (Chapter 4)

cutter Uses electronic machines, knives, or scissors to precisely cut around the pattern pieces through layers of fabric, often several inches in thickness. (Chapter 4)

deaccession The removal of items from a museum collection because of repetition of artifacts, the receipt of better examples, loss, or decay. (Chapter 13)

decentralized buying The process used by individual stores or groups of stores within a retail chain that have a buyer who selects from the company's primary buyer's purchases. (Chapter 6)

demographic data Consumer data that can be interpreted as numbers (e.g., age, income, education attained, and number of family members). (Chapter 1)

department manager Oversees a specific area or department within a store and maintains the sales floor by supervising sales associates, placing new merchandise on the sales floor, adding signage for promotions, recording markdowns, and executing floor sets. (Chapter 10)

design-driven brand A brand that is led by a designer expressing a personal artistic vision and sense of taste. (Chapter 6)

design process The conception of a style, to include its inspiration or theme, the color palette, fabric selection, form, and fit. (Chapter 6)

diffusion labels Secondary clothing lines, often priced much lower than the designer's original line, such as Vera Wang's Simply Vera line for Kohl's. (Chapter 8)

digital marketing manager Works to further develop and manage a company's digital marketing presence and oversees the digital marketing strategy for the brand. This person is responsible for managing online brand and product campaigns to raise brand awareness. (Chapter 8)

digital twin Refers to a solution to fit preference in which a scanner takes a customer's measurements digitally; *body scanning*. (Chapter 4)

digitizer An electronic tool that is used to manipulate the size and shape of pattern pieces. (Chapter 5)

direct competition A manufacturer producing or a retailer selling a similar product at roughly the same price point as another, targeted toward the same customer or market niche. (Chapter 6)

direct market brand Describes a brand that is the name of the retailer. Often, this brand is carried by a specialty store chain, such as Ann Taylor, IKEA, and Banana Republic. (Chapter 6)

director of product development Ultimately responsible for strategic planning of the division, this person specifies exactly what the company will make and market, as well as when it will do this. (Chapter 6)

distribution Concerned with making sure that the product is available where and when it is wanted; includes determining how much inventory to hold, how to transport goods, and where to locate warehouses. (Chapter 8)

distribution manager Also referred to as an *allocator* or a *replenishment analyst*, this position is responsible for planning and managing the flow of goods received from the vendors, as ordered by the buyers, to the retail locations. (Chapter 9)

divisional merchandising manager (DMM) Works under the general merchandising manager and provides leadership for the buying staff of a division or a related group of departments, such as menswear, women's wear, or home furnishings. (Chapter 11)

draping method Process in which a patternmaker shapes and cuts muslin or the garment fabric on a dress form or a live model to create a pattern. (Chapter 5)

educational event A presentation during which a fashion event planner, a manufacturer's representative, or an employee hired by the planner educates an audience about a product. (Chapter 7)

electronic data interchange (EDI) Refers to the transfer of computer-generated information between one company's computer system and another's. (Chapter 4)

end product The final product to be purchased by the customer. (Chapter 4)

entrepreneur The business owner who is financially responsible for the company and oversees all aspects of the retail business. (Chapter 10)

exclusive An item limited to a retailer in a trade area. In some cases, a retailer may negotiate to be the only one in a geographic region to carry a particular item or the only one in the country to carry a particular color. For example, the label may read: "Burberry Exclusively for Neiman Marcus." (Chapter 6)

exports Products that are bought by an overseas company from a vendor in the United States and sent out of the country. (Chapter 3)

Family and Consumer Science Education (FCSEd) Certification for an instructor who teaches high school, vocational, or college courses in textiles, fashion, interior design, consumer education, personal financial literacy, clothing construction, careers in the fashion industry, and similar topics. (Chapter 13)

fashion blog Online coverage of fashion topics through which a narrator discusses and shares opinions and information about products, retailers, designers, and anything else related to clothing and accessories. (Chapter 11)

fashion bloggers Are much like *fashion writers*, but with a definitive online presence, a distinct personality, and an informal writing style. (Chapter 11)

fashion curators Work within historical and socioeconomic frameworks to educate others about fashion through accessing and archiving fashion artifacts, then sharing many of these with the public. (Chapter 13)

fashion design The development and execution of wearable forms, structures, and patterns. (Chapter 5)

fashion designer A creative who supervises a team of design assistants at a company, works under the label of a big-name designer or manufacturer, freelances for others while creating a personal line, or produces a line under his or her own name. (Chapter 5)

fashion director Responsible for determining the trends, colors, themes, and textures for piece goods or fabrics that a firm will feature for a specific season. In retailing, this position is responsible for designating the trends, themes, colors, and fabrics that the buyers will purchase for the retail operation. (Chapter 2)

fashion event producer Someone who increases the visibility of a design house, organization, brand, product, or fabric by coordinating special events, such as fashion shows and seminars, which provide exposure for these products; works with budgets, media, and customers in producing cost-effective and high-profile events. Also known as *fashion show producer*. (Chapter 7, Chapter 12)

fashion exclusivity Refers to having merchandise that is unique to a particular company. (Chapter 6)

fashion journalists Develop stories and materials such as articles, advertisements, and product descriptions, for books, magazines, newspapers, and online Web sites and blogs. Also known as *fashion writers*. (Chapter 11)

fashion photographer Takes photographs of models wearing the latest apparel, accessories, hairstyles, and makeup, or highlighting the newest home furnishings and other fashion products, primarily for commercial use. (Chapter 12)

fashion photostylist Responsible for bringing to life a photographer's or director's vision for a fashion photography shoot, magazine layout, music video, television or film commercial, or print advertisement. (Chapter 7)

fashion production planner A person who projects timelines for manufacturing the products in a line. (Chapter 3)

fashion scholar A person who studies, researches, writes, and teaches students in a classroom or online about the industry (past, present, and future), its careers, and the skills needed to succeed in it. (Chapter 13)

fashion shoot Photography session of models and/or fashion items. (Chapter 7)

fashion stylist Consults with clients on hair, makeup, footwear, jewelry, and apparel to create total looks, often for specific events. (Chapter 7, Chapter 12)

fashion visual Refers to the images used in the fashion industry, such as photographs, trend boards, and magazine clippings. (Chapter 12)

fashion writer See *fashion journalist*. (Chapter 11)

fast fashion Apparel and accessories trends that are designed and manufactured quickly, and in an affordable way, to allow the mainstream consumer to take advantage of current fashions at a lower price. (Chapter 6)

fiber house A company, also called a *fabric house*, that represents a fiber source or a fabric. (Chapter 1)

findings Functional product components that may not be visible when viewing the final product; they include zippers, thread, linings, and interfacings. (Chapter 3)

findings buyer Person responsible for purchasing zippers, threads, linings, and such for a manufacturer. (Chapter 3)

finishing Enhances the appearance of fabric and also adds to its suitability for everyday use or durability. Finishes can be solely mechanical, solely chemical, or a combination of the two. (Chapter 2)

first cost Wholesale price in the country of origin. (Chapter 3)

first pattern Used to cut and sew the prototype. (Chapter 5)

fit model This is the model on whom a designer may drape, cut, and pin fabric and on whom the designer will check the sizing and proportion of garments. Also referred to as the *fashion house model*. (Chapter 12)

flat pattern method Uses angles, rulers, and curves to create patterns. (Chapter 5)

floor set The arrangement of fixtures and merchandise on the sales floor to create a fresh look and highlight brand-new or undersold merchandise. (Chapter 10)

foundations Similar to museums, they are institutions formally set up with endowment funds. (Chapter 13)

freelance costumer Hired for specific productions by a theater company or production studio and may or may not actually be local to the theater for which he or she is designing. (Chapter 12)

functional finish A finish that imparts special characteristics to the cloth (e.g., durable press treatments). (Chapter 2)

funder Financing source, such as a bank or the Small Business Administration, used by a prospective business owner with a well-written business plan that justifies financing due to a good potential for profit, minimized risk, and a strong long-range plan. (Chapter 10)

general finish A finish, such as scouring or bleaching, that simply prepares the fabric for further use. (Chapter 2)

general merchandising manager (GMM) Leads and manages the buyers of all divisions in a retail operation. (Chapter 9)

globalization The process of interlinking nations of the world with one another; this is a growing trend in the fashion industry. (Chapter 3)

global sourcing Refers to the process of locating, purchasing, and importing or exporting goods and services from around the world. (Chapter 3)

gross margin Actual profit after cost of goods, markdowns, and other expenses are deducted. (Chapter 9)

import production coordinator Works as a liaison between the domestic apparel or home furnishings company and the overseas manufacturer or contractor. (Chapter 3)

imports In North America, products that are purchased from an overseas vendor and shipped to the United States or Canada. (Chapter 3)

informal fashion show is a show without extravagant staging and technical assistance, often taking place in a conference center, hotel, or restaurant in which models circulate among the tables as refreshments are served. (Chapter 7)

interactive display Exhibit ancillary in which viewers can press a button to run a video or actively participate in the exhibition's subject matter. (Chapter 13)

internal theft Refers to merchandise or money stolen by employees within the company. (Chapter 10)

international store manager Supervises store sales and staff performance in a different country, or group of countries, not in the company's country of residence. (Chapter 10)

inventory The selection of products available for sale in a fashion operation; this is also referred to as *merchandise assortment*. (Chapter 9)

inventory replenishment Reorders and stock placement on the sales floor to replace or fill in merchandise sold. (Chapter 4)

key account For a manufacturer, this term refers to a large retailer, in terms of sales volume, which carries the manufacturer's line consistently and in depth. (Chapter 4)

key vendor Manufacturers' lines featured as the greatest proportion of inventory in a retail operation. (Chapter 9)

knockoff A copy of another style, often of lesser quality and with minor modifications. (Chapter 6)

labdip A swatch of dyed fabric sent by mills to the product development team for color approval prior to dyeing large yardages of fabric. (Chapter 6)

landed costs The actual price of goods after taxes, tariffs, handling, and shipping fees are added to the cost of imported goods. (Chapter 3)

lead time Number of days, weeks, months, or years needed for the intricate planning and production steps that are implemented before fashion products actually arrive at the retail store; it is also the amount of time needed between placing a production order and receiving the shipment of products. (Chapter 1, Chapter 4)

letter of credit A document issued by a bank authorizing the bearer to draw a specific amount of money from the bank, its branches, or associated banks and agencies. (Chapter 3)

license An agreement in which a manufacturer is given exclusive rights to produce and market goods that carry the registered name and brandmark of a designer, celebrity, character, or product line. (Chapter 3)

licensee The manufacturer of a licensed product. (Chapter 3)

licensing director Responsible for overseeing the look, quality, labeling, delivery, and distribution of the company's licensed product lines. (Chapter 3)

licensor The owner of the name or brandmark who receives a percentage of wholesale sales or some form of compensation based on a licensing agreement. (Chapter 3)

lifestyle trends A population segment's values, interests, attitudes, dreams, and goals. (Chapter 1)

line plan Shows the number of styles in the line, the number and general types of fabrics and yarns to be used, colors per style, anticipated stock-keeping units (SKUs), and approximate preferred costs. (Chapter 6)

mall manager Responsible for everything in the mall from formulating its budget and planning promotional activities to developing its mix of tenants and building community relations. (Chapter 14)

management The process of organizing and controlling the affairs of a business or a particular sector of a business. (Chapter 10)

manager-in-training (MIT) An employee who is being trained to move into a management position. (Chapter 10)

manufacturer's representative Also referred to as a manufacturer's rep, this person is a wholesale salesperson who is often independent. (Chapter 4)

marker The layout of pattern pieces on the fabric from which the pieces will be cut. (Chapter 4)

marker maker Traces pattern pieces by hand or by computer into the tightest possible layout, while keeping the integrity of the design in mind. (Chapter 4)

marketing director Develops, implements, and facilitates the marketing plan in fashion retailing. (Chapter 8)

marketing manager A position that is just below that of marketing director in the executive hierarchy and has qualifications similar to those of marketing director. (Chapter 8)

marketing mix The Four Ps of marketing include: price, product, placement, and promotion. A fifth P of marketing can be added—the people or consumers who are targeted as potential customers or product users, referred to as the target market. (Chapter 8)

marketing plan Helps to define and quantify user benefits; establishes the market size as well as potential customer interest; and addresses the competition. (Chapter 8)

market week Scheduled at the apparel and trade marts throughout the year in conjunction with the introduction of the new, seasonal lines presented by manufacturers. Also called a *trade show*. (Chapter 4)

mass customization Strategy that allows a manufacturer or retailer to provide individualized products to a consumer. (Chapter 4)

master pattern Final pattern; often evolved from adjusting and perfecting a sample pattern. (Chapter 4)

media planner Determines prices, including quantity discounts, for a media buy that may include several venues, such as radio, television, and newspaper. The media planner determines how the advertising budget is best spent to generate the most exposure and sales. (Chapter 7)

merchandise coordinator Employed by a manufacturer and works in retail stores carrying the manufacturer's line within a certain geographic area, restocking products, installing displays, reordering top-selling styles, and educating sales staff and customers on the product line. (Chapter 4)

merchandiser Collaborates with the director of product development to decide what to produce and organizes and manages the entire product development process; this person is responsible for the development of a balanced, marketable, profitable, and timely line. (Chapter 3, Chapter 6)

merchandising Refers to all of the activities involved in the buying and selling of a product line. (Chapter 9)

merchandising calendar The product development team's schedule, created to deliver the right product (i.e., style, quality, and price) at the right time. (Chapter 6)

merchandising-driven brand Void-filling brand; a market-based brand designed to fill a niche in a market (i.e., an underserved customer) and create products to appeal to a distinct customer. (Chapter 6)

merchandising executive training program Designed for new hires, former interns, college recruits, or current employees who have shown skills in merchandising, to prepare them for their first assignment as assistant buyers; also referred to as *merchant executive training program*. (Chapter 9)

micro blogs Provide shorter stories that are easy to read and are accompanied by video clips and links that are smaller in size and easy for readers to share with one another; often focused on a specific niche in the industry. (Chapter 11)

modeling and talent agency director Ultimately responsible for locating and contracting new models, training them, and securing modeling jobs for them. (Chapter 12)

multiline representative An independent salesperson who carries a number of lines, often working with noncompetitive product lines and manufacturers. (Chapter 4)

museological training Instruction that covers how to preserve, maintain, and interpret museum collections. (Chapter 13)

museum conservator Manages, cares for, preserves, treats, and documents works of art, artifacts, and specimens; with regard to fashions or costumes, conservators acquire and preserve important visuals (e.g., photographs, illustrations, or sketches), costumes, accessories, furnishings, and other valuable items for permanent storage or display; this position may be referred to as a *restoration and preservation specialist*. (Chapter 13)

museum curator Works under the supervision of the museum director. A curator directs the accession, deaccession, storage, and exhibition of collections. This position may also be referred to as a *museum keeper*. (Chapter 13)

museum director Runs the business of the museum, manages the general operations and staffing of the organization, and coordinates the public affairs mission of the museum. (Chapter 13)

museum managerial training Educational program for a museum curator on how to run a museum, from personnel to finances to operations. (Chapter 13)

open-to-buy The amount of money allocated for the buyer to make new merchandise purchases each month, based on sales and inventory amounts. (Chapter 9)

operations manager Develops and maintains effective sales and operational programs with a focus on superior customer service for all of the retail units in the company or for units in a region. (Chapter 10)

outsourcing Having an aspect of a company's work performed by nonemployees in another company and, perhaps, in another country. (Chapter 2)

partnership A business owned by two or more people. (Chapter 10)

partnership event An event in which a fashion firm collaborates with another company outside of the fashion industry with the intent of drawing in customers. (Chapter 7)

party planning Can involve manufacturer, a designer, a PR director, or an organization hiring a fashion event producer to put together a celebratory event. (Chapter 7)

pattern grader Develops a pattern in the full range of sizes offered by the manufacturer. (Chapter 4)

patternmaker Translates the design concept into a flat pattern to create an actual garment. (Chapter 5)

philanthropic fashion show A fashion show with ticket sales and/or donations that benefit a nonprofit or charitable organization. (Chapter 7)

photographic model Hired to be photographed in the studio or on location. Although a select few top models work in high-fashion magazines, most opportunities exist through mail-order catalogues, newspaper advertisements, and television. Also known as a *print model*. (Chapter 12)

photography stylist Works with teams of people such as photographers, designers, lighting technicians, and set builders. Sets up the shoot for the photographer, scouts locations, and selects appropriate props, fashions, accessories, and, perhaps, the models to enhance the shoot. (Chapter 12)

physical inventory The merchandise actually in the retail or manufacturing operation. (Chapter 10)

piece goods Fabrics or materials, such as leather, used to create products. (Chapter 2)

piece goods buyer Purchases the textiles used in the production of final products. (Chapter 3)

planner Works in collaboration with the buyer to develop sales forecasts, inventory plans, and spending budgets for merchandise to achieve the retailer's sales and profit objectives. (Chapter 9)

planning manager Provides leadership, direction, and support at the merchandise division level to plan appropriately; this person also distributes and monitors inventory within a company's various retail locations to maximize sales. (Chapter 9)

planning module A chart constructed by a planner that details inventory ratios, such as top-to-bottom ratios of junior sportswear. (Chapter 9)

plan-o-gram Floor plan showing the placement and types of racks, fixtures, display units, and/or merchandise in order to create an easy flow of traffic and present the merchandise most effectively. (Chapter 14)

pop-up shop A project that is like a hide-and-seek boutique that pops up within other retail locations or at vacant retail spaces with few preliminary announcements. They quickly draw crowds, are open for a limited period of time, and then disappear or morph into something else. (Chapter 7)

portfolio A collection of work that illustrates a job candidate's range of skills and outcomes. This is also referred to in some sectors of fashion as a *book*. (Chapter 12)

press photography Also known as *photojournalism*, this focuses on images directly related to news stories, both events and personalities. (Chapter 12)

print service Company that sells print designs to mills, wholesalers, product developers, and retailers. (Chapter 2)

private brand A name owned exclusively by a particular store that is extensively marketed with a definite image, such as Target's Mossimo and Isaac Mizrahi brands. (Chapter 6)

private label A line name or brand that the retailer develops and assigns to a collection of products and that is owned exclusively by a particular retailer, such as Antonio Melani at Dillard's. (Chapter 6)

product development Creating and making a product, such as a dress, belt, or chair, from start to finish. (Chapter 6)

product development designer The creator of a product or product line; he or she is a trend forecaster in his or her own right by determining what the customer will be ready for next. Going through the design process with each new season, this person in a retail firm is also referred to as a *private label designer*. (Chapter 6)

product development patternmaker Takes accurate measurements and develops a pattern, either by using draping, CAD, or flat pattern methods, to create a pattern that, if correctly developed, ensures that the designer's vision will be implemented. (Chapter 6)

product manager Responsible for all products within a company's product lines or for a specific product category within the line. (Chapter 4)

product marketing manager Anticipates when to get into a fashion style, color, or theme and when to get out. (Chapter 8)

product void Merchandise category in which there are few, if any, items to fill consumer needs and desires. (Chapter 4)

production assistant Supports the production manager with detail work and record keeping. This person may track deliveries, assist development of production schedules, and communicate the workflow of the factory to the production manager. (Chapter 4)

production authorization The process of selecting and quantifying styles that will be manufactured. (Chapter 6)

production efficiency manager Responsible for monitoring the speed and output of a manufacturing facility and for managing waste. (Chapter 4)

production manager Also referred to as a *plant manager*, this person is responsible for all operations at the manufacturing plant, whether it is a domestic or overseas location and whether contracted or company owned. Job responsibilities of a production manager include supervising or completing the estimation of production costs, scheduling workflow in the factory, and hiring and training production employees. (Chapter 4)

production planner Estimates the amount and types of products a company will manufacture, either based on previous seasonal sales or on orders being received from the sales representatives on the road and in the showroom. (Chapter 4)

professional development Includes continuing education, perhaps toward a higher degree; internships within a field; conference participation; and memberships in trade and educational organizations. (Chapter 13)

promotion The endorsement of a person, a product, a cause, an idea, or an organization; these activities communicate a company's or product's attributes to the target consumers using two primary tools: publicity and advertising. (Chapter 7)

promotion director Guides the marketing activities of a fashion operation and finds hooks, or topics of interest, for a network of media sources. (Chapter 7)

promotion product Can refer to an item, such as a press release or an advertisement, or an event, such as a fashion show or music video, used as an endorsement tool. (Chapter 7)

prop house Firm that rents furniture, fixtures, mannequins, and décor accessories to visual merchandisers, saving the company money on limited-use display pieces while reducing the amount of warehouse space and labor needed to inventory and store visual merchandising props. (Chapter 14)

prototype First sample garment, accessory, or home product. (Chapter 5)

psychographics Refers to lifestyle choices, values, and emotions of a population. (Chapter 1)

public affairs As a mission in museums, this refers to collaborating with the community, the government, industry, and social and academic organizations to develop exhibitions and collections that appeal to and educate the community and its visitors. (Chapter 13)

public relations director Responsible for finding cost-effective ways to promote the company he or she represents. (Chapter 7)

puck A mouselike device used for computer-aided design. (Chapter 5)

purchase order (PO) A contract for merchandise between the buyer, as a representative of his or her firm, and the vendor. (Chapter 3)

quality control manager Also known as the *quality control engineer*, this person develops specifications for the products that will be manufactured and is responsible for the final inspection of garments from the manufacturer, checking fabric, fit, and construction for quality and adherence to product specification guidelines. (Chapter 4, Chapter 6)

radio-frequency identification technology (RFID) Increases supply-chain management through the tagging of containers, pallets, and individual items so that they can be accurately tracked as they move through the supply chain. (Chapter 4)

reference librarian Responsible for managing the inventory of books, samples, and resources of a company, such as a large apparel manufacturer, a fashion publisher, or a fiber/fabric house, and for procuring new ones. (Chapter 2)

regional store manager Responsible for the retail stores of a particular company that are located in a segregated area of the United States and/or overseas; this position is also referred to as a *district manager*. (Chapter 10)

residential costumer Hired by a specific theater to design and develop costumes for an extended series of productions. (Chapter 12)

resource room Reference library of product samples and sources, such as books, photographs, and other images. (Chapter 2)

resource room director Responsible for managing the inventory of books, fabrics, garments, and resources and for procuring new ones for a fashion library or resource room. (Chapter 2)

retail label A brand with the retailer's name on it, such as Neiman Marcus, Custom Interiors, or Saks Fifth Avenue. A retailer may negotiate with a manufacturer to put its label on a group of items instead of or in addition to the manufacturer's label, although the retailer may not have anything to do with the design or development of the items. (Chapter 6)

retailer A business that sells products to the ultimate consumer and can include the vast range of brick-and-mortar stores (e.g., department stores, mass merchants, specialty stores, boutiques, discount stores, and outlet stores), as well as catalogue, brick-and-click, and online stores. (Chapter 6)

retail store manager Oversees all aspects of a retail store's operation, from promotions and inventory to the customers and employees, often consisting of assistant managers, department managers, sales associates, and staff. (Chapter 10)

sales forecast Includes projections of sales by category, style, color, and size based on historical data and statistical analysis. This information may be used to place preliminary fabric and trim orders and block out production time in factories. (Chapter 6)

sample line Includes a prototype of every style available in the final product line and is used by sales representatives to show and sell the line to buyers. (Chapter 4)

sample size Used for testing fit and appearance, in addition to selling purposes. (Chapter 5)

secondary vendor Manufacturers' line featured in a retailer's inventory in small quantities. (Chapter 9)

security Refers to the safekeeping of the merchandise in the store. (Chapter 10)

security manager Works to prevent merchandise theft; collaborates with receiving, accounting, and management to be certain that accurate accounting procedures are in place and true losses are identified when the physical inventory is taken. (Chapter 10)

show model Employed by a modeling agency that takes bookings from clients who need to display clothes at fashion shows, exhibitions, or trade markets; also referred to as a *runway model*. (Chapter 12)

showroom A place where product lines are displayed; usually caters only to the trade. (Chapter 4)

showroom salesperson Also referred to as a *showroom representative*, this person works at a manufacturer's and/or designer's place of business, where he or she meets with visiting retail buyers and presents the latest product line to them. (Chapter 4)

shrinkage Merchandise losses due to theft. (Chapter 10)

single-line representative Manufacturer's representative who prefers to sell solely one manufacturer's line as an independent salesperson, rather than as a company employee. (Chapter 4)

social media The tools and social Web sites of the Internet that are used to communicate online with others. (Chapter 7)

social media director Develops, manages, and oversees the implementation of public relations programs in the social media venue. This includes creating content and generating coverage for social media efforts in all forms. (Chapter 7)

social networking The online communication of individuals, often with relationships or similar interests. (Chapter 7)

social Web site A Web site that functions like an online community of Internet users (e.g., Facebook and LinkedIn). (Chapter 7)

sole proprietorship A business owned by an individual. (Chapter 10)

sourcing The activities of determining which vendor can provide the amount of product needed, negotiating the best possible price and discounts, scheduling deliveries, and following up on actual shipments to make certain due dates are met and that quality control is maintained. (Chapter 3)

sourcing manager Director of the activities related to locating goods and producers of goods. (Chapter 3)

spec pack Contains detailed information taken from the designer's sketch, translated into measurements in order to ensure desired fit and styling details, such as the placement of pockets, the length of zippers, the size of buttons, etc. Also called a *tech pack*. (Chapter 5)

spec sheet Specification list; typically provides detailed measurements and construction guidelines. (Chapter 6)

specification technician Also known as *spec tech*, attends the fittings of the sample garments, takes measurements, and compiles these measurements into packets to hand off to production. (Chapter 5)

spreader Lays out the selected fabric for cutting. (Chapter 4)

stabilizing Saving and maintaining museum artifacts. A museum curator stabilizes artifacts when preparing them for storage or an exhibition. (Chapter 13)

stock-keeping unit (SKU) Identification data for a single product. (Chapter 3)

street style blogs Encompass fashion trend, environments, and styles seen on the streets. Whether an object, a group, or an individual, they can be action shots or posed, usually taken in the middle of a city. (Chapter 11)

strike-off A few yards of fabric printed by a mill and sent to the product developer (i.e., colorist, designer, and sample maker) to be made into a sample. (Chapter 2, Chapter 6)

stylus A computerized pen. (Chapter 5)

surface designer Knitters, weavers, or embroiderers for industries ranging from apparel to upholstery. (Chapter 2)

supply-chain management (SCM) All of the activities required to coordinate and manage every step needed to bring a product to the consumer, including procuring raw materials, producing goods, transporting and distributing those goods, and managing the selling process. (Chapter 4)

sustainability The practice of maintaining profitability while avoiding depletion or exploitation of natural, human, and economical resources. (Chapter 4)

sustainability officer Charged with building a business case in the organization to make improvements that enhance profitability as well as improve the company's public image. (Chapter 4)

target market The people or consumers who are targeted as potential customers or product users. (Chapter 8)

tearsheet A page that has been pulled from a newspaper, model book, or magazine. They are excellent to include in the portfolio for the photographer who has been published. (Chapter 12)

technical design Use of drawings, measurements, patterns, and models to develop the "blueprints," or technical plans, needed for the manufacturing of products. (Chapter 5)

technical designer Liaison between the designer and factory, responsible for working closely with the designers to communicate their specific product requests to the factory overseas. (Chapter 5)

technical photographer Produces photographs for reports or research papers, such as textile durability analyses. (Chapter 12)

technical writers Translate highly technical information into easy-to-understand text. (Chapter 11)

terminal degree Highest educational degree available in a particular field. (Chapter 13)

textile colorist Chooses the colors or color combinations that will be used in creating each textile design. (Chapter 2)

textile design The process of creating the print, pattern, texture, and finish of fabrics. (Chapter 2)

textile designer Creates original patterns, prints, and textures for the fabrics used in many types of industry, from fashion to interiors. (Chapter 2)

textile engineer Works with designers to determine how a design can be applied to a fabric in terms of more practical variables, such as durability, washability, and colorfastness. (Chapter 2)

textile stylist Modifies existing textile goods, altering patterns or prints that have been successful on the retail floor to turn them into fresh, new products. (Chapter 2)

textile technical designer Creates new textile designs or modifies existing fabric goods, altering patterns or prints that have been successful on the retail floor to turn them into fresh, new products. (Chapter 6)

textile technician Works with the issues that are directly related to the production of textiles, such as care factors, finishing techniques, and durability. (Chapter 2)

trade mart Houses temporary sales booths and permanent showrooms leased either by sales representatives or manufacturers. Also called an *apparel mart*. (Chapter 4)

trade publication Periodical designed for readers interested in or employed in specific professions, vocations, or merchandise classifications. (Chapter 7)

trade school An institution that may offer fashion programs and provide certificates, rather than degrees, upon the student's completion of the program, including programs in such areas as fashion design, illustration, retailing, photography, and merchandising. (Chapter 13)

traffic manager Supervises workflow on the factory floor, monitoring the product from start to finish. (Chapter 4)

transparency Full disclosure of information from the company regarding all aspects of the product, including materials used in the product, human rights and wage issues related to production processes, and impact to the environment along the supply chain. (Chapter 4)

transparency officer Monitors, ensures compliance, identifies gaps, develops, and provides open communication of all aspects of a company's product, including materials used in the product, human rights and wage issues related to production processes, and impact to the environment along the supply chain. (Chapter 4)

trend board The tool forecasters use to communicate seasonal fashion moods and trends to designers, buyers, product developers, and manufacturers. Key terms and images of the trend's fabrications, colors, and styling details are composed on a "board." In the past, these boards were created by hand; today, they are more likely created and disseminated to design and merchandising personnel digitally. (Chapter 1)

trend book Design resource publication intended to assist creative teams and manufacturers in developing future product lines. Trend books may include photos, fabric swatches, materials, color ranges, drawings of prints, product sketches, silhouettes, commentaries, and related materials. (Chapter 1)

trend forecaster Continually monitors the consumer and the industry through traveling, reading, networking, and, most important, observing; this person creates formal reports that summarize important fashion trends with seasonal themes. The trend forecaster in the product development division of a retailer identifies the fashion trends and then interprets them for the retailer's particular customer or market. (Chapter 1)

trendspotter A person located at a university or other location worldwide who provides information to a forecasting company, such as WGSN, on the latest trends in the locale. (Chapter 1)

trimmings Decorative components designed to be seen as part of the final product (e.g., buttons, appliqués, and beltings). (Chapter 3)

trimmings buyer Person who is responsible for locating and ordering decorative components for products. (Chapter 3)

trunk show Consists of a fashion event planner and/or a manufacturer's representative bringing a manufacturer's full seasonal line to a retail store that carries that particular manufacturer. (Chapter 7)

vendor The person selling a product or service, or a manufacturer or distributor from whom a company purchases products or production processes. (Chapter 3)

visual merchandisers Responsible for the window installations, displays, signage, fixtures, mannequins, and decorations that give a retail operation aesthetic appeal and a distinct image. This position is also known as *visual merchandising director*. (Chapter 14)

visual merchandising Design, development, procurement, and installation of merchandise displays and the ambiance of the environment in which the displays are shown. (Chapter 4, Chapter 14)

vocational school Provides training for students who elect not to participate in a four-year college degree program upon high school graduation. Courses taught include commercial clothing construction, apparel alteration, patternmaking, and retailing. (Chapter 13)

volume driver Top-selling merchandise for a manufacturer or retailer. (Chapter 3)

wholesale A company that sells the goods to the retailer for subsequent resale to the consumer. (Chapter 8)

writers See *journalist* (Chapter 11).

yardage A given amount of fabric, based on its length in yards. (Chapter 3)

CREDITS

Chapter 1

1.0 Victor VIRGILE/Gamma-Rapho via Getty Images
1.1 Pascal Le Segretain/Getty Images
1.2 Arun Nevader/Getty Images for VFW Management INC
1.3 Kristy Sparow/Getty Images for Premiere Vision
1.4 Sardella/WWD/© Conde Nast
1.5 Ollyy/Shutterstock.com
1.6 Goran Bogicevic /Shutterstock.com
1.7 Dan MacMedan/Getty Images
1.8 © Marleen Daniëls
1.9 Jeff Kravitz/FilmMagic/Getty Images
1.10 Matthew Sperzel/Getty Images
1.11 Han Myung-Gu/WireImage/Getty Images
Box 1.1 and 1.2 Courtesy of Henry Doneger Associates, Inc.
Box 1.3 © Philippe Munda

Chapter 2

2.0 Jaguar PS/Shutterstock
2.1 © 2015 Lectra S.A. All rights reserved. www.lectra.com
2.2 Pinzauti/Grazianeri/WWD/© Conde Nast
2.3 Giannoni/WWD/© Conde Nast
2.4 and 2.5 Courtesy of Lectra
2.6 Courtesy of Ellis Develpments Ltd; design by Peter Butcher
2.7 Photo by Patrick Cline for Lonny LLC
2.8 Fairchild Books
2.9 Courtesy of Cotton Incorporated
2.10 Courtesy of the Woolmark Company
2.11 Courtesy of Fur Council of Canada
2.12 Courtesy of Mohair Council of America
Box 2.1a–c Courtesy of Lectra
Box 2.2 Courtesy of ITP—Inkjet Textile Printing, LLC

Chapter 3

3.0 Betsie Van Der Meer/Getty Images
3.1 Baird/WWD/© Conde Nast
3.2 Erin Fitzsimmons/Fairchild Books
3.3 Adisa/Shutterstock.com
3.4 Peter White/WireImage/Getty Images
3.5 David Livingston/Getty Images
3.6 Iannaccone/WWD/© Conde Nast
3.7a Thornton/Footwear News/© Conde Nast
3.7b Guzel Studio /Shutterstock.com

Chapter 4

4.0 Delbo/ WWD/© Conde Nast
4.1a Caroline McCredie/Getty Images for Fenty Beauty by Rihanna
4.1b Jacopo Raule/Getty Images for Fenty x Puma
4.1c Victor Boyko/Getty Images for Fenty x Puma
4.1d Presley Ann/Patrick McMullan via Getty Images
4.2 Barbara Davidson/Los Angeles Times via Getty Images
4.3 JEAN-CHRISTOPHE VERHAEGEN/AFP/Getty Images
4.4 © Diana Hirsch/iStockphoto.com
4.5–4.7 Courtesy of Lectra
4.8 © S.G/Alamy
4.9, 4.10a and b Churchill/WWD/© Conde Nast
4.11 Michael Brochstein/SOPA Images/LightRocket via Getty Images
4.12a–c Mark Peterson/Corbis via Getty Images
4.13 YOSHIKAZU TSUNO/AFP/Getty Images
Box 4.3 GREGOR FISCHER/AFP/Getty Images

Chapter 5

5.0 Mitra/WWD/© Conde Nast
5.1 David M. Benett/Dave Benett/Getty Images for Tiffany & Co.
5.2 Giannoni/WWD/© Conde Nast
5.3 Anton Oparin/Shutterstock
5.4 Jun Sato/WireImage/Getty Images
5.5 Thierry Chesnot/Getty Images
5.6 Jamie McCarthy/WireImage/Getty Images
5.7 Keenan/WWD/© Conde Nast
5.8 Courtesy of Fairchild Books
5.9 Ariel Skelley/DigitalVision/Getty Images
Box 5.1 Jean Catuffe/GC Images

Chapter 6

6.0 Dimitrios Kambouris/Getty Images for Kohl's
6.1 Kim Kulish/Corbis via Getty Images
6.2 Alhovik /Shutterstock
6.3 Iannaccone/WWD/© Conde Nast
6.4 John Lamparski/Getty Images
6.5 Justin Sullivan/Getty Images
6.6a Thomas Concordia/Getty Images
6.6b Peter White/Getty Images
6.6c ANGELA WEISS/AFP/Getty Images
6.7 Aquino/WWD/© Conde Nast
6.8 Gareth Brown/Corbis via Getty Images
6.9 Dodds/WWD/© Conde Nast
6.10a and b Courtesy of Lectra
6.11 Courtesy of Fairchild Books

Chapter 7

7.0 Kevork Djansezian/Getty Images
7.1 WWD/© Conde Nast
7.2a Moviestore Collection Ltd/Alamy Stock Photo
7.2b Peter White/WireImage/Getty Images
7.2c Peter White/WireImage/Getty Images
7.3 anouchka/iStock.com
7.4 Hero Images/Getty Images
7.5 omgimages/istockphoto
7.6 Kevin Mazur/Getty Images for Giorgio Armani Beauty
7.7 Keenan/WWD/© Conde Nast
7.8 Rebecca Sapp/WireImage/Getty Images
7.9 Phillip Faraone/Getty Images for Showpo

Chapter 8

8.0 winhorse/Getty Images
8.1 Fairchild Books
8.2 Jennifer Graylock/Getty Images for Kohl's
8.3 J2R /Shutterstock
Box 8.1a and b © I Love Fashion Retail, All Rights Reserved.

Chapter 9

9.0 Action Sports Photography /Shutterstock
9.1a Lucas Schifres/Getty images
9.1b Eugene Gologursky/Getty Images
9.1c Michael Gottschalk/Photothek via Getty Images
9.2 Mark Ganzon/Getty Images for Fenty Beauty
9.3 Mitra/WWD/© Conde Nast
9.4 Keenan/WWD/© Conde Nast
9.5 Yoshiyoshi Hirokawa/DigitalVision/Getty Images
9.6 xPACIFICA/Corbis NX/Getty Images
Box 9.1 Lauren Wzorek Earl

Chapter 10

10.0 Andresr/Shutterstock
10.1 matejmm/iStock.com
10.2 Jay Freis/Getty Images
10.3 Hero Images/Getty Images
10.4 DmitriMaruta /Shutterstock
10.5 Thomas Barwick/DigitalVision/Getty images
10.6 Bikeriderlondon /Shutterstock

Chapter 11

11.0 Johnny Greig/Getty Images
11.1 ERIC BARADAT/AFP/Getty Images
11.2 BONNINSTUDIO /Shutterstock
11.3 man-repeller.com
11.4 Charley Gallay/Getty Images for AKID Brand
Box 11.1 Monica Schipper/Getty Images

Chapter 12

12.0 Michael Kovac/Getty Images for Paley Center
12.1 Paul Warner/WireImage/Getty Image
12.2 Oscar Gonzalez/NurPhoto via Getty Images
12.3 Micro Discovery/Corbis Documentary/Getty Images
12.4 Jesse Grant/Getty Images for Vanity Fair
12.5 Hero Images/Getty Images
Box 12.3 Alberto E. Rodriguez/Getty Images for Disney

Chapter 13

13.0 Peter Macdiarmid/Getty Images
13.1 Rob Stothard/Getty Images
13.2 Mark Clifford/Barcroft Media/Getty Images
Box 13.1 Chomel/WWD/© Conde Nast
Box 13.2 Ericksen/WWD/© Conde Nast
Box 13.3 Maitre/WWD/© Conde Nast
Box 13.4 Maestri/WWD/© Conde Nast

Chapter 14

14.0 Cristina Arias/Cover/Getty Images
14.1 Andrew Toth/Getty Images for The Recording Academy
14.2a–14.4c WindowsWear PRO
14.5 Maitre/WWD/© Conde Nast

Appendix B

R1 Courtesy Fairchild Books
R2 Courtesy Fairchild Books
R3 Courtesy Gretchen Von Koenig
R4 Courtesy Fairchild Books
R5 Courtesy Carly E. Minis

INDEX

spreader, 60, 236
Springs Global, 36
Sprout Social, 159
stabilizing, 198, 236
stock-keeping unit (SKU), 43, 236
store manager, 152
    job search, 156
    salary and wage resource, 216
store owner, 160
store planning director, 208, 210
    career challenges, 210
    qualifications, 210
    salary and wage resource, 216
Streep, Meryl, 183
street style blogs, 169, 2369
strike-off, 23, 100, 236
stylist, 180–2
    career challenges, 182
    job search for Internet stylist, 181
    qualifications, 182
    salary and wage resource, 216
stylus, 82, 2396
Sui, Anna, 91
supplier, 39
supply-chain management (SCM), 64, 236
surface designers, 23, 236
sustainability, 115, 236
sustainability officer, 67–8, 236
    qualifications, 68
    salary and wage resource, 216

T

Talbots, 64
TAL Corporation of Hong Kong, 30
Target, 91, 128
target market, 124, 236
tearsheet, 180, 236
tech design, 79
technical design, 79, 236
technical designer, 236
    career challenges, 80, 82
    day in the life of, 81
    qualifications, 80
    salary and wage resource, 217
technical photographer, 179, 236
technical writers, 166, 236
tech packs, 82
Tender Buttons, 41
terminal degree, 199, 236
textile/apparel cutter, salary and wage
    resource, 217
textile colorist, 21, 26–7, 236
    career challenges, 27
    qualifications, 27
textile companies
    Australian Wool Services Limited
        (Woolmark Company), 34

classified advertisement for, 33
Cone Mills, LLC, 36
Cotton Incorporated, 33–4
DuPont, 36
Fur Council of Canada, 34–5
International Luxury Outerwear Expo,
    35
Mohair Council, 35–6
Springs Global, 36
textile design, 21, 23, 26, 236
textile designer, 21, 237
    salary and wage resource, 217
textile engineer, 21, 29–30, 237
    career challenges, 30
    qualifications, 30
    salary and wage resource, 217
textile house, 4
textile stylist, 26, 237
textile technical designer, 101–2, 237
    career challenges, 102
    qualifications, 102
textile technician, 21, 27, 29, 237
Tiffany, 203, 204
Todd & Duncan, 101
Tory Burch, 47, 48, 98
trade associations, 222
trade marts, 61, 237
trade publications, 109, 222, 237
trade schools, 199, 237
trade shows, 9, 61
traffic managers, 56, 217, 237
transparency, 68, 237
transparency officer, 68, 237
    qualifications, 68
    salary and wage resource, 217
travel, 14
trend board, 4, 237
trend book, 9, 237
trend forecasters, 3, 237
    career challenges, 17–18
    career path of, 16–17
    job market for, 17
    job of, 4, 8–9, 12, 14–16
    Li Edelkoort, 4, 10–11
    qualifications, 16
trend forecasting
    consumer behavior and, 8
    examples of companies, 17–18
trendspotters, 17, 237
Trend Union, 18
trimmings, 41, 237
trimmings buyer, 41–2, 237
    career challenges, 42
    qualifications, 42
trunk show, 117, 237
Twitter, 74, 114, 135

U

U.S. Bureau of Labor Statistics, 166

V

Valentino's Spring 2019 Haute Couture, 3
Van Noten, Dries, 14
vendor, 39, 237
Versace, 47, 107
Versace, Gianni, 191
Victoria and Albert Museum, 189, 192
Victoria's Secret, 151, 152
Vine, 114
Vionnet, Madeleine, 191
visual merchandiser, 204, 208, 209, 237
visual merchandising, 66, 163, 204, 237
visual merchandising assistant, 217
visual merchandising director/manager, 217
visual merchandising professionals, 204,
    212
    career challenges, 208
    future outlook for, 208
    growing career opportunities, 204, 206
    qualifications, 206, 208
vocational schools, 199, 237
Vogue (magazine), 3, 77, 107, 109
void-filling brands, 94
volume drivers, 43, 237

W

W (magazine), 107, 109
Wang, Vera, 76, 77
wardrobe stylists, 180
The Washington Post (newspaper), 166
web site designer/developer, salary and
    wage resource, 217
wedding planner, 174, 175
wholesale, 128, 216, 237
#whomademyclothes, 69
W. L. Ross and Company, 36
Wolfe, David, 5–7
Women's Wear Daily (magazine), 109, 113
Woolmark Company, 34
Worth, Charles, 193
Worth Global Style Network (WGSN), 15,
    17–18
writer, 166, 217, 237

Y

yardage, 40, 237
YouTube, 74

Z

Zappos, 135, 140–1
Zara, 64, 90, 123, 124, 125, 128, 133, 170
Zodiac, 98
Zooey In The City, fashion blog, 170